Anthropology, Public Policy, and Native Peoples in Canada

Edited by
Noel Dyck and James B. Waldram

McGill-Queen's University Press
Montreal & Kingston • London • Buffalo

© McGill-Queen's University Press 1993
ISBN 0-7735-0961-5 (cloth)
ISBN 0-7735-0978-X (paper)

Legal deposit second quarter 1993
Bibliothèque nationale du Québec

Printed in the United States on acid-free paper

Publication of this book has been supported by
grants from The University of Saskatchewan
and the Publications Fund Committee of Simon
Fraser University.

Canadian Cataloguing in Publication Data

Main entry under title:
  Anthropology, public policy, and native
  peoples in Canada
  Includes bibliographical references.
  ISBN 0-7735-0961-5 (bound) –
  ISBN 0-7735-0978-X (pbk.)
  1. Native peoples – Canada – Government
  relations. 2. Native peoples – Canada – Ethnic
  identity. 3. Anthropology – Canada. I. Dyck,
  Noel. II. Waldram, James B. (James Burgess)
  E78.C2A54 1993   323.1'197071   C92-090714-8

Contents

Abbreviations

ACND	Advisory Council on Northern Development
AFN	Assembly of First Nations
CAGSL	Canadian Arctic Gas Study, Limited
CARC	Canadian Arctic Resources Committee
CASCA	Canadian Anthropological Society/La société canadienne d'anthropologie
CC	commission counsel
CEARC	Canadian Environment Assessment Research Council
CESCE	Canadian Ethnology Society/La société canadienne d'ethnologie
CMA	Canadian Museums Association
CMC	Canadian Museum of Civilization
COPE	Committee for Aboriginal Peoples Entitlement
CYI	Council for Yukon Indians
DIAND	Department of Indian Affairs and Northern Development
DIANR	Department of Indian Affairs and National Resources
DP	Delta Gas Producers
DPMO	Deputy Prime Minister's Office
EIA	environmental impact assessment
FSIN	Federation of Saskatchewan Indian Nations
IBNWT	Indian Brotherhood of the Northwest Territories (now Dene Nation)
ICA	Indian Chiefs of Alberta
ICME	International Committee for Museums of Ethnography

ICOM	International Council of Museums
IODE	Imperial Order of the Daughters of the Empire
ITC	Inuit Tapirisat of Canada
JBNQ	James Bay and Northern Quebec Native Harvesting Research Committee
KIA	Keewatin Inuit Association
MAA	Metis Association of Alberta
MIB	Manitoba Indian Brotherhood
MMF	Manitoba Metis Federation
MNC	Metis National Council
MNSI	Metis and non-status Indian
MSB	Medical Services Branch
NIB	National Indian Brotherhood (after early 1980s, Assembly of First Nations)
PCO	Privy Council Office
PMO	Prime Minister's Office
P-O	participant-observation (research)
SAAC	Society for Applied Anthropology in Canada
SIA	social impact assessment

1 Anthropology, Public Policy, and Native Peoples: An Introduction to the Issues

NOEL DYCK and JAMES B. WALDRAM

INTRODUCTION

The issues that concern us in this volume can be conveniently introduced by a familiar ethnographic device, the recounting of a social situation – in this case, one that occurred while this volume was being written. In the autumn of 1989 the attention of the news media both in France and Canada focused for a few days on a crew of Haida Indians from the Queen Charlotte Islands as they paddled a magnificently carved war canoe up the River Seine to honour Claude Lévi-Strauss, France's world-renowned anthropologist.[1] This improbable episode had its beginnings in a request from the Musée de l'homme in Paris to Bill Reid, a Haida artist, to display some of his jewelry and larger works at a special exhibition to recognize Lévi-Strauss as he turned eighty. Reid, who had fantasized several years earlier of passing under the Pont Neuf (the oldest bridge in Paris) in a canoe, took this opportunity to offer the museum his fifteen-metre war canoe (known as *Lootaas* or "wave eater" in Haida), provided that it could be paddled up the Seine, into the heart of Paris, by a Haida crew. Museum officials eagerly undertook to raise the funds required for the expedition.

Near the end of its eventful voyage the *Lootaas* stopped to take on Lévi-Strauss before passing the Eiffel Tower and arriving for an official reception at the city hall, where the delegation was met by the mayor of Paris and the Canadian ambassador to France. Changing into traditional costumes, members of the crew performed

Haida dances that had been received enthusiastically by French audiences at each stop on the trip. French television crews who interviewed members of the expedition were especially interested in determining whether the Haida paddlers still lived in a traditional fashion. Canadian reporters pursued a quite different angle in covering the episode. A story that appeared on the front page of the *Vancouver Sun* (2 October 1989) was concerned first and foremost with the manner in which a supposedly cultural undertaking had been transformed into a political statement about the distance between the Haida and governments in Canada with respect to the resolution of Native[2] land claims. Indeed, on the first day of the voyage, the Haida delegation had unceremoniously hauled down Canadian flags (supplied by the Canadian embassy) from the escort boats that accompanied the canoe and replaced them with Haida flags. Haida spokespersons explained to reporters that the Queen Charlotte Islands comprised a Native homeland which they called Haida-Gwaii: "We have our own flag, our own identity, our own constitution, and our own passports."

When the expedition finally landed in front of city hall, officials with the Canadian embassy responded diplomatically to questions from Canadian reporters – yes, the Haida were entitled to fly "whatever flag they want" – and congratulated members of the expedition (which had been financed in part by grants from the governments of Canada and British Columbia) for carrying a message of "peace and friendship" to France. In Canada, news of the voyage provoked heated statements in letters to the editor (e.g., *Vancouver Sun*, 10 October 1989, A-11). Some of these letters were sharply critical of the disrespect shown to the Canadian flag, while others endorsed both the objectives of the Haida and the dramatic tactics they had employed to express their position.

Among Canadian anthropologists the voyage of the *Lootaas* evoked a sense of familiarity, irony, and ambiguity. On the one hand, the use of the voyage – or, more specifically, the media coverage of the voyage – by the Haida to promote their political objectives vis-à-vis the Canadian state was readily recognizable as an instance of what anthropologists have identified as ethnodrama (Paine 1985a), a political stratagem much favoured by aboriginal leaders both in Canada and in other "fourth world" settings (Dyck 1985). On the other hand, such a spectacular celebration of an anthropologist by Native peoples some two decades after Deloria's (1969) pungent critique of the discipline was, to say the least, ironic. Moreover, given the political agenda of the Haida, the choice of Lévi-Strauss as a recipient for such recognition was even more curious. Unlike many of his anthropological colleagues in Canada, Lévi-Strauss had neither carried out land claims research on behalf of aboriginal communities nor analysed public policy and government administration as it pertains to Native peoples.

Yet to the extent that this episode illustrates the complexity and ambiguity that surround relations between anthropology, public policy, and Native peoples, it serves to locate some of the central concerns dealt with in this volume. During the past three decades a growing number of anthropologists in Canada have dedicated themselves to investigating and, when asked to do so, intervening in one capacity or another in various relations and dealings between Native peoples and the agencies and institutions of the Canadian state. This departure from the discipline's traditional preoccupation with ethnological research has had an inescapable effect upon the scope, purposes, and practice of anthropology. In this introductory essay we shall briefly outline the conditions that have prompted this reshaping of the anthropological enterprise and identify some of the problems and possibilities that have arisen from this process.

The questions raised here are vital and challenging ones that engender lively debate, even between co-editors and co-authors. We have chosen not to "smooth over" or ignore some of the marked differences in our individual appraisals of the current state of and future prospects for anthropological practice, but to identify these as matters that deserve to be opened up for frank discussion within the discipline. Accordingly, we should identify the sections "Reshaping Anthropological Practice," "The Anthropological Contribution," and "The Implications of Engagement" as having been written by Dyck, and "A Critical Perspective" by Waldram; "Introduction," "Anthropologists and Native Peoples," and "An Overview of the Volume" present the views of both co-authors.

ANTHROPOLOGISTS AND NATIVE PEOPLES

The innovations within Canadian anthropology during the past thirty years reflect both wide-reaching developments in the overall field of aboriginal peoples' dealings with governments in Canada and a parallel expansion of new forms of anthropological involvement with Native communities and issues. Since the 1960s, Canada's Department of Indian Affairs has undergone a series of administrative reforms designed to rid this essentially nineteenth-century institution of its unacceptable features. In consequence, a series of government initiatives – including the ill-fated 1969 federal proposal that the Department of Indian Affairs be simply abolished (cf. S.

Weaver 1981) – have been mounted, ostensibly to rectify the social, economic, and political marginality of Canadian Indians. These initiatives, along with other public policy measures directed toward not only registered Indians but Native peoples generally, have had a fundamental impact on Native communities, often as a result of the intense resistance these actions have generated among aboriginal peoples.

Anthropologists' attempts to recognize these developments within their writings have gradually altered the character of their published accounts. Fieldwork studies of "traditional" cultures and processes of "acculturation" have been superceded by new interests or made to speak to highly politicized issues such as aboriginal land claims. Today the challenge of analysing bureaucratized relationships and novel forms of political action that reach from Ottawa to Indian reserves and back again – occasionally even via Paris – demands the attention of anthropologists, such as analyses of kinship organization once preoccupied their predecessors. What is more, professional anthropologists are no longer confined to universities or museums. Professors of anthropology and ethnological curators have been joined by a growing number of anthropological practitioners who work as consultants or as salaried employees of band and tribal councils, provincial and national aboriginal peoples' organizations, and a variety of federal and provincial government agencies. The balance within the definitively anthropological practice of "participant-observation" has, as Cruikshank notes (this volume), taken a decided shift in favour of "participation" in recent years.

Paradoxically, during this same period anthropology's standing as the academic discipline most interested in and knowledgable about aboriginal cultures and peoples has been overtaken by the work conducted on Native issues by a growing number of representatives of other disciplines, including political science, history, sociology, law, geography, and the emerging discipline of Native studies. This is, of course, a predictable development, for the nature and needs of aboriginal peoples reach beyond the bounds of any one discipline (Tremblay 1983:335; Hedley 1985:100). Nevertheless, the appearance of academic competitors, along with the emergence of new ethnographic interests and professional roles, has obliged anthropologists to rethink the purposes and practice of their discipline.

Some of the disciplinary matters which today concern anthropologists originate in criticisms made by aboriginal peoples of individual anthropologists, as well as of anthropology in general; more will be said of these below. Others have surfaced when anthropologists working either inside or outside academia have found themselves at odds with traditional disciplinary expectations, particularly with respect to anthropological participation in advocacy activities. In any case, anthropologists are now reassessing the practical implications, costs, and benefits of anthropological involvement in Native issues and asking themselves some searching questions. For instance, what are the analytical and methodological weaknesses, strengths, and possibilities of anthropology? What should anthropologists study, and which questions and issues would be best left to practitioners of other disciplines? How can anthropologists better equip themselves to comprehend the workings of the nation-state in its various manifestations? In what forms, under what restrictions, and to whom should anthropologists present their findings? How can anthropologists working outside academia have their work acknowledged within the discipline? Should anthropologists seek to join the developing field of public policy studies, should they attempt to transform their discipline into one devoted to advocacy on behalf of aboriginal peoples, or should they instead restrict themselves to producing politically independent ethnographies which will serve as a form of social criticism?

Elsewhere in this introduction we shall examine some current responses to these questions. Before turning to these, however, we need to review certain particularly salient features of the longstanding relationship between anthropology and Native peoples in this country. While aboriginal peoples in Canada and elsewhere have served anthropology well, what has anthropology done for them? Who or what does anthropology seek to serve? These are abiding questions that must be acknowledged and readdressed by each generation of anthropologists for as long as we involve ourselves in the study of Native communities, cultures, and issues. To come to terms with these essential matters we must take account of the discipline's largely colonial origins and recognize that some of our current purposes oblige us to struggle with contradictions inherent in these origins (Herzfeld 1987:13). By examining the development of the practice of anthropology in one country we hope to extend the basis for subsequent comparative analyses of anthropology in a range of "fourth world" settings.[3]

Anthropology's involvement with aboriginal peoples in Canada has, arguably, always reflected considerations of public policy, even though anthropologists have not always recognized that this was the case. Until recently, anthropology in Canada was housed primarily within university departments and museums (or government agencies which carried out museum functions) and directed toward ethnological research and collection. During the nineteenth century and much of the twentieth century, the discipline's primary goal was to salvage material and ethnographic representations of "authentic" aboriginal cultures before these were swept away by the "inevitable" forces of "progress" as manifested by Euro-Canadian settlement and economic development. In consequence, recorded ethnological texts, artifacts, and photographs were assiduously gathered in order to document ways of life and peoples who were believed to be "vanishing." What was generally ignored or excluded from these ethnological accounts was the manner in which Euro-Canadian institutions were actively engaged not only in occupying aboriginal lands and resources but also in devising and implementing programs of coercive tutelage (Dyck 1991) which were intended to "save" aboriginal peoples by ridding them of their aboriginality. Public officials' presumption of the inevitability of these outcomes was, for the most part, accepted at face value by anthropologists who focused their attention on those cultures and traditions which, it was thought, were about to disappear rather than upon the circumstances of their disappearance. A telling illustration of this approach was provided in the early part of the twentieth century when officers of the newly formed Anthropology Division of the Geological Survey of Canada formally requested that new amendments to the Indian Act (which sought to prohibit traditional Indian dances and religious ceremonials) not be enacted in a manner that would interfere with the ethnological investigations undertaken by the division (Pettipas 1988:302–3). The request did not, however, dispute the appropriateness of the amendments' denial of Indian religious and political rights.

By the fourth decade of the twentieth century, when it was obvious that aboriginal peoples in Canada were not vanishing and that government programs were not readily transforming Indians into "brown white men," anthropologists began to adopt a new paradigm which focused on problems and processes of "acculturation." Studies which adopted this approach tended to treat individual Native persons as "culture bearers," thereby dichotomizing "authentic" aboriginal cultures from contemporary aboriginal persons. In ethnographic practice, aboriginal persons were viewed primarily as individuals whose behaviour could be examined and understood without much or any reference to the larger sociopolitical context within which they were located. By concentrating their studies either on "traditional" cultures and histories of "culture contact" or upon the dilemma said to be confronting aboriginal individuals – the so-called dilemma of being "caught between two cultures" – anthropologists for the most part continued to overlook pertinent economic and power relations and to take for granted the operation of public policies that subjected Native peoples to regimes of coercive tutelage and marginalization within Canadian society.[4]

In the wake of the Second World War and the European Holocaust, a determination arose throughout the western world to dismantle colonial structures and to eliminate officially sanctioned systems of racial segregation. Canada's archaic system of Indian administration came under intense and continuing scrutiny from members of the public and, in due course, from politicians who were persuaded of the need to reform this repressive bureaucratic structure and to speed the "integration" of Native peoples into Canadian society. Two major parliamentary inquiries into federal stewardship of Indian affairs led to a series of long overdue revisions to the Indian Act. Testifying before the first of these committees in 1947, Diamond Jenness, the head of the ethnology division of the National Museum of Canada, unequivocally recommended a phased termination of federal Indian administration (including the system of Indian reserve lands) and a program of forced integration of Indians into Canadian society (Johnson 1984:24–5). His proposals for eliminating the special status of registered Indians sharply contradicted the views expressed by Indian representatives who were forced to overcome formidable political and logistical obstacles even to be permitted to appear before the committee. In the end, the assimilationist position propounded by Jenness and other anthropologists gained a more receptive hearing from the parliamentarians than did the Indian presentations (Pettipas 1988:412–13).

During the 1950s and 1960s, a series of anthropological community studies were mounted to assess the current situation and problems of Native communities (e.g., Dunning 1964; Shimpo and Williamson 1965). A common feature of many of these anthropological studies was the inclusion of policy recommendations to improve the future prospects of Native people. The best-known and certainly the most ambitious study conducted within this genre was the two-volume Hawthorn-Tremblay report (Hawthorn 1967), a largely anthropological study commissioned by the federal government in the mid-1960s to provide a national survey of Canadian Indians' economic, political, and educational needs and policies. Notwithstanding the apparently limited impact of this report on subsequent government policy making (see Weaver, this volume), its publication established a high-water mark of self-confidence within Canadian anthropology concerning the ability of anthropologists to understand and improve Canadian public policy toward Native peoples.

Although proposing what amounted to a new policy for Canadian Indians, no formal meeting was ever held with Indian representatives to discuss the report's wide-reaching policy recommendations (La Rusic 1985:22–3). The perceptiveness of many of the observations and proposals made in this report was accompanied by an implicit assumption that the authors were capable of assessing and representing Indians' best interests to the Minister of Indian Affairs.

Within two years of the publication of the Hawthorn-Tremblay report, the conditions that had sustained these kinds of assumptions began to change significantly. The publication in the United States of Deloria's (1969) denunciation of anthropology prompted squeals of indignation but also much introspection among anthropologists on both sides of the border. The year 1969 also marked the beginning of a new era in Canadian Indian administration: the unveiling of the federal government's White Paper proposals to eliminate the Department of Indian Affairs along with the special legal status of registered Indians ignited an Indian-led protest movement which captured the attention of the news media and the public across Canada. The publication late in 1969 of Harold Cardinal's bestselling book, *The Unjust Society*, left little doubt about the ability of Canadian Indians to articulate their interests directly and most effectively to politicians and to members of the public.

Since 1969 anthropologists have had to adjust themselves not only to the rapidly changing state of relations between Native peoples and governments but also to the willingness of Native leaders to criticize some aspects of anthropology while making increasing use of others. As Weaver (this volume) notes, anthropologists have been taken to task for their frequent failure to return the products of their research to Native communities as well as for a tendency to depict Indians as culturally static people (e.g., Ahenakew 1985). Individual anthropologists have also been publicly rebuked for publishing controversial accounts of Native communities (Ames 1986:43–4). Out of these experiences has come a recognition among anthropologists of the ways in which ethnographic studies of Native communities also comprise "political facts" (Sansom 1985b: 9–12) which may subsequently be used by government officials or local non-Native groups against these communities.

At the same time, anthropological writings have also been used extensively by Native leaders; indeed, the notion of Indians as "citizens plus," first coined in the Hawthorn-Tremblay report, was used to good effect by the National Indian Brotherhood in rejecting the White Paper. Moreover, the development of publicly funded Indian, Metis, non-status Indian, and Inuit political bodies at the local, regional, and national levels created many opportunities for anthropologists and other non-Natives to serve as paid or unpaid consultants, advisors, and researchers.[5] Anthropologists, along with practitioners of other disciplines, offered Native communities and organizations particular skills and knowledge which were initially in short supply among aboriginal peoples. While requests made of anthropological researchers by their aboriginal "subjects" to provide technical advice and, occasionally, political assistance were certainly not unknown prior to 1969 (e.g., Pettipas 1988:345), since then expectations of some form of reciprocal assistance from anthropologists has become virtually a condition of fieldwork in aboriginal communities (see Waldram, this volume).

Anthropological publications today reflect the increased interest and involvement of the discipline in relations between aboriginal peoples and the nation-state. Ethnographic accounts also demonstrate both a greater circumspection in dealing with sensitive topics (Dyck, this volume) and the rising popularity of a new analytical approach emphasizing the manner in which aboriginal people, both past and present, have sought to resist governments' attempts to strip them of their cultures and to force their assimilation into the "mainstream," non-Native society (Bruner 1986). The perspective now favoured in anthropological publications is decidedly deferential in its treatment of aboriginal peoples and issues.

RESHAPING ANTHROPOLOGICAL PRACTICE

During the 1970s and 1980s anthropologists published a number of studies (e.g., Brody 1975, 1981; Ryan 1978; S. Weaver 1981; Tanner 1983; Asch 1984; Salisbury 1986; Culhane Speck 1987; Waldram 1988) that explored different facets of the relationship between aboriginal peoples and public policy in Canada.[6] Anthropologists also played active and important roles in the Mackenzie Valley Pipeline Inquiry (Berger 1977; Usher, this volume) and the negotiation of the James Bay and Northern Quebec Agreement, two events which have had lasting significance for Native peoples' relations with the Canadian nation-state. Nonetheless, there remain doubts both inside and outside the discipline concerning the general capacity of anthropologists to understand, let alone influence or assist, the making of public policy in this or in any field. What is the basis for this reticence? What are seen to be the limitations of anthropology? Why is anthropological knowledge discounted?

An abbreviated list of the alleged shortcomings of anthropology – especially, but not exclusively, with respect to its depiction of and influence on Canadian policy towards aboriginal peoples – would include the following: an inability to respond quickly or practically to outsiders' requests for information (Buchignani 1986); an individualistic approach to field research and analysis which ill prepared anthropologists to serve as members of interdisciplinary research teams (Sansom 1985b); an unacceptable level of naïvety concerning the nature of the bureaucratic world, the needs and interests of policy makers, and of decision-making processes within the institutions of contemporary nation-states (LaRusic 1985); a disinclination to provide "objective" statistical data, a corresponding reliance upon "soft" qualitative data, and a general inability to communicate findings in a manner that satisfies public policy makers (T. Weaver 1985); the lack of an established professional profile and recognized expertise to contribute either to practical decision making or to the emerging field of policy sciences (Salisbury 1976); and a tendency to concentrate on local-level political processes at the cost of ignoring macro-level institutional structures and considerations.[7] To this list should be added the frequency with which anthropology has been singled out for public criticism by aboriginal peoples. Anthropologists are probably the most visible and easily caricatured of all academics and professionals who work with aboriginal peoples. In addition to instances where charges of unethical practice have been levelled at individual anthropologists, the discipline as a whole has been accused of exploiting aboriginal peoples not only by trafficking in their artifacts (Cole 1985) but, nowadays, also by stealing their stories, their experience, and their right to represent their own heritage.[8] Together, these factors might conceivably even be construed as providing a rationale for anthropologists to abstain from any further involvement in the messy and contentious field of contemporary public issues. Anthropologists might, then, take refuge in arguments that their discipline is manifestly not "suited" to dealing with these troublesome issues and retreat to quieter realms of scholarship.

Another way to respond to this statement of purported disciplinary shortcomings is to confront it directly in order to discern the nature of the criticisms being made. What several of these criticisms amount to is a claim that anthropology is limited in its ability to contribute to public policy analysis or policy making because anthropologists are as yet relatively inexperienced in the ways of the world of policy science. There is, of course, always some scope for any discipline to expand its repertoire of research methods, its understanding of complex institutional settings, and its intended audiences. But this is already happening in anthropology, as was demonstrated by the work of anthropologists in the course of the James Bay negotiations and the Berger Inquiry where considerations of teamwork, speed, and practicality of research were essential (cf. Asch 1982; Feit 1982; Salisbury 1986; Usher, this volume). The observation that these kinds of anthropological research undertakings are not so common as they ought to be may tell us more about the generally low level of public support devoted to anthropological research in Canada than it does about the alleged shortcomings of the discipline. Substantial resources are required in order to conduct policy-relevant research and effective anthropological intervention. Good anthropology, in any field, cannot be done on the cheap.

Another criticism of anthropology is even less understanding or tolerant, for it asks whether anthropological knowledge is intrinsically unreliable and irrelevant to the needs of policy makers and policy scientists. This positivisticly based criticism amounts to a rejection of the need for and validity of the knowledge anthropological theories and methods are designed to produce. This criticism not only fails to appreciate the epistemologically distinctive fashion in which anthropology seeks to relate to the people and processes its practitioners study but also refuses to recognize the "interested" nature of all "knowledge," including that produced by policy makers and policy scientists. This critique can, perhaps, be rephrased less grandly along the lines of "don't tell me what I don't want to know."

Because of its distinctive fieldwork methods and analytical approach (about which more will be said below), anthropology has had to confront a difficult methodological problem that other disciplines interested in public policy have largely ignored: the management of the operating distance created between a discipline and the people, practices, and processes it studies. Anthropologists have long struggled with the implications of two quite different ways of dealing with this problem. As a first option, anthropologists could seek to maintain the traditional conceptual distance between themselves and their subjects by a variety of means, including the use of non-reflexive concepts and measures, thereby placing themselves above their subjects, in a position of epistemological superiority. This was the traditional assumption that underlay the creation of ethnological museums throughout the western world in which aboriginal cultures were, in Ames's (1986) term, "museumified" as an exhibition of the power of westerners to objectify, represent, and display the lives and cultures of their "inferiors." To maintain a discipline's distance from and superiority over those whom it studies is to enhance the professional "authority" and "expertise" of its practitioners.

The second option is to acknowledge these problems of distance and representation and to confront the impact of our investigations and writings on those whom we study (cf. Brizinski, this volume). This approach recognizes the "interested" nature of all knowledge and commits its practitioners to create knowledge in such a manner as to assist the people we study (or with whom we work) to exercise greater control over managing their lives and social arrangements. In seeking to decrease the distance between the anthropologist and the subject, this approach consciously seeks to deconstruct postures of professional "authority" and "expertise" and to share knowledge with the people we study. It amounts to what Sansom (1985a) has termed the surrender of a disciplinary "concession" (or "franchise") which was once thought to enable anthropologists uniquely to "know" and to represent the nature and interests of aboriginal peoples.

In choosing to demystify their discipline, to decrease the distance between themselves and their subjects, and to situate themselves beside rather than above aboriginal peoples, anthropologists have recognized the interested nature of all social knowledge. This is not, however, in any sense the equivalent of "going Native": distinct analytical purposes still serve to distinguish the purposes of anthropology as a comparative discipline from those of the people whom anthropologists seek to understand and with whom they undertake to share their understandings. Nor does this entail any decrease in the discipline's commitment to the search for objectivity (Harries-Jones 1991). Instead, what it marks is acceptance of the proposition that objectivity is not to be achieved by hiding the relationship between investigators and the investigated behind a screen of abstract, depersonalized, and ostensibly "unbiased" concepts, procedures, or quantitative measures; objectivity is, rather, the outcome of continuous scholarly comparison and assessment that demands free and open discussion both inside and outside a given discipline or profession. From this perspective, objectivity is not a static entity or a "thing" which can be enjoyed only by a privileged few who purport to be uniquely empowered by specialized knowledge-producing procedures "owned" (cf. Gusfield 1981) by their disciplines; objectivity is, instead, an ideal which is to be sought through continuing exchange and evaluation of concerns, observations, and interpretations.

Anthropology's relationship with the people it studies is both unusually important for this particular discipline and professionally demanding of anthropologists. In closing the distance between themselves and their subjects, anthropologists may be permitted access to situations and concerns which lend depth and richness to our understanding and analysis of contemporary issues (cf. Scott, this volume). Yet this reliance on close working relationships with aboriginal peoples increases the vulnerability of anthropologists to sanctions that are less likely to be applied to, or to be as troubling for, practitioners of other disciplines. Anthropological research today tends to be more accessible and comprehensible to non-anthropologists than is generally the case with research conducted within other disciplines: ethnographic accounts usually yield more easily to non-professional readers than do statistical charts or legal arguments.

The more that anthropologists strive to make both the processes and products of their research open to scrutiny and involvement by aboriginal peoples, the greater the possibility that particular anthropological research tasks such as the recording of oral histories (see Cruikshank, this volume; Ignace, Speck, and Taylor, this volume) may be gradually repatriated by Native researchers. This shifting division of intellectual labour between anthropologists and their subjects creates a sense of contingency within anthropology that serves to challenge claims of exclusive possession of specialized professional expertise and knowledge. It makes the practice of participant-observation research methods far more demanding and the writing of ethnographic accounts far less certain in outcome than was once the case. But it also permits – nay, obliges – anthropologists to grapple with some essential questions about their discipline: what knowledge and knowledge for what? In facing these concerns anthropologists avail themselves of opportunities to produce scholarship that is both intellectually penetrating and socially responsible. The cost of realizing these opportunities is the abandoning of a professional posture designed first and foremost to enhance the prominence, rewards, and protective distancing of a discipline from those it studies.

THE ANTHROPOLOGICAL CONTRIBUTION

What particular capabilities and knowledge does anthropology have to offer? The principal strengths of the discipline can be attributed to its commitment to scientific humanism and its methodological reliance on participant-observation and the comparative perspective. While each of these represents an ideal that cannot always be realized and may not be entirely unproblematic, together they account for most of what is distinctive about anthropology as a discipline, as a way of seeing.

The mission of scientific humanism within anthropology has been to deliver the message that the ways of our society, or of any given society, are not the only imaginable or acceptable ones (Richardson 1975:524). Historically, anthropological expressions of this cultural relativism may have been more likely to produce generalized critiques of ethnocentrism than to expose existing colonial power relations. Nevertheless, an implicit corollary of the finding that social and cultural customs are varied and mutable has been the supposition that "we," too, are capable of changing our ways and our society. It should also be noted that the anthropological approach to cultural relativism has promoted not an unstinting avoidance of evaluating other cultures but a postponement of doing this until an informed judgment can be made (Maybury-Lewis 1985:134).

A number of characteristic features of anthropology derive from participant-observation research methods. Simply by virtue of "being there," by conducting field research in particular places for extended periods of time, anthropologists are more likely to be exposed to interests and activities that may not have been part of their initial research design (Lithman 1984:29–30). By not relying entirely or even primarily upon the collection of statistical data, the analysis of historical documents, or the administering of questionnaires, anthropologists interject themselves into unanticipated relationships and situations that may initially perplex them, but which ultimately demand explanation. By staying around any given community or interactional arena long enough to learn how to detect and situate local perceptions on complex issues, anthropologists practise research within an astutely cultivated interface between themselves and those whose lives they seek to understand (cf. O'Neill, Kaufert, et al., this volume). In discovering what they weren't initially looking for, anthropologists render themselves capable of being informed and instructed by their subjects. This provides an ongoing reflexivity and a capacity for discovery which is, in a number of respects, beyond the methodological charters or capabilities of other disciplines.

The anthropological practice of seeking to immerse oneself within fieldwork situations also encourages the development of a holistic perspective on social life. Interconnections between fields of activity that are, according to externally defined academic categories, supposed to be separate and distinct, emerge and force the participant-observer to recognize relationships that would otherwise tend to be overlooked. For instance, symbolically scripted local activities in Canada and elsewhere frequently furnish the rhetorical means by which aboriginal peoples endeavour to pursue their interests vis-à-vis national societies and state institutions (Dyck 1979,

1983a; Paine 1985); yet these ethnodramatic processes and performances have often been ignored in non-anthropological accounts of
political relations between Native peoples and governments.[9] The
continuing need to link communities to issues, localities to nations,
and the micro-level situation to macro-level forces and processes demands that anthropologists develop intrinsically holistic descriptive
and analytical techniques which are envied by non-anthropologists
(e.g., McNab 1986).

Finally, anthropologists are experienced in seeking to interpret
different societies and cultures to one another, for comparison has
always been an integral part of the discipline. Within anthropology
there is an abiding assumption that one ought to search out social
and cultural differences that will require investigation and explanation. The minimal frame of comparison has been the difference
between "us and them," the society of the anthropologist and that
of the "other" which he or she has undertaken to investigate. In
order to establish the nature and extent of differences, as well as to
demonstrate sometimes unanticipated similarities, anthropology has
encouraged the collection and analysis of detailed empirical data.

This empirical bent within the discipline fosters not only a
continuing concern with devising more effective methods for
gathering and interpreting information but also a proclivity for
breaking down stereotypical and categorical images of peoples,
institutions, and contexts. The inclination of anthropologists to
record and ponder their particular experience in investigating
relations between aboriginal people and the nation-state has slowly
but steadily led to an increased awareness within the discipline that
governments are by no means monolithic structures and that
aboriginal communities may also be divided in subtle and not so
subtle ways by internal cleavages.

Individual practitioners of other disciplines may employ some of
these approaches in their investigations, but they do so without
much encouragement or assistance from their disciplines. Anthropology, however, recognizes and promotes these as being appropriate and powerful tools for examining social life, even though
individual anthropologists may not always make full or effective use
of them. The power of basic anthropological modes of investigation
and explanation continues to attract people who initially encounter
field situations as historians, journalists, meteorologists, or teachers
but who subsequently become anthropologists in order to pursue
concerns with which their previous training had not equipped them
to deal. And the experience of conducting field research continues
to transform anthropologists who were initially concerned with
academically defined research interests into advocates (Schensul and

Schensul 1978:154) who are unable to ignore disquieting questions about the manner in which public policies and administrative measures frustrate the aspirations and constrain the life chances of aboriginal peoples.

But how, specifically, can anthropologists contribute to explaining and improving relations between aboriginal peoples and the nation-state in Canada? To begin with, anthropology offers a distinctive perspective on public policy and government administration that complements, balances, and extends the insights offered by other disciplines interested in social policy issues. Thus, while political scientists tend to focus primarily on the activities, responsibilities, and strategies of centrally located decision makers, anthropologists are inclined to be more attentive to considerations of the local-level impacts of particular policies and administrative measures.

While not denying the obvious importance of what occurs within formally constituted political arenas and institutions, the emerging anthropological approach to public policy seeks to reach beyond taken-for-granted definitions of purposes and of reality generated by government task forces, legislatures, and bureaucratic programs. Anthropologists are becoming experienced in detailing the often overlooked consequences of particular policies on aboriginal communities (e.g., Henriksen 1973; Driben and Trudeau 1983; Lithman 1983). At the same time, in tracing the evolution of government policies toward Native peoples, anthropologists have become acutely aware of the need to be not only well informed about the composition and operations of agencies such as the Department of Indian Affairs but also mindful of the historical and ideological forces that have determined the direction of these agencies (cf. Dyck 1991; Smith, this volume).

Yet the work of Sally Weaver (e.g., 1981, 1982, 1984a, 1984b, 1985a, 1985b, 1986a, 1986b, and this volume) amply demonstrates the capacity of ethnographers to make the adjustments needed to conduct research effectively in centres and offices of political and bureaucratic power, whether in Ottawa, Canberra, or elsewhere. Other anthropologists have investigated the workings of Native political organizations (Sawchuk 1978, 1985, and this volume; Dyck 1983b). By working at various levels both within aboriginal communities and organizations and with government bodies, anthropologists are developing a broadly based and increasingly sophisticated understanding of various dimensions of public policy processes and of Native-state relations in Canada. Individual anthropologists may be better suited to working at one level rather than another or on one side of the relationship rather than the other. Still, because of its intrinsically holistic and comparative nature, the discipline as a whole seeks to comprehend, integrate, and explicate the diversity of interests and insights gleaned from research conducted in these different locations.

The practical contributions of anthropologists to understanding and improving aboriginal peoples' relations with the nation-state reflect both longstanding and recent anthropological concerns. First,[10] there has been considerable demand for the services of anthropologists to record traditional and contemporary ways of aboriginal life, particularly with respect to the documentation of land use patterns in support of land claims (e.g., Kayahna Tribal Area Council 1985; Elias, this volume). In some parts of the country anthropologists are being asked to conduct relatively traditional forms of ethnological research on behalf of tribal councils (Ignace, Speck, and Taylor, this volume). These modest but important and demanding research tasks deserve greater recognition within the discipline than they are sometimes granted (Salisbury 1976). Since permission to conduct anthropological fieldwork at the local level must now be negotiated through local Native authorities, we can expect more anthropologists to be asked to reformulate the focus of their investigations so that their findings will be of use to the community as well as to the anthropologist (cf. Cove 1987).

A second means by which anthropologists may contribute to their discipline, to aboriginal peoples, and to Canadian society in general is through their activities as advisers or employees of band and tribal councils or regional, provincial, or national Native peoples' organizations or government agencies. Involvement in these kinds of applied activities is by no means unproblematic either for the anthropologists who engage in them (see Sawchuk, this volume) or for other members of the discipline who may not approve of such active forms of anthropological "participation" (Hedican 1986). The value of the practical advice or services rendered to clients or employers by individual anthropologists is, presumably, a matter to be determined by the parties concerned. Anthropologists are by no means the only persons who are willing or able to serve as consultants or employees in this field, although the contacts and information obtained by anthropologists through previous field research may place them in an advantageous position when interesting and/or lucrative contracts or positions become available. To earn a living in this highly competitive field, anthropologists will have to acquire skills that were not covered by their college textbooks (LaRusic 1985; Elias, this volume; Sawchuk, this volume), but this is the case for graduates of other disciplines as well.

Whether anthropologically trained persons who are employed outside museums or educational institutions ought to be considered to be "real" anthropologists is a question professional bodies such as the Canadian Anthropology Society/La société canadienne d'anthropologie (CASCA) and the Society for Applied Anthropology in Canada (SAAC) answer in the affirmative. Yet, since mutterings overheard in the corridors at anthropological conferences indicate that this view is not universally shared by all university- or museum-based anthropologists in this country, it is perhaps worth considering the question briefly. The determining of an appropriate balance between "participation" and "observation" within anthropology will always be a potentially contentious matter. Nevertheless, surely the measure of a contributing anthropologist – as opposed to a person who has anthropological training but who is no longer engaged in practising the discipline – revolves around whether or not he or she is still reading, writing, and discussing anthropology in any of the variety of ways in which this can be done. The information, experience, and analytical questions generated by applied anthropologists' involvement in the world of practical affairs can, when these are described, analysed, and published (or otherwise made available to members of the discipline and other interested readers) undoubtedly enrich anthropological scholarship.[11] It is hoped that anthropological analyses (such as the ones presented in this volume) of the dilemmas encountered by practitioners will, in turn, help to improve the calibre of anthropological praxis.

A third area of activity for anthropologists involves their ability to serve as cultural interpreters, whether as "expert witnesses" in court cases or simply as sympathetic observers who help to articulate the positions of Native communities to non-Native audiences. Well-documented ethnographies (e.g., Brody 1981) can, of course, do much to inform interested Canadians about the situation and aspirations of aboriginal communities and to interpret Natives and non-Natives to one another. Under certain conditions, anthropologists might even be able to serve as social ombudspersons (Salisbury 1976) who would undertake to mediate between communities and government agencies. But drawing the line between interpretation and representation can be a slippery matter, as Waldram (this volume) demonstrates: repeated acts of cultural translation can transform aboriginal peoples into clients whose ability to represent their own interests is further undermined each time an anthropological advocate speaks on their behalf (Henriksen 1985:121–4).

A fourth way in which anthropologists may help to improve the situation of aboriginal peoples in Canadian society is by conducting problem-oriented research which seeks to investigate sensitive but important issues in a manner which strives to be both objective and useful to Native communities. An excellent example of this type of work is provided by Dara Culhane Speck's (1987) study of the politics of medical care within a British Columbia community; on the other hand, a much criticized study conducted along these lines is Shkilnyk's (1985) account of the impact of relocation, mercury poisoning, and alcoholism upon an Ojibwa community in Ontario. Researchers who undertake to write social criticism must discover ways to combine tact and frankness and to balance the interests of the communities they wish to aid with the demands of scholarship (Dyck, this volume). In the long run, however, the ability of anthropologists to satisfy these demands and produce ethnographic studies which offer fresh and critical insights into matters other disciplines consider to be too difficult or controversial to discuss will determine whether or not anthropology will become a discipline of the twenty-first century.

THE IMPLICATIONS OF ENGAGEMENT

What has been said above outlines the emergence of a discipline which is vitally engaged in studying and seeking to improve relations between Native peoples and the nation-state. Yet there remains a number of unresolved questions and problems concerning the nature and implications of these various forms of engagement. Some of these will be identified, if not resolved, in this section.

Thus far we have spoken about the practice of anthropology without distinguishing between "applied anthropology" and "advocacy anthropology." Within the discipline generally there is little consistency in defining these terms (cf. Schensul and Schensul 1978; Chambers 1985; Van Willigen 1986; Wulff and Fiske 1987). Within Canadian anthropology, concerns about the practical implications of different forms of disciplinary involvement are beginning to emerge out of the collective experience of anthropological practitioners.

On the one hand, some anthropologists (Harries-Jones 1985; Mayberry-Lewis 1985; Van Esterik 1985) contend that engaging in advocacy through one's research and/or direct political participation need not detract from and, indeed, may well enhance the value of one's work both to the discipline and to the communities for which advocacy is undertaken. Other anthropologists (e.g., Salisbury 1976, 1986; Asch 1982, 1983; Feit 1982) suggest that one of the principal possible contributions of anthropologists to Native peoples is the lending of their expertise and societal legitimacy to support, albeit in a "professional" manner, aboriginal positions and claims. From this perspective, the prospect of declaring a personal commitment to "advocacy anthropology" is fraught with practical difficulties. To identify an anthropologist as an advocate within a courtroom or before a public inquiry may be to label him or her as "biased" and thus to strip that person of whatever "expert" knowledge or capacities she or he might otherwise be able to bring to bear in support of aboriginal peoples. This conflict between the immediate demands of being asked to "act like an expert" and the longer-term gains to be achieved by anthropologists through acknowledging and revealing the interested nature of all knowledge clearly warrants further discussion within the discipline.

Increased attention also needs to be given to the impact of anthropological praxis upon anthropological theory, methodologies, and writing. Feit (1982) has argued persuasively about the scholarly benefits that are being realized through anthropologists' engagement in the social and political issues that engulf aboriginal communities; the revising of theories of social change; the connection of macro and micro levels of analysis; and the sharpening of our understanding of the ways in which aboriginal communities seek to organize their lives within and around the intrusive institutional apparatus of the nation-state. Participation in debates outside academia also raises important epistemological issues that would not so readily surface if anthropologists spoke only to one another (Asch 1983:209). Questions of how anthropologists know what they know and how we can present our knowledge so that it can be understood outside the discipline are beginning to expand the horizons of anthropological perspective and reveal new ways in which we can make the so-called "soft" knowledge of ethnography speak to an otherwise "hard" world.

Finally, since anthropologists both inside and outside academia work not with cold, impersonal "data" but with living individuals and communities, one can expect ethical questions and problems to be matters of continuing concern for the discipline. In recent years several cases have raised concerns that are not covered by existing statements of professional ethics or by university committees for monitoring research ethics. One case involved an application by an alliance of tribal councils in British Columbia (including the Sto:lo Tribal Council and Nation, Nl'akapmx Tribal Council, and three bands of the Shuswap Nation) to obtain an injunction to prevent two anthropological researchers from working as researchers for either the Canadian National Railways (CNR) or the federal or provincial governments on a court case which was to determine whether the CNR could proceed with plans to double-track its lines through the Thompson-Fraser rivers corridor.[12] After working with and for B.C. Indian bands for some fifteen years, during which period the two researchers became recognized as "authorities" on many Native issues, and after being specifically contracted the year before to conduct research in support of the Nl'akapmx case against the CNR, the two decided to switch sides and to work for the railway. Indian leaders were shocked by this action, which they viewed as being grossly unethical; the B.C. Supreme Court granted their application for an injunction against the two.[13]

A second case (discussed in Harrison's essay, this volume) involved a boycott mounted by the Lubicon Indians of northern Alberta against an exhibition of Canadian Native art organized by the Glenbow Museum in conjunction with the staging of the 1988 Winter Olympic Games in Calgary. The oil company that sponsored the exhibition held a major interest in the traditional lands of the Lubicon people, lands that had been denied to them for decades despite official recognition of the legitimacy of their claim. The decision of the Glenbow Museum to carry on with its exhibition despite the boycott sparked intense debate within both the museum community and the Canadian Ethnology Society (the precursor to the Canadian Anthropology Society). A nationally broadcast radio debate between two senior anthropologists on the issue was continued in *Culture*, the journal of the Canadian Anthropological Society (Trigger 1988a, 1988b; Ames 1988) Such publications[14] identify some of the difficult choices that museum-based anthropologists have to face today.

These and the other complex, thorny concerns dealt with in this volume demonstrate the extent to which anthropology and anthropologists are in touch with, if not fully in control of, the issues that emerge from anthropology's attempts to study and influence for the better the relationship between aboriginal peoples, public policy, and the Canadian nation-state. By recognizing and responding to the challenging theoretical, methodological, political, and ethical questions raised by anthropological research and involvement in these fields, the contributors to this volume seek to extend the scope and utility of their discipline. In the next section James B. Waldram offers his personal critique of anthropological research and Native public policy.

A CRITICAL PERSPECTIVE

It would be fair to state that anthropology over the past century has had relatively little impact on the formation of Native public policy, through either the analyses of issues relevant to policy making or through more active participation in the policy field. This fact is quite remarkable given the paramount place of Native North Americans in the development of ethnological theory and methodology, and the rather large number (relative to the other social sciences) of anthropologists whose careers have been largely based on researching these peoples. Certainly there have been exceptions, and the great work of anthropologists involved in the Mackenzie Valley Pipeline Inquiry and the James Bay hydroelectric project springs to mind. But even these examples underscore an important point: the anthropologists involved were either on the fringe, as "expert witnesses" giving testimony within their narrowly defined areas of expertise (that is, as ethnographers; see Salisbury 1986; Usher, this volume), or were involved in comprehensive research activities that required them to develop understandings far beyond anthropology, including a variety of theoretical, methodological, and epistemological perspectives representative of the legal profession, the physical sciences, and the other social sciences. In both cases it was the prior existence of anthropological ethnographers that facilitated anthropological input into the policy process. There was a strong element of chance in this: the right people, anthropologists willing to become actively involved, happened to be in the field (or had recently conducted their research) when these political issues of national importance literally exploded around them. In this critique I wish to address some of the limitations of current anthropological research in the Native public policy arena, and describe where I believe the discipline must move if it is to have a greater impact. I use the term "policy process' to describe public policy formulation in its widest possible sense. In the case of Native Canadian research, this would include the participation of anthropologists in the actual decision-making process, as well as their research activities and the effects these have on policy.

It is essential first to delineate the kinds of anthropological research and activity that have been, and can be, undertaken in the policy process. Some research activity, for instance, may be timely and relevant but essentially undirected (that is, a product of the anthropologist's own intellectual curiosity). A good example of this type of research is Sally Weaver's work on Native policy making in Canada (see S. Weaver, this volume, 1981, 1986a, and 1986b). The research is exhaustive, and most certainly has the potential to inform public policy; that is, it is policy relevant. But time is not of the essence in this type of research, and it is frequently historical in nature, reviewing the development of past policy. At the other end of the scale is directed research, or research requested or contracted for specifically to address a developing policy issue. Work on Native land claims is a good example of this type of research. Time factors are more important in the completion of this research, although perhaps not crucial, and the anthropologist may still be afforded great opportunity to undertake the necessary work. Still further along the scale of directed research is that in which time is of the essence. This is particularly true of research required to meet the demands of legal action, such as injunctions to stop development on Native lands, or informing or reacting to imminent policy decisions. The anthropologist may not have the time, nor be afforded the resources (money, equipment, staff, etc.) to undertake a comprehensive research program in the ethnographic tradition. He or she must be able to respond to the needs of the policy process, and especially the Native community, for quick research. The simple fact is that much Native policy research is directed in one way or another by Native groups themselves, engaging anthropologists in contract research or through other arrangements, and is framed by shortages of both time and funds. If anthropologists are to be involved, they must be willing, and able, to respond accordingly.

The major limiting factor of much current anthropology is also one that many perceive to be its strength relative to other social sciences, that is, the participant-observation (P-O) methodology. The P-O technique is, of course, the signature method of the discipline, one that evolved essentially out of the Boasian tradition in North America, and with some of the early British ethnographers, such as Malinowski and Radcliffe-Brown. The technique required the anthropologist to spend a great deal of time in a particular locale, to participate in local life while simultaneously observing it. Comprehensive, primarily qualitative, fieldnotes were taken, and it was axiomatic that data analysis could not be properly undertaken until much data had been accumulated. Anthropology was "holistic," meaning that its practitioners felt compelled to investigate a wide variety of disparate cultural phenomena in a search for patterns and linkages. Such inquiry usually led to descriptions by cultural anthropologists of whole cultures, or by social anthropologists of significant segments of those cultures, written for a Euro-American, and invariably scientific, audience. Whether these accounts were, indeed, comprehensive and accurate reflections of the culture, particularly as the Natives themselves saw it, has only recently become an issue within the discipline (Marcus and Fischer 1986; Clifford and Marcus 1986).

Much anthropology in Canada is still strongly rooted in the ethnographic tradition, and it still has value in certain contexts where ample time is available for research. Indeed, some ethnographers have modified the classic ethnographic approach, developing community-based methodologies which involve the local people at all stages of research planning, data gathering, and analysis (see O'Neil, Kaufert, et al., this volume). The problem with P-O and the ethnographic approach is that it is a slow methodology. The public policy process in Canada moves much more quickly than the ability of many anthropologists to conduct research into questions of vital importance to that process.

In order to have some input into this hyper-policy process, characterized by very intense and rapidly paced activity, anthropologists wishing to be involved in this kind of work must present the necessary skills and techniques. While P-O strategies can still guide the anthropological inquiry, it is essential for the anthropologist of today to be well versed in a variety of research techniques, and this means borrowing liberally from other social sciences. First and foremost, the anthropologist must be able to undertake culturally appropriate survey research in combination with quantitative data analysis. These techniques can be most readily borrowed from sociology, a discipline with a relatively long quantitative tradition, and modified for use in the Native context. This modification is essential since Native communities present a variety of cultural and linguistic challenges to the researcher, and here anthropology finds itself in a good position to comprehend this pluralism. Related to the adoption of these quantitative techniques, of course, must be a change in attitude of many methodologically hostile anthropologists, who continue to argue that such strategies are not "anthropological" and are best left to other disciplines.[15]

Many of the papers in this volume also point out the need for anthropologists interested in policy-relevant work to have knowledge of, and research skills in, a wide variety of other areas. Since a great many of the current policy issues facing Native peoples are in the legal realm (e.g., land claims, treaty rights, constitutional issues, control of resource development), law and ethnohistory, which are informed by history and the policy actions of the past, are particularly important. However, current land and resource issues require a knowledge of geography, economics, and methodologies appropriate to these disciplines. Again, anthropologists are in an excellent position to modify the techniques of these disciplines to suit the Native context, and to respond to the methodologies of others used in the policy process.

While adopting quantitative techniques is essential, the anthropologist need not surrender the insights that the ethnographic tradition can offer. Indeed, in recent years some medical anthropologists have developed a methodology of "rapid ethnographic assessment" which is equally relevant to other areas of anthropological research (Bentley, Pelto, et al. 1988). Employing a variety of methodological strategies, including some borrowed from other areas (such as the use of focus groups, borrowed from marketing research), those involved in rapid ethnographic assessment are able to develop a body of cultural data that can inform a fast-paced policy process. This is particularly important where human and environmental disasters are indicated, such as the outbreak of life-threatening diarrhea described by Bentley, Pelto et al. (1988), or the type of "quick response" research described by Dyer, Piscou, and Gill (1990) in the context of the Exxon Valdez oil spill in Alaska. At the 1990 Society for Applied Anthropology meetings in York, England, it was evident that "disaster anthropology" had emerged recently as an important sub-area of the discipline. The ability to move quickly, to design and execute research rapidly, to expeditiously analyse the data and inject the results into the policy process can quite literally be matters of life and death for some people.

The ability to respond to a variety of conditions is the true hallmark of good anthropological research in the policy context. It is no longer acceptable to use P-O as an excuse to avoid research activities that prevent us from employing the ethnographic approach, or that require huge grants from funding agencies. Those anthropologists wishing to engage in this type of work must be able to respond to the many factors that govern the research process: time or urgency, money, staffing, and so on. The anthropologists should have the ability to develop and employ the necessary techniques to provide the best quality data given these factors. In this sense, the good anthropologist is a good social scientist, and anthropological training should reflect this fact. Furthermore, while the benefits of a team approach to research, which may or may not be multidisciplinary in nature, are obvious, the simple fact is that it is often not financially feasible and the anthropologist must be able to work effectively with a variety of techniques. The training of local residents in specific components of the research has become a common alternative; in effect the anthropologist builds his or her own team from the ground up. It is essential that the relevant parties in the policy process be made aware of the limitations of these factors in the execution of the research and the types and quality of data that can be produced, to allow them to make an informed decision with respect to approving the research or altering some of the factors. But this obligation on the part of the anthropologist is no different from the obligations of accountability already described in the literature (e.g., Freeman 1977; Ryan 1985).

There is no question that anthropology, grounded as it is in the ethnographic tradition and guided by the principle of holism, provides an excellent base for the production of policy-relevant research input into the public policy process. However, it is no longer sufficient to train students to be primarily ethnographers, and to count on the discipline's having some policy input almost inadvertently, as in the Mackenzie Valley and James Bay cases. The anthropologist of today must be skilled and inclined to undertake the best possible research, given the constraining factors, to meet the demands of a rapidly moving policy process. The discipline as a whole must shed its collective abhorrence of quantitative techniques and applied or advocacy research. There are those in other disciplines who, in the past, have filled the void left by anthropologists unable to respond to the policy process, yet many anthropologists have been critical of their work.

Intellectually, we need also to free ourselves from the view that there must be a theoretical benefit to the discipline from applied work. Applied and advocacy anthropology, done for its own sake by trained anthropologists, should be accepted for what it is, basic praxis of the discipline. Of course it is appealing for theoretical or ethnographic benefits to derive from applied, policy-relevant research, but the existence of such benefits should not be the standard by which the quality of the work itself is measured.

Anthropologists who have undertaken research among Native Canadians, and who in many cases have built their careers on such research, must recognize their moral obligation to assist these peoples to achieve their goals. In the case of largely inactive anthropologists, this obligation may consist of simply promoting in their own departments the kinds of approaches and methodologies discussed here. For the rest of us, it means being willing to help when requested to do so, in a context in which there may be little or no theoretical benefit to the discipline, nor any monetary or other professional benefit to the anthropologist. A purely self-serving anthropology is, in reality, a neocolonial anthropology.

If anthropologists believe they do have something to contribute to the policy process, that indeed their ethnographic perspective best informs the other methodologies required, then the time to act is at hand. Otherwise, the discipline and its practitioners are likely to remain at the fringe of the public policy process, wringing their hands and wondering why they are never consulted.

Certainly the future is going to provide ample opportunity for anthropologists to become involved in the public policy process as it pertains to Native Canadians. Indeed, Canada may well be on the threshold of a new era of Native participation in the policy arena, and the events of the summer of 1990 bear this out. The action of the Assembly of Manitoba Chiefs and Elijah Harper in scuttling the Meech Lake Accord is perhaps the most significant of recent instances where Native peoples have influenced the policy process through peaceful, democratic means. In contrast, the efforts of the Mohawks from Kanesatake and Kahnawake to protect their land through militant action indicates a profound frustration with this process, and may inspire similar efforts throughout the country in the near future.

But some important policy-related issues remain unresolved. The Lubicon Indians are fighting against a logging and milling plan in northern Alberta. The James Bay Cree are gearing up to oppose Phase Two of the James Bay hydroelectric project. The Indians and Metis on the Ontario side of James Bay have formed a coalition to facilitate their effective participation in environmental assessment hearings concerning Ontario Hydro plans to construct generating facilities on the rivers in the Moose River Basin. The report of Manitoba's Aboriginal Justice Inquiry recommended broad changes to the justice system. And British Columbia Chief Justice Allan McEachern's decision against the land claim of the Gitksan-Wet'su-wet'en has dramatically altered the whole comprehensive claims process. Given that a 1990 public opinion poll indicated only 48 percent of Canadians supported the notion of aboriginal self-government (*Globe and Mail*, 30 October 1990), it will continue to be difficult for the Native peoples in Canada to affect public policy in a manner that will readily result in the recognition of their aboriginal rights, the resolution of their land claims, and the implementation of self-government structures. Despite progress on the constitutional front, these are public policy issues in which anthropology can make a contribution. Indeed, we would suggest that anthropology has a responsibility to Native Canadians in this regard.

AN OVERVIEW OF THE VOLUME

The essays in this volume examine a wide range of historical and contemporary issues related to anthropology and public policy in the Native Canadian context. Presented here are both historical studies and case studies of contemporary activity by anthropologists. They speak to the theoretical, methodological, and ethical issues of relevance to the public policy arena.

If anthropologists are to have any input into the policy-making process in Canada, they must have a sound understanding of how they, and their data, have been utilized in the past. Part One of this volume, therefore, contains three papers that examine Native public policy in the historical context. The first paper, by Derek Smith, on the implementation of the Eskimo Disk List System in the North, demonstrates the manner in which anthropologists can undertake ethnohistorical research into areas of public policy. Sally Weaver's examination of the Hawthorn report, a 1960s effort to utilize anthropologists and other social scientists in the formulation of Indian policy, provides a detailed examination of the manner in which anthropologists and their data were utilized, and offers some concrete lessons to be heeded by anthropologists working in the policy arena in the future. Peter Usher provides an overview of impact assessment and social change in the North, focusing on the Mackenzie Valley Pipeline, or Berger Inquiry to describe the manner in which this important policy issue affected both social science theory and methodology.

Part Two examines the relationship between anthropology and Native peoples from the personal perspective of each practitioner and of those affected. Julie Cruikshank and Peggy Brizinski deal with the process of conducting ethnography in the Canadian North, and the effects of ethnography on both the discipline of anthropology and the Native residents. Cruikshank presents a macro-level analysis of the politics of ethnography, addressing such key questions as the manner in which cultures have been, and can be, portrayed by anthropologists and the role of collaborative research in producing both sensitive and useful texts from the Native perspective. Brizinski, in contrast, offers a micro-level, candid, discussion of her investigation of the perceptions of northern Natives of anthropological and related social science researchers, including personal observations of reactions to her as an anthropologist. The next paper presents a critical discussion of anthropologists and their work by three British Columbia Natives, Ron Ignace, George Speck, and Renee Taylor. These individuals bring to the discussion a solid knowledge of academic anthropology combined with practical experience in the Native public policy arena, and are therefore able to offer insiders' perspectives on the many questions raised by other non-Native authors in the volume. Noel Dyck, in his contribution, questions why anthropologists tend to shy away from certain areas of research that, while apparently sensitive in nature, would nevertheless have great salience for questions of public policy. For Dyck, it is neither useful, nor responsible, for anthropologists to ignore these difficult issues.

The papers in Part Three describe various practical applications of anthropology, and of the work of anthropologists, in the Native policy arena. The first three papers tackle questions of research in Native public policy from somewhat different angles. John O'Neil, Joseph Kaufert, Patricia Kaufert, and William Koolage describe a variety of medical research projects in the North which have had as their focus a community-based approach involving collaboration with Native researchers and staff. Doug Elias provides a comprehensive discussion of the methodological expertise and limitations that anthropology offers Native communities involved in land claims research, emphasizing the complexities involved that dictate the adoption, where resources are available, of a multidisciplinary team approach. Finally, Sawchuk provides us with an inside look at the trials and tribulations of an anthropologist involved in land claims research, and offers a critical evaluation of the future role of anthropologists working for Native political organizations.

The final three papers in the volume provide a variety of perspectives on anthropological issues and Native public policy. James B. Waldram presents a case study of his own role as an appointed delegate for a Native community involved in negotiations with a provincial government and describes the limits to which he could go as a non-resident community representative/advocate anthropologist. Colin Scott's examination of the politics of "culture" in the Indian policy arena examines the manner in which concepts such as "custom" and "tradition" are manipulated by both Indian and non-Native politicians as they seek to achieve their respective political ends, and he describes the manner in which anthropology has historically contributed to these static views of both concepts.

Julia Harrison's essay, the final paper in the volume, concerns an event that polarized the Canadian anthropological community in 1987 and 1988. The event was the Glenbow Museum's exhibition *The Spirit Sings*, which was mounted in conjunction with the 1988 Calgary Winter Olympic Games. The exhibition was the target of a boycott attempt by the Lubicon Lake Indian Band and its supporters, including many Canadian anthropologists. Harrison describes her own personal view of the controversy, as the curator of the exhibit and as an anthropologist, and both describes and analyses the opposition that developed. Perhaps more so than any other issue in recent years, the Glenbow boycott demonstrates the degree to which some anthropologists are prepared to enter into the political process in a direct way, eschewing the traditional role of researcher to become politically active. The papers in this volume clearly indicate that such activity is by no means without controversy or complications.

NOTES

1 See, for instance, the following newspaper articles on the episode: "Haida canoe trip up the Seine native artist's fantasy come true' (*Globe and Mail*, 30 September 1989, C-4) and "Paddlers enter Paris flying the Haida flag" (*Vancouver Sun*, 2 October 1989, A-1).

2 The terms "Native" and "aboriginal" are used throughout this introduction to refer to the different peoples of indigenous ancestry in Canada. These overarching terms, which are used to refer generally to a range of peoples of indigenous ancestry, including Indians (who are registered as such under the terms of the Indian Act), non-status Indians, Metis, and Inuit peoples, are best paired with the plural "peoples" in order to recognize the commonalities among particular peoples who remain, nonetheless, distinct from one another in other ways.

3 A recent issue of *Practicing Anthropology* (1990, 12[2]) examines the relationship between anthropologists and American Indians.

4 There were, of course, some notable exceptions to this general pattern; see especially Hanks and Hanks (1950), a much undervalued anthropological analysis that was largely completed before World War Two.

5 See Macgregor (1989:65, 75, 134) and Hodgins and Benidickson (1989: 268) for reports of both positive and negative appraisals by Native peoples of the performance of particular anthropologists.

6 See Dyck (1990) for a review of anthropological writings on Native issues before and since the 1960s.

7 The latter comment was made by Sally Weaver in her capacity as a discussant of papers presented on "The State of the Art of Native Studies" at the Canadian Ethnic Studies Association Conference held in Calgary, Alberta, 20 October 1989.

8 This type of argument has most recently been levelled at non-Native writers by critics who claim that "their culture is one of the only valuable commodities natives own in this country, and for white writers to keep telling their stories is inevitably appropriation." "Minorities go toe to toe with majority" (*Globe and Mail*, 30 September 1989, C-1).

9 Jhappan (1990) is an exception to this general observation. See also Pal for a revealing admission by a political scientist that "the [public policy] analyst's art is a curious alchemy of smoke and substance" (1987:244).

10 The following listing of practical activities or roles that can be played by anthropologists is based largely, but not exclusively, upon Feit (1982).

11 In the interests of fairness, the same criteria ought to be applied to tenured university professors who, for whatever reasons, choose to retain teaching positions even though they have effectively withdrawn from reading or writing anthropology.

12 "Researchers criticized," *Vancouver Sun*, 17 September 1986, A-2.

13 While the injunction was granted to prevent the two researchers from

working for the CNR on the project, they were also awarded $60,000 in compensation for their loss of income through the decision.

14 See the special issue of the *Native Studies Review* (1987, 3[2]) on Native peoples and museums.

15 Dell Hymes (1974:29) once identified in anthropology "a trained incapacity to rise above one's professional subject and into the modern world and a view of anthropology as equivalent only to ethnology." I would argue that the situation has not changed much in the years since his remark. The volume in which this article appears, also cited by Hymes, presents a now dated, but essentially accurate, critique of anthropology as a whole; it seems that the lessons of this volume have been forgotten.

BIBLIOGRAPHY

Ahenakew, David. 1985. "Aboriginal Title and Aboriginal Rights: The Impossible and Unnecessary Task of Identification and Definition." In *The Quest for Justice: Aboriginal Peoples and Aboriginal Rights*, ed. M. Boldt and J.A. Long, 24–30. Toronto: University of Toronto Press.

Ames, Michael M. 1986. *Museums, the Public and Anthropology: A Study of the Anthropology of Anthropology*. Vancouver: University of British Columbia Press. New Delhi: Concept Publishing Company.

– 1988. "The Liberation of Anthropology: A Rejoinder to Professor Trigger's 'A Present of their Past.'" *Culture* 8(1):81–5.

Asch, Michael. 1982. "Dene Self-Determination and the Study of Hunter Gatherers in the Modern World." In *Politics and History in Band Societies*, ed. E. Leacock and R.B. Lee, 347–71. Cambridge: Cambridge University Press.

– 1983. "Native Research and the Public Forum: Implications for Ethnological Theory." In *Consciousness and Inquiry: Ethnology and Canadian Realities*, ed. F. Manning, 201–10. Ottawa: National Museums of Canada.

– 1984. *Home and Native Land: Aboriginal Rights and the Canadian Constitution*. Toronto: Methuen.

Bentley, Margaret E., G. Pelto, W. Strauss, et al. 1988. "Rapid Ethnographic Assessment: Applications in a Diarrhea Management Program." *Social Science and Medicine* 27(1):107–16.

Berger, Thomas R. 1977. *Northern Frontier, Northern Homeland: The Report of the Mackenzie Valley Pipeline Inquiry*, vol. 1. Ottawa: Supply and Services Canada.

Brody, Hugh. 1975. *The People's Land: Eskimos and Whites in the Eastern Arctic*. Harmondsworth: Penguin

– 1981. *Maps and Dreams: Indians and the British Columbia Frontier*. Vancouver: Douglas & McIntyre.

Bruner, Edward M. 1986. "Ethnography as Narrative." In *The Anthropology of Experience*, eds. V. Turner and E.M. Bruner, 139–55. Urbana/Chicago: University of Illinois Press.

Buchignani, Norman. 1986. "Some Practical Points on Doing Contract Research in One's Own Society." In *Anthropology as Praxis*, ed. P. Spaulding, 145–61. Calgary: Department of Anthropology, University of Calgary.

Cardinal, Harold. 1969. *The Unjust Society: The Tragedy of Canada's Indians*. Edmonton: Hurtig.

Chambers, Erve. 1985. *Applied Anthropology: A Practical Guide*. Englewood Cliffs, New Jersey: Prentice-Hall.

Clifford, James, and G.E. Marcus, eds. 1986. *Writing Culture: The Poetics and Politics of Ethnography*. Berkeley: University of California Press.

Cole, Douglas. 1985. *Captured Heritage: The Scramble for Northwest Coast Artifacts*. Vancouver/Toronto: Douglas & McIntyre.

Cove, John. 1987. *Shattered Images: Dialogues and Meditations on Tsimshian Narratives*. Ottawa: Carleton University Press.

Culhane Speck, Dara. 1987. *An Error in Judgement: The Politics of Medical Care in an Indian/White Community*. Vancouver: Talonbooks.

Deloria, Vine, Jr. 1969. *Custer Died For Your Sins: An Indian Manifesto*. New York: Macmillan.

Driben, Paul, and R.S. Trudeau. 1983. *When Freedom is Lost: The Dark Side of the Relationship Between Government and the Fort Hope Band*. Toronto: University of Toronto Press.

Dunning, R.W. 1964. "Some Problems of Reserve Indian Communities." *Anthropologica* 6:3–38.

Dyck, Noel. 1979. "Powwow and the Expression of Community in Western Canada." *Ethnos* 44(1–2):78–98.

– 1983a. "Political Powwow: The Rise and Fall of an Urban Native Festival." In *The Celebration of Society: Perspectives on Contemporary Cultural Performance*, ed. F. Manning, 165–84. Bowling Green, Ohio: Bowling Green University Popular Press.

– 1983b. "Representation and Leadership of a Provincial Indian Association." In *The Politics of Indianness in Canadian Society*, ed. A. Tanner, 197–305. St John's: Institute of Social and Economic Research, Memorial University of Newfoundland.

– 1985. "Aboriginal Peoples and the Nation-State: An Introduction to the Analytical Issues." In *Indigenous Peoples and the Nation-State: Fourth World Politics in Canada, Australia and Norway*, ed. N. Dyck, 1–26. St John's: Institute of Social and Economic Research, Memorial University of Newfoundland.

– 1990. "Culture, Communities and Claims: Anthropology and Native Studies in Canada." *Canadian Ethnic Studies* 22(3):40–55.

– 1991. *What is the Indian "Problem": Tutelage and Resistance in Canadian*

Indian Administration. St John's: Institute of Social and Economic Research, Memorial University of Newfoundland.

Dyer, Christopher L., J.S. Picou, and D. Gill,. 1990. "Social Relations and Subsistence Tradition Disruption among Native Alaskans." Paper presented to the Society for Applied Anthropology Conference, York, England, 28 March–1 April 1990.

Eddy, E.M., and W.L. Partridge, eds. 1987. *Applied Anthropology in America*. 2d ed. New York: Columbia University Press.

Feit, Harvey. 1982. "The Future of Hunters within Nation-States: Anthropology and the James Bay Cree." In *Politics and History in Band Societies*, eds. E. Leacock and R.B. Lee, 373–411. Cambridge: Cambridge University Press.

Freeman, Milton M.R. 1977. "Anthropologists and Policy-Relevant Research: The Case for Accountability." In *Applied Anthropology in Canada*, ed. Sally Weaver. Ottawa: Canadian Ethnology Society.

Gusfield, Joseph R. 1981. *The Culture of Public Problems: Drinking-Driving and the Symbolic Order*. Chicago: University of Chicago Press.

Hanks, L.M., and J.R. Hanks. 1950. *Tribe under Trust: A Study of the Blackfoot Tribe of Alberta*. Toronto: University of Toronto Press.

Harries-Jones, Peter. 1985. "From Cultural Translator to Advocate – Changing Circles of Interpretation." In *Advocacy and Anthropology: First Encounters*, ed. R. Paine, 224–48. St John's: Institute of Social and Economic Research, Memorial University of Newfoundland.

– 1991. *Making Knowledge Count: Advocacy and Social Science*. Montreal and Kingston: McGill-Queen's University Press.

Hawthorn, H., ed. 1967. *A Survey of the Contemporary Indians of Canada: Economic, Political, Educational Needs and Policies*, 2 vols. Ottawa: Queen's Printer.

Hedican, Edward J. 1986. "Anthropologists and Social Involvement: Some Issues and Problems." *Canadian Review of Sociology and Anthropology* 23(4): 544–58.

Hedley, Max. 1986. "Community-Based Research: The Dilemma of Contract." *Canadian Journal of Native Studies* 6(1):91–103.

Henricksen, Georg. 1973. *Hunters in the Barrens: The Naskapi on the Edge of the Whiteman's World*. St John's: Institute of Social and Economic Research, Memorial University of Newfoundland.

– 1985. "Anthropologists as Advocates – Promoters of Pluralism or Makers of Clients?" In *Advocacy and Anthropology – First Encounters*, ed. R. Paine, 119–29. St John's: Institute of Social and Economic Research, Memorial University of Newfoundland.

Herzfeld, Michael. 1987. *Anthropology Through the Looking-Glass: Critical Ethnography in the Margins of Europe*. Cambridge/New York: Cambridge University Press.

Hodgins, Bruce W., and J. Benidickson. 1989. *The Temagami Experience:*

Recreation, Resources and Aboriginal Rights in the Northern Ontario Wilderness.
Toronto: University of Toronto Press.

Hymes, Dell. 1974. "The Use of Anthropology: Critical, Political, Personal."
In *Reinventing Anthropology*, ed. Dell Hymes, 3–79. New York: Vintage.

Jhappan, C. Radha. 1990. "Indian Symbolic Politics: The Double-Edged
Sword of Publicity." *Canadian Ethnic Studies* 22(3):19–39.

Johnson, Ian. 1984. *Helping Indians to Help Themselves – A Committee to Investigate Itself: The 1951 Indian Act Consultation Process.* Ottawa: Treaties and
Historical Research Centre, Department of Indian and Northern Affairs.

Kayahna Tribal Area Council. 1985. *The Kayahna Region Land Utilization and
Occupancy Study.* Big Trout Lake, Ontario: Kayahna Tribal Area Council.

LaRusic, Ignatius. 1985. "Reinventing the Advocacy Wheel." In *Advocacy
and Anthropology: First Encounters*, ed. R. Paine, 21–7. St John's: Institute
of Social and Economic Research, Memorial University of Newfoundland.

Lithman, Y.G. 1983. *The Practice of Underdevelopment and the Theory of
Development: The Canadian Indian Case.* Stockholm: Department of Social
Anthropology, University of Stockholm.

– 1984. *The Community Apart: A Case Study of a Canadian Indian Reserve
Community.* Winnipeg: University of Manitoba Press.

Macgregor, Roy. 1989. *Chief: The Fearless Vision of Billy Diamond.* Markham,
Ontario: Viking.

McNab, David T. 1986. "Some Reflections on the Life and Hard Times of
an Indian Land Claims Researcher.' *Canadian Journal of Native Studies*
6(1):129–39.

Marcus, George E., and M.M.J. Fischer. 1986. *Anthropology as Cultural
Critique: An Experimental Moment in the Human Sciences.* Chicago: University of Chicago Press.

Maybury-Lewis, David. 1985. "A Special Sort of Pleading – Anthropology at
the Service of Ethnic Groups." In *Advocacy and Anthropology – First
Encounters*, ed. R. Paine, 130–48. St John's: Institute of Social and
Economic Research, Memorial University of Newfoundland.

Paine, Robert. 1985a. "Ethnodrama and the 'Fourth World': The Saami
Action Group in Norway, 1979–81." In *Indigenous Peoples and the Nation-
State: Fourth World Politics in Canada, Australia and Norway*, ed. N. Dyck,
191–235. St John's: Institute of Social and Economic Research, Memorial
University of Newfoundland.

– 1985b. *Advocacy and Anthropology – First Encounters.* St John's: Institute of
Social and Economic Research, Memorial University of Newfoundland.

Pal, Leslie A. 1987. *Public Policy Analysis: An Introduction.* Toronto: Methuen.

Pettipas, Katherine A. 1988. "Severing the Ties That Bind: The Canadian
Indian Act and the Repression of Indigenous Religious Systems in the
Prairie Region, 1896–1951." Ph.D. diss., University of Manitoba.

Richardson, Miles. 1975. "Anthropologist – The Myth Teller." *American Ethnologist* 2(3):517–33.

Ryan, Joan. 1978. *Wall of Words: The Betrayal of the Urban Indian*. Toronto: Peter Martin Associates.

– 1985. "Decolonializing Anthropology." In *Advocacy and Anthropology – First Encounters*, ed. R. Paine, 208–14. St John's: Institute of Social and Economic Research, Memorial University of Newfoundland.

Salisbury, Richard F. 1976. "The Anthropologist as Societal Ombudsman." In *Development from Below: Anthropologists and Development Situations*, ed. D.C. Pitt, 255–65. The Hague: Mouton.

– 1983. "Applied Anthropology in Canada: Problems and Prospects." In *Consciousness and Inquiry: Ethnology and Canadian Realities*, ed. F. Manning, 192–200. Ottawa: National Museums of Canada.

– 1986. *A Homeland for the Cree: Regional Development in James Bay, 1971–1981*. Kingston and Montreal: McGill-Queen's University Press.

Sansom, Basil. 1985a. "Aborigines, Anthropologists and Leviathan." In *Indigenous Peoples and the Nation-State: Fourth World Politics in Canada, Australia and Norway*, ed. N. Dyck, 67–94. St John's: Institute of Social and Economic Research, Memorial University of Newfoundland.

– 1985b. "Canons of Anthropology?" In *Advocacy and Anthropology – First Encounters*, ed. R. Paine, 3–12. St John's: Institute of Social and Economic Research, Memorial University of Newfoundland.

Sawchuk, Joe. 1978. *The Metis of Manitoba: Reformulation of an Ethnic Identity*. Toronto: Peter Martin Associates.

– 1985. "The Metis, Non-Status Indians and the New Aboriginality: Government Influence on Native Political Alliances and Identity." *Canadian Ethnic Studies* 17(2):135–46.

Schensul, S.L., and J.J. Schensul. 1978. "Advocacy and Applied Anthropology." In *Social Scientists as Advocates: Views From the Applied Disciplines*, eds. G.H. Weber and G.J. McCall, 121–65. Beverly Hills: Sage Publications.

Shimpo, M., and R. Williamson. 1965. *Socio-Cultural Disintegration Among the Fringe Saulteaux*. Saskatoon: Centre for Community Studies, University of Saskatchewan.

Shkilnyk, Anastasia M. 1985. *A Poison Stronger than Love: The Destruction of an Ojibwa Community*. New Haven: Yale University Press.

Stull, D.D., and J.J. Schensul, eds. 1987. *Collaborative Research and Social Change: Applied Anthropology in Action*. Boulder, Colorado and London: Westview Press.

Tanner, Adrian, ed. 1983. *The Politics of Indianness in Canadian Society*. St John's: Institute of Social and Economic Research, Memorial University of Newfoundland.

Tremblay, M.-A. 1983. "Anthropology in Question: What Knowledge and

Knowledge for What?" In *Consciousness and Inquiry: Ethnology and Canadian Realities*, ed. F. Manning, 332–47. Ottawa: National Museums of Canada.

Trigger, Bruce G. 1988a. "A Present of Their Past? Anthropologists, Native People and Their Heritage." *Culture* 8(1):71–9.

– 1988b. "Reply to Michael Ames." *Culture* 8(1):87–8.

Van Esterik, Penny. 1985. "Confronting Advocacy Confronting Anthropology." In *Advocacy and Anthropology: First Encounters*, ed. R. Paine, 59–77. St John's: Institute of Social and Economic Research, Memorial University of Newfoundland.

Van Willigen, John. 1986. *Applied Anthropology: An Introduction*. South Hadley, Massachusetts: Bergin and Garvey.

Waldram, James B. 1988. *As Long as the Rivers Run: Hydroelectric Development and Native Communities in Western Canada*. Winnipeg: University of Manitoba Press.

Weaver, Sally M. 1981. *Making Canadian Indian Policy: The Hidden Agenda, 1968–70*. Toronto: University of Toronto Press.

– 1982. "The Joint Cabinet/National Indian Brotherhood Committee: A Unique Experiment in Pressure Group Relations." *Canadian Public Administration* 25(2):211–39.

– 1984a. "A Comment on the Penner Report." *Canadian Public Policy* 10(2): 215–21.

– 1984b. "Struggles of the Nation-State to Define Aboriginal Ethnicity: Canada and Australia." In *Minority and Mother Country Imagery*, ed G.L. Gold, 182–210. St John's: Institute of Social and Economic Research, Memorial University of Newfoundland.

– 1985a. "Federal Difficulties With Aboriginal Rights Demands." In *The Quest For Justice: Aboriginal Peoples and Aboriginal Rights*, eds M. Boldt and J.A. Long, 139–47. Toronto: McClelland & Stewart.

– 1985b. "Political Representivity and Indigenous Minorities in Canada and Australia." In *Indigenous Peoples and the Nation-State: Fourth World Politics in Canada, Australia and Norway*, ed. N. Dyck, 113–50. St John's: Institute of Social and Economic Research, Memorial University of Newfoundland.

– 1986a. "Indian Policy in the New Conservative Government, Part 1: The Neilson Task Force of 1985." *Native Studies Review* 2(1):1–43.

– 1986b. "Indian Policy in the New Conservative Government, Part 2: The Neilson Task Force in the Context of Recent Policy Initiatives." *Native Studies Review* 2(2):1–45.

Weaver, Thomas. 1985. "Anthropology as a Policy Science: Part 1, A Critique." *Human Organization* 44(2):97–105.

Wulff, R.M., and S.J. Fiske, eds. 1987. *Anthropological Praxis: Translating Knowledge Into Action*. Boulder, Colorado and London: Westview Press.

PART ONE

Historical Perspectives on Native Policy Issues

The analysis of historical Native policy issues is essential if we hope to understand the role anthropology might play in such areas on the future. Toward this end, the three papers in this section examine a variety of policy related issues in historical context. The opening paper, by Derek Smith, focuses on the ill-fated attempts of the federal government to implement a "disk list" system for registering Inuit (or "Eskimos," the term used at the time) in a manner similar to the system for registering Indians. Smith's paper demonstrates how public policy in this instance was guided primarily by the concerns of the administrators, who felt they needed a more efficient system for keeping track of the Inuit. He investigates the unintended but serious consequences of the introduction of this bureaucratic identification for the Inuit.

Sally Weaver examines the development of Indian policy in the late 1960s, paying special attention to the "White Paper" and the use of anthropological data presented in the "Hawthorn report." Like Smith, Weaver demonstrates how government has made policy with respect to Native peoples in the absence of, or while ignoring, anthropological and other available information on such peoples. Both papers stress the fact that government policy often appears to develop in an information vacuum. We are left to ponder how anthropologists and their work can break through, where appropriate, to inform such policy.

The final paper in this section, by Peter Usher, looks back at the Mackenzie Valley Pipeline Inquiry and its role in reshaping both theoretical and methodological understandings of social impact assessment. The experience of addressing the inquiry forged a new relationship between social scientists, many of whom were bridging the gap between theoretical and applied approaches, and the Native community. The resulting new paradigm of social and economic development directly challenged the existing modernization/acculturation paradigm that had its roots in earlier anthropological depictions of Native peoples, and, in so doing, sparked a much needed shift in anthropological thought. The relationship between theory development and practical applications of anthropological and social scientific approaches is clearly articulated in the highly public nature of the inquiry.

2 The Emergence of "Eskimo Status": An Examination of the Eskimo Disk List System and Its Social Consequences, 1925–1970

DEREK G. SMITH

INTRODUCTION

In February 1941 a formal decision the Northwest Territories Council[1] voted to adopt a system of identification for all Eskimos[2] of the Territories. Intended to facilitate the maintenance of virtually all governmental and administrative records, the decision made particular mention of records of "hunting, education, hospitalization and relief"[3] and also included provision both for the issue of "numbered identification discs to Eskimos" which would bear the Canadian coat of arms and for a sufficient number of disks to be struck.[4] Census enumerators were equipped with supplies of disks, registration forms, and detailed instructions in order to link up the initial Eskimo registration with the conduct of the 1941 Canadian Census.[5] This registration system, the outcome of discussions and debates extending back into the 1920s, remained in force until the early 1970s.

My purpose here is essentially two-fold: (a) to outline the history of the Eskimo Disk List System from available archival records and (b) to suggest how this system may have entailed social consequences for the Eskimo/Inuit population, particularly those concerning structured inequalities in Canada, which helped to create a stigmatized ethnic underclass of Northern persons.

My approach to these purposes is guided by theoretical perspectives derived from several sources: (a) from the kind of analysis of the relationship among forms of knowledge and power developed by Foucault (e.g., 1979), (b) from the analysis of "modes of domination" and "symbolic violence" in the work of Bourdieu (1989: 183–97), and (c) from the analysis of the impact of imperial/colonial structures (and especially "structural violence") in the work of Galtung (1980).

Social inequality in the Canadian Arctic is surely one of the area's most important and most visible social issues. It has been widely documented and studied from a variety of theoretical perspectives, including "relations of tutelage" (Honigmann and Honigmann 1965, 1970); "patronage, brokerage, and clientage" (Paine 1971, 1977); "plural society" relations (D.G. Smith 1975a); and relations of ethnic inequality (Vallee 1967). While each of these has some insight to bring to the problem, I believe each to be inadequate in some important respect. These perspectives do, however, point to the kind of social inequality that I now believe to be more fruitfully dealt with in *theories of practice* than in either structural/organizational/institutional analyses, or in sociological and social-psychological actor-centred theoretical constructions.

Foucault (1990, but esp. 1979), for example, clearly shows that projects of governance by the state are accomplished in several ways, among them the forging of direct links between the state and the individual and the exercise of "intensive surveillance" over the population to be governed through the acquisition of particular kinds of knowledge about its constituent members. Richard Saumarez Smith (1985) takes up Foucault's insights and applies them with great effect to the development of British Imperial rule in India after 1860 by relating "the two instruments of British Imperial rule in India, village records and district reports, to a wider discourse between knowledge and administrative control" (R.S. Smith 1985: 153). Smith shows that underlying this system were a number of assumptions: "that society could be represented as a series of facts, that the form of these facts was self-evident, and that administrative power stemmed from an accurate knowledge and an efficient use of these facts. As an instrument of the government, these records were always bound up with the technologies of governing" (R.S. Smith 1985:154).

This analysis was further postulated on the idea that "to 'know' Indian society was to know what was good for it" (R.S. Smith 1985:154). Smith shows that these systems of record and report have a "construction of reality embedded within them" (R.S. Smith 1985:154). He also draws the conclusion that "once society had been broken down into a group of individuals, by means of censuses and surveys, it was no longer necessary to delegate the function of the government contractually through privileged instruments of mediation, whether families or the "little republics" of village communities. An individual's relation to the State could be defined instead by his [or her] status" (R.S. Smith 1985:156). The analogy to the projects of governance by the Canadian state in the Arctic is arresting – certainly not in detail, but in the fundamental strategies of governance and their impacts on the population.

Dorothy E. Smith (1990, esp. ch. 4) explores the relationships among knowledge, "textual realities," and power in practices of ruling. The relevance of many of her insights to the case material I present here is remarkable. She refers to state records as "textual realities," which, she argues, "are not fictions or falsehoods; they are normal, integral, and indeed essential features of the relations and apparatuses of ruling" (D.E. Smith 1990:83). But she does go on to argue that "such textual surfaces presuppose an organization of power as the concerting of people's activities and the uses of organization to enforce processes producing a version of the world that is peculiarly one-sided, that is known only from within the modes of ruling, and that defines the objects of its power" (D.E. Smith 1990:83–4).

Dorothy Smith shows as does Foucault (1990, 1979) that the organization of knowledge is "foundational to the relations of ruling," often as "bodies of knowledge" vested in government and other agencies (D.E. Smith 1990:84). She goes on to connect the relations of ruling to such "factual surfaces of textual realities" as bodies of demographic data acquired by the organized practices of state agencies (D.E. Smith 1990:84). Once again, I take the relevance of such theorization to my case material to be quite striking.

In drawing on such theoretical works and case analyses, my analysis of the Eskimo Disk List System indicates how the assignment of unique personal identification numbers through that list forged a direct state-to-individual link that rendered ineffective and irrelevant for most state purposes virtually all traditional Eskimo structures of social solidarity, including the family. The only legitimate way for a person designated as an Eskimo to interact with the state was as a solitary individual identified by a unique Disk List number. This constituted an "atomization" or "individuation" of the Eskimo population, but also a homogenization or "totalization" (Foucault 1990) of the population since precisely the same kinds of knowledge were gathered about each person. The massive accumulation by the state of information concerning each Eskimo person was facilitated by linking a wide variety of personal information through the Disk List numbers. This created a system of knowledge by which the Canadian state exercised an "intensive surveillance" over the Eskimo population. Quite literally, "the Eskimo population" became a creation of state practice in order to meet state interests of governance.

Pierre Bourdieu's (e.g., 1989:183–97) examination of the "modes of domination" based in a theory of practice rather than in political economy or in more traditional structural analysis of social institutions, organizations, and social relations has, I believe, much to offer in the analysis of practices of governance in the Canadian Arctic. The practices involved in enumerating, registering, defining, and acquiring knowledge of populations in order to administer/govern them are inherently rooted in, and productive of, social inequality. Indeed, they are so intensely dominating as to constitute what Bourdieu (1989:196) identifies as "symbolic violence ... the gentle, hidden form which violence takes when overt violence is impossible."[6] Practices such as the collection of vital statistics, registrations of populations, and the creation of legal or quasi-legal ethnic statuses are not necessarily malevolent in intent, but their net social impact as experienced by under-privileged, over-administered, over-regulated, and over-controlled populations is surely violent in Bourdieu's terms. Governing practices are usually so "euphemized" (Bourdieu 1989:191–6), rationalized, justified, legitimated as the "just and right," the "efficient and effective," the "socially recognized and acceptable," as "for the good of the people," and "in the collective interest" that in their "taken-for-grantedness" they are treated as unquestionably "right." They are violent, because of their role in the creation and maintenance of social inequality, sometimes of an intense form; symbolic because they are embedded in overtly just, acceptable, well-intentioned, and benign (euphemized) practices. I maintain that the Eskimo Disk List embodies just such symbolically violent but euphemized practices of governance.

While I am convinced that giving priority to the theorization of practices of domination is important, I also believe that it can be immensely useful to maintain some degree of integration between analyses based in theories of practice and more traditional (e.g., structuralist, political economic) analyses, especially in considering the sources of social inequality. Johan Galtung's (1980, cf. esp. ch. 10) analysis of the "structures of imperialism," a distinctive and recognizable structure of relations which are structurally violent, also has much to add to the present analysis. According to Galtung structural violence is rooted in self-perpetuating structures and patterns of social relations. It is not necessarily explicit in the intentions of actors, but it is "structure-to-person" rather than "person-to-person" violence (1980:43, 67–8). Built into legitimated, justified, and rationalized political and economic structures, its sociocultural sources are not necessarily clearly visible or obvious (and are often detected only by careful, even labourious analysis). Its sources are frequently misrepresented as located in the immediate social context or in the personal qualities of the actors (as in blame-the-victim types of analysis). Structural violence is usually most easily perceived in its net effects, which may be extremely varied. These may include, for example, impoverishment, unequal life expectancy, unequal participation in educational structures, poorer health, differential employment rates, and so on. All of these are readily discernible in (and are extensively documented for) Canadian Arctic populations. I maintain that the Eskimo Disk List played an instrumental role in the conduct of political, economic, and social structural relations between Eskimos and the larger Canadian social system, the *net effects* of which for the Eskimo population can only be seen as structurally violent.

METHODOLOGY

In this brief study I concentrate on archival sources, with the guiding argument that the Eskimo Disk List System was entirely a creation of the administrative system and was designed to deal with problems engendered by that system's operations. Eskimo people had no part in designing the list, and it answered none of their perceived needs. It created an administrative-legal definition of the Eskimo population that was only partially related to racial and linguistic realities and had no connection to the sociopolitical and sociocultural realities of the Native people themselves. In short, my analysis of the Eskimo Disk List System will necessarily deal far more with bureaucratic policies and operating procedures than with Inuit cultural characteristics or social organization. Naturally, a full study of the Disk List System and its effects would examine in detail accounts of Eskimo peoples' experiences with it. But here my task is more limited, for I focus on those aspects of the development of the Eskimo Disk List and its social consequences that can be known through an examination of archival sources.

It may well be objected that this is an unconventional approach for an anthropologist, and that such analyses are the domain and speciality of historians. But while the style of this analysis is indeed much closer to the conventional methods and procedures of historians than those of anthropologists, it is clear that historians, in Canada's North at any rate, simply do not deal with issues and phenomena on the scale of the Eskimo Disk List – they are preoccupied with much larger issues than the kind of issues in northern history and administrative policy which concern anthropologists more immediately in their attempts to understand the social position of Native people.

Anthropologists have, of course, effectively studied archival materials. To name but a few striking examples, Trigger's (1976, 1987) studies of Huron and St Lawrence Iroquois ethnohistory make admirable use of archival materials, as do Morantz's (1983a, 1983b) studies of the fur trade in eastern James Bay. Paine (1971, 1977) and his collaborators have made some remarkably detailed studies of relations at and across ethnic boundaries in the North. Many anthropological works make extensive use of the Hudson's Bay Company archives, such as studies by Morantz (1983a, 1983b), Bishop (1974), Hickerson (1967, 1970), among many others of the fur trade period. Waldram's (1988) study of the impact of hydroelectric development on Native communities makes extensive use not only of ethnographic research but of archival and unpublished materials.

Relatively few anthropological studies of administrative policy and practice as such have been based on internal government documents, for the tendency has been to rely on published works and documents, typically in conjunction with ethnographic fieldwork. This is true both for the historic periods for which documentary materials are available in public archives and for very recent times for which it is now possible to examine documentation under access to information legislation. Hence Paine's (1971, 1977) analyses of administration in the North rely heavily on published government documents and ethnographic fieldwork, as does my own work (e.g., D.G. Smith 1975a), Sally Weaver's (1981) study of Canadian Indian policy formation, and Hugh Brody's (1975) study of ethnic relations in the North. Most of the data used in Ponting and Gibbin's (1980) study of Indian administration consist of published sources, as does the work of Frideres (1974, see esp. ch. 1). The same is true of Jenness's (1962, 1964, 1965, 1967, 1968) landmark studies of the administration of Inuit peoples in Alaska, Canada, and Greenland and of Hawthorn's (1967) equally landmark study of Indian administration. Naturally, studies of administrative practices are of immense value, especially when supplemented by ethnographic data and analysis of government administrations' own internal correspondence and memoranda. There is definitely an attempt at impression management in published government documents which must be taken into account and corrected by reference to original documents where possible. That, however, involves issues of method which we cannot pursue here. The point is that direct analysis of original documents often sheds vivid light on issues concerning anthropologists' attempts to understand public policy issues related to Native people. A recent, superb example may be found in Seguin's (1989) immensely detailed anthropological analysis of the origin and development of the government reindeer herd in the Western Arctic.

BACKGROUND TO THE ESKIMO DISK LIST SYSTEM

The Eskimo Disk List System has not been analysed in detail before, although some northern historians and anthropologists have commented on it briefly in passing. While my present study of it attempts to sketch its origins and development, we must not lose sight of the fact that it is only one part of a much larger historical and administrative reality. Canada's Native people, including the Inuit, have been subject to a steady encroachment of administration on their daily lives far beyond that experienced by other Canadians with the continued growth of the institutions of government within the Canadian state.

The course of Canada's relations with Native people has witnessed their transformation from the sovereignty envisaged by the Royal Proclamation of 1763 into "intensely administered" peoples under government wardship and trusteeship. An essential element in that intense administration has been the question of membership as shown through band lists or central registers for Indians, scrip books for the Metis, and the Eskimo Disk List for the Inuit. For many important purposes, it has been the administration who has defined and decided who is or is not a Native person, not Native persons themselves.

In the North, the largest government-defined sociopolitical reality, which has provided the backdrop for many major administrative measures, has been the question of Arctic sovereignty. This has been a matter of increasing concern since Great Britain's transfer of sovereignty over the Arctic to Canada in the late nineteenth century, and most especially since Canada's own reassertions of that sovereignty (for example in the Bernier expedition of 1910–11, see Zaslow 1988:198, 322). Canada claimed sovereignty over the Arctic and its islands and seas from the continental mainland to the North Pole on the polar sector principle, a principle only tacitly recognized by Great Britain but rejected by the United

States and other countries until the present day. A number of non-Canadian activities in the North have been considered to be slights or affronts, in various degrees, to Canada's claim to Arctic sovereignty on the sectoral principle (Zaslow 1988:12–14, 16–21, 28, 199–202). These include activities of American whalers in the 1890–1908 period in the western Arctic (Bockstoce 1986: ch. 12); of European explorers and scientists (for example the Greenland-based expedition of the American D.B. MacMillan, successor to Peary); of the European government-supported Thule Expedition in Canada's eastern and central Arctic in 1919–20; and of oil exploration by the American Imperial Oil company at Fort Norman on the Mackenzie River in 1921.

These and other events led to the decision by 1921 to establish a separate administration, located in the North and in Ottawa, for the Northwest Territories (Zaslow 1988:28). An important function of this administration was to demonstrate "effective sovereignty" over the North, especially the Arctic islands and seas. This would involve a large series of measures to show that Canada not only claimed sovereignty in the Arctic but maintained active patrol and administration of its waters, lands, resources, and peoples. It is in this context that we must understand the political implications of the establishment of both the Royal Canadian Mounted Police in 1920 as a visible testament of Canadian presence in the Arctic and the Eastern Arctic Patrol in 1922; the revival of the Northwest Territories Legislature in 1921–22, and the consolidation of government control in such matters as postal, health, and wildlife administration in the same period. Ultimately, this period saw Canada's Inuit population placed under "government trusteeship" (Zaslow 1988: 151–73), as, in my terms, an intensely administered population. The origins of the Eskimo Disk List System are intimately bound up with the activities of the Eastern Arctic Patrol and of the RCMP in the early 1920s, both of whom felt an urgent need to be able to identify precisely any Inuit person for various administrative purposes. In turn, the administration of Canada's northern peoples is intimately connected to the establishment of "effective sovereignty" in the North, and the Eskimo Disk List was an important instrument toward that end.

HISTORICAL DEVELOPMENT OF THE ESKIMO DISK LIST SYSTEM

The report of the Eastern Arctic Expedition for 1932, an annual government ship expedition taking supplies and medical and administrative services to Eastern Arctic communities, contained a suggestion that the Department of the Interior (then in charge of Arctic administration) "adopt some universal system of identification of the Eskimo population."[7] The memorandum goes on to say that "this is nothing new, as Dr MNO[8] pointed out some years ago that the difference in spelling native surnames on vital statistics forms would possibly lead to confusion, but no action was ever taken to find a solution of the difficulty."[9]

It seems highly likely that the suggestion of an Eskimo identification system originated with medical personnel in the Arctic who, understandably enough perhaps, required a clear and unequivocal system for identifying patients in order to ensure that medical care and procedures were administered to the correct person, and to facilitate the maintenance of patient histories. While this system seems to have been mentioned as early as the 1920s, a memorandum dated 21 May 1935, over the signature of a Medical Officer at Pangnirtung, NWT outlines specific suggestions and reasons for creating such a system.[10] It also seems clear that such a system had been widely discussed among northern administrative personnel, police forces, and missionaries as early as 1920 or 1921.[11] Their interests and administrative requirements are also reflected in the identification system that came into being.

Major ABD had discussed the matter with Royal Canadian Mounted Police officers and personnel, resulting in the 1935 suggestion "that if all the Eskimo [sic – the usual plural at this time] were fingerprinted it would be a start in the right direction."[12] This suggestion had "met with approval of the Police authorities [they appear to have initiated it] ... and I understand General [military rank] NDB is prepared to issue instructions to have all Eskimo fingerprinted by members of the Force [the RCMP], without expense to the Department [of the Interior]."[13] While there was considerable enthusiasm in several quarters over this decision, it was to cause some problems over the next two or three years.

What had begun as a proposed system of medical patient identification now became linked to the maintenance of other sorts of records on Eskimo people, as it was to become linked with more and more administrative and legal records through the period of its existence as the Eskimo Disk List System. It is proper to note, however, that when the suggestion for identifying and fingerprinting all Eskimos was made in 1935, it did not meet with universal approval. A handwritten marginal notation to the 1935 memorandum states, "Critics of the Departmental Administration would be sure to find some reason for condemning this suggestion. It looks to me to be unnecessary,"[14] apparently referring to all the suggestions contained in the memorandum. Indeed, the original memorandum acknowledged that there would be objections from those "strongly opposed to the system of fingerprinting. They seem to think that there is some connection between criminals and fingerprints and that there might be questions asked in Parliament concerning it."[15] But this objection was countered by the view that because "very few Eskimo can read or write ... the fingerprints would serve as his [sic] mark."[16] The memorandum goes on to argue the suitability of such a system for the administration of "all matters pertaining to native welfare ... [and] records of hunting, trapping, education, hospitalization, special qualifications as interpreter, boatsman, dog driver, reindeer herder, etc."[17] A simple and necessary system of medical patient identification had grown into something different and much more comprehensive, if not also much more insidious.

Deputy Minister of the Interior FLS reacted very guardedly to the suggestion that all Eskimos be fingerprinted. His reply to the original memorandum directs that "for the present we might restrict the fingerprinting of Eskimos to those who are assisted in any way and to those who are willing to have their fingerprints taken,"[18] stating his hope to have the matter discussed with the Northwestern Territories Council before anything was done, but arguing that "a start may be made this year and we will see how it works out."[19] The Eastern Arctic Report for 1933 records that only a small number of sets of fingerprints were taken (seventeen), all by the RCMP, and from all posts visited.[20] This would hardly add up to more than one or two persons fingerprinted at each port of call. The report states that "only the more important cases were fingerprinted, and in some ports ... no fingerprints were taken at all."[21] The criteria for identifying "important cases" are not given, but probably were the most severe medical cases, since the statement occurs in the middle of a long section on medical matters. In the opinion of the report's author (Major ADB?), "The procedure hardly justified itself. The matter caused overcrowding of already cramped examination quarters, *and in many cases frightened the natives quite noticeably*"[22] (emphasis added). Native people knew quite clearly that fingerprinting was a procedure involved with criminal proceedings, and were probably alarmed in this case because the RCMP were in charge of making the fingerprints. Remembering that these seem to have been taken only from the most severe medical cases, one does not need a highly active imagination to see the implied connection between serious illness and criminality. In any case, the author of the Eastern Arctic Report (1933) goes on to say, "I further believe that it requires an expert to interpret the prints, and he is stationed in Ottawa. As a means of identification it is, unquestionably, infallible, but is hardly adaptable, in my opinion, to the north."[23] By the end of 1933, a total of twenty-two sets of fingerprints had been collected. However, by April 1935 the same author (Major ABD) reports much more enthusiastically that "the experiment in fingerprinting, inaugurated in the Eastern Arctic, has been an unqualified success and can be extended by the Royal Canadian Mounted Police to embrace all Eskimos in Canada. The reports of births by Registrars of Vital Statistics (R.C.M. Police) will take care of infants until they reach the eight or nine years of age when their finger prints can be taken."[24] This report includes a recommendation to fingerprint all Eskimos in Canada, and that the RCMP be placed in charge of the operation. A handwritten marginal notation on this memorandum, apparently by the deputy minister, succinctly states, "Concur."[25] However, the question of fingerprinting does not continue to appear in correspondence after the late 1930s. It was displaced by a greater concern to link Eskimo identification to the collection and maintenance of vital statistics, and the conduct of the impending 1941 Census of Canada. The Eskimo identification and registration project had expanded in scale once more.

The original necessity for clearly identifying medical patients is spelled out in detail in several documents. Reasons included (a) the fairly low literacy rates of the Eskimo population of the time; (b) the tendency for Eskimos to have only one name known to non-Eskimos (no surname or family name, although the situation was highly variable – some had European surnames or had adopted place names as surnames); (c) the inconsistency of common (or first) names, since the same person could pick up and abandon several in the course of years, sometimes including two or more nicknames as usual first names; (d) the inconsistent use of baptismal names (usually biblical) and European surnames (both often given by missionaries, not necessarily chosen by the persons concerned and therefore sometimes not routinely used), which rather than replacing traditional names were often simply acquired as one more name for use in certain social circumstances.[26]

A medical officer at Pangnirtung, NWT addressed two memoranda to the deputy minister, Department of the Interior,[27] enumerating the various problems in identifying Eskimo patients, and suggested a number of measures to deal with them. Apart from suggesting certain measures, some of great historical significance, his line of argument clearly reveals some of the attitudes toward Native people among administrators of the time. On the matter of names, he states that there are "three requirements to be met in names, – First: Spelling; Second: Identification and Third: Some practical system of filing."[28] He refers to a continuing problem concerning Eskimo names extending well back into the 1920s, making specific reference to a local census made by the RCMP in 1924,[29] written both in Roman characters and syllabics, identifying each person, household group, camp, and "headman." Apparently a constantly updated version of the 1924 police census was used to facilitate medical administration in the Pangnirtung and Blacklead Island vicinities. Regarding the role of the Native people, the medical officer says, "I think that if left to get the names from the natives each has a different spelling for each name. The native certainly can not spell his own name and when it comes to remembering the names of their children, it appears to be too much of a mental effort for them to clutter up their minds with."[30] He immediately tempers this statement by saying "This is not true of all the natives, but it is true in isolated cases," but almost immediately returns to his original tone by asserting that "the native cannot get his sounding mechanism" around certain sounds in English names, such as the "R" in Ruth. He says that this inability of Eskimos to get their tongues around English sounds is at the base of a good many of the problems in identifying Native people clearly and consistently. He is entirely mute on the problems caused by English speakers trying to get their tongues around Eskimo names.

That traditional Eskimos did not have family names is also identified as a major source of difficulty, as well as the Eskimo practice of having names in childhood which are replaced by more adult forms as the child matures through various life stages.[31] In addition, naming practices in traditional Inuit societies seem to have varied quite considerably by region, and European names (when adopted) were by no means adopted in standardized ways.

Dr CFQ's solution to the various problems of "identification, spelling, and filing"[32] was decisive in determining the historical course of the Eskimo identification system. "My humble suggestion would be, that at each registration [of vital statistics by the RCMP] the child be given an identity disk on the same lines as the army identy [sic] disk and the same insistance [sic] that it be worne [sic] at all times."[33]

While Dr CFQ may have discussed the matter with other officers, he certainly seems to be the first to make the formal suggestion of a disk registry and to have it accepted. During the late 1930s there was very little further action on the matter, although the idea of a Disk List System seemed to gain more and more favour. It even appeared for a time that the United States Department of the Interior was considering adopting the proposed Canadian system for use among Eskimos in Alaska, and possibly also for Indian populations there.[34] Little seems to have come of the matter. It would be interesting to know the reasons for this apparent rejection, particularly since the Canadian system was about to develop into a major administrative venture. While there was a general and growing acceptance of Dr CFQ's Disk List proposal, there was some opposition. This may in part have been produced by some shifts in policy regarding the North and concerning the status of Eskimo populations.

In 1939, the Supreme Court of Canada ruled in a *Reference Re: Eskimos* that Eskimos were included in the generic term "Indian" which had been so widely applied to the Native peoples of North America. The reference investigates and establishes the historic usage, and concludes that since Eskimos belonged to the generic category "Indians," they were the specific responsibility of the federal (not provincial) government under the constitutional provisions of The British North America Act (1867). The reference had arisen out of a dispute between the federal government and the Province of Quebec over which government had constitutional power over the Eskimos in that province, particularly as to the provision of social welfare programs. The significance here is that the administration of all Eskimo matters was amalgamated in the same federal government department, and the identification system (which had been developing so far only within the Northwest Territories) was now extended to all Eskimos in Canada, including the adoption of the Disk List proposal.[35]

In 1940 there were still misgivings concerning the adoption of a Disk List System, although it was now almost a reality. Major ABD stated in a memorandum: "The suggestion that metal discs be worn either around the neck or wrist has not met with favour, because ... (a) Indians do not wear them; (b) Misunderstandings might easily arise if Eskimos wore chains; and (c) So far as we know, wards of other Dominions do not wear identification discs."[36] He proposed instead that Eskimos carry "a small identification card (linen) enclosed in celophane [sic] – similar to the credit card issued by the oil companies."[37] He argues that the "Eskimos as a race are instinctively careful of their belongings," and he ventured the opinion "that the idea of an identification card would appeal to them generally."[38] Significantly, he now saw as an additional benefit to an identification system "the commencement of a general licensing system and [by it] Eskimos would be taught to keep records of game seen and killed. By this means they would be taught conservation and gradually come to realize that the Arctic regions are their own and they will be responsible for their development."[39]

Hence, what began as a medical patient identification system now became linked to a general licensing system to hunt and trap. MLN annotated a memorandum on 10 May 1940 with the note that the proposed disk would be "a numbered identification disc, something of the shape of a twenty–five cent piece, with two holes punched in it in case the Eskimos wish to attach same to their clothing or wear same around their neck or wrist."[40] He suggested that the Forestry Service (a part of the Department of Mines and Resources to which the Northern Administration also belonged at that time) might be able to suggest a design similar to the metal tags used to mark and identify trees.

A "card system of record" had been gradually introduced in the late 1930s to deal with all northern residents other than Treaty Indians and was judged to be "working out perfectly so far as whites, half-breeds and those who have regular recognized names ... but considerable difficulty has been experienced in connection with the natives [here implying Eskimos] because of lack of uniformity in the spelling of their names, lack of names, etc."[41] This was considered a strong argument to proceed (a) with a distinctive identification system for Eskimos; (b) with the issuance of identification disks; and (c) with the correlation of the identification disks and records with "a complete census of the Eskimos and those living the life of a native for whom this administration is responsible"[42] (i.e., for offspring of Eskimo persons by "fathers unknown"). An estimate of the numbers of disks required was also offered, as was a suggestion that the disks should bear the image of a wild goose or other appropriate northern symbol (since the coat of arms of Canada had been ruled inappropriate, despite its potential usefulness as a sign of Canadian sovereignty in the Arctic). Some further debate ensued about the material of the disk, its decoration, and its possible parallels with those used by the Canadian Armed Forces,[43] with yet further estimates of numbers and costs. A marginal notation on one memorandum suggested that full estimates be prepared for presentation at a meeting of the Northwest Territories Council, which, in its One Hundred and Twenty-Second Session, passed the necessary ordinance to establish the Eskimo Disk List System, and provided that the initiation of the system coincide with the 1941 Census of Canada.[44] With further deliberation, and in consultation with the federal Department of the Secretary of State, it was ruled that disks should be modeled on the identification disks used in the Royal Canadian Navy, and that "a sufficient number of discs be struck bearing the Canadian coat of arms [sic – despite the previous decision that this was inappropriate] to be distributed to all Eskimos in Canada." By 26 March 1941 final arrangements of design were made, insisting that the disks bear the words "Eskimo Registration Certificate" (a very telling phrase) and ordering a stock of 10,000 disks to be "ready for distribution on the opening of navigation" and to be supplied to enumerators for the 1941 Census of Canada.[45] The Eastern Arctic Report[46] indicated that "census enumerators had been instructed and supplied with schedules ... [and that] everywhere the idea of native identification has been welcomed by all concerned."[47]

Problems with the administration of such a system of identification arose immediately. Various memoranda appeared: asking for instructions on the compulsory return of identification disks of deceased Eskimos;[48] clarifying the purposes of the Disk List System as approved by the Northwest Territories Council;[49] complaining that RCMP staff in the North were failing to enter Disk List numbers on correspondence concerning Eskimo persons;[50] reporting that supplies of disks had not arrived in the Mackenzie Delta Region even by December 1942, eighteen months or so past the 1941 Census enumeration, and that none of the Eskimos in the Mackenzie Delta had disks;[51] repeating the necessity of recovering disks from deceased persons to prevent misuse of wartime ration allowances; and reporting that "certain Eskimos on Boothia Peninsula destroyed their discs after receiving them,"[52] thereby disrupting the operation of the Disk List System.[53] Other correspondence concerns the misuse of Disk List data for purposes not intended by the Territorial Council, such as the administration of hunting and trapping privileges, requiring restatement of the basic principle that the Disk List was designed to interlock with vital statistics, and "school, hospital, relief, ration and crime returns."[54] The overzealous use of Disk List information seems not to have extended to local RCMP personnel, who may, for reasons not fully clear, have resisted the use of the Disk List System. An order to ensure its use was issued on 4 November 1943 requiring local RCMP detachments to submit revised Disk List data to the commanding officer in the Western Arctic on an annual basis by 31 July each year.[55] Other directives clarified the administration of the system, especially the matter of official registrars of Disk List data in order to avoid duplicate registrations and to ensure consistent application of administrative directives.[56] Provision was made to establish a central registry, with necessary staff and clerks, in Ottawa.[57] The system experienced many difficulties and anomalies, however, since more and more Eskimos were living outside traditional Eskimo territories or in southern Canada. How were they to be identified, issued disks, and consistently administered? Such problems continued throughout the existence of the Disk List System.

By 1945 questions directed to Disk List registrars suggested that, in practice, some people were beginning to treat the Disk List System as a means to define Eskimo status. This potential problem was foreshadowed by the 1941 suggestion that the disks bear the legend "Registration Certificate."[58] The tendency – one must emphasize that it was more in day-to-day administrative practice than in official policy or law – was to treat possession of a disk number as evidence of Eskimo status, and lack of such a disk as evidence of lack of eligibility for Eskimo status. In 1945 the matter arose in relation to administration of children's allowance payments, as in a memorandum from the director of Lands, Parks and Forests Branch, Department of Mines and Resources:

Lt Commander POM of the Department of National Health and Welfare called me this morning to see how we could describe Eskimos for the purposes of the regulations under the Children's Allowance arrangement. I explained that every Eskimo was issued an itentification [sic] disk by the Bureau of Northwest Territories and Yukon Affairs and is described as an Eskimo in the vital statistics records. I pointed out that some of these Eskimos are listed in the vital statistics records of the provinces but that all of them are issued identification disks whether in the Northwest Territories, the Yukon or the provinces.[59]

There is at the very least an *implication* here that possession of an Eskimo Disk somehow defines its possessor as being an Eskimo, at least for some administrative purposes.

Yet another shift in registration practice occurred at about this time (late 1945). Discussions were beginning to take place about the actual necessity of each Eskimo having personal possession of a disk, particularly in light of the administrative confusions caused by loss or duplication, or by persons being in possession of disks not personally issued to them. Major ABD, in a memorandum to a director of his department, declared that "the original idea for the issue [of discs] was for temporary purposes only. There was never any intention in my mind, that the identification disc could be described or used as a token" (i.e., as a registration certificate], and "there will be no need for the Eskimo to wear identification discs for a longer period than is required for him [sic] and his [sic] family and friends to memorize the number."[60] This seems to be an extraordinary claim, since there was no previous mention or hint, at least in archival documents, that the identification disks were to be a temporary measure, and, as we have seen, clear instructions had been given when the discs were ordered that they bear the legend "Eskimo Registration Certificate." In any case, the claim marks an important shift away from the use of actual disks to an emphasis on the registration number assigned to each Eskimo and its uses in administrative records. In addition, efforts were being made by the deputy commissioner of the Northwest Territories to recall all previous disks and numbers and to assign new numbers and disks, because it "has been reported to me that it is impossible to reconcile to any satisfactory degree the record of identification discs issued with the vital statistics record. Under the circumstances [it is recommended] that we proceed to issue a new set of identification discs this year, tying the number to the vital statistics record in each and every case ... inasmuch as [the disks] are to be an integral part of our record, it would seem that we should make them of white metal and possibly with a dignified design on them."[61] The administrative disorder surrounding the whole question of disks and registration numbers and their uses (as well as hints in the records of resistance by Eskimo people) hardly seems to justify Major ABD's claim that "they have proven an unqualified success,"[62] and the suggestion to replace the original fibre disks with more permanent white metal disks seems to connote permanent rather than temporary use.

Very detailed instructions were provided to district registrars for the registration of all vital statistics.[63] A lengthy section deals with the registration of Eskimos and "Nomads."[64] Records were to be prepared in duplicate under seven headings: (1) registration district; (2) number of new identification disk issued; (3) number of old identification disk recalled; (4) name of native; (5) date of birth (estimated if necessary); (6) birth certificate registration number; or (7) delayed birth certificate registration number. One copy was to be forwarded to the Bureau of Northwest Territories and Yukon Affairs, Ottawa, and the other was to be retained in the registration area. It is of interest to note that it was now considered necessary to divide the Arctic into four registration areas: (a) Eastern Arctic, the portion under territorial jurisdiction; (b) Eastern Arctic, the portion under jurisdiction of the Province of Quebec; (c) Western Arctic (Mackenzie Basin); (d) Yukon Territory.[65] Registration districts, which increased in number in succeeding years, were in effect throughout the lifetime of the Eskimo Disk List System.

The definition of "Nomad" is clarified in a related document, the Family Allowance Regulations, submitted to the Governor General to be approved by Order in Council by the minister of National Health and Welfare.[66] According to this document " 'Nomad' means a person of mixed Indian or Eskimo blood, residing in the Northwest Territories or the Yukon Territory, who is neither an Eskimo nor an Indian, but who follows the Indian or Eskimo mode of living."[67] In administrative practice, two categories of persons of Eskimo ancestry were effectively being created – what many government officials in the North were calling "status Eskimo" and "non-status Eskimo"[68] in the 1960s (D.G. Smith 1975a:2–5). Whether these expressions were already in general use in the 1940s is as yet difficult to ascertain. The determination of who was an Eskimo or Nomad was critical to the administration of family allowances in the North, because persons of these categories were paid the allowance "in the form of controlled supplies in lieu of cash,"[69] and any person who met the criteria but for some reason was not actually registered on the Disk List could receive payments in cash.

By 1946, the disorder and confusion surrounding the assignment and use of Eskimo Disk numbers, particularly in the Western Arctic where the ethnic situation was always more complex than in most other Arctic areas, seems to have become more evident. Several memoranda and letters allude to the problems. An administrative officer in Aklavik, NWT reported that "in trying to sort out hospital accounts and other matters concerning Eskimo I am encountering more confusion than should be necessary. There seems to be no clear lines exactly as to who is counted as a native Eskimo and thus a charge on the Department and who is of white status [i.e., Nomad] and not. I find children of white men with disc numbers and children of Eskimo without. I find at least two cases where Indians also have Eskimo discs."[70] The same officer also reported another problem for Registrars in the Western Arctic – that is, the difficulty of knowing the proper administrative procedures for dealing with the Eskimos of Alaskan origin who had been moving into the Mackenzie Delta area over a number of years.[71] Directives were issued for yet another recall and reissue of disk numbers by the RCMP, and rules of eligibility for Alaskan Eskimos or their children domiciled or resident in Canada were clarified.[72] All school principals were also instructed to maintain meticulous Disk List data under the threat that payment of the "various returns, accounts, etc." would be withheld unless "positive identification of each child attending school" could be established, especially in matters relating to family allowances.[73] Cases arose in which children of registered Eskimos had been born outside the traditional areas of Eskimo occupation and were not registered on a Disk List since there was no standardized way of recording their births or other vital statistics with the registrar-general of the Northwest Territories and ensuring that they were issued with disk numbers.[74]

In 1966, a case came to the attention of the office of the commissioner of the Northwest Territories which may have marked a real turning point in policy regarding the Disk List. In a letter to the commanding officer, "G" Division (Western Arctic) of the RCMP, the Commissioner wrote:

You may be familiar with the case of Mr NNN of Tuktoyaktuk. Mr NNN was issued with a disc as an Eskimo. I understand it was later taken from him on the grounds that his father was not an Eskimo. Mr NNN has lived all his life as an Eskimo and wants to continue to do so. It appears to me that as he was born and brought up as an Eskimo, has always lived the Eskimo way of life, has been known as an Eskimo, calls himself an Eskimo, and wishes to continue to live as an Eskimo we should accept his situation and return his disc. *More to the point, not to be officially recognized as an Eskimo in this situation could seriously affect his living and opportunities.*[75] (emphasis added)

Cases such as these led to a reconsideration of the Disk List System in the years following 1965 (the system was completely abandoned by the early 1970s), aided by Project Surname, a program under which all Eskimos chose surnames and the spelling of all personal and surnames was standardized.

Before leaving this historical sketch of the Eskimo Disk List System we must return briefly to a crucial issue which had pursued the administration of the system throughout its existence. In practice, especially at the local level of administration in the Arctic – and in public understanding – possession of a disk number was repeatedly (if not exactly consistently) taken to mean that its owner was of Eskimo status in some legal or quasi-legal sense. Despite repeated reminders to the contrary to local administrative personnel, this practice gradually hardened into a routine interpretation, and eventually even became embedded in legal terminology in various federal government regulations and in *The Ordinances of the Northwest Territories* (Northwest Territories 1956a, 1956b). For example, regulations under The Family Allowance Act (1945) tersely defined an Eskimo in the following way: " 'Eskimo' means a person who is listed as an Eskimo on the roll of records of, *and to whom an identification disc has been issued* by, the Bureau of Northwest Territories and Yukon Affairs of the Department of Mines and Resources"[76] (em-

phasis added). Here the possession of an Eskimo Disk was considered to define who was and who was not an Eskimo for purposes
of family allowance payments (made to Eskimos at that time only in
the form of supplies, not in cash). The Northwest Territories Game
Ordinance (Northwest Territories 1956a) and the Liquor Ordinance
(Northwest Territories 1956b) both contain definitions of Eskimo,
which differ in significant ways. The Game Ordinance definition
reads:

"Eskimo" includes:

(i) a male person who is a direct descendant in the male line of a male
person who is or was of the race of aborigines commonly called
Eskimos,

(ii) the legitimate child of a person described in paragraph (i),

(iii) the illegitimate child of a person described in (ii), and

(iv) the wife or widow of a person described in (i), (ii), or (iii), but does not
include the Eskimo wife of a person other than an Eskimo, unless she
has been deserted by or divorced from that person or has become the
widow of that person, except that any person who, upon the coming
into force of this Ordinance, was considered to be an Eskimo for the
purposes of the game laws of the Territories shall, unless he elects not
to be so considered, be deemed to continue to be an Eskimo.[77]

The Liquor Ordinance of the Northwest Territories contains a
similar, but by no means identical definition:

"Eskimo," for the purposes of this Ordinance, means

(i) the son of a male person belonging to the race of aborigines
commonly referred to as Eskimos,

(ii) the legitimate child of a person described in subparagraph (i),

(iii) the illegitimate child of a female person belonging to the race of aborigines commonly referred to as Eskimos, unless the Commissioner has,
by order issued at the child's bequest, declared such child to be not an
Eskimo, and

(iv) the wife of a person described in subparagraphs (i), (ii) and (iii), but
does not include the Eskimo wife of a person other than an Eskimo,
nor a person who in the opinion of the Commissioner has for the previous eighteen months immediately preceding his application for a
permit earned his livelihood chiefly by means other than hunting and
trapping and in other respects has ceased permanently to follow the
Eskimo mode of life.[78]

While both these definitions significantly echo the definition of Indian in The Indian Act (1951) (see D.G. Smith 1975b:158–61), and were probably explicitly modeled on it, they differ in two notable respects from its definition of Indian: first, the definitions of Eskimo' are special purpose definitions, provided for the administration of particular regulations and laws, while the definition of Indian is a much more general and encompassing definition, partly for the administration of the Indian Act but also providing a general definition to be used in a comprehensive way to define a status in the Canadian polity; and second, the definition of Indian is very closely tied to equity in Indian lands, while the definition of Eskimo has no such connection. Nevertheless, the various definitions of Eskimo *taken together* constitute a quasi-legal definition in actual practice, and while not entirely consistent either in terms or in application, have played a very significant role in constituting Eskimos as an ethnic status group with access to or exclusion from a large number of privileges and administrative programs. I argue at more length below that the net effect was negative, despite the benefits and privileges intended by government.

Several features of the definitions of Eskimo may now be identified. Taken together, they constitute the definition of an Eskimo ethnic status: (1) to which persons may be admitted or from which they may be excluded; (2) which has features of a racial definition; (3) which has features of a way of life (or cultural) definition; (4) which has features of a community consent definition; (5) which has features of a personal choice of identity definition; (6) which is signified by enrolment in the Eskimo Disk List. Perhaps most significantly, it is a status which can be lost by marriage (of an Eskimo woman to a non-Eskimo man), or acquired by marriage (of a non-Eskimo woman to an Eskimo man). Mostly for this reason (of marriage to a non-Eskimo male), many persons who were in all other respects Eskimo were excluded from the status, and persons who were in no respect Eskimo other than by entering a marriage relationship with an Eskimo man were included in the status.

Eskimo status was a reality not only in local administrative understandings and practices in the North and in legal provisions, it was also recognized by senior policy officials in southern Canada. A director of the Department of Indian Affairs and Northern Development in 1966 asserted in a memorandum to the legal adviser of the Department: "*Ownership of a disc number defines a person of Eskimo Status.* Although, disputes have arisen on occasion, disc numbers are normally issued to persons who are not of Eskimo blood, i.e. the father or mother may have been "white," as long as they are living as part of an Eskimo family or following the traditional Eskimo way of life"[79] (emphasis added)

DISSOLUTION OF THE DISK LIST SYSTEM

The problem of legal definitions of Eskimo status had arisen in the late 1960s concerning legal protection for Eskimo arts and crafts, especially those produced by arts and crafts co-operatives in the North. In addition, questions were being asked by members of the public about the legal aspects of Eskimo status.[80] Answers given were in terms of disk numbers and ordinance definitions. One memorandum contains the following revealing (but not necessarily consistent) assertions:

The policy of the Department [of Indian Affairs and Northern Development] in defining an Eskimo could possibly be summarized in this way: "*An Eskimo is a person the Department considers to be an Eskimo*" ... [on] the question of how one loses his [or her] Eskimo status, [we] could answer by the dictum: "Once an Eskimo always an Eskimo." The issuance of a disc does not change a person's status or race, and even though an Eskimo may surrender his [or her] disc or opt out of certain programs established by the administration for the benefit of Eskimos, he [or she] still is an Eskimo and as such may take advantage of any of the programs established to assist Eskimo[81] [sic]. (emphasis added)

The legal adviser of the Department of Indian Affairs considered these questions from the public "to be of great importance" and recommended that the "question be resolved in consultation between the Northern Administration Branch and the Indian Affairs Branch";[82] indeed, he had already forwarded the matter to the deputy minister for attention. It may be of interest that there is no indication that he suggested discussion of the matter with Eskimo persons or organizations. In any case, the Disk List System was by now well on the way towards dissolution. The commissioner of the Northwest Territories had already clearly stated his position on the matter, certainly within the Territorial government and the Department of Indian Affairs and Northern Development: "It seems to me that there is only one justification for assigning a number to people and actually putting it on a disc. That is, if an absolute requirement exists for identifying people and the alternatives would be an unacceptable level of confusion. It strikes me that we should discontinue the number system and the disc system as soon as possible. I do not know when this will be the case. Indeed, for all I know it is possible to discontinue the system now ... I wish ... to be free of identifying any other racial groups."[83]

Clearly the level of dissatisfaction with the Eskimo Disk List System, at least among administrators and policy makers, had reached such a level that it had outlived any administrative useful- ness it may have had. It was soon to be done away with entirely through Project Surname undertaken by the territorial and federal governments with a conspicuous presence and role for the Native people who carried it out. That is another story, and one very much worth documenting, but which can only concern us briefly here.

Project Surname undertook to dismantle the Eskimo Disk List System principally by making provisions for all Inuit persons to adopt permanent surnames of their choice in addition to their usual first names. These surnames were assembled during a massive pro- gram of public meetings and door-to-door visitations. All names so adopted were registered with local, territorial, and federal govern- ment agencies. By the time this project was completed, each Inuit person was identified for administrative purposes in precisely the same way as every other Canadian citizen – that is, by surname, usual first name, and social insurance number.

Dissatisfaction with the Disk List System had come from several sources. Over the years many Native people had complained of its injustices. By the late 1960s, it had become one of the first issues to which emerging Native political organizations committed themselves for among other reasons, the existence or not of an Eskimo status (and possession of it or not by specific persons) had clear legal im- plications for land claims settlements and related matters. By this time it was probably not in the interest of the federal government to admit to the existence of Eskimo status. Some impetus to resolve the Canadian situation came from the Alaskan land claims settle- ment procedures, for many Inuit in the Western Arctic in particular were also entitled to benefits under the Alaskan settlement. These considerations, combined with the internal administrative dissatis- faction with the Disk List in both federal and territorial governments led to its demise. I must also point out that these events coincided almost exactly with the discontent over the Indian registration sys- tem which was such a prominent part of the major Indian Affairs policy debates of the late 1960s analysed by Sally Weaver (1981).

CONCLUSIONS

In my brief examination of archival materials on the Eskimo Disk List, I have outlined the emergence of Eskimos as a subject population (i.e., one to be administered), a population based on a quasi-legally constituted ethnic status, and a population constituted by the practices of the state in terms that serve primarily the interests of the state. The criteria for inclusion in and exclusion from that population are entirely of an administrative origin. The idea for the Eskimo Disk List arose out of problems in administering the Eskimo population because administrators were incapable of learning, pronouncing, or distinguishing Eskimo names, or maintaining a clear sense of kin relations among Eskimo people, despite their allegations that it was the Eskimos who had these problems. One readily grants that, in medicine, where the Disk List began as an instrument of patient identification, the clear distinction and identification of persons was an absolute necessity. But a system that began in order to facilitate medical records became, with astonishing rapidity, a comprehensive administrative system of identification pervading all aspects of government's interaction with Eskimo people, and ultimately came to define the quasi-legal Eskimo status which had an impact on virtually all aspects of Eskimo social life as an intensely administered population within the Canadian polity. That system included the administration of records of vital statistics, welfare programs, family allowance records, crime records, education records and privileges, licences to hunt and trap, rights to consume alcohol, marriage regulations, and many others.

Unlike the Indian Band List and general registry system which identifies each Indian person with a unique number and regulates equity in Indian lands and claims on land, the Eskimo system had no relation to equity in land or other demonstrable positive advantages. It was purely a system of state origin, and in the interests of the state, to facilitate the administration of a population which had unique sociocultural, demographic, and geographical features – a system based on criteria entirely selected by the northern administration. Especially in the latter part of its existence, inclusion in the Disk List conferred more and more the features of a quasi-legal ethnic status, to and from which persons could be included or excluded on the decision of the administration. There was and is no constitutional basis in Canada for the creation of such an ethnic status, unlike the Indian status system which, for good or for bad, was quite carefully embedded in Canada's constitutional documents (such as The British North America Act of 1867). Without any legal sanction whatsoever, the definition of Eskimo status was fairly closely modeled on the definition of Indian legal status in The Indian Act (1951), Sections 2, 5–16; and subsequent amendments (see D.G. Smith 1975b). To mention but one of the problems created by this, non-Eskimo women who married Eskimo men were considered to have Eskimo status, while some persons otherwise entirely of Eskimo origin were excluded because they could not be shown, on administrative-legal grounds, to qualify for Eskimo status, and women in all other aspects Eskimo were excluded at the time of their marriage to non-Eskimo men. Apart from being a cumbersome (at times almost chaotic) system which consumed an enormous amount of administrative energy and resources, the only authenticity the Disk List System could claim was in terms of administrative policy and practice.

Erected on a basis of racial descent criteria ("descent from a male person in the male line"), inclusion in the list was based on an unsteady combination of criteria – marital status, cultural identification ("follows an Eskimo way of life"), self-identification ("wishes to follow the Eskimo way of life"), and community acceptance ("is generally accepted by the local community to be an Eskimo") – but the final decision as to whether any particular person held Eskimo status rested entirely in the hands of the administration.

Yet another feature of the system was that it did not provide a comprehensive definition of Eskimo status which was valid for all purposes. A person could conceivably qualify for Eskimo status under the Northwest Territories Game Ordinance, but not under the Liquor Ordinance, and thereby be relegated to an administrative limbo wherein he or she would be neither Eskimo nor non-Eskimo, creating a problematic relation to the Disk List which regulated so many other features of life. The result was confusion and a simmering sense of inequality and injustice. The net effect of the system was to regulate eligibility for virtually all government programs concerning the Eskimo population, resulting in unequal access to the benefits of Canadian society. In some cases Eskimo status was a clear benefit, in other cases (probably the majority), a liability. Eskimo status and membership in the Disk List outlined what we may call an "inauthentic ethnic category" – one whose authenticity did not derive from its members and their own conceptions of themselves but from criteria generated entirely within an administrative framework and to fulfil its purposes alone.

The net sociological effect of Eskimo status and Disk List membership was to contribute to substantial socioeconomic inequalities. The exact weight of Eskimo administrative identity in such inequalities cannot be demonstarted on the basis of our archival investigation – or indeed of *any* archival data considered alone. What our analysis has provided is a sketch of the sociopolitical framework of administrative policy and practice in which these inequalities were generated and legitimated, at least insofar as these can be known from archival sources.

In Galtung's (1980: e.g., 109–39) terms, the Eskimo Disk List and its administration was an important structural focus for the promotion of social inequality and sociopolitical subordination which he calls structural violence, because of its devastating socioeconomic effects. It was structurally violent because small, routine, everyday administrative decisions had major, disruptive, negative, and subordinating socio-political and socioeconomic effects among Inuit people which could have massive impact on the daily life of Eskimo people. While the assignment of social insurance numbers to all members of the Canadian state has certain parallels, they are superficial. In the Eskimo case, we are dealing with the intensive administration of a small, generally impoverished, and politically subjugated regional population enclave. The demographic contrast of the two situations accounts in part for the intense administration in the Eskimo case, an intensity that I maintain was violent both symbolically and structurally.

The Eskimo Disk List and the intense administration it entailed were structurally violent because the instruments of governance developed for administering the Eskimo population became key instruments in the Canadian state's prosecution of its policies of sovereignty in the Arctic. While Foucault (1979:11) maintains that "sovereignty is exercised ... above all on a territory and consequently on the subjects who inhabit it,"[84] I suggest that in the case of the Canadian Arctic (and possibly other colonial/imperial situations) the reverse was true – that the annexation, governance, atomization, and surveillance of the population were the key instruments by which territorial sovereignty was exercised.

When a small, traditional people is administered with such intensity (primarily to serve interests other than their own, in this case the annexation of a vast territory in the interest of the Canadian state); when people are registered, identified, required to wear or possess numbered identification disks, contacted about personal information again and again with the information received collated into a huge network of administrative knowledge about them through which they are to be governed, the results can only be described as violent. In this case, the violence is clearly of the kind identified as symbolic violence inhering in the modes of domination analysed in the work of Bourdieu (1989:183–96). The symbolic violence lies in four aspects of the system:

1   the assignment of unique personal identification numbers, which not only identify the person but also facilitate the collation of

state information and knowledge (surveillance) of him or her and the totalization of the population to which he or she belongs, creates the grounds of a massive sociopolitical inequality;

2 the use of a person's unique identification as the only legitimate ground for dealing with the state, which renders virtually all traditional structures of collective solidarity ineffective for state purposes and may prevent the formation of new structures, leads to atomization or individuation of the population;

3 the reduction of the Eskimo population to identical constituent atoms of the same type for the purposes of state operations leads to homogenization of the Eskimo population; and

4 the use of rationalization such as "in the public interest," "for the good and protection of the Eskimo people," "in the interest of national sovereignty," and so on permits the euphemitization (Bourdieu 1989:191–6), legitimation, justification, and acceptance of the whole system and its sorry effects.

This system was violent because its real effects were symbolized (and in effect concealed) in a system of administrative practices that were virtually unchallengeable by the people who were so intensely administered, indeed dominated, by them.

NOTES AND UNPUBLISHED REFERENCES

The Department and Northern Affairs Canada has kindly given permission for the quotation of unpublished memoranda and other documents in this study. This permission does not imply that the department or any of its officers is in any way in agreement with or supports all or any of the interpretations offered here.

I wish to acknowledge with thanks the comments of several colleagues and friends who have read this study and a shorter version of it which was presented at the Canadian Anthropology Society/ La société canadienne d'anthropologie (CASCA) Meetings at the University of Ottawa in May 1989. They include: Vic Valentine, Bruce Cox, Caryll Steffens, Roy Joe Inglangasuk, Scott McLean, Lorna Weir, Bruce Curtis, Katherine D. Kelly, Valda Blundell, John Cove, Frank Vallee, Alan Hunt, Ian Roderick, Stephen Richer, Rob Shields, and students in the master's level proseminar in anthropology at Carleton University. I have also drawn on papers given at CASCA meetings in May 1990 (University of Calgary) and May 1991 (University of Western Ontario). Joel D. Reimer patiently assisted in preparing the final text, for which I am very thankful. I owe special thanks to Noel Dyck and James B. Waldram for a close reading of the text and very detailed constructive comments. I have incorporated some of the comments and criticisms of my colleagues, but the final version, and especially its limits, defects, and some of its contentious conclusions, must be considered entirely my own.

1 Extract, minutes of the One Hundred and Twenty-Second Session of the Northwest Territories Council held 11 February 1941, Sec. (x).

2 The term "Eskimo" is frequently used here along with the more contemporary term "Inuit" because it is the term used throughout the historic period described and analysed in this chapter and throughout the archival sources involved. The term "Inuit" came into usage after the period under consideration here.

3 See note 1 above, Ibid., Sec. (v).

4 Ibid.

5 Extract, Major ABD's Report, HMS *Nascopie*, 12 August 1941 (The Eastern Arctic Report). Permission of the Department of Indian and Northern Affairs to cite from archival documents for this study stipulates that none of the persons mentioned may be identified by name. Accordingly, all names are indicated by fictitious initials which bear no relation to the real names of the persons concerned.

6 "Symbolic" and "structural" violence (see below) are, I would think, usually concurrent; both proceed from hidden sources, both are perceivable mainly in their *net effect*.

7 Memorandum, Chair of the Lands Board to Deputy Minister FLS, Department of the Interior, 26 June 1933.

8 Dr MNO, an experienced medical officer in the Arctic, who served in many communities over a long period.

9 Memorandum, Chair of the Lands Board, to Deputy Minister FLS, Department of the Interior, 26 June 1933.

10 Memorandum, CFQ, MD, Medical Officer, to UVW, Director, Dominion Lands Administration, Department of the Interior, dated Pangnirtung, NWT, 21 May 1935.

11 Memorandum, Chair of the Lands Board to Deputy Minister FLS, 26 June 1933; and Memorandum, CFQ, MD, Medical Officer to UVW Director, Dominion Lands Administration, Department of the Interior, 21 May 1935.

12 Memorandum, Chair of the Lands Board to Deputy Minister FLS, Department of the Interior, 26 June 1933.

13 Ibid.

14 Ibid.

15 Ibid.

16 Ibid.

17 Ibid.

18 Memorandum, Deputy Minister of the Interior to FLS, Chair, Dominion Lands Board, Ottawa, 27 June 1933.

19 Ibid.

20 Extract, Eastern Arctic Report, HMS *Nascopie*, 1933 (Major ABD is the author?).

21 Ibid.

22 Ibid.

23 Memorandum, General NDB, Commissioner, RCMP, to UVW, Deputy Minister, Department of the Interior, Ottawa, 4 December 1933.

24 Memorandum, Major ABD, Department of the Interior, to UVW, Director, Dominion Lands Administration, Department of the Interior, Ottawa, 11 April 1935.

25 Ibid.

26 Memorandum, Chair of the Lands Board to Deputy Minister FLS, 26 June 1933; memorandum, CFQ, MD, Medical Officer to UVW, Director, Dominion Lands Administration, Department of the Interior, 21 May 1935; and memorandum, CFQ, MD, Medical Officer, to UVW, Director, Dominion Lands Administration, Department of the Interior, dated Pangnirtung, NWT, 8 September 1936; and memorandum, Major ABD to UVW, Director, Lands Administration, Department of the Interior, Ottawa, 11 April 1935.

27 Memoranda, CFQ, MD, Medical Officer, to UVW, Deputy Minister, Department of the Interior, dated Pangnirtung, NWT, 21 May 1935 and 8 September 1936.

28 Ibid., 8 September 1936.

29 Ibid., 8 September 1936.

30 Memorandum, CFQ, MD, Medical Officer to UVW, Deputy Minister, Department of the Interior, 21 May 1935.

31 Ibid.

32 Memorandum, CFQ, MD, Medical Officer, to UVW, Director, Lands Branch, Department of the Interior, 8 September 1935.

33 Memorandum, CFQ, MD, Medical Officer, to UVW, Director, Lands Branch, Department of the Interior, 21 May 1935.

34 Letter, DXI, Assistant to the Director, U.S. Department of the Interior, Office of Indian Affairs, to UVW, Director, Lands Branch, Department of the Interior, dated Juneau, Alaska, 14 June 1935.

35 Memorandum, Major ABD, Lands, Parks and Forest Branch, Department of Mines and Resources, to MLN, Ottawa, 9 May 1940.

36 Ibid.

37 Ibid.

38 Ibid.

39 Ibid.

40 Ibid.

41 Ibid.

42 Memorandum, KEO to Major ABD, Ottawa, 30 October 1940.

43 Ibid.

44 Memorandum, Major ABD, Department of Mines and Resources, to MLN, Ottawa, 21 January 1941.

45 Extract, Minutes of the One-hundred and Twenty-first Session of the Northwest Territories Council, 11 February 1941, Sec. (x).

46 Memorandum, Major ABD to MLN, Ottawa, 26 March 1941.

47 Extract, Major ABD's Eastern Arctic Report, HMS *Nascopie*, 12 August 1941.

48 Memorandum, MLN, Deputy Commissioner of the Northwest Territories, to the Commissioner, RCMP, Ottawa, no clear date, probably late 1941.

49 Memorandum, Major ABD to Mr. ACD, Ottawa, 2 December 1942.

50 Memorandum, Major ABD to Mr ACD, Ottawa, 2 December 1942; and memorandum, MLN, Deputy Commissioner of the Northwest Territories, to the Commissioner, RCMP, Ottawa, no clear date, probably late 1941.

51 Memorandum, EKN, Inspector, Officer Commanding "G" Division, RCMP, to Commissioner, RCMP, Ottawa, dated Aklavik, NWT, 30 December 1942.

52 Ibid.

53 Ibid.

54 Memorandum, Major ABD to MLN, Ottawa, 29 March 1943.

55 Circular Memorandum, EKN, Inspector, Officer Commanding "G" Division, RCMP, to all Detachments in the Eastern Arctic and on the Western Arctic Coast, dated Ottawa, 4 November 1943.

56 Memorandum, Major ABD to MLN, Ottawa, 16 November 1943.

57 Ibid., see especially the marginal notation by Deputy Commissioner, Northwest Territories.

58 Memorandum, Major ABD to MLN, Ottawa, 26 March 1941.

59 Memorandum (cited in full), MLN, Director, Lands, Parks and Forests Branch, Department of Mines and Resources, to Major ABD, Ottawa, 5 March 1945.

60 Memorandum, Major ABD to MLN, Bureau of Northwest Territories and Yukon Affairs, Ottawa, 19 April 1945.

61 Memorandum, MLN, Deputy Commissioner of the Northwest Territories, to Major ABD, Ottawa, 11 April 1945.

62 Memorandum, Major ABD to MLN, 19 April 1945.

63 "Explanatory Memorandum for District Registrars, Northwest Territories and Yukon Territory, Relative to the Registration of Vital Statistics and the Payment of Family Allowances," seven legal-size pages, no date or department provenance indicated, but apparently from the Deputy Minister of Welfare, since it is referred to as enclosed with a letter from him to MLN, Deputy Commissioner, Northwest Territories, Department of Mines and Resources, dated Ottawa, 13 July 1945.

64 "Nomads" in the administrative parlance of the day denoted persons who followed a traditional Eskimo way of life, but were not eligible for registration as Eskimos.

65 "Explanatory Memorandum" (see note 63), Ottawa, 13 July 1945.

66 Draft copy exists in file 431 v.45, Department of National Health and Welfare, indicating only July 1945 as date.

67 Ibid., Part Seven Sec. 30.

68 Personal field-notes from research in the Mackenzie Delta, 1965, 1966–1967; see D.G. Smith (1975a).

69 Memorandum, MLN, Registrar-General of Vital Statistics for the Northwest Territories, to Deputy Minister, Department of National Health and Welfare, Ottawa, 13 March 1946.

70 Memorandum, IUY to MLN, Deputy Commissioner of the Northwest Territories, Aklavik, NWT, 31 August 1946.

71 Ibid.; for a discussion of the Alaskan Eskimo migrations into the Canadian Western Arctic see D.G. Smith (1984).

72 Memorandum extract attached to memorandum, IUY to MLN, 31 August 1946, see note 70.

73 "Circular Letter to All School Principals in the Northwest Territories and Eskimo Territory of the Province of Quebec," from MLN, Deputy Commissioner of the Northwest Territories, Ottawa, 6 December 1946.

74 See, for example, memorandum, BDE, Deputy Registrar-General of Vital Statistics for the Northwest Territories, to Registrar of Vital Statistics, RCMP Detachment, Hay River, NWT, 2 February 1966.

75 Letter, EOT, Commissioner of the Northwest Territories, to Chief Superintendent EKN, Commanding Officer, "G" Division, RCMP (originally signed by SOM), Ottawa, 14 June 1966.

76 "Family Allowances Regulations" 431/v.45 submitted to the Governor General for approval by order-in-council by the Minister of National Health and Welfare, July 1945.

77 "An Ordinance Respecting the Preservation of Game in the Northwest Territories" (Game Ordinance), *Revised Statutes of the Northwest Territories* 1956, Chapter 42, Part I, Paragraph 2 (c).

78 "An Ordinance to Provide for the Control and Sale of Liquor in the Northwest Territories" (Liquor Ordinance), *Revised Statutes of the Northwest Territories* 1956, Chapter 60 Sec. 2 (1) (c).

79 Memorandum, POG, Director, to ICH, Legal Adviser, Department of Indian Affairs and Northern Development, Northern Administration Branch, Ottawa, 14 March 1967.

80 For example, letter, Prof. FLY, University of British Columbia, to Information Officer, Government of the Northwest Territories, Vancouver, 1 June 1967; and letter, RMC, Director, Northern Administration Branch, Department of Indian Affairs and Northern Development, to Prof. FLY, 11 June 1967.

81 Letter, RMC to FLY, see note 80.
82 Memorandum, ICH, Legal Adviser, to RMC, Director, Northern Affairs Branch, Department of Indian Affairs and Northern Development, Ottawa, 4 July 1967.
83 Memorandum, EOT, Commissioner of the Northwest Territories, to Administrator of the Arctic, 19 May 1966.
84 Foucault (1979:11) is speaking of a "juridical principle which throughout the Middle Ages down to the 16th century had defined sovereignty in public right," namely of the establishment and maintenance of sovereignty in the European state context. It seems to me that the juridical and other state practices are likely to be rather (even very) different in the case of different colonial and imperial situations, and that therefore some of Foucault's assertions would have to be re-examined and appropriately modified for application to these contexts.

BIBLIOGRAPHY

Bishop, Charles. 1974. *The Northern Ojibwa and the Fur Trade*. Toronto: Holt.
Bockstoce, John R. 1986. *Whales, Ice, and Men: The History of Whaling in the Western Arctic*. Seattle: University of Washington Press.
Bourdieu, Pierre. 1989. *Outline of a Theory of Practice*. Cambridge Studies in Social Anthropology, no. 16. Cambridge: Cambridge University Press.
Brody, Hugh. 1975. *The People's Land: Eskimos and Whites in the Eastern Canadian Arctic*. Harmondsworth: Penguin.
Fisher, Robin. 1977. *Contact and Conflict: Indian-European Relations in 1774–1890*. Vancouver: University of British Columbia Press.
Foucault, Michel. 1979. "Governmentality." *Ideology and Consciousness* 6:5–21.
–   1990. *Power/Knowledge: Selected Interviews and other Writings, 1972–1977*, ed. Colin Gordon. New York: Pantheon.
Frideres, J.S. 1974. *Canada's Indians: Contemporary Conflicts*. Scarborough, Ontario: Prentice-Hall.
Galtung, Johan. 1980. *The True Worlds: A Transactional Perspective*. New York: Free Press.
Hawthorn, Harry B. 1967. *Survey of the Contemporary Indians of Canada: A Report on Economic, Political, and Educational Needs and Policies*. 2 vols. Ottawa: Indian Affairs Branch, Department of Indian Affairs Northern Development.
Hickerson, Harold C. 1967. *Land Tenure of the Rainy Lake Chippewa at the Beginning of the 19th Century*. Smithsonian Publications 2, no. 4. Washington, D.C.: Smithsonian Institution.
–   1970. *The Chippewa and Their Neighbours: A Study in Ethnohistory*. New York: Winston.

Honigmann, John J., and I. Honigmann. 1965. *Eskimo Townsmen*. Ottawa: Canadian Research Centre for Anthropology, St Paul University.

– 1970. *Arctic Townsmen: Ethnic Backgrounds and Modernization*. Ottawa: Canadian Research Centre for Anthropology, St Paul University.

Jenness, Diamond. 1962. *Eskimo Administration: I. Alaska*. Arctic Institute of North America Technical Paper no. 10. Montreal: Arctic Institute of North America.

– 1964. *Eskimo Administration: II. Canada*. Arctic Instituteof North America Technical Paper no. 14. Montreal: Arctic Institute of North America.

– 1965. *Eskimo Administration: III. Labrador*. Arctic Institute of North America Technical Paper no. 16. Montreal: Arctic Institute of North America.

– 1967. *Eskimo Administration: IV. Greenland*. Arctic Institute of North America Technical Paper no. 19. Montreal: Arctic Institute of North America.

– 1968. *Eskimo Administration. V. Analysis and Reflections*. Arctic Institute of North America Technical Paper no. 21. Montreal: Arctic Institute of North America.

LaViolette, F.E. 1961. *The Struggle for Survival: Indian Cultures and the Protestant Ethic in British Columbia*. Toronto: University of Toronto.

Morantz, Toby E. 1983. *An Ethnohistoric Study of Eastern James Bay Social Organization, 1700–1850*. Canadian Ethnology Service Mercury Series, no. 88. Ottawa: National Museums of Canada.

–, and F. Daniel. 1983. *Partners in Furs: A History of the Fur Trade in Eastern James Bay, 1600–1870*. Montreal and Kingston: McGill-Queen's University Press.

Northwest Territories. 1956a. "An Ordinance Respecting the Preservation of Game in the Northwest Territories (Game Ordinance)," *Revised Statutes of the Northwest Territories* 1956, Chapter 42, Part I, Paragraph 2(c).

– 1956b. "An Ordinance to Provide for the Control and Sale of Liquor in the Northwest Territories (Liquor Ordinance)," *Revised statutes of the Northwest Territories* 1956, Chapter 60, Section 2(1)(c).

Paine, Robert, ed. 1971. *Patrons and Brokers in the Eastern Arctic*. Newfoundland Social and Economic Papers, no. 2. St John's: Memorial University of Newfoundland, Institute of Social and Economic Research.

– 1977. *The White Arctic: Anthropological Essays on Tutelage and Ethnicity*. Institute of Social and Economic Research Monograph no. 7. St John's: Memorial University of Newfoundland.

Ponting, J. Rick, and R. Gibbins. 1980. *Out of Irrelevance: A Socio-Political Introduction to Indian Affairs in Canada*. Toronto: Butterworths.

Reference Re: Eskimos. 1939, Canada Law Reports: Supreme Court of Canada. Queen's Printer, 104–24.

Séguin, Gilles. 1989. "Reindeer for the North: A Preliminary Study of the Role of Government, 1907–1960." Master's thesis, Institute of Canadian Studies, Carleton University.

Smith, Derek G. 1975a. *Natives and Outsiders: Pluralism in the Mackenzie River Delta*. Mackenzie Delta Research Reports, no. 12. Ottawa: Department of Indian Affairs and Northern Development.

–, ed. 1975b. *Canadian Indians and the Law: Selected Documents, 1663–1972*. Carleton Library, no. 87. Toronto: McClelland and Stewart.

– 1984. "Mackenzie Eskimo." *Handbook of North American Indians*, vol. 5 (Arctic), 347–58. Washington: Smithsonian Institution.

Smith, Dorothy E. 1990. *The Conceptual Practices of Power: A Feminist Sociology of Knowledge*. Toronto: University of Toronto Press.

Smith, Richard Saumarez. 1985. "Rule-by-records and Rule-by-reports: Complementary Aspects of the British Rule of Law." *Contributions to Indian Sociology* 19 (1):153–76.

Trigger, Bruce. 1976 *The Children of Aatentsic: A History of the Huron People to 1660*. Montreal and Kingston: McGill-Queen's University Press.

– 1987. *Natives and Newcomers: Canada's Heroic Age Reconsidered*. Montreal and Kingston: McGill-Queen's University Press.

Vallee, Frank G. 1967. *Kabloona and Eskimo in the Central Keewatin*. Ottawa: Canadian Research Centre for Anthropology, St Paul University.

Waldram, James B. 1988. *As Long as the Rivers Run: Hydroelectric Development and Native Communities in Canada*. Winnipeg: University of Manitoba Press.

Weaver, Sally. 1980. *Making Canadian Indian Policy: The Hidden Agenda, 1968–1970*. Toronto: University of Toronto Press.

Zaslow, Morris. 1988. *The Northward Expansion of Canada, 1914–1967*. Canadian Centenary Series, no. 17. Toronto: McClelland & Stewart.

3 The Hawthorn Report: Its Use in the Making of Canadian Indian Policy

SALLY M. WEAVER

INTRODUCTION

If anthropologists seek to influence the policy-making process through their research, they must first understand the political and bureaucratic nature of governments and how the policy-making process operates within that context. One way to gain this knowledge is to discover how our work has been used by governments in the past, a long-neglected aspect of applied anthropology (Chambers 1985:viii). This paper analyses the life cycle of one research report, not with the intent of proclaiming indignation at the government's treatment of our work, but in a serious attempt to understand how our research is perceived and used by policy makers in the complex process of policy formulation. I have chosen a report with which I am familiar, the classic Hawthorn report, the two-volume, government-commissioned national survey of Canadian Indians, *A Survey of the Contemporary Indians of Canada* (Hawthorn 1967).[1] I will follow the history of the work from its inception in 1963 through to its use during the formulation of the 1969 White Paper on Indian policy – the controversial and soon-shelved proposal to terminate the special rights and legal status of First Nations Indians in Canada (Department of Indian Affairs and Northern Development [DIAND] 1969). It is important to understand from the outset, however, that the Hawthorn report was not commissioned with the White Paper in mind. Its use during the formulation of the White Paper met with highly mixed responses from various agencies within the government. On the basis of this reaction, I draw some observations about the treatment and utility of anthropological research for Indian policy. I conclude with a brief sketch of subsequent national surveys of First Nations conditions and programs, a sketch which highlights the uniqueness of the Hawthorn report.

THE RESEARCH STAGE OF
THE HAWTHORN REPORT

The context in which the Hawthorn report was commissioned in 1963–64 is important for understanding its scope and its eventual reception within government.

In 1963 "the Indian problem" was just beginning to take shape in Canadian society. A greater awareness among the public of the mere existence of First Nations peoples, a hitherto unknown minority, was a significant change. First Nations were beginning to express their disenchantment with government administration and their marginal position in society, but the Indian movement had yet to establish a national focus and an organizational base (Cardinal 1977:182). Within government, the Indian Affairs Branch, then a part of the Department of Citizenship and Immigration, was beginning to examine its programs in the context of its overarching policy of Indian integration, keeping in mind the joint parliamentary committee's 1961 recommendations to accelerate Indian integration into Canadian society (Senate and House of Commons 1961:605). Adé Tremblay, Hawthorn's associate director, recalled that rising pressures for change were coming from many quarters:

There were pressing demands on the part of the indigenous communities to have sizable increases in their share of the "national income" and ... there were rising conflicts in the federal-provincial relations concerning their respective jurisdictions in the fields of health and welfare, education and economic development. It was at a time, too, when many Indian leaders expressed their concern over the fact that despite growing capacity for self-government Indian communities were submitted to greater bureaucratic, administrative and economic controls. There were also, on the part of many whites, a growing fear that the "economic burden" of the indigenous communities was to become intolerable on the part of the white taxpayer.[2]

The net effect of all these forces was an increasing frustration among senior officials in the Indian Branch with the limited effectiveness and outreach of their programs. As one official explained: "We were at a dead end; nothing more was happening. We needed some feedback on where to go from here."[3] The growth of the welfare state was raising expectations among Canadians of increased social services but the provinces, which delivered most of these services to Canadians, largely ignored Indians who remained a federal responsibility under the Canadian constitution (BNA Act 1867, Sec. 91(24)). In effect, First Nations were being by-passed by the provinces, and less than adequately served by the federal government according to its own policies.

The Hawthorn report was clearly the result of a convergence of two events: the disenchantment among senior branch officials with their programs, and a fortuitous incident of public demand. In early 1963, Colonel H.M. Jones, who was about to retire as the director of the branch, decided that the branch needed concrete and usable information about the condition of Indians upon which to reformulate and improve its programs. At the same time, the national executive of the Imperial Order of the Daughters of the Empire (IODE) approached the minister, Richard Bell, urging him to undertake a three- to five-year study on how Indians in Canada could achieve equal opportunity with other citizens.[4] Officials used the IODE's timely request as a pressure point on the minister who agreed to undertake a major research project.[5] The research component of the branch at that time was extremely weak, so the decision to turn outside the government for information was understandable.

When the branch decided to commission the study its officials were already familiar with Hawthorn's study on British Columbia Indians (Hawthorn, Belshaw, and Jamieson 1958) as well as his earlier report on the Doukhobors (Hawthorn 1955), both studies having policy and program implications (Inglis 1975:4–5). Finding the Indian study useful, Colonel Jones contacted Hawthorn to inquire whether he would organize the project or recommend others who might be suitable. Although Hawthorn was at first extremely reluctant to consider the project, mainly because he understood the massive proportions of the task and had normal full-time commitments at the University of British Columbia, he eventually agreed.[6]

The branch set few limits on the scope of the project other than the need for the information to bear directly on the present conditions of First Nations and to be usable by officials in a practical program sense. The terms of reference were mutually shaped by Hawthorn and senior officials, and they were exceedingly broad. As Hawthorn recalled: "The agreement allowed any scope, including recommendation for the abolition of the department. The fact that we did not arrive at such a conclusion derived from our findings and judgement; we considered the point.'"[7] When the contract was signed in June 1963, it included a guarantee to publish the final report and it identified four areas for concentration: (1) economic development, (2) constitutional and administrative matters, (3) education, and (4) local government and leadership. This was a large task given the two- to three-year time frame allowed.[8]

Hawthorn proceeded to select a core of senior researchers who spearheaded the major lines of inquiry while maintaining their full-time commitments to their universities. Stuart M. Jamieson, a UBC economist, wrote the economic development sections of the report. Alan C. Cairns, a UBC political scientist, did the work on administrative and constitutional matters, and Kenneth Lysyk, then at the UBC Law School, wrote the sections on the legal status of Indians. These men, with Hawthorn, authored volume one of the report, the part which had the greatest implications for policy-making. Marc-Adélard Tremblay, an anthropologist at Laval University who joined the team as co-director at a later date due to prior commitments, did the educational analysis with Joan Ryan, then a graduate student in educational psychology at UBC. Frank Vallee, the third senior editor of volume two and an anthropologist at Carleton University, wrote the sections on band government and leadership. Including these senior researchers, Hawthorn's team totaled fifty-two social scientists, mostly anthropologists, who undertook specific studies on reserves as consultants.

Despite the large size of the team and the breadth of the mandate, the work proceeded smoothly from its inception in late 1963 to its completion in October 1967. Senior officials, eager, even over anxious, for the findings at the outset, provided full access to files and personnel and easy and informal exchange of views, which led to the mutual shaping of many recommendations. Some of the team's recommendations were incorporated into programs before the report was finalized, reflecting the fact that changes occurring in the branch threatened to overtake the research. Co-ordination of the project was undertaken by Hawthorn who held periodic seminars and informal sessions among the researchers. The final reports by the senior researchers were edited to various degrees by Hawthorn and submitted to the government on time: volume one was submitted in October 1966, volume two in October 1967.

In style, the research operation had many of the qualities of a task force: the mandate had been mutually worked out by Hawthorn and officials, and the good rapport between the team and the branch facilitated the exchange of ideas. While differences of opinion between them certainly existed, the researchers found senior officials amenable to new ideas, in contrast to the mid-range civil servants from whom they often encountered opposition. When Hawthorn submitted each volume, it was reviewed by branch officials with only minor editorial changes suggested, mainly of a factual nature. In short, no "political editing" occurred as some social scientists might have suspected.

In content, the report was firmly rooted in a philosophy of enhancing special status or "citizens plus" status for First Nations – meaning that "in addition to the normal rights and duties of citizenship, Indians possess certain additional rights as charter members of the Canadian community" (Hawthorn 1967:6). The report sought ways to give "practical meaning" to citizen plus status (1967:12), at the same time rejecting the notion that special legal status prevented the delivery of provincial services to Indians. Instead, it proposed increased provincial involvement in Indian affairs (1967:15–16) and cautioned government against confusing legal equality with socio-economic equality, fearing serious hardship to First Nations if such occurred (1967:392). In general, the report laid bare many problems in programs and argued that the branch should assume the role of advocate-ombudsperson for First Nations until they were sufficiently skilled to protect their own self-interests against those of the powerful political and corporate forces in society (1967:13, 17, 397–8). In the meantime, it stressed, the government should encourage and support the growth of Indian political organizations-pressure groups (1967:11–12, 17). Central to the report's philosophy was the position that goals such as integration were not properly the domain of the government; these decisions could only be taken by Indians for Indians, and only when Indians were in a position of equal opportunity to make these real life choices (1967:6, 13). Indeed, "choice" was a key value informing the report: "The prime assumption of the Report has been that it is imperative that Indians be enabled to make meaningful choices between desirable alternatives; that this should not happen at some time in the future as wisdom grows or the situation improves, but operate now and continue with increasing range" (1967:5).

Generally, the Hawthorn report was significant as the first national scale social science survey of First Nations conditions in Canada, and as the first major substantiation of the socio-economic components of "the Indian problem" in the 1960s. It was a multidisciplinary study, broad in topic, and it provided 151 specific recommendations for government action. In fact, it had most of the qualities of a "usable" study:

1 It directly addressed the concerns of government officials, not those of academics.

2 It was multi-disciplinary, avoiding the bias of a single discipline approach.
3 It was based on current data (gathered between 1964 and 1966).
4 It was written in plain, readable English, free of jargon, (although the French translation proved problematic).
5 It was based on a national sample of reserves (thirty-five), selected on the basis of their geographic location, size, and urban proximity, as well as on selected in-depth studies of specific reserves for certain purposes.
6 Its recommendations were practicable or capable of being implemented.

In sum, the report had all the formal qualities of social science research felt to be of utility to policy makers. How, then, was it received by branch officials, other social scientists, and the public?

THE REPORT'S RECEPTION

Upon completion of each volume, Hawthorn and the senior researchers met with branch officials in Ottawa and discussed the recommendations in considerable detail. Branch officials found most of the recommendations acceptable.[9] Cairns' interpretation of the federal mandate for Indians as a permissive one which did not prevent the delivery of provincial services to First Nations was novel and welcomed, despite the anticipated difficulties of persuading the provinces to accept this view. Jamieson's basic approach, that programs focus on enhancing marketable skills rather than developing Indian reserves, was met more guardedly. But the notion that the Indian Branch should act as advocate and ombudsperson for First Nations within government was accepted in principle. In all, of the 151 recommendations the branch agreed with 110, partly agreed with nine, disagreed with ten and was undecided about the final eight.[10] The work fared less well among social scientists.

Within the year William Dunning, an anthropologist at the University of Toronto, published a review of the first volume of the report in *Canadian Forum* (Dunning 1967). While Dunning found no difficulty with the research base, he took exception to the enhanced role given the Indian Affairs Branch in the future, arguing that the researchers should have questioned the branch's monopoly on Indian affairs. He was highly critical of the report's philosophy, stating that its approach was "worthy of 1867," not 1967 (Dunning 1967: 52). In his view the report was too cautious and conservative an approach to the branch which, in his opinion, was excessively paternalistic and authoritarian. In short, Dunning thought the report should have examined the structure of the Branch. The extent to which his views representated the opinions of Canadian social scientists is not known to me, but I suspect some of them shared his perspective largely because of the critical position they normally take on the branch's activities in their writings. Dunning's review, it can be noted here, subsequently had an interesting history in later developments on the White Paper.

The public response to the Hawthorn report is most easily gauged by its reviews in the press and popular magazines. Hawthorn leaked the first volume to George Mortimore, then a reporter for the Toronto *Globe and Mail*, who gave it a favourable and prominent review there and elsewhere (Mortimore 1967a, 1967b). The few other reviews I was able to find were also positive (e.g., Katz 1967) and *all* of them treated the report as a substantiation of the "Indian problem."

In summary, the report seems to have had a mild but positive response from the media and a critical reception by social scientists. Within government, its immediate impact was severely handicapped by the steady succession of ministers through the Indian Affairs program (six ministers since the start of the project), and by the fact that Arthur Laing, the minister to receive both volumes of the work, was a strong-willed, business-oriented minister disinclined to put much credence in social science.

Determining the degree of implementation of the report's recommendations is a thorny problem and I will side-step this by simply noting that officials say they put many of the recommendations into effect in programming. It is obvious, however, that some of those of a more general nature were not implemented. The Indian Progress Agency, for example, an independent body to monitor annually the progress of Indians was not instituted (Hawthorn 1967:9). The more basic point, however, is that the task force quality of the research led some branch officials to think in new ways and to approach both programs and policy in a different light than they would have without the interchange of ideas and information with the research team. This is probably the strongest form of "implementation" brought about by the Hawthorn project in the end. The longer range impact of the report for general Indian policy can be assessed only against the fast moving political climate of the period 1967–69.

THE INDIAN ACT

In 1967, when the Hawthorn report was complete, the "Indian problem" was taking firmer shape in Canadian society. Public awareness of Indians as a poor and powerless minority was increasing, and public opinion was quickly focusing on the Indian Act as an instrument of legal oppression and racism. It is important to note that white liberals who promoted the "Indian cause" failed to understand the long-standing ambivalence First Nations held toward the act; the fact they valued it because of certain Indian rights it provided, and yet resented it because of its excessive constraints on self-determination. The culmination of these public pressures, evident in MPs' statements in the Commons as well as the press, was the decision by the Pearson government to revise the Indian Act. Thus, under Arthur Laing, the act was to be liberalized, to become a more flexible and adaptive instrument by offering a series of options for band government, land use, and local-level decision-making powers. In short, by 1967, the act had become a political embarrassment to the government, an administrative hindrance to the branch, and in Laing's view "a fortress or prison" for Indians (Laing 1967).

It must be stressed, however, that the decision to revise the Indian Act was taken in 1966–67 *within* the traditional policy framework of retaining special rights for First Nations; honouring the treaties, retaining the reserves, and establishing an Indian Claims Commission. Although the demise of the Indian Department was the ultimate goal of the government, this was not foreseen in the near future, as it was in the 1969 White Paper. Furthermore, Indians were to be consulted on the revisions (DIAND 1968) and in the absence of representative Indian organizations, the department set up an elaborate system of consultation meetings intended to obtain Indian opinion. These consultations were originally scheduled for the spring of 1968 because Laing was anxious to move quickly through the process and introduce amendments to the Indian Act in late 1968. But these plans were immediately disrupted by the announced retirement of Lester Pearson and the April 1968 Liberal leadership race which brought Pierre E. Trudeau to power. Consequently the consultations were postponed until after the Liberal leadership race and the June federal election which returned Trudeau to power with a majority government.

THE NEW TRUDEAU ADMINISTRATION

The Trudeau administration brought a new ethos to government which valued fundamental change and political, not bureaucratic, leadership. This resulted in the establishment of new procedures for policy-making within the cabinet and extensive policy reviews in most federal fields of operation. Indian policy was among those affected. One result was that the Hawthorn report became judged by a new set of politicians and officials who sometimes shared Trudeau's own personal philosophy against special rights for cultural minorities (e.g., French Canada) (Trudeau 1968) but who also held different views on the policy-making process itself. In short, the political context for evaluating the Hawthorn report had changed dramatically with the advent of participatory democracy, Trudeaumania, and expansive hopes for far-reaching changes in most fields of federal policy.

Events moved rapidly in the summer and fall of 1968 as the new Trudeau government settled into office. Indian policy was given high priority by the cabinet together with other policies such as national unity and regional economic expansion. Trudeau introduced extensive changes in the cabinet structure designed to enhance the government's capacity to produce more effective and well-planned policies. In his view policies were to be made by politicians, not civil servants whom he generally distrusted (Doern 1971). Furthermore, policies were to be far sighted, to foresee future changes, and to avoid creating further problems. These were heady months in Ottawa, and both politicians and senior officials had high expectations that many social problems, ignored in the past, would finally receive the serious examination they deserved. Because of this ethos, incremental policies were disparaged and fundamental change highly valued. This explains, in part, how the exercise to revise the Indian Act turned into an exercise which questioned the foundations of the act and produced the 1969 White Paper.

THE WHITE PAPER AND
THE HAWTHORN REPORT

The process of developing the White Paper was an extremely complex and tangled one, and it will be simplified here in an effort to determine the precise fate of the Hawthorn report in its deliberations.

Briefly, the policy-making process took two different but increasingly divergent paths. Publicly, DIAND's consultation meetings with First Nations began in the summer of 1968, becoming the major instrument for raising Indian expectations that their views on special rights would be considered by the government in revising the Indian Act. Privately, within the government at the cabinet level, a dramatically different exercise began which questioned both the philosophical and practical basis of a separate Indian administration and special rights for First Nations. This second exercise took place in the central advising agencies around the cabinet: the Prime Minister's Office (PMO), which provided Trudeau with *political partisan* advice on policy, and the Privy Council Office (PCO), which provided Trudeau and the cabinet with *bureaucratic* advice from an *overall* governmental perspective rather than from a specific department's perspective (Lalonde 1971, Robertson 1971). It is important to realize that the PMO and the PCO were expanded in size and given much more powerful roles in advising the cabinet on policies under the Trudeau administration. Consequently, when the White Paper was being shaped, senior DIAND officials were facing, *for the first time*, powerful countervailing pressures from these agencies which expected them to produce far-sighted policy proposals that were well rationalized in terms of wider government priorities. If DIAND officials failed to comply, the PMO and the PCO were there to ensure the work was done. In short, the department's ability to shape new policies was severely limited at this time.

As the policy-making process began in the summer of 1968 all three agencies – the PMO, the PCO, and the department – were expected to propose new ways in which the government should begin to approach the "Indian problem." This involved the basic question of how broad in scope the new policy should be; for example, should it be a global Indian policy, or should it focus mid-range on sectoral policies such as social services, education, and housing? Should it include Metis and Inuit as well as Indians? Should it be shaped largely by the department, or should it be shaped by a special task force in the PCO as was increasingly common in those years? In September 1968 the prime minister focused the process by asking the department to undertake a thorough and critical policy review of Indian Affairs which would indicate possible policy directions the government could consider. In responding to the prime minister's request, the department used the Hawthorn report to substantiate its proposals, and it was in this context of a far-reaching policy review that the report was introduced during the development of the White Paper. It soon became evident that the three agencies – the department, the PMO, and the PCO – had very different views of its utility.

THE DEPARTMENT'S USE OF
THE HAWTHORN REPORT

With the exception of Colonel H.M. Jones who had retired by mid-1968, the senior officials who had commissioned the Hawthorn report were still in place in the department's hierarchy when the White Paper was formulated. The only major change was the insertion, above them, of a new deputy minister, John A. MacDonald, who had worked closely with Arthur Laing and, like him, had a strong business orientation to Indian affairs. Thus the department was headed by Jean Chrétien, its new young minister, Robert Andras, a new minister without portfolio, the forceful deputy minister, MacDonald, and the "old guard," the half-dozen senior officials who had commissioned the Hawthorn report and who had spent most of their careers in the Indian service.

To back track a moment. When MacDonald became deputy minister in the spring, he had initiated a total program review in the department in an effort to take stock of its needs for the next five years. By the fall of 1968 this assessment produced a five-year plan (a program forecast) which he submitted to the PMO and PCO as a response to the prime minister's request for a far-sighted policy review. The Hawthorn report figured significantly in the plan in that it had been minutely examined by senior departmental officials who were required to comment in detail on each of the 151 recommendations and indicate future program and policy directions that might flow from them. In this context the department referred to the Hawthorn report as "an important point of reference in the conceptualization of policy."[11] Much of the substantive data in the report was also used in the department's five year plan. In essence, then, the department's first step in shaping the White Paper was to forward this plan to the PMO and PCO in an attempt to promote a *continuation* of its current programming, as well as to test opinion in the central agencies. Had the plan been accepted its effect would have been to expand and strengthen the bureaucracy.

PCO RESPONSE

The PCO's job was to review this plan and advise the cabinet and the prime minister on whether the department had in fact produced the thorough and far-sighted policy review the prime minister had requested. The PCO's role was to examine policies in terms of overall government priorities, not just those of a department, and its powers were extensive. The officials in the PCO (social policy unit) who handled Indian policy were decidedly activist in their ideology; they strongly advocated Indian participation in any policy-making effort. They also questioned the assumptions underlying traditional Indian policy and the separate bureaucracy. The key person in the PCO to evaluate the department's proposal was Walter Rudnicki, a former DIAND official. His formal training was in social work and he had mounted the community development program in the Indian Affairs Branch in 1964, staying there long enough to see it terminated by the old guard officials. He was highly critical of the department's authoritarian treatment of First Nations and, because of its abolition of the community development program, he distrusted the department's claims to relinquish patronage over Indians. From his vantage point in the PCO he was in an ideal position to criticize the department's proposals; he was familiar with the department's operations and ideology and his job required him to critically assess departmental proposals. Above all he was an adept political craftsperson who was highly skilled in arguing his position and justifying his views in terms of the values then being promoted by the Trudeau administration – especially that of participatory democracy.

When the department's proposal came to him for review, Rudnicki prepared an extensive and well-received evaluation of it for the PMO. His assessment, for the most part, was incisive and devastating, and he concluded that the department was suffering from the naïve assumption that more bureaucracy would solve the "Indian problem." Nor was he impressed with the department's use of the Hawthorn report to substantiate its position. To put it bluntly, Rudnicki had little respect for academic experts and even less for the Hawthorn report. He saw the report as inherently conservative; he set out to discredit it.

His first criticism, following Dunning (1967), was that the research had failed to include in-depth studies of single reserves. He argued that had such work been done, the basic recommendations might have been quite different. The irony here was that in-depth studies abounded in the academic literature and had been included in the Hawthorn research; the particular strength of the report lay in its attempt to go beyond individual case studies to a national coverage of the problems Indians experienced across Canada.

The second point of attack was more interesting. Rudnicki disagreed strongly with the report's recommendation of an enhanced role for the department and, in expressing his views, he used the language of Bill Dunning's published critique of the Hawthorn report. He wrote: "The study seems to have started with the assumption that the Indian Affairs Department is the only available agency to assist Indians. This is a philosophy worthy of 1867. Although the study does express some mild reservations about the department, it stops short of analyzing its structure, its resources, its policies or the qualifications of its personnel."[12] Rudnicki's final criticism of the Hawthorn report reflected his antipathy to academic experts and to the department's failure to solicit Indian opinion on the report's recommendations: "It is relevant to note that none of Hawthorn's recommendations have ever been referred to Indian leaders and spokesmen [sic] for comments or discussion. The Indians were simply bystanders in a scene where experts had a conversation among themselves and arrived at their own consensus."[13] The allegation that researchers had not dealt with Indians in collecting data was simply incorrect, but he was right in saying that Indian leaders had not been asked to evaluate the report for the government. However, the implication that Indians would not have supported it can be partly questioned because they subsequently used its philosophy to substantiate their own counter-proposals to the White Paper in 1969 and 1970 (see below).

Rudnicki's indictment of the Hawthorn report reflected more widely held views of it by other activist officials who were later involved in formulating the White Paper. These men considered the report to be a conservative document with a philosophy that was out of tune with the prevailing notion of participatory democracy espoused by the Trudeau government and society in general. One described the report as "promoting acculturation through bureaucracy instead of acculturation through Indians," and another said it was "philosophically dated" (S. Weaver 1981:128). The report's proposal that the department become the advocate-ombudsperson for Indians was at the centre of their rejection, for they were convinced that the department would promote its own continuation at the expense of Indian self-determination and would not agree to Indian participation in policy formulation. They were also convinced that it was incapable of far-reaching change and unable to understand what Indians were trying to communicate.

THE RESPONSE OF THE PMO

Rudnicki's evaluation of the department's proposals was well received in the PMO, the most powerful agency in the policy-making process. The key figure in the PMO guiding Indian policy was Jim Davey, a major strategist for Trudeau's leadership and election campaigns. He was a physicist and computer specialist by training and shared Trudeau's liberal ideology and cybernetic approach to policy-making. Davey's main job was to advise Trudeau on the political-partisan implications of policies which included the prospects for re-election. Davey was led to the Hawthorn report in a particular context which is important for understanding his evaluation of it.

In addition to the proposals Rudnicki had forwarded from the PCO, Gordon Robertson, the head of the PCO and the most powerful civil servant in Ottawa, had suggested that Indian policy be transferred to a Royal Commission for further inquiry (S. Weaver 1981: 91–2). Robertson felt this would allow more thorough examination of the issues and that it would distance the proceedings from the prime minister if the matter became politically explosive. It would also buy time, although this was *not* his basic reason for proposing a commission.

Although Jim Davey agreed with Robertson on many issues regarding the "Indian problem," he did not like the notion of a Royal Commission. Thus Davey assessed the Hawthorn report in the context of a proposed Royal Commission. He wrote: "I have recently looked at the Hawthorne [sic] Report, a voluminous document prepared by academics from across Canada on Indian problems. They talk about treating Indians as citizens plus and make other recommendations whose political ramifications are enormous and endless. I shudder to think that any Royal Commission might bring out such a similar document."[14] To this he added: "1972 is also the probable date of the next election. I would hate to see a Royal Commission report coming out around or prior to that date."

Although Davey's views on the Hawthorn report reflect his opinion of academic experts, they also reflect the basic liberal ideology in the PMO: a strong system of ideas and values favouring individualism and legal and political *equality*. Throughout the policy-making process the PMO had equated the "special status" issue with Quebec to the "special status" issue with Indians, and Trudeau's own personal philosophy against protecting cultural groups by legislation – or special governmental arrangements – was well known to the policy-makers. In Davey's view the political implications of special status for Indians were boundless – and groundless. He saw the Indian Act as legislated discrimination, and the Hawthorn report, which supported special status, was consequently set aside as a statement of philosophy *and* as a substantive guide for developing the new policy.

In summary, the Hawthorn report was used at the outset of the formulation process that produced the White Paper. It was evaluated from three perspectives, each producing a different judgment of its utility.

The department had commissioned the study four years earlier to improve its programming and had found the report useful in this regard. Because the department wanted to enlarge its administrative operation, it used the report to substantiate its proposal for a five-year plan. But because the department was cautious and conservative in its approach, its proposed plan failed to meet the requirements of the new ethos for fundamental and far-sighted policy formulations. As a result the department's plan was set aside, and more significantly, its policy competence was discredited in the eyes of the PCO and to a lesser extent the PMO.

PCO activists, especially Rudnicki, distrusted academics and the department, and discredited the Hawthorn report because it failed to emphasize Indian participation in the policy-making process. The activist ideology held that a new Indian policy would succeed only if it were the product of mutual exchange and agreement between Indian leaders and cabinet ministers. For this exchange to occur Indians had to bypass the bureaucracy, and particularly the department. Because the Hawthorn report dealt with Indian-bureaucratic relationships, it was dismissed as a useful approach to a new policy. It was also discredited on the grounds that the department used its "expert" opinion as a substitute for Indian involvement in policy-making.

The PMO, in the person of Jim Davey, took yet another approach to the report. He reacted to the report's philosophy, its emphasis on special rights for First Nations. The report was quickly dispensed with because it contradicted the value of equality in the liberal ideology that prevailed in the PMO and because it was felt to have unacceptable political implications in terms of election timing and Quebec's demands for special status.

The attitudes in the PMO and the PCO toward external experts or academics can be summarized in a more general way. "Experts" were seen to be too narrow in their comprehension of the problems facing government, too insensitive to political "realities," and too removed from government to understand the political implications of their own recommendations. Overall, experts were viewed as idealistic, theoretical, and philosophically conservative. More significantly they were considered outmoded in their thinking. These attitudes, matched with the determination to keep secret the formulations of the White Paper, greatly diminished the chances of bringing in external experts, let alone First Nations people. For these reasons, not only were none of the Hawthorn researchers involved in the formulation of the White Paper, they did not know it was being developed until it was publicly released in June 1969.

CONCLUSIONS

Although many implications for social science research could be drawn from the treatment of the Hawthorn report, I will mention only a few, ones which are not usually noted in the policy literature (see also S. Weaver 1985).

First, we should realize that federal policy is developed not in government departments, but in a complex relationship between departments and the central agencies advising the cabinet (e.g., the PMO, PCO, the departments of finance and justice). None of these central agencies may share departmental perspectives. In other words, it is not possible to assume a homogeneous "governmental" perspective of anthropologists' work. Rather, we should expect selective treatment – as the experience of the Hawthorn report has demonstrated.

Second, we should be prepared for rapid shifts in governmental approaches to policies occasioned by federal elections, quickly changing climates of public opinion, etc. If possible, we should anticipate the effects of these changes on the reception of our work. If changes occur unexpectedly, we should address them directly and promptly, otherwise our positions will appear outdated and ignorant of the political realities of the day and, therefore, will be easily disregarded as passé.

Third, we should understand that the formulation of a particular policy can be significantly influenced by the development of concurrent policies in other fields (e.g., the effect of separate status policies for Quebec on Indian policy). Consequently we should make ourselves aware of the overall field of government policies and search out the ways in which these may impact on the policy with which we are concerned.

Fourth, we should make a serious effort to predict the political implications of our recommendations not just on – in this case – First Nations Indians in Canada, but on the government as well. Although this is difficult, it is a useful exercise in trying to determine the chances of our recommendations being implemented, and in trying to target recommendations with the maximum chance of their being accepted. In this vein some of the strategies used by well-established pressure groups provide effective models for us to explore.

Fifth, we must realize that today, unlike the 1960s, Indian policy is increasingly made by governments influenced by First Nations political organizations. Hence the policy field has become much more complex. One result of this change has been the greater need for policy research by Indian organizations, a process Salisbury (1975) recognized several years ago in terms of social science involvement and utility in the policy process.

Finally, I believe that the most important factor in the fate of the Hawthorn report is the special rights ideology which informs it. It is obvious that our research will be evaluated not only in terms of the personal philosophies of the policy-makers but also in terms of the political ideologies prevailing inside government. Consequently, we must rationalize our approach against the dominant ideology and policy thinking of the day, using the instances of agreement to advantage, and arguing against the shortcomings of government ideology when such is felt necessary. Beyond that, there is little we can do without direct personal involvement in the policy process.

After the release of the White Paper in June 1969, the Hawthorn report was used for political purposes by the Indian movement, and for administrative purposes by DIAND. Briefly, although national Indian leaders have understandably disliked the failure of anthropologists to return the products of their research to their host First Nations communities (e.g., Manuel and Posluns 1974:158–61), and equally disapproved of their tendency to cast Indians into some culturally fossilized time frame (e.g., Ahenakew 1985:28), First Nations leaders used the Hawthorn report to support their initial request to government for funds to sustain the emergent National Indian Brotherhood (NIB) in 1968,[15] and to repudiate the White Paper immediately after its public release (NIB 1969:4). More prominent was the Indian adoption of Hawthorn's term "citizens plus" as the title of their official national counter-proposal to the White Paper (Indian Chiefs of Alberta [ICA] 1970:19–20). And George Manuel, the first president of the National Indian Brotherhood, gave the report high praise for its valuable information on the government's activities, revealing the real extent of government commitment to Indian well-being (Manuel and Posluns 1974:163). Generally, the educational sections of the Hawthorn report had the greatest appeal to Indian leaders in supporting their demands to government (e.g., Cardinal 1969:58–9; ICA 1970:75–85; Manuel and Posluns 1974:190), although Manuel did make reference to economic development and Indian Act recommendations as well (Manuel and Posluns 1974:150–1, 123).

Within DIAND, the Hawthorn report was used in a limited way in the department's next attempt to assess Indian socio-economic conditions and government programs on a national scale. This in-house study, based on already existing data, was titled *Indian Conditions: A Survey* (DIAND 1980). Where possible, the statistical data and observations of the Hawthorn report were used as a base line for identifying long-term trends in Indian circumstances (DIAND 1980:1). The survey's major finding was that the federal government was spending less per capita each year on Indians than on social programs for any other group (DIAND 1980:5). It was hoped that this information would persuade Treasury Board and cabinet to increase DIAND's budget. The basic argument was that although Indians had shown certain gains in socio-economic circumstances, there were problems related to alcohol and family breakdown, among other matters, indicating that First Nations were still in need of support programs. Despite being leaked to *Maclean's* magazine by DIAND officials for a sympathetic review (Anderson 1980), the study received little public recognition.

The 1980s ushered in a new era in Indian affairs in many ways. The economic recession in the early 1980s was paralleled by efforts to reform the Canadian constitution in which First Nations played a unique role both during and after its patriation from Britain (e.g., Schwartz 1986, CARC 1988). During these years (1980–84) policy advice on Indian issues to the Trudeau government derived more directly from Indian political organizations and, in the case of self-government, from a special committee of the House of Commons chaired by Keith Penner (Penner 1983). But even here, Penner's recommendations contained many ideas from the Assembly of First Nations (AFN) – the National Indian Brotherhood reformed by Indians in the early 1980s. In contrast, the proposed national survey of Indian programs by Senator Austin, announced by Trudeau during the 1984 first ministers' conference on aboriginal rights (Trudeau 1985:154–5), died as a federal initiative. Indian and other aboriginal organizations boycotted the effort, seeing it as a government attempt to divert their attention from the key agenda item of political rights, not program needs.

With the coming to power in September 1984 of the Progressive Conservative government of Brian Mulroney, Indian programs were included in the highly unpopular review of government departments launched by deputy prime minister Eric Nielsen (Deputy Prime Minister's Office [DPMO] 1986). Conducted in secrecy and well removed from DIAND's control, Nielsen's task force made recommendations highly similar to those in the infamous 1969 White Paper – that Indians be transferred to the provinces and that DIAND be abolished in a few years' time. Known as the Nielsen report, it was leaked in cabinet document form[16] to the press in April 1985. The subsequent public controversy embarrassed the prime minister, who had recently promised to consult Indians on policy initiatives (Mulroney 1985:158), and severely strained relations between First Nations and the new government (S. Weaver 1986a, b). The Nielsen report was ideologically hostile to special rights and to any recognition of contemporary First Nations cultures. As part of a broader exercise to cutback government spending and ultimately reduce the national deficit, the report recommended capping the expenditures on various Indian programs. Although the prime minister quickly denied that the cabinet document represented government policy (PMO 1985), doubts continued about his sincerity in regard to Indian policy (Erasmus 1986), particularly as his government continued to "downsize" DIAND's bureaucracy, and to cap or cutback program expenditures in certain areas (e.g., post-secondary educational assistance, Native media and political organizations) (AFN 1989, 1990).

In retrospect, the twenty-five years following the Hawthorn report have seen limited government success in establishing national program surveys. Furthermore there has been no anthropological involvement at the national level in any of these initiatives. Generally, anthropologists have ideologically aligned themselves with First Nations positions and have tended to concentrate their efforts at the local level, largely on land claims research. Since the Hawthorn report, but particularly during the constitutional discussions on aboriginal rights, lawyers and to a lesser extent academics in political science and public administration have entered the Indian policy field, writing about self-government issues as much as about aboriginal rights. In their self-initiated research, anthropologists have not tended to address policy issues at the national level, nor have they taken heed of the admonitions of LaRusic (1985:25) and Thomas Weaver (1985:198) to study the decision-making structures of government. Until anthropologists have seriously examined both the policy issues and the policy process, we must remain bystanders at the national level of Indian policy discourse.

NOTES AND UNPUBLISHED REFERENCES

1 This paper draws on my previous published work (S. Weaver 1976, 1981) and my unpublished 1979 paper on the Hawthorn report titled "The Life-Cycle of a Research Report: Lessons to be Learned from the Fate of the Hawthorn Report," presented at the conference on Social Science and Social Policy organized by the Western Association of Sociology and Anthropology, Lethbridge, Alberta, 2 March 1979. I have updated this paper by current research on government policy. My 1976 paper contains much information not included in this paper on the relationship between the Hawthorn team and Indian Branch officials.

Many colleagues generously helped me with the initial drafts of this paper in 1975-76. I am particularly grateful to Harry Hawthorn, Adé Tremblay, Alan Cairns, Stuart Jamieson, Frank Vallee, Joan Ryan,

George Parsons, and Gordon Inglis for their willingness to discuss the history of the project with me. To Henry Rogers and John Leslie of the Department of Indian Affairs I am equally indebted for their kind help in accessing the Hawthorn materials in the department's record division. To David Hume of the Public Archives of Canada I owe equal thanks for his assistance in locating relevant documents. To the Social Sciences and Humanities Research Council of Canada I gratefully acknowledge financial support for this and subsequent research.

2 Personal communication, Dr Marc-Adélard Tremblay, 13 November 1975.

3 Confidential interview with a senior Indian Affairs Branch official, Victoria, B.C., 1976.

4 H.M. Jones to Hon R. Bell, 7 January 1963 (National Archives of Canada, henceforth NA, RG 10, vol. 7983), and IODE Presentation to Minister R. Bell, "Re. A Proposal for a Research Programme to Assist Canadian Citizens of Indian Origin" (NA, RG 10, vol. 7983).

5 Hon. R. Bell to Mrs P. Robinson, President of the IODE, 30 January 1963 (NA, RG 10, vol. 7983).

6 Personal communication, Dr Harry Hawthorn, 17 February 1976.

7 Personal communication, Dr Harry Hawthorn, 21 October 1975.

8 Pressure on the Hawthorn team to expand the already large scope of the work persisted. Some topics were simply set aside (Hawthorn 1967:8), while others, such as criminal justice, were transferred to other agencies, in this case the Canadian Corrections Association which produced the first study of *Indians and the Law* (1967).

9 Personal communication, Dr Harry Hawthorn, 21 October 1975.

10 DIAND, Draft Cabinet Memorandum, "Canadian Indian and Eskimo Affairs," October 1968, and background document, "Policy and Program Proposals for Indian and Eskimo Affairs; Brief to Cabinet Committee on Social Policy," October 1968.

11 Ibid., Draft Cabinet Memorandum, 67. For full discussion of this period of policy-making see S. Weaver (1981:74-97).

12 Memo, "Policy for Native Peoples," W. Rudnicki to Gordon Robertson, 13 November 1968, 24.

13 Ibid., see note 12.

14 Memo, Jim Davey to the Prime Minister, 25 November 1968.

15 Letter, Walter Dieter, President of the National Indian Brotherhood, to Mr R.F. Battle, DIAND, 3 September 1968. See page 2 of the enclosed submission entitled "Proposal: Canadian Indian Brotherhood," 30 August 1968.

16 Draft Cabinet Memorandum, "Report of the Ministerial Task Force on Native Programs," 12 April 1985, Deputy Prime Minister's Office.

17 Academics in law and public administration also have a paramount role to date in research commissioned by the Royal Commission on Aborigi-

nal Peoples. The Royal Commission was established in August 1991 by Prime Minister Mulroney to study the "economic, social and cultural circumstances" of aboriginal (Indian, Inuit, and Metis) peoples. The commission's detailed terms of reference, prepared for the prime minister by Brian Dickson, former chief justice of the Supreme Court of Canada, are as wide ranging in scope as those of the Hawthorn team (Prime Minister's Office, "Royal Commission on Aboriginal Peoples." Press Release. Ottawa, 27 August 1991). The commission's report is expected in three years' time.

BIBLIOGRAPHY

Assembly of First Nations (AFN). 1989. "Letter to the Prime Minister." Full page advertisement in the *Globe and Mail*, 4 April 1989.

–   1990. *Budget in Grief*. Ottawa: AFN.

Ahenakew, David. 1985. "Aboriginal Title and Aboriginal Rights: The Impossible and Unnecessary Task of Identification and Definition." In *The Quest for Justice*, eds. Menno Boldt and J.A. Long, 24–30. Toronto: University of Toronto Press.

Anderson, Ian. 1980. "Third World on the Doorstep." *Maclean's* 30 June: 18–19.

Canadian Arctic Resources Committee (CARC). 1988. *Aboriginal Self-Government and Constitutional Reform: Setbacks, Opportunities and Arctic Experiences*. Ottawa: CARC.

Canadian Corrections Association. 1967. *Indians and the Law*. Ottawa: The Canadian Welfare Council.

Cardinal, Harold. 1977. *The Rebirth of Canada's Indians*. Edmonton: Hurtig.

Chambers, Erve. 1985. *Applied Anthropology*. Englewood Cliffs, NJ: Prentice-Hall.

Department of Indian Affairs and Northern Development (DIAND). 1968. *Choosing a Path*. Ottawa: Queen's Printer.

–   1969. *Statement of the Government of Canada on Indian Policy 1969*. (The White Paper). Ottawa: Queen's Printer.

–   1980. *Indian Conditions: A Survey*. Ottawa: DIAND.

Deputy Prime Minister's Office (DPMO). 1986. *Improved Program Delivery, Indians and Natives: A Study Team Report to the Task Force on Program Review*. April 1985. Ottawa: Deputy Prime Minister's Office.

Doern, G.B. 1971. The Development of Policy Organizations in the Executive Arena. In *The Structures of Policy-Making in Canada*, eds. G.B. Doern and P. Aucoin, 39–78. Toronto: Macmillan.

Dunning, William. 1967. "The Hawthorn Report." *The Canadian Forum*. June:52–3.

Erasmus, Georges. 1986. "Commentary." *Native Studies Review* 2(2):52–63.

Hawthorn, H.B. 1955. *The Doukhobors of British Columbia*. Report presented by the Doukhobor Research Committee to the Government of British Columbia. Vancouver: University of British Columbia Press.

–, C.S. Belshaw, and S.M. Jamieson. 1958. *The Indians of British Columbia*. Toronto: University of Toronto Press.

– 1967. *A Survey of the Contemporary Indians of Canada: Economic, Political, Educational Needs and Policies*, 2 vols. Ottawa: Queen's Printer.

Indian Chiefs of Alberta (ICA). 1970. *Citizens Plus*. (The Red Paper). Edmonton: Indian Chiefs of Alberta.

Inglis, Gordon. 1975. "Harry and Audrey Hawthorn: An Appreciation." In *Papers in Honour of Harry Hawthorn*, ed. V.C. Serl and H.C. Taylor, Jr., 1–9. Bellingham, WA: Western Washington State College.

Katz, Joseph. 1967. "The Hawthorn Report: A Review." *Canadian Welfare* 43 (July–August):30–2.

Laing, Arthur. 1967. *The Indian People and the Indian Act*. Speech given to the Ryerson's Men's Club, Vancouver, B.C., 16 October. Ottawa: DIAND Press Release.

Lalonde, Marc. 1971. "The Changing Role of the Prime Minister's Office." *Canadian Public Administration* 14:509–37.

La Rusic, Ignatius. 1985. "Reinventing the Advocacy Wheel?" In *Advocacy and Anthropology*, ed. Robert Paine, 22–7. St John's: Institute of Social and Economic Research, Memorial University of Newfoundland.

Manuel, George, and M. Posluns. 1974. *The Fourth World: An Indian Reality*. Toronto: Collier-Macmillan.

Mortimore, George E. 1967a. "Vast Aid Urged to Enable Indians to Move from Depressed Reserves." *Globe and Mail*, 22 February:1–2.

– 1967b. "The Indians Were Here First: Treat Them As 'Citizens Plus.'" *Human Relations* (Ontario Human Rights Commission) 7(15):4–6.

Mulroney, Brian. 1985. "Notes for an Opening Statement to the Conference of First Ministers on the Rights of Aboriginal Peoples." (2–3 April 1985.) Reprinted in *The Quest for Justice*, eds. M. Boldt and A. Long, 154–64. Toronto: University of Toronto Press.

National Indian Brotherhood (NIB). 1969. "Statement on the Proposed New 'Indian Policy,' " 26 June. Ottawa: National Indian Brotherhood Press Release.

Penner, Keith. 1983. *Report of the Special Committee on Indian Self-Government in Canada*. House of Commons Standing Committee on Indian Affairs and Northern Development, Minutes of Proceedings, 12 and 20 October 1983. Issue no. 40.

Prime Minister's Office (PMO). 1985. "Statement of Prime Minister Regarding Development of Aboriginal Policy," 18 April. Ottawa: PMO Press Release.

Robertson, Gordon. 1971. "The Changing Role of the Privy Council Office." *Canadian Public Administration* 14:487–508.

Salisbury, R.F. 1975. "Policy Regarding Native Peoples: An Academic Social Scientist's Perspective." In *Social Science and Public Policy Conference*, 20–2 November 1975. Ottawa: Social Science Research Council of Canada.

Schwartz, Bryan. 1986. *First Principles, Second Thoughts: Aboriginal Peoples, Constitutional Reform and Canadian Statecraft*. Montreal: Institute for Research on Public Policy.

Senate and House of Commons. 1961. *Joint Committee on Indian Affairs* (Final Report to Parliament) Minutes of Proceedings, no. 16, 30 May–7 July. Ottawa: Queen's Printer.

Trudeau, Pierre E. 1968. *Federalism and the French Canadians*, ed. J.T. Saywell. Toronto: Macmillan.

– 1985. Statement by the Prime Minister of Canada to the Conference of First Ministers on Aboriginal Constitutional Matters, 8–9 March 1984. Reprinted in *The Quest for Justice*, eds. M. Boldt and J. Anthony Long, 148–56. Toronto: University of Toronto Press.

Weaver, Sally M. 1976. "The Role of Social Science in Formulating Canadian Indian Policy: A Preliminary History of the Hawthorn-Tremblay Report." In *Proceedings of the Third Annual Congress of Canadian Ethnology Society, The History of Canadian Anthropology*, 50–98. Hamilton: Department of Anthropology, McMaster University.

– 1981. *Making Canadian Indian Policy: The Hidden Agenda 1968–70*. Toronto: University of Toronto Press.

– 1985. "Impediments to the Creation and Use of Research for Social Problem Solving: A Perspective from Anthropology and Native Studies." In *Social Science Research in Canada: Stagnation or Regeneration?* 160–6. Ottawa: Science Council of Canada.

– 1986a. "Indian Policy in the New Conservative Government, Part I: The Nielsen Task Force of 1985." *Native Studies Review* 2(1):1–43.

– 1986b. "Indian Policy in the New Conservative Government, Part II: The Nielsen Task Force in the Context of Recent Policy Initiatives." *Native Studies Review* 2(2):1–45. (Weaver's Reply to the Commentators, 79–84.)

Weaver, Thomas. 1985. "Anthropology as a Policy Science: Part II, Development and Training." *Human Organization* 44:197–205.

4 Northern Development, Impact Assessment, and Social Change

PETER J. USHER

INTRODUCTION

The study of social change has preoccupied social scientists working in northern Canada since World War II. This is because of both the growth of economic development and social change as fields of study in the social sciences generally, and the evident rapidity and pervasiveness of change in the North itself. To the end of the 1960s most of the relevant literature was set in a framework of modernization and acculturation. While it documented the nature and difficulties of the transition from hunter to proletarian (e.g., La Rusic 1970), the outcome – assimilation by the national economy and culture – seemed in little doubt.

During the 1970s both the perspective and the objectives of northern social science changed profoundly. By no coincidence this transformation occurred in the context of the rise of Native political movements and organized resistance to several proposed mega-projects in the North. Northern scholars were also influenced by changing perspectives in the social sciences generally. Social impact assessment – a more focused and applied form of the study of social change – became the means by which much ethnographic research was done. As well, the review of development issues attracted the attention of other social scientists, with the result that human research in the North is no longer primarily the preserve of anthropologists.

This paper explores the emergence and use of social impact assessment (SIA) in the North, its contributions to our understanding of social change there in both theory and practice, and its limitations as presently constituted.[1] I give special attention to the use of SIA in the review of the proposed Mackenzie Valley gas pipeline during the mid-1970s because of my own involvement in the process, as both an expert witness and as co-ordinator of the social and economic evidence on behalf of the Committee for Original Peoples Entitlement (COPE) of Inuvik. Other struggles going on at the same time, however, such as that of the James Bay Cree and Inuit, were important in the development of scholarship on social change in the North.

The Mackenzie Valley Pipeline Inquiry (1974–77) was the first formal, systematic assessment in Canada of the socio-economic effects of a major industrial development on northern Native peoples,[2] and it became a virtual Royal Commission on northern development. The Berger Inquiry is well known for its major recommendations, for its innovative approaches to assessing social and environmental effects, and for its popularization of the North as a homeland as well as a frontier. The inquiry served to recast the issue of northern development from a technical problem of economic development and the modernization of "primitive" peoples to a more fundamental political question of the rights and interests of Native northerners vis-à-vis those of other Canadians and of corporate and bureaucratic interests. Those questions, and the environmental issues addressed at the Berger Inquiry, are with us still.

The inquiry also became a forum in which profoundly differing views on the nature and ethics of social change, cast in the broadest sense of the impact of industrialization, were advanced and judged. It was a test of the application of these ideas about social change in a practical context: the emerging field of social impact assessment (SIA). Because social scientific ideas and practice are so rarely tested in this way, it is useful to consider the effect of this episode upon their development. There emerged from those years both a new paradigm of development and social change in the North and new processes of directing their course, although these in turn have their own limitations which must be assessed and overcome.

THE EMERGENCE OF SOCIAL IMPACT ASSESSMENT

Social impact assessment is generally understood to be a means of determining how and to what extent specified social groups will become better or worse off as a result of certain externally generated actions. It must therefore be able to specify the nature and circumstances of the social group and the changes that occur as a result of these actions. It must also be able to distinguish these changes from ones that might occur independently. Finally, it must make some value judgments about the changes predicted.

Social impact assessment is an applied science intended to have direct application to public policy. Yet it suffers from a lack of consensus about its content and methods, and from considerable uncertainty with respect to prediction and to the determination of cause and effect. This was especially so in the 1970s when, as a new technique, SIA had not yet had the opportunity to verify its predictions through post-project monitoring and evaluation. Rooted in such practical techniques as cost-benefit analysis, economic evaluation, and the development of social indicators, SIA is also informed by theories or concepts of social change.

Because SIA has emerged in Canada primarily as a response to concerns about the effects of major industrial projects in rural and northern areas, it has assumed a distinctive focus. Typically, the agent of impact is conceived of as a single industrial project undertaken (or catastrophic event caused) by an identifiable party. The target of impact is one or more community or place which due to its location is likely to be materially affected by the project. How the agent of change and its likely targets are identified in the first place is critical to determining effects.

This collective or community focus is perhaps the most distinctive feature of SIA and it sets it apart both from the determination of private or individual losses (which have traditionally been the focus of legal actions for trespass, damage, or violation of rights) and from the calculation of the value of these losses according to neo-classical economics or accounting principles. Those procedures, which have also involved anthropologists and other social scientists, tend to be ahistorical and positivist, and assume as given what is in fact a normative framework of private property and market concepts, the values of possessive individualism, and the precedence of individual over collective rights. The individual, conceived of as *homo economus*, is the essential unit of analysis. If there can be said to be a group loss, it is neither more nor less than the sum of individual losses.

In practice SIA has proceeded at three distinct levels of analysis or abstraction: inventory, hypothesis testing, and theory. Which one is emphasized in any particular SIA depends on the paradigm of social change that informs the exercise. Again, the Berger Inquiry provides a useful focus for examining these, because it remains the only instance to date in which all three levels were explicitly addressed in the same proceedings, and in which competing paradigms were most directly and explicitly contested. It was also a notable example of the successful mobilization of both cultural identity and social theory in recasting SIA from a positivist, technical exercise to a normative, political one.

At the most elementary level, SIA consists of taking inventory to establish a base line against which to measure change. In the early 1970s the variables normally considered relevant by industry proponents and governments were limited to jobs, training, and income as benefits, and to loss of property (and to a limited extent, loss of livelihood) and requirements for public investment in infrastructure as costs.[3] Research on social indicators, then a newly developing field, suggested that such social variables as criminal convictions, education, health, demographics, migration, and political participation should also be considered (e.g., Wood 1974). Essential as such inventories may be in aid of establishing baseline conditions, they contribute nothing to the theory of social change, and at best only raw data for hypothesis testing.

A second or intermediate level of social impact analysis involves the attempt to determine cause and effect relationships through hypothesis testing in order to predict the effects of certain actions. In this view (which in the early 1970s had been barely articulated), social impact assessment seeks not simply to measure costs and benefits, but to predict adverse impacts based on a systematic understanding of the phenomena and processes under review.

This conception of SIA, although not necessarily value neutral, is empiricist, and most closely approximates the principles of environmental impact assessment (EIA), of which it is often an adjunct in public review processes. Like EIA, it is preoccupied with accurate identification of the pre-impact or "base line" conditions from which change can be measured, and of the agent of change, so as to forecast the new, post-impact condition. Within this view there are substantial methodological differences about the selection and measurement of variables, but there is a common commitment to measurement and hypothesis testing.

Whether or not the sponsors or authors acknowledge it, every SIA is informed by high-level theories or paradigms about social change. Some researchers are explicit in their orientation, but even the most positivist reveal their choice of paradigm by the very selection of variables for analysis. SIAs which are explicit about their theoretical perspective often also use the case study as confirmation of the theory. These SIAs engage in a third level of analysis: the application of major theoretical models to a specific problem. The testing of these models is of a different order than testing locally specific hypotheses about cause and effect.

The choice of paradigm is paralleled by the choice of perspective on SIA itself. These perspectives or models have been identified as the technical and political (Lang and Armour 1981; Canadian Environmental Assessment Research Council [CEARC] 1985). The philosophy of the first is positivist, of the second, critical. In the first model, SIA is a technical component of a rational planning and decision-making process: the research must therefore be reductionist and value free. In the second model, SIA is a community action component of the political process. It is intended to make the process of development more equitable by empowering the community to control it, and the research – holistic in conception and participatory in execution – results in an advocacy document. The Berger Inquiry became a contest not only of theories of social change, but also of these models of SIA.

In the early 1970s, there was no practical experience with the second model, and its advocacy and implementation were a matter of struggle. SIA, when conducted at all, was then funded and controlled exclusively by government and industry who perceived it as a technical, positivist exercise.[4] It was not necessarily seen as an exercise requiring social scientific knowledge, and it was often done by engineers (or engineers recently retreaded as environmental scientists). Terms of reference for SIA research were highly restricted in scope and content. Where social scientists were involved, their attempts to go beyond these terms of reference and take account of local concerns resulted in the suppression of results and even disciplinary action (Stucki 1972; Usher 1974a). "Consultation" with Native communities about major projects consisted of government and industry arriving together at meetings to announce their plans, and to suggest how people could accommodate themselves to these (Usher and Noble 1977; Usher 1978; Waldram 1988).

It was only when Berger ruled that he would hear from northern residents at informal hearings in each community, as well as from expert witnesses at formal hearings, and that there would be public funding of non-government organizations to enable their full participation in the inquiry, that the regional Native organizations believed that it would be in their interest to take seriously the formal process of SIA.[5]

It is at the third level of analysis that SIA and political protest converge, because the major paradigms of social change suggest very different interpretations of the causes and of the costs and benefits of change (as well as of what to do about it), and also provide potent symbols and rhetoric for public debate. The most memorable and persuasive SIA studies or reviews from the public perspective are those that engage the issue at this level, and it is for this reason, as well as its innovative procedures and recommendations, that the Berger Inquiry has come to be regarded as "one of the half dozen most important public inquiries since Confederation" (Page 1986:123).

Native leaders have long understood the instrumental value of SIA, not least in the ways they chose to participate in and utilize the Berger Inquiry. The choice of paradigm in SIA must conform to the political objectives of those who commission it. It may be up to the social scientists to articulate it, and to support it with fact and argument, but they do not choose the paradigm itself. This does not mean that Native leaders (or any other decision makers who commission SIA) are themselves intimately familiar with the major paradigms of the social sciences. These paradigms are, however, well understood in their essence, even if in vulgar or common sense form, by almost every adult member of society, and strongly influence people's political perspectives.

TWO VIEWS OF CHANGE

Two paradigms of social change were considered and developed at the Berger Inquiry. Here I examine how both the specific cases advanced for and against the pipeline, and the perspectives that informed them, were based in existing knowledge of the North, how they were employed and developed by the participants in the inquiry, how they related to SIA, and how these paradigms emerged from the inquiry episode.

Modernization/Acculturation: The Case for the Pipeline

The advocates of oil and gas development – industry, all levels of government, and local business interests – characterized the North as a frontier awaiting development, which could only benefit from the pipeline. In both formal impact statements and informal advocacy, Native people were said to suffer from too much unemployment and welfare, too little income, and too little education and training to take advantage of wage employment opportunities; hence they would especially benefit from industrialization. The fur trade and life on the land were dying, and in any event the youth did not want such a life. Only industrial employment generated by the extraction of oil, gas, and minerals could provide for the needs of the growing population.

Industry promised training programs that would enable Native northerners to take maximum advantage of these opportunities. Adverse effects (when their possibility was even acknowledged) were downplayed. The pipeline would require only a small area of land, therefore its environmental effects would be very limited, and those few who wanted to could still make a living from the land. To the extent that either industry or government acknowledged Native claims as a legitimate issue, they saw these as real estate transactions: a clearing of title so that progress could continue. Hence both industry and government asserted that construction of the pipeline would not prejudice a settlement.

Both the modernization/acculturation model (which was then virtually the sole paradigm of social change and economic development) and a large body of contemporary anthropological research in the North appeared to support this case. In this view, the concepts of modernization and industrialization were virtually interchangeable. Both were the universal experience, beyond politics and ideology, of capitalism and socialism alike. Both required the breakdown and eventual replacement of whatever social forms had existed before. For industrialization to occur, there would have to be profound ideological and institutional change and a radical reordering of both the social organization of work and the prevailing conceptions of property and mutual obligations among persons. The social contract would need rewriting (implicitly, it seemed, by those with the vision to recognize that necessity).

Out of such change is said to emerge a higher standard of living, a better quality of life, and greater personal choice. Although fraught with transitional difficulties at certain stages, industrialization and its benefits are seen to meet certain fundamental and perhaps even innate human needs and wants. The evidence is straightforward: people apparently accept the trappings of industrial development when these are made available. People like the material benefits, and they will take wage employment and move to urban areas to get them. The majority of people are thus alleged to be "voting with their feet," and their economic behaviour, taken as the indication of their true or "revealed" preference, confirms the essentially benign and beneficial nature of the transition.

When these changes are externally generated, as in the case of a small, foraging society coming into contact with a large, industrial society, acculturation is said to occur. The smaller and less advanced group adapts, in response to the models and incentives for change which are provided by both a free market economy and directed social change, the latter intended to ease the transition from the old to the new. There will be massive cultural replacement, particularly in the spheres of work, institutional life, and social relations, resulting in individual behaviour which is more functional to the modernized, industrialized economy.

This model of economic development and cultural change informed much of the theory and practice of economic and social development, as promoted by western nations, in both the Third World and in their own rural and remote areas. Certainly it informed the ideas of those responsible for the development of northern Canada during the post-war era. It is the intellectual foundation of the more popular view that sees industrialization as inevitable, desirable, and beneficial – the more the better, and anyone not yet on the train should certainly hurry aboard. Indeed, this model is the essence of what is called "development" in everyday discourse.

Applied to northern Canada, the model led to the conclusion that major industrial projects were in principle a good thing. In this view, the fur trade, the missionaries, government activity, the education system, urbanization, and the media had already resulted in acculturation, and set Native people irreversibly on the road to modernization.

Negative consequences of these changes, and major disparities of income and social well-being compared to fully industrialized parts of Canada, were acknowledged. The problem with the project of modernization was not that it was begun, however, but that it was never completed. Hence no interruption or relaxation of the cure could be prescribed until the patient was brought completely into the modern world, kicking and screaming if necessary. Continued blockage could only lead to deepening dependency and a culture of poverty. The solution lay with the provision of employment opportunities and a modern social and economic infrastructure, promoted by interventionist government policies if necessary.

These ideas appeared in government policy statements (e.g., Robertson 1961), in influential policy studies (Jenness 1964; Rea 1968), and in seminal anthropological studies of social change (e.g., Murphy and Steward 1956; Van Stone 1965; Honigmann and Honigmann 1965, 1970). More recently publicized research in the Mackenzie Delta was easily interpreted as supporting this view (e.g., Wolforth 1971; Smith 1974). The case was articulated in detail on behalf of industry at the inquiry by Charles Hobart (1976Ea,b,c),[6] and carried forward by critics of the Berger report, almost all of whom, incidentally, advocated the technical approach to SIA (e.g.,

Stabler 1977, 1985). These themes continue to be reiterated in social impact statements by project proponents.

Since, in this view, Native northerners have already "crossed the Rubicon" on their march towards modernization, neither industrialization in general, nor its specific development projects, which are latecomers to the scene, can be regarded as the cause of major social change. Rather, these projects are the means by which full participation in industrial society can be assured. It remains only to work out the details.

From this perspective, it is entirely appropriate to restrict SIA to a verification of the proponent's claims about the extent to which the project in question will raise the local standard of living. Beyond this cost-benefit approach, the impact assessment need only recommend the most effective ways of maximizing local benefits and mitigating adverse effects. Canvassing local opinion is unnecessary because actual preferences are revealed in behaviour which, as measured by standard demographic and economic indicators, shows that people want and benefit from industrialization.

Hinterland as Homeland: The Case Against the Pipeline

The Native organizations[7] responded to this argument by challenging its factual content and the validity of its conclusions. They also shifted the grounds of the debate by calling into question the conventional view of development, and posing both a revised explanation of the present and an alternative agenda for the future, in order to mobilize public sentiment in favour of Native culture, identity, and rights, and against the pipeline.

The pipeline, it was argued, would be just another episode of boom and bust, like the fur trade, the whale fishery, the gold rush, and military construction before it. Native people would be neither trained nor hired in any numbers, and those who were would become unemployed with no locally useful skills when the oil and gas fields were depleted. It was inappropriate, the argument continued, to consider the impact of only a pipeline, when its construction was in fact predicated on marine exploration and production, feeder lines, gas plants, roads, and an overwhelming influx of non-Natives. The project as a whole was an unprecedented venture which would open the door to massive development with incalculable and irreversible effects, like the settlement of the Prairies or the Amazon rain forest.

This massive assault on the land base of Native northerners threatened their basic economic resources and the way of life that these resources sustained. While people were no longer living solely off the land as earlier generations had done, they still relied on the land for their food, their enjoyment, and the maintenance of their culture and identity. The massive influx of temporary workers (and the associated expansion of government and business activity) would also constitute an assault on Native communities, especially the smaller ones, which remained the hearth of Native culture. The lesson of earlier booms was that there would be adverse effects on physical, social, and mental health, and a loss of cultural values and integrity. Nor would these effects be moderated by government or industry, whose unwillingness or inability to listen to the people or to regulate industrial activity were already well known.

When all the riches were taken out from under them by foreign companies, Native land and culture would have been destroyed and people left with nothing. It was precisely for these reasons, and in order to right historic injustices and take control of their own future, that the settlement of land claims was essential and urgent. The construction of a pipeline would therefore not merely prejudice the settlement of Native claims, it would jeopardize the very existence of Natives as a people. Whatever the national benefits of a pipeline might be (and these were also questioned), there were certainly no benefits to Native northerners.[8]

In advancing this case, the two Native organizations relied on both recent empirical research in the North (much of it recast as expert testimony on the impact of development by the social scientists who had done this research) and on emerging theoretical perspectives on social change, industrial impact, and economic development. COPE and the Indian Brotherhood of the Northwest Territories (IBNWT) made broadly similar, and in many respects complimentary cases. Yet there were also some significant differences in approach, based on their respective experiences with development, their strategies with regard to aboriginal claims, and the political views and tactics of their leadership.

THE CONTENT OF THE NATIVE CASE

The evidence against the pipeline focused on four major areas: the continuing reliance of Native communities on their traditional lands and resources, the adverse effects of development on those lands and resources and hence on the Native economy, problematic aspects of training and employment on industrial projects, and the adverse effects of major projects on health, social well-being, and cultural integrity. I focus here on the social scientific evidence given at the formal hearings, as individuals at the community hearings addressed a wide range of concerns, not all of which they attributed to the project.

Land Use and Occupancy

The Inuit and the Dene of the Northwest Territories had already documented the nature and extent of their use of the land, as a basis for negotiating land claims settlements with the federal government. The results showed that people had not abandoned the land, but made continuing extensive (and in some cases revived) use of almost all of the lands and waters of the Northwest Territories (Freeman 1976, Nahanni 1977). The research also demonstrated the social and cultural significance of the land to Native northerners, and their continuing attachment to it (Usher 1974b; Brody 1976). Contrary to the popular view of the North as a vast, empty treasure house of riches waiting to be tapped, all the lands and waters proposed to be taken up for development were already occupied and used by people who could assert legal title to them.[9]

Country Food and the Native Economy

Development advocates placed little or no economic value on "country food" (food obtained for household consumption by hunting and fishing). Yet Native people regarded this as a major value at risk from the environmentally and socially disruptive effects of the project. Government and industry estimates of the volume and value of existing production, prepared for the inquiry, were successfully challenged on both methodological and theoretical grounds (Usher 1976a, Ea). The principle of replacement or substitution value (derived from welfare economics), was established at the inquiry (Berger 1977b), and has since become widely accepted.[10] Properly accounted for, hunting and fishing were neither economically irrational nor the last-resort pursuit of the otherwise unemployed, but contributed a large proportion of the effective income of most Native households.

Yet restricting the case to economic arguments invited compensation for their loss, rather than avoidance of it. Therein lay the importance of the many statements by local residents at the community hearings about the social and cultural significance not only of country food, but of livelihood; of hunting and life on the land itself. Significantly, those statements were supported by recent ethnographic research both within the region (Usher 1971; Asch

1976E, 1977; Rushforth 1977) and in the Eastern Arctic (Brody 1975), which elaborated the outlines of a distinctive mixed, subsistence-based "Native economy."

Training and Employment

Two lines of evidence were advanced to challenge the industry/government case. One was that in the past, development had not provided training and jobs to Native people. They were the last hired and first fired, and when they got jobs, it was only at the lowest end of the occupational structure (Wolforth 1971). Even where major efforts had been made to train and employ Native people, as on the DEWline and at the Rankin Inlet nickel mine, the jobs did not last and people returned to their communities with skills they could not use.[11]

The second line of evidence dealt with the nature and effects of wage employment itself, and suggested that even if industry did provide training and jobs, the effect would be negative. This argument, which focused on the disruptive effects of industrial employment and the private nature of wage income on the household economy, the social organization of labour, and the transmission of knowledge in the Native economy, was made most succinctly by Brody (1975, 1976Ea, 1977) and Asch (1977).[12]

Social Effects on Communities

The Native organizations argued that the enormous influx of temporary workers, and the expansion of business and government activity that would accompany construction, would have major distorting effects on the local economy and public services, and would lead to a deterioration of physical, mental, and social health in the communities. Further, neither industry nor government would be able to control these consequences.

Evidence was presented about the results of similar industrial developments elsewhere, such as mining and highway construction in the Yukon (Cruikshank 1976E; McClellan 1976E; Sharp 1976E), hydro development in Quebec and Manitoba, and especially those of the construction of the oil pipeline in Alaska, then nearing completion (Baring-Gould 1976E; Dixon 1976E; Forrest 1976E; Worl 1976E). Adverse effects were identified with respect to, among other things, health and nutrition (e.g., Hildes 1976E; Schaefer 1976E), health services (Noble 1976E), housing (Clarke 1976E), and alcohol (Brody 1976Eb).

In their specific critique of the project and its outcomes, the Native organizations presented what amounted to a social impact statement authored by a wide spectrum of social scientists. Leaving aside for the moment the treatment of the general paradigms of development and social change, it was on a technical and scientific level by far the most comprehensive impact statement in Canada to that time, and in its breadth not matched since. It was particularly innovative in two respects.

One was its direct co-ordination with and complementary relationship to the statements (at the community hearings) of the people who would be affected by the project (COPE and IBNWT fieldworkers, as well as commission counsel staff, visited the communities extensively during the inquiry). The other was the extensive use of comparative evaluation based on research findings and practical experience from other areas.

STRATEGY AND THEORY OF THE NATIVE CASE

Some differences in approach between COPE and IBNWT have already been noted, particularly those based on their historical experience with development. The basic political objectives of the two organizations at the inquiry, however, were the same: no development before claims settlements. Further, both stated that this did not imply their approval of the project as described if claims were settled. IBNWT, however, was unwilling to respond to the project itself, basing its case on aboriginal title and political rights.

COPE was willing to consider the issue at two levels. The Inuit did not want the project, but also did not believe that oil and gas development could be stopped, because for them it was already a reality.[13] The idea that development would jeopardize the claim was not a hypothetical one – the effects on the land and the people were being felt every day. Better to move now, and save what could be saved. Berger had created the opportunity to make the case in public to a wide audience; it was therefore prudent to make the best of it in the most practical ways possible. Leave it to the Dene to talk of colonialism, nationalism, and the Third World, ideas that the COPE leadership believed meant nothing to the ordinary Inuit family. COPE preferred to speak in its own language, relying on those who could speak from specific experience and knowledge of the Arctic. It used the inquiry as the opportunity to write the terms and conditions for a project that it fully expected to be approved regardless of the inquiry's outcome.

Beyond the specific critique of the project, both COPE and IBNWT sought to advance an overarching perspective or framework through which the inquiry could understand both the experience of Native northerners and why the settlement of aboriginal claims had to involve the recognition of Native sovereignty, including control of the land itself. The two key elements of this framework constituted theories of northern economic history and of the state in the North.

The framework advanced for understanding the history and characteristics of the northern economy was in essence a critique of capitalism and industrialism. It was strongly informed by emerging theoretical perspectives on metropolis and hinterland, dependency, development and underdevelopment, capitalism as a world system and its significance for race and class, and forms of resistance to imperialism and colonialism. While IBNWT advanced the themes of colonialism and underdevelopment more explicitly than did COPE (invoking especially the ideas of André Gunder Frank, Harold Innis, Paulo Freire, and Franz Fanon), the models were similar.

COPE and IBNWT both sought to explain that the present situation was neither an unfortunate aberration nor a case of modernization unfulfilled. Brody's seminal work on the development of colonialism in the Eastern Arctic (1975) provided an important foundation, not least because it could not be dismissed as an inappropriate analogue. The major themes advanced at the inquiry and in later publications were that industrial development required the destruction of the traditional economy by appropriating land and labour, that each major stage of historical development had deepened the dependency of Native people, and that the widespread introduction of wage labour would proletarianize them and render them further dependent (see especially Usher 1976b,Ec, 1981a, 1982a,b; Asch 1977, 1979a, 1982; Brody 1977, 1981, 1987; Watkins 1977).

The recent experience of Native people with industrial development and their concerns about its future prospects were explained by a neo-marxist perspective of the state as an instrument of capital. The state was not a neutral arbiter with respect to development, and hence could not be entrusted to regulate it. The evidence was to be found generally in the role of government in resource development and Native administration (Fumoleau 1973, Beakhust 1976Ea; Bean 1977), and specifically in the failure of government to regulate industrial activity effectively through impact assessment, statute, monitoring, or enforcement (Usher 1971, 1976Ea; Usher and Beakhust 1973; Beakhust 1976Eb, Zemansky 1976E).

A VISION OF THE FUTURE

The Native organizations' response to the case for the pipeline in particular, and to the modernization/acculturation model in general, amounted to an alternative vision of the future, which required for its fulfilment an alternative mode of development. A substantially separate, community-based path of development was proposed, relying on renewable resources, intermediate technology, and small enterprise (Berger 1977a,b). It would be financed by rents on limited and Native-regulated development of subsurface resources.

The minimum conditions that would allow Native society to control the direction and rate of change, if not indeed its own destiny, were identified as:

- maintenance of the traditional land base;
- maintenance of a Native political majority;
- control of key instruments of economic power and decision making;
- maintenance of the viability of the small, predominantly Native communities;
- development of a cash flow to support Native self-government and enterprise.

The implication for the inquiry, and SIA, was that the proposed pipeline project had to be evaluated not according to technical or value-free criteria, but rather in terms of the vision of the people whose communities it would affect. The question was better cast in terms of whether the project would help or hinder the realization of that vision (Usher 1978). Where the technical model of SIA focused on economic well-being as measured by income and employment, the political model emphasized social well-being, self-determination, and the centrality of cultural values and social institutions.

THE LEGACY

The New Paradigm

From the Mackenzie Valley pipeline and other energy project controversies, there emerged not only a critique of the old paradigm of modernization/acculturation, but also the foundations of a substantially new paradigm, based in a synthesis of new empirical research.

As articulated in the inquiry report itself, the Northern Frontier/ Northern Homeland theme gave this new paradigm a popular cachet. As articulated by those who had pressed it at the inquiry, and by others around the same time (e.g., Elias 1975; Ballantyne, Brook, et al. 1976; Zlotkin and Colborne 1977; Loxley 1981), its core elements were more explicitly those of political economy: metropolis and hinterland, imperialism and dependency.

Thus emerged a union among anthropology, geography, and political economy which, as a means of advocacy, reversed the telescope. "Value-neutral" investigation of "primitive" societies from the academic centre could be replaced by an examination of external institutions as *agents* of change on behalf of aboriginal groups. As a consequence of both the Mackenzie Valley and James Bay episodes there arose among anthropologists in Canada a concern with hunting *societies* (Asch 1982; Feit 1982): the emergence of gesellschaft through struggle, and of the possibilities for their self-governance and economic advancement in ways compatible with cultural survival. The social organization and economic basis of these societies were conceptualized in terms of modes of production and subsistence (Asch 1979b; Usher 1981b), also core themes of the new paradigm. Yet despite the interrelatedness of all these themes, the new paradigm has to date not been named, and there is not yet consensus about its categories and terminology (Usher and Weinstein 1991).

The paradigm shift that occurred in the mid-1970s raised new questions for the study of social change at both the theoretical and methodological levels. What constitutes significant or irrevocable change, and to whom is it significant? What is the relationship between such change and adverse effects, and are these effects experienced only by individuals or can we speak of cultural impairment? Are there especially critical points of change, and if so, what are their diagnostic indicators? How do we know when they have occurred and what caused them, and more important, how can we predict these events? These questions are significant not only for theory but also for resolving major controversies in northern development, from both a policy and a legal perspective.

Since under the evolutionary/acculturation model, the "final" outcome of change could not be redirected, the central question was the effect of altering the rate of change, and the proper role of intervention through tutelage or guidance in that process. Change was the continuous passage from ancient to modern, marked by no single significant event. Progress could be measured by such indicators as income, wealth, energy consumption, technology, and complexity of social organization, while its handmaiden, acculturation, could be measured by the loss of traditional traits.

The model of change that emerged from the Berger Inquiry and similar events was more catastrophic, yet at the same time the outcome could be changed by struggle. It was a neo-marxist model in two senses. First, it was an evolutionary model which explained the overarching passage from ancient to modern, or in this case precapitalist to capitalist, society. Second, the passages from one stage (mode of production) to another were seen as the product of contradiction and conflict. Yet this new model also departed from the classical one. The North provided a different setting, which might enable industrialization and its ill-effects to be bypassed. Hence the interest, especially by IBNWT and its supporters, in non-European models and in the experience of post-colonial development.

That the North had become contested terrain probably contributed to an overly deterministic view of the contemporary forces of change, and to exaggerated predictions about the outcome. The project focus of impact assessment contributed to a sense, at that time, among the opponents of the Mackenzie Valley Pipeline, as among the opponents of other developments such as James Bay Hydro, of an all or nothing struggle. This, as I elaborate below, has created some problems for SIA if not also the larger paradigm itself.

What did the mode of production concept mean for the consideration of contemporary change? One proposition that emerged from the Berger Inquiry was that the critical event marking the passage from a domestic or petty commodity mode of production to an industrial one was not the fur trade (production for exchange), but wage employment (the sale of labour power). In contrast to the acculturation perspective, core features of the existing social formation – such as the system of land tenure and resource management, and the social organization of labour – although altered by the fur trade, were seen to have survived it in non-capitalistic form (Asch 1979b, 1984).[14] The fur trade's compatibility with foraging and subsistence was emphasized, as was the extent to which Native people incorporated it to their benefit and as a means of maintaining a sphere of autonomy. In Polanyi's terms, economy remained embedded in society, land and labour were not yet fully marketable commodities, and the Great Transformation had not yet occurred in the North (Usher 1982a,b). It was the widespread introduction of wage labour, coupled with the dispossession of land, that would entrain a deepening and irreversible dependency and proletarianization.

These ideas have been criticized from within the political economy paradigm, particularly by Daniels (1981), Bourgeault (1983), and Tough (1988). As well, neither recent experience nor historical inquiry lends them unambiguous support. During the late 1970s and early 1980s, the oil and gas industry provided much more employment to Native people in the Western Arctic, and this employment was incorporated more successfully into the mixed, subsistence-based economy, than critics had anticipated. As well, subsequent examination of the historical record suggests that wage labour is a much less recent phenomenon among Native northerners than commonly appreciated. It has been as surely a part of their historical experience with the world economy as trade, albeit not so pervasive a one. In many parts of the subarctic, wage labour was if anything more common in the early twentieth century, before the restructuring of the Depression and the post-war era squeezed Native people out of employment in transport, guiding, and woods work.

Like the fur trade stereotype, the labour stereotype is not entirely without foundation. Both did and do constitute significant change with detrimental effects under certain conditions. Recent fur trade scholarship, whether of the ethnohistorical or political economy variety, has forced a rethinking of fur trade history and fur trade relations. It is now possible to be much more precise about the fur trade as an agent of change. A new labour scholarship is required that will help to specify the conditions under which wage labour is or is not problematic for Native communities.[15] Unlike much of the contemporary labour scholarship pertaining to the industrialized parts of Canada, this new work will have to focus less on the labour process and more on the role of wage labour in the household, in a kin-based organization of economic activity, and in a mixed, subsistence-based economy.

Another benefit of recent ethnohistorical research on the fur trade (e.g., Ray and Roberts 1985; Yerbury 1986) is the corrective it provides to the view of the long, stable "contact-traditional" period marked by the absence of change – or in its more vulgar form, of Native people living in a timeless "ethnographic present" until some recent stage of contact with capitalism kick-started their motor of history.

Without this corrective, the critique of industrial development in the North can too readily be interpreted as a critique of history and a glorification of life before history. If Native people do not make their own history until the advent of capitalism, then they are easily seen as the perpetual victims of history. And if the triumph of capitalism in the North is said to be heralded by whatever project is currently under review, then impact predictions are liable to be apocalyptic, but as time passes, less credible.

Worse, the critique of industrialization is too easily trivialized or vulgarized, especially as used in popularizations or political advocacy. Change itself, rather than control over it, comes to be seen as problematic, if not indeed fatal to aboriginal peoples. Their allegedly pristine and seamless life on the land must collapse, and all that will be left is an acculturated, anomic people on the brink of social disintegration. The beginning of history becomes trauma, akin to the departure from Eden or the Freudian view of birth. Such a position easily leads to despair (e.g., such popular accounts as Mc-Mahon 1988), and to the view that because nothing in the history or culture of Native people enables them to deal with this "trauma," they are in dire need of all that modernization can bring them (Shkylnik 1985).

Change has indeed been rapid in the North (it is commonly said that socio-economic changes that took two or three centuries in industrialized societies have been compressed into two or three decades in the North, and some Native people themselves are prone to characterizing their recent experience as a leap from the stone age to the space age). Yet, there remains a need to be more precise about what the problem with rapid change really is, and whether the problem might not better be seen as one of control over change, which was the essence of the case advanced by the Native organizations at the Berger Inquiry.

SIA in Practice

The Berger Inquiry has become widely regarded as a landmark in the public assessment and review of industrial development. Many Native and other citizens' organizations, when confronted with similar problems of development, have called for a "Berger-type inquiry," although what they really wanted was a Berger-type result. The intervening years have shown that one does not necessarily guarantee the other.[16] The key innovations and principles of the Berger inquiry have not been fully institutionalized, nor has their subsequent application always been fruitful.

SIA has become an integral part of the impact assessment process in practice, although not necessarily by legislation. However, the range of evidence normally considered by public review agencies, and more important, the paradigm or framework within which they consider this evidence, remains largely confined to the norms of southern industrial society. The new paradigm is by no means ascendent in the public arena. Scope, content, and approach to SIA constitute a matter of renewed and not always successful struggle in each case.

It is now widely recognized that industrial development in the Canadian North has the sharpest effects on the small, largely Native communities (of which there are at least 200 in the Arctic and subarctic), because their socio-economic characteristics, and the cultural and historical forces that created them, differ significantly from those of southern Canadian communities, rural or urban. As a consequence, it is now much more widely accepted that SIA must involve project-affected communities directly, not only through participation in hearings, but also in the research process itself, and especially in identifying impact issues and hypotheses. SIA is now, if not actually commissioned, at least authorized by the affected communities, and much of the information comes from residents themselves through interviews, questionnaires, or authorization for access to existing data. Yet neither public participation in the review process nor intervenor funding is a matter of right.

The community focus of SIA is also a source of difficulty. Community becomes reified as a fundamental social category which obscures significant social and economic boundaries (and hence varying effects, both real and perceived) within it. The emphasis on the colonial experience at the Berger Inquiry left the impression of communities speaking with a single voice. While that was very often true, such homogeneity of interest and opinion cannot be assumed to exist in other times and places.

While the existing framework of public policy review focuses on single industrial projects, there is no theoretical reason that SIA should not focus just as appropriately on institutional changes (Craig and Tester 1982). The structures established in response to major projects – whether they be Native claims settlements, or arrangements like the Northern Flood Agreement in northern Manitoba, or the expansion of government activity – all have social and economic effects. The Mackenzie Valley, for example, has experienced major social and economic changes since the mid-1970s even though the large-diameter gas pipeline was never built. This was partly because of its decreasing isolation from the world economy, but also because major public and private institutions planned for and implemented the changes that the pipeline and associated developments were expected to entrain.

Yet, the more the review process broadens, the more one is led into a debate on the general effects of industrialization and technology on human society and on the natural environment. These are fundamental political questions that can sometimes be illuminated, but not resolved, by SIA or EIA as these processes are presently constituted. Interesting as some might find it to hold regular judicial or administrative hearings on the overall development of industrial capitalism, this is not a reasonable expectation in the context of project review. The fundamental consideration of what Torgerson (1980) has described as the over-arching project of industrialization in the North, as the Berger Inquiry became, may be effective once in a generation, but not in association with every new development proposal.[17] There were about seven major project reviews in the territorial North, and a similar number in the subarctic regions of the provinces, in the decade after the Berger Inquiry. Increasingly one heard the same predictions about social and environmental effects, and indeed often the same experts making them, from one set of hearings to another, like a travelling circus.

The problem is the lack of continuity between the pre-project assessment review and the actual management and monitoring of projects once under way. Impact assessment seemed to involve nothing more than making predictions about project effects, based on general principles and some hastily assembled base line (pre-project) data, rather than on a sound understanding of the affected social and environmental systems. In the post-Berger years, these predictions were having almost no effect on whether or how projects went ahead, and little subsequent effort was made to verify them.

The response by both affected communities and responsible government agencies has been increasing indifference. If review panels are called on again and again to pronounce judgment on the same predictions, with no provision for testing or verification, the result can only be an increasing distrust of the validity and utility of both the social and environmental sciences as useful instruments for determining public policy. The danger for SIA, and the new paradigm, is that they will be seen increasingly as polemic in scientific disguise.

One solution is the use of hypothesis testing and monitoring, that is, to shift SIA from the first level of analysis described earlier to the second. However, some forms of industrial development must proceed in order for this to happen, and in fact many have since the 1970s. Unfortunately, monitoring, hypothesis testing, and post-project evaluation have so far been the exception rather than the rule. Yet it is only in this way that SIA can become an accumulative, self-improving process that will have a beneficial effect on public policy, and generate new knowledge rather than merely utilize what is already known. This knowledge can actually be used to modify problematic effects and even be incorporated into the design of other projects (see Beanlands and Duinker 1983 on monitoring in EIA, and LGL, ESL, et al. 1986 for an attempt to extend this principle to SIA). This approach, however, is not compatible with all-out opposition to industrial development in principle.

Raising SIA from the level of inventory to hypothesis testing will also lead to modification and improvement of the basic paradigm of social change. Hypothesis testing (by which I do not include "all against all" statistical tests for association among ill-conceived survey variables) will depend on continued improvement in the understanding of the social and economic processes at work in the North, and of how the forces of change are mediated locally by history, institutions, and values. Without this we have no basis for understanding, let alone predicting, the effects of development of any kind as they will be experienced and perceived by the affected population.

One corrective is to reassert the importance of ethnographic and ethnohistorical methods. Under normal time requirements for SIA, field research methods tend to be restricted to surveys and questionnaires, or worse, anecdotal information obtained in public meetings.

There is also the question of how to isolate, for analytical purposes, the particular phenomenon under review from the more general processes of industrialization of which it is an integral part. This requires the use of control groups or communities,[18] and the identification of key diagnostic indicators, although as indicated earlier, of a much more sophisticated and qualitative nature than jobs and income.

CONCLUSIONS

The chief contributions of the Berger Inquiry to social scientific understanding and practice in the North were the emergence of the new paradigm, and its effects on the practice of SIA. Its contributions to the store of knowledge were more incidental. Many social scientists used their existing research results as the basis for expert evidence[19] – indeed they were pressed into the then unfamiliar role of predicting project impacts on the basis of research that was neither conceived nor designed with that purpose in mind. Very little impact research was actually commissioned by the intervenors (or by the commission itself), and like much SIA then and since, it has remained in the grey literature.

Although the new paradigm that emerged from the inquiry and related processes has been widely elaborated, the modernization/acculturation model continues to have many adherents. Certainly the latter continues to inform public policy, even where some elements of the frontier-homeland concept have received quasi-official recognition. In 1977, a colleague who played a central role in the inquiry expressed to me the hope that the modernization/acculturation paradigm had been finally consigned to the trash bin of history. Such has not been the case. The two paradigms run on parallel tracks in separate journals. Sometimes they provide stimulation and challenge for each other, other times they are unhappily married with the sometimes trivial results noted above. As much as the inquiry and similar events stimulated the development of new ideas and perspectives, some of these now seem as dated as their predecessors, while others, more productive and provocative, have since been modified, refined, or transcended.

As for practice and implementation, the record is mixed. Both SIA and public review practices have, mercifully, come a long way since the early 1970s. There is a model, but its implementation is incomplete. We may wait a long time, however, before a single event so captures public imagination, and gives the actors so great a stage and so great an impetus, as did the Mackenzie Valley pipeline proposal. The social scientists' tool box is larger and better equipped than before, but so too is the job ahead more complex and demanding. In the long run, the chief lesson of the Berger episode for social scientists is that from struggle emerges creativity. But the generals who continue to rehearse for the last war are always the losers. The next struggle will be different.

NOTES

My thanks to Frances Abele, Jill Torrie, Martin Weinstein, and Pamela White for ideas and for critical observations on earlier drafts. I am also grateful for the financial assistance of the Social Sciences and Humanities Research Council of Canada. I would like to take this opportunity to acknowledge the contribution of others involved in COPE's intervention at the Berger Inquiry, in particular my co-workers, Gaile Noble, John Bayly, and the late Lorraine Allison, and the guidance of Nellie Cournoyea and the late Sam Raddi.

1 I include in SIA both scientific and political processes: on the one hand the preparation of a social impact statement (a formal document containing evidence and predictions about the effects of the project under review), as well as the subsequent monitoring and evaluation of these predictions, and on the other, the public review and assessment of the proposal and impact statement.

2 Similar issues were considered with regard to the construction of the James Bay hydro-electric project in Quebec in 1973, but before a court

of law. A federal-provincial study board was established in 1971 to assess the impact of hydro-electric development in northern Manitoba, but there was no public review of the project. A 1958 proposal to create a harbour in northwest Alaska by atomic blasting was the occasion of the first impact assessment of a major project anywhere in northern North America (Wilimovsky and Wolfe 1966), but there was no formally constituted public review.

3 See, for example, the federal government's guidelines for northern pipelines (DIAND 1972).

4 Examples include the SIA reports of the Lake Winnipeg, Churchill and Nelson Rivers Study Board (Manitoba 1974); the James Bay Hydro assessment (Salisbury, Filion, et al. 1972); and the various background studies on the Mackenzie Valley pipeline commissioned by industry (Gemini North Ltd. 1974, Van Ginkel Associates 1975) and the Federal Government's Task Force on Northern Oil Development (DIAND/MPS 1974, Stager 1974 – although the last study was a model for community involvement at the time).

5 In his preliminary rulings of July 1974, Berger also stated that he would hear evidence about Native claims and how these would be affected by the gas pipeline project as well as evidence about the effects of proposed related facilities such as the gas plants and gathering systems and a Mackenzie Valley transport corridor. All these innovations had been urged upon the inquiry in preliminary submissions by COPE and IBNWT, and were indeed the essential preconditions of their participation. In the outcome, the inquiry met the spirit as well as the letter of these undertakings.

6 Evidence given at the inquiry by social scientists which was not subsequently published elsewhere is cited here as 1976E. The list of evidence cited is found after the literature references.

7 The Committee for Original Peoples Entitlement (COPE) represented the Inuit of the Western Arctic (now Inuvialuit) and also acted for Inuit Tapirisat of Canada, of which COPE was a regional affiliate. The Indian Brotherhood of the Northwest Territories (IBNWT, now Dene Nation) represented the Dene of the Mackenzie Valley, and also acted for the Metis and non-status Indians of the N.W.T. The Council for Yukon Indians (CYI) was a minor participant and opposed the pipeline on similar grounds. In referring to the actions and positions of each at the inquiry, I have used the names in common use at that time.

8 Many of these arguments were taken up by sympathetic individuals and organizations outside the North concerned with Native rights, the environment, and economic nationalism (e.g., McCullum and McCullum 1975; Dosman 1976; Pimlott, Brown, and Sam 1976; Fuller 1977; Jackson 1978). The issues and atmosphere of the time may be gleaned from such works as Pimlott, Vincent, and McKnight (1973), Usher and

Beakhust (1973), Pearse (1974), Usher (1974a,b,c, 1978), Alexander (1976), O'Malley (1976), Usher and Noble (1977), Stabler and Olfert (1980), and Page (1986).

9 The Inuit research also emphasized the patterned and systematic nature of land use and occupancy, constituting a *lex loci* or customary law which, in the light of recent historic court decisions, was, "on the evidence, of a class which can be presumed to have survived the assertion of a territorial sovereignty by the Crown" (Lester 1977:367). These arguments were first presented at the inquiry. The facts of use, if not always the *lex loci*, have been accepted in most adversarial proceedings since then without challenge (see Elias 1989); the body of work as a whole is now widely accepted as a major contribution to ethnographic knowledge of the North.

10 Studies undertaken on behalf of the Cree and Inuit of James Bay and northern Quebec at around the same time produced similar critiques of administrative harvest records, as well as the first systematic documentation of Native harvests over a large region by means of surveys (JBNQ 1982a,b). Similar debates occurred in connection with hydroelectric development in northern Manitoba and Saskatchewan (see especially Ballantyne, Brook, et al. 1976).

11 Industry's proposals for training and employment, and its claims about the benefits of its rotational employment programs in Inuit communities (Hobart 1981, 1982) and the role that unions might play, were held up to rigorous scrutiny by commission counsel as well as by the Native organizations.

12 For an extended discussion of the significance of Asch's testimony for the orientation and methodology of SIA, see Torgerson (1980).

13 The Inuit of the Western Arctic already had concrete experience with both the environmental and social effects of development. The construction of the DEWline and the new town of Inuvik were matters of recent memory, and for the previous ten years there had been extensive oil and gas exploration including seismic work. The magnitude and effects of development would be much greater in the Western Arctic because oil and gas fields there would be continuing zones of heavy industrial activity, whereas in the Mackenzie Valley, the effects would be more restricted to the pipeline itself. The Dene experience with the oil and gas industry was, for the most part, much less immediate, and the prospects more abstract.

14 The requirements of claims research also promoted this view (Elias 1989; 1990).

15 Knight (1978) provides an important beginning, although one too little recognized by Arctic and subarctic anthropologists.

16 For example, although Native organizations continue to introduce

evidence with respect to their aboriginal or treaty rights at impact assessment reviews, it is difficult to avoid the conclusion that this evidence is largely ignored and has had no substantive effect on any project since the Berger Inquiry.

17 Experience with such broad "concept" or multi-project reviews as Ontario's Royal Commission on the Northern Environment, and the federal Beaufort Sea Environmental Assessment Review confirms this view. The risk is that the nature of development becomes too easily ill-defined, SIA (like the larger question of social change) becomes trivialized, and the problem of cumulative and synergistic effects of a broad range of developments is, despite lip service, given short shrift.

18 See, for example, Usher, Anderson, et al. 1979, in which a control community was used to isolate the effects of the loss of an Ojibwa fishery due to mercury pollution by comparing a variety of social indicators.

19 The role of the social scientist as expert witness, an increasingly familiar one since the mid-1970s and a significant topic discussed elsewhere in this volume, is beyond the scope of the present discussion.

REFERENCES

Alexander, C. 1976. *Angry Society*. Yellowknife: Yellowknife Publishing.

Asch, M. 1977. "The Dene Economy." *Dene Nation – The Colony Within*, ed. M. Watkins, 47–61. Toronto: University of Toronto Press.

– 1979a. "The Economics of Dene Self-Determination." In *Challenging Anthropology*, eds. D. Turner and G. Smith, 339–510. Toronto: McGraw-Hill Ryerson.

– 1979b. "The Ecological-Evolutionary Model and the Concept of Mode of Production." In *Challenging Anthropology*, eds. D. Turner and G. Smith, 81–99. Toronto: McGraw-Hill Ryerson.

– 1982. "Dene Self-Determination and the Study of Hunter-Gatherers in the Modern World." In *Politics and History in Band Societies*, eds. E. Leacock and R. Lee, 347–72. Cambridge: Cambridge University Press.

– 1984. *Home and Native Land*. Toronto: Methuen.

Ballantyne, P., P. Brook, P. Burns, et al. 1976. "Aski-puko – The Land Alone. A report on the expected effects of the proposed hydro-electric installation at Wintego Rapids upon the Cree of the Peter Ballantyne and Lac La Ronge Bands." Report prepared for the Federation of Saskatchewan Indians.

Bean, W. 1977. "Colonialism in the Communities." In *Dene Nation – The Colony Within*, ed. M. Watkins, 130–41. Toronto: University of Toronto Press.

Beanlands, G.E., and P.N. Duinker. 1983. *An Ecological Framework for*

Environmental Impact Assessment in Canada. Halifax: Institute for Resource and Environmental Studies, Dalhousie University.

Berger, Thomas R. 1977a. *Northern Frontier – Northern Homeland, The Report of the Mackenzie Valley Pipeline Inquiry.* Ottawa: Supply and Services Canada.

– 1977b. *Northern Frontier – Northern Homeland, The Report of the Mackenzie Valley Pipeline Inquiry.* Vol. 2, *Terms and Conditions.* Ottawa: Supply and Services Canada.

Bourgeault, R. 1983. "The Indian, the Metis and the Fur Trade: Class, Sexism and Racism in the Transition from 'Communism' to Capitalism." *Studies in Political Economy* 12:45–80.

Brody, H. 1975. *The Peoples' Land.* Harmondsworth: Penguin

– 1976. "Land Occupancy: Inuit Perceptions." In *Report, Inuit Land Use and Occupancy Project,* vol. 1, ed. M.M.R. Freeman, 185–242. Ottawa: Department Indian Affairs and Northern Development.

– 1977. "Industrial Impact in the Canadian North." *Polar Record* 18(115):333–9.

– 1981. *Maps and Dreams.* Vancouver: Douglas & McIntyre.

– 1987. *The Living Arctic.* London: Faber and Faber.

Canada-Manitoba. 1974. "Social and Economic Studies (Appendix 8)." *Report of Lake Winnipeg, Churchill & Nelson Rivers Study Board.* N.p.

Canadian Environmental Assessment Research Council [CEARC]. 1985. *Social Impact Assessment – A Research Prospectus.* Hull: Supply and Services Canada.

Craig, F.E., and F.J. Tester. 1982. "Indigenous Peoples: Reassessing Directions for SIA." In *Indian SIA: The Social Impact Assessment of Rapid Resource Development on Native Peoples,* eds. C.C. Geisler, R. Green, D. Usner, P.C. West, 16–40. N.p.: University of Michigan.

Daniels, D. 1981. "The High Cost of Avoiding Political Economy: A Belated Review of Rolf Knight's *Indians at Work. Canadian Journal of Native Studies* 1(1):209–16.

Department of Indian Affairs and Northern Development [DIAND]. 1972. *Expanded Guidelines for Northern Pipelines.* Ottawa: DIAND.

– and MPS Associates Ltd. [DIAND/MPA]. 1974. *Regional Impact of a Northern Gas Pipeline,* 6 vols. Ottawa: DIAND.

Dosman, E.J. 1975. *The National Interest.* Toronto: McClelland & Stewart.

Elias, P.D. 1975. *Metropolis and Hinterland in Northern Manitoba.* Winnipeg: Manitoba Museum of Man and Nature.

– 1989. "Rights and Research: The Role of the Social Sciences in the Legal and Political Resolution of Land Claims and Question of Aboriginal Rights." *Canadian Native Law Reporter* 1:1–43.

– 1990. "Wage Labour, Aboriginal Rights, and the Cree of the Churchill River Basin, Saskatchewan." *Native Studies Review* 6(2):43–64.

Feit, H. 1982. "The Future of Hunters Within Nation-States: Anthropology and the James Bay Cree." In *Politics and History in Band Societies*, eds. E. Leacock and R. Lee, 373–412. Cambridge: Cambridge University Press.

Freeman, M.M.R., ed. 1976. *Report, Inuit Land Use and Occupancy Project*. 3 vols. Ottawa: Department of Indian Affairs and Northern Development.

Fuller, W.A. 1977. "Land Use in Canada's North." In *Managing Canada's Renewable Resources*, eds. R.R. Krueger and B. Mitchell, 194–209. Toronto: Methuen.

Fumoleau, R. 1973. *As Long as This Land Shall Last*. Toronto: McClelland & Stewart.

Gemini North Ltd. 1974. *Social and Economic Impact of Proposed Arctic Gas Pipeline in Northern Canada*, 4 vols. N.p.: Canadian Arctic Gas Pipeline Ltd.

Hobart, C. 1981. "Impacts of Industrial Employment on Hunting and Trapping Among Canadian Inuit." In *Renewable Resources and the Economy of the North*, ed. M.M.R. Freeman, 202–18. Ottawa: Association of Canadian Universities for Northern Studies and Canada Man and the Biosphere Program.

– 1982. "Industrial Employment of Rural Indigenes: The Case of Canada." *Human Organization* 41(1):54–63.

Honigmann, J., and I. Honigmann. 1965. *Eskimo Townsmen*. Ottawa: Canadian Research Centre for Anthropology, University of Ottawa.

– 1970. *Arctic Townsmen*. Ottawa: Canadian Research Centre for Anthropology, University of Ottawa.

Jackson, T. 1978. "Resisting Pipeline Imperialism: The Struggle for Self-determination in the Canadian North." *Alternatives* 7(4):40–51.

James Bay and Northern Quebec Native Harvesting Research Committee [JBNQ]. 1982a. *The Wealth of the Land – Wildlife Harvests by the James Bay Cree, 1972–73 to 1978–79*. Quebec City: JBNQ.

– 1982b. *Research to Establish Present Levels of Native Harvesting – Harvests by the Inuit of Northern Quebec. Phase II. Yrs. 1979 and 1980*. Montreal: JBNQ.

Jenness, Diamond. 1964. *Eskimo Administration: II, Canada*. Montreal: Arctic Institute of North America.

Knight, R. 1978. *Indians at Work*. Vancouver: New Star Books.

Lang, R., and A. Armour. 1981. *The Assessment and Review of Social Impacts*. Ottawa: Federal Environmental Assessment Review Office.

La Rusic, I. 1970. "From Hunter to Proletarian." In *Developmental Change Among the Cree Indians of Quebec*, ed. N.A. Chance, Bi-B59. Ottawa: Department of Regional Economic Expansion.

Lester, G. 1977. "Primitivism versus Civilization: A Basic Question in the Law of Aboriginal Rights to Land." *Our Footprints are Everywhere*, ed. C. Brice-Bennett, 351–74. Nain, Labrador: Labrador Inuit Association.

LGL Limited, ESL Environmental Sciences Limited, ESSA Environmental and

Social Systems Analysts Ltd., and P.J. Usher Consulting Services. 1986. "Mackenzie Environmental Monitoring Project 1985–86 Final Report." Report prepared for Indian and Northern Affairs Canada, Environment Canada, Fisheries and Oceans Canada, Government of the Northwest Territories and the Yukon Territorial Government.

Loxley, J. 1981. "The 'Great Northern Plan.' " *Studies in Political Economy* 6:151–80.

McCullum, H., and K. McCullum. 1975. *This Land is Not for Sale*. Toronto: Anglican Book Centre.

McMahon, K. 1988. *Arctic Twilight*. Toronto: Lorimer.

Murphy, R., and J. Steward. 1956. "Tappers and Trappers: Parallel Processes in Acculturation." *Economic Development and Cultural Change* 4:393–408.

Nahanni, P. 1977. "The Mapping Project." In *Dene Nation – The Colony Within*, ed. M. Watkins, 21–7. Toronto: University of Toronto Press.

O'Malley, M. 1976. *The Past and Future Land*. Toronto: Peter Martin Associates.

Page, R. 1986. *Northern Development – The Canadian Dilemma*. Toronto: McClelland & Stewart.

Pearse, P.H., ed. 1974. *The Mackenzie Pipeline – Arctic Gas and Canadian Energy Policy*. Toronto: McClelland & Stewart.

Pimlott, D.H., K.M. Vincent, and C.E. McKnight, eds. 1973. *Arctic Alternatives*. Ottawa: Canadian Arctic Resources Committee.

–, D. Brown, and K.P. Sam. 1976. *Oil Under the Ice*. Ottawa: Canadian Arctic Resources Committee.

Puxley, P. 1977. "The Colonial Experience." In *Dene Nation – The Colony Within*, ed. M. Watkins, 103–19. Toronto: University of Toronto Press.

Ray, A.J., and A. Roberts. 1985. "Approaches to the Ethnohistory of the Subarctic: A Review of the *Handbook of North American Indians: Subarctic*." *Ethnohistory* 32(3):270–80.

Rea, K.J. 1968. *The Political Economy of the Canadian North*. Toronto: University of Toronto Press.

Robertson, G. 1961. "The Future of the North." *North* 8(2):1–13.

Rushforth, S. 1977. "Country Food." In *Dene Nation – The Colony Within*, ed. M. Watkins, 32–46. Toronto: University of Toronto Press.

Salisbury, R.F., F. Filion, R. Rawji, and D.A. Stewart. 1972. *Development and James Bay: Social Implications of the Proposals for the Hydroelectric Scheme*. Report prepared for the James Bay Development Corporation. Montreal: McGill University, Programme in the Anthropology of Development.

Shkilnyk, A. 1985. *A Poison Stronger than Love*. New Haven: Yale University Press.

Smith, D.G. 1974. *Occupational Preferences of Northern Students*. Social Science Notes 5. Ottawa: Northern Science Research Group, Department of Indian Affairs and Northern Development.

– 1975. *Natives and Outsiders: Pluralism in the Mackenzie River Delta, Northwest Territories*. Ottawa: Northern Science Research Group, Department of Indian Affairs and Northern Development.

Stabler, J.C. 1977. "The Report of the Mackenzie Valley Pipeline Inquiry, Volume I: A Socio-Economic Critique." Review of the Berger report. *The Muskox* 20:57–65.

– 1985. "Development Planning North of 60: Requirements and Prospects." In *The North*, ed. M.S. Whittington, 23–51. Toronto: University of Toronto Press.

–, and R. Olfert. 1980. "Gaslight Follies: The Political Economy of the Western Arctic." *Canadian Public Policy* 6(2):374–88.

Stager, J.K. 1974. *Old Crow, Y.T. and the Proposed Northern Gas Pipeline*. Report no. 74-21. Ottawa: Environmental-Social Committee, Northern Pipelines, Task Force on Northern Oil Development.

Stucki, L.R. 1972. "Canada's 'Unemployable' Northerners: Square Pegs in Round Holes in the System to be Created for the International Transfer of Energy by Pipeline from Northern Canada to the United States." Paper presented at the meeting of the American Anthropological Association, Toronto.

Torgerson, D. 1980. *Industrialization and Assessment – Social Impact Assessment as a Social Phenomenon*. Toronto: York University Publications in Northern Studies.

Tough, F. 1988. "The Northern Fur Trade: A Review of Conceptual and Methodological Problems." *The Muskox* 36:66–79.

Usher, P.J. 1971. *The Bankslanders: Economy and Ecology of a Frontier Trapping Community*. 3 vols. Ottawa: Northern Science Research Group, Department of Indian Affairs and Northern Development.

– 1972. "Hinterland Culture Shock." *Canadian Dimension* 8(8):26–31.

– 1974a. "Environmental Impact Assessment – Social Perspective." In *National Conference on Environmental Impact Assessment, Proceedings*, eds. C.G. Morley and B. Odlum, 72–81. Winnipeg: Agassiz Centre for Water Studies.

– 1974b. "The Significance of the Land to Native Northerners." In *Proceedings of the 1973 National Convention, Canadian Society of Exploration Geophysicists*, Calgary, 170–7. (Reprinted as "Northerners and the Land." *Canadian Dimension* 11(2),1975:23–30.)

– 1974c. "Geographers and Northern Development: Some Social and Political Considerations." *Alternatives* 4(1):21–5. (Reprinted in R.R. Krueger, and B. Mitchell, eds. 1977. *Managing Canada's Renewable Resources*, 210–18. Toronto: Methuen.

– 1976a. "Evaluating Country Food in the Northern Native Economy." *Arctic* 29(2):105–20.

– 1976b. "The Class System, Metropolitan Dominance and Northern Development in Canada." *Antipode* 8(3):28–32.

- 1978. "Evaluating Change: the Case of the Mackenzie Valley Gas Pipeline." In *Evaluating Change (Proceedings of the Symposium on Evaluating Change, Edmonton June 1975)*, eds. J.G. Nelson and C.A. Gray, 97–113. Ottawa: Social Science Federation of Canada.
- 1981a. "Staple Production and Ideology in Northern Canada." In *Culture, Communication, and Dependency*, eds. W.H. Melody, L. Salter, and P. Heyer, 177–86. Norwood, NJ: Ablex Publishing.
- 1981b. "Sustenance or Recreation? The Future of Native Wildlife Harvesting in Northern Canada." In *Renewable Resources and the Economy of the North*, ed. M.M.R. Freeman, 56–71. Ottawa: Association of Canadian Universities for Northern Studies and Canada Man and the Biosphere Program.
- 1982a. "Assessing the Impact of Industry in the Beaufort Sea Region." Report prepared for the Beaufort Sea Alliance (evidence to Beaufort Sea Hydrocarbon Production and Transportation Proposal Environmental Assessment Review Panel). Ottawa.
- 1982b. "The North: One Land, Two Ways of Life." In *A Geography of Canada – Heartland and Hinterland*, ed. L.D. McCann, 411–56. Scarborough, Ont: Prentice-Hall.
-, and P. Anderson, H. Brody, et al. 1979. "The Economic and Social Impact of Mercury Pollution on the Whitedog and Grassy Narrows Indian Reserves, Ontario." Report prepared for Anti-Mercury Ojibwa Group (Kenora, Ontario). Ottawa.
-, and G. Beakhust. 1973. *Land Regulation in the Canadian North*. Ottawa: Canadian Arctic Resources Committee.
-, and G. Noble. 1977. "New Directions in Northern Policy Making: Reality or Myth?" In *Mackenzie Delta: Priorities and Alternatives*, 87–105. Ottawa: Canadian Arctic Resources Committee.
-, and M.S. Weinstein. 1991. *Towards Assessing the Effects of Lake Winnipeg Regulation and Churchill River Diversion on Resource Harvesting in Native Communities in Northern Manitoba*. Canadian Technical Report of Fisheries and Aquatic Sciences no. 1794. Winnipeg: Fisheries and Oceans Canada.
Van Ginkel Associates. 1975. "Communities of the Mackenzie – Effects of the Hydrocarbon Industry." Prepared for Canadian Arctic Gas Study Ltd. N.p.
Van Stone, J.W. 1965. *The Changing Culture of the Snowdrift Chipewyan*. National Museum of Canada Bulletin 209. Ottawa: Department of Secretary of State.
Waldram, J. 1988. *As Long as the Rivers Run*. Winnipeg: University of Manitoba Press.
Watkins, M. 1977. "From Underdevelopment to Development." In *Dene Nation – The Colony Within*, ed. M. Watkins, 84–99. Toronto: University of Toronto Press.

Wilimovsky, N.J., and J.N. Wolfe. 1966. *Environment of the Cape Thompson Region, Alaska.* Oak Ridge, TN: United States Atomic Energy Commission.

Wolforth, J. 1971. *The Evolution and Economy of the Delta Community.* Ottawa: Northern Science Research Group, Department of Indian Affairs and Northern Development.

Wood, K.S. 1974. *An Approach to Social Reporting in the Canadian North.* Halifax: Institute of Public Affairs, Dalhousie University.

Yerbury, J.C. 1986. *The Subarctic Indians and the Fur Trade, 1680–1860.* Vancouver: University of British Columbia Press.

Zlotkin, N. and D.R. Colborne. 1977. "Internal Canadian Imperialism and the Native Peoples." In *Imperialism, Nationalism, and Canada,* ed. C. Heron, 161–85. Toronto and Kitchener: New Hogtown Press and Between the Lines.

DIRECT EVIDENCE AT THE MACKENZIE VALLEY PIPELINE INQUIRY

References followed by "E" are listed below. Text and cross-examination are contained in the transcripts of the inquiry. Summaries are provided in:

Mackenzie Valley Pipeline Inquiry, Summaries of Proceedings. 1976. Ottawa: Department of Indian Affairs and Northern Development. See vol. 3, *Mackenzie Delta and Beaufort Sea,* and vol. 5, *The Human Environment.*

Unless otherwise indicated all evidence cited below was presented at formal hearings in Yellowknife in 1976. Initials in brackets indicate the organization on whose behalf the evidence was given. In addition to the Committee for Aboriginal Peoples Entitlement (COPE) and Indian Brotherhood of the Northwest Territories (IBNWT), there are the Council for Yukon Indians (CYI), Commission Counsel (CC), Delta Gas Producers (DP), and Canadian Arctic Gas Study Ltd. (CAGSL). IBNWT evidence subsequently published in Watkins (1977) is cited in the references above.

Asch, M. Land use by Slavey Indians (IBNWT). 29 April.

Baring-Gould, M. Social impact of the Trans-Alaska Pipeline construction on Valdez, Alaska (CC). 4 October.

Beakhust, G. Overview – political development (COPE). 21 July.

– Environmental compliance and control (COPE). 15 October.

Brody, H. Overview (one and two) (COPE). 20–1 July.

– Alcohol. (CC). 22 July.

Clarke, L. Impact of the proposed Mackenzie Valley Gas Pipeline on housing in Inuvik and Fort Simpson (COPE-IBNWT). 9 September.

Cruikshank, J. Social impact of the Alaska Highway on Yukon Indians (CYI). 5 May.

Dixon, M. Impact information centres, Alaska (CC). 17 August.

Forrest, A. Alaska Native Claims Settlement Act (IBNWT). 30 June.

Hildes, J. Health care and health care delivery (COPE). 15 September.

Hobart, C. Socio-economic overview of the Mackenzie Delta region (DP). 21 January (Inuvik).

– Socio-economic overview of the Mackenzie River corridor (CAGSL). 5 July.

– Sociological aspects of construction and operation (CAGSL). 13 July.

McClellan, K. Social impact of the Alaska Highway on Yukon Indians (CYI). 5 May.

Noble, G. Health care and health care delivery (COPE). 15 September.

Schaefer, O. Health care and health care delivery (COPE). 15 September.

Sharp, R. Impact of mining activity upon Indian people at Ross River, YT (CYI). 7 May.

Usher, P.J. Assessment and Consultation: Analysis and Conclusions (COPE). 8 April.

– The Traditional Economy of the Western Arctic (COPE). 20 July.

– Overview (COPE). 21 July.

Worl, R. Subsistence impacts and land claims in Alaska (COPE). 21 September.

Zemansky, G. Environmental compliance and control (COPE). 15 October.

PART TWO

The Politics of Anthropological Research

The four papers in this section examine the practice of anthropology and public policy questions from a more personal perspective. In many ways they are inspired by recent work on a "post-modern" anthropology which returns the researcher to a more open and reflexive role in describing, understanding, and communicating culture to a wider audience. Julie Cruikshank's examination of the politics of ethnography in the north challenges us to consider carefully the effects of anthropology's "enduring objects," its data and reports, when research is undertaken. Brizinski tackles a similar issue, but from an even more personal perspective. Her article describes the process whereby such research actually takes place. The two essays raise important questions about the process, and implications, of anthropological research.

The reflections of Ron Ignace, George Speck, and Renee Taylor on anthropology and public policy resulted from interviews which were subsequently transcribed and edited. As members of Native communities who also happen to be familiar with anthropology, they are able to offer well-informed and searching assessments of anthropological work in this field. In this sense, their views are complimentary to those of Brizinski: we obtain the perspective of both an anthropologist and Native activists examining anthropological research activities.

The final paper in this section, by Noel Dyck, focuses our attention on the fact that anthropologists tend to shy away from research in certain sensitive areas. This, of course, is not surprising, and the previous papers in this section clearly articulate why this is so. Yet, by being evasive, anthropologists in effect reduce the extent to which their work can be useful in resolving certain public policy issues. These issues cry out for systemic, objective analysis of the type that anthropologists can provide. Reluctance to address the more pressing social, economic, and health issues of Native communities in both historical and cultural contexts has led to a diminishing of the discipline's capacity to contribute to the understanding and improvement of the public policy process.

5 The Politics of Ethnography in the Canadian North[1]

JULIE CRUIKSHANK

One of the liveliest areas of discussion in contemporary anthropology centres on how to convey authentically, in words, the experience of another culture. Anthropology's claims to provide authoritative interpretations of cultural experience are being challenged from both inside and outside the discipline (Rabinow 1977; Said 1979; Rosaldo 1980; Ellen 1984; Clifford and Marcus 1986; Marcus and Fischer 1986; Clifford 1988). The issue of how culture can be translated is also a subject of considerable discussion in the communities where ethnographers conduct research. In fact, the development of a critical and articulate local audience is changing the shape and direction of ethnographic research and writing, certainly in northern Canada and Alaska.

If this debate sometimes carries a reflexive "post-modernist" tone in academic circles, indigenous peoples are expressing their concerns much more directly. Their growing emphasis upon land claims, self-government, and repatriation of cultural symbols has given them ample opportunity to observe the public significance attributed to ethnographic images. For example, one need only spend a few days listening to scholars called as expert witnesses at the ongoing Gitksan-Wet'suwet'en land claims case currently before the Supreme Court of British Columbia to recognize that the texts are on trial while the plaintiffs remain cast in the role of courtroom spectators. Anthropologists are cross-examined about ethnographies written a generation ago, while lawyers venture legal interpretations of those texts several steps removed from the intentions of their authors, often deceased.[2]

Written accounts, then, seem to carry a startling amount of power in the range of policy issues, large and small, arising from the relationships between Native peoples, the nation-state, and Canadian society in general. Inevitably, the question of how these accounts are constructed in the first place is being raised. The issue, at least for some Native northerners, centres on who controls the images, the representations of their lives portrayed to the larger world. In this context, some of the modest experiments in ethnographic research and writing occuring in northern Canada may contribute to this discussion. Because they involve the energy and enthusiasm of significant numbers of Native and non-Native northerners, such experiments deserve to be part of the dialogue about trends in ethnographic research.

The cultural context of fieldwork is changing in ways that may seem disconcerting to some researchers who worked in the North a generation ago. Organizers of a symposium on subarctic research at the 1986 meetings of the American Anthropological Association, for example, expressed concern about a diminishing contribution of Arctic and subarctic ethnography to cultural anthropology in recent years, suggesting that northern studies have been consigned to oblivion (Balikci and Myers 1987). Yet from the perspective of researchers based in the North during the 1970s and 1980s, there has actually been an explosion of critical local interest in ethnographic research during these decades, generating a new audience for ethnographic writing and lively discussion about research questions and methods. There are a number of reasons for this – the weight attributed to ethnographic evidence in land claims negotiations, concern by Native peoples about language loss, and attempts to introduce cultural history and oral literature into northern classrooms.

At the same time there is growing tension between goals of university-based anthropology and local stipulations for fieldworkers. This is particularly noticeable because the Arctic and subarctic were viewed as a ready-made laboratory for so long. Anthropologists no longer have the power to decide unilaterally where and how they will do fieldwork. Instead, research strategies negotiated locally and based on a model of *collaboration* are replacing more conventional models of university-initiated research. Increasing numbers of anthropologists and linguists are choosing to spend a significant portion of their professional careers based in northern Canada or Alaska. While the demands of working in a local context

may preclude publication in academic journals, much of this collaborative research does fall within long-established traditions in
subarctic ethnography.

My own perspective comes from living in the Yukon Territory
and in Alaska during ten of the last eighteen years, much of that
time working with a locally based project, the Yukon Native Language Centre. During those years, specific changes seem to have
occurred in the kinds of questions ethnographers are asking, the
methods they use, and the writing genres they select to present
their work. In each case this can be illustrated most clearly by
examples of locally based collaborative projects.

RESEARCH QUESTIONS

The history of ethnographic research in the Arctic and subarctic
seems always to have reflected an interplay between detailed ethnographic documentation and general questions posed far from the
North. What we saw in the 1980s seemed to be an intensification of
that process.

During the 1950s and 1960s northern societies were considered
primarily as providing evidence for or against specific hypotheses
about social organization. Julian Steward, for example, based his
formulations about band organization at least in part on observations by Speck (1915) and Osgood (1936), and set terms of a debate
carried on by Leacock (1954), Helm (1965), Knight (1965), and
others over the years. In fact, questions about band organization
continue to provide the unifying theme of the recently published
Subarctic Handbook (Helm 1981).

But as ethnographers began to utilize Athapaskan and Algonkian
studies as their research focus rather than just as evidence for more
general theory, they were confronted with individual differences.
Firm definitions of band society seemed to evaporate. Every attempt
to produce a normative account generated further questions. People
in northern communities did not always agree with one another,
offering thoughtful but seemingly idiosyncratic responses. Following
conferences on hunter-gatherers in the 1960s (Damas 1969; Lee and
Devore 1968), efforts to document the *variety* of possible options
available for social organization replaced some of the earlier determination to define general principles that would be broadly appli-
cable to northern hunter-gatherers. By the 1960s a general post-
war interest in acculturation models reached the subarctic. Murphy
and Steward's influential paper (1956) on tappers and trappers used
an acculturation model to predict inevitable assimilation of band

societies into national industrial economies. So entrenched was this model by the 1960s that a whole series of Arctic and subarctic studies, many of them sponsored by the Canadian government, took acculturation as their main theme (Balikci 1963; Chance 1963; Van Stone 1965; Honigmann 1966; Hoseley 1966).

By the 1970s Native northerners were becoming politically vocal about their own views of their society. In the mid-1970s hundreds of Dene addressed the Mackenzie Valley Pipeline Inquiry, and Yukon Indians spoke to the Alaska Highway Pipeline Inquiry protesting that they were not societies in transition but strongly committed to continuing their traditional way of life in the present (Berger 1977; Lysyk 1977; Asch 1982). Across the North, attention to land claims has sparked a corresponding interest in documenting cultural persistence (Feit 1982), a notion that ultimately has strong roots in archaeology and field ethnology.

There seems to be an unresolved conflict between models of stability and models of change in Arctic and subarctic anthropology (see also Ray 1986). Native northerners have been quick to draw attention to shifting fashions by pointing to studies they find misleading; for example, acculturation studies of the 1960s have come under intense criticism. Northerners are suggesting that if anthropologists want to work in their communities, local people should have a role in defining some of the questions for research.

FIELDWORK METHODS

If research questions are being re-evaluated, so are the methods anthropology uses to derive its data. Since the 1920s, participant-observation has been the cultural activity that defined anthropology. Fieldworkers have long recognized the inherent contradiction posed by simultaneously participating in the life of a community and dispassionately observing daily events; however, as long as the demands of the academic institution were stronger than the demands of the community, observation was the component most valued. Increasingly aboriginal people have their own ideas about the kind of relationship they want to establish with an anthropologist. They emphasize the participatory component of fieldwork, suggesting that ethnographers who want to work in their communities should be prepared to do so in ways and during times specified by the community. While this is certainly a contentious issue, it has to be addressed by every ethnographer working in the North.

The model being negotiated in some northern communities is one based on collaboration between participants rather than research by the anthropologist on the community. Such collaboration has local people and the ethnographer jointly specify terms under which research will be conducted and a final report produced. While the resulting demands may be extremely time consuming and long term for the ethnographer, such work does provide perspectives on questions central to anthropology. One of the more interesting questions may be how subjective and objective realities become blurred in such research, and how the personal reaction of the investigator to collaboration affects the kinds of questions asked.

ETHNOGRAPHIC WRITING

Writing is the other side of fieldwork. Readership of classic northern ethnographies is shifting from an academic audience to a politically astute Native audience, particularly as land claims negotiations in the North begin to attribute unexpected weight to ethnographic evidence. However, the contradiction between the strict limitations imposed by any fieldwork situation and the model of authority that written ethnographies are expected to emulate means that books with titles like *The Han Indians* (Osgood 1971) or *The Kaska Indians* (Honigmann 1954) or *The Upper Tanana Indians* (McKennan 1959) have a tendency to disappoint this new readership.

Attention to various ways of writing about cultural experience has generated a good deal of experimentation in recent years (Clifford and Marcus 1986). In the North issues of authorship, ownership and copyright are all being redefined. One possibility involves working with local people to prepare their own version of a research report under their own authorship. Another option, particularly appropriate for documenting language and oral tradition, involves assigning copyright to the narrator and producing publications under that narrator's authorship. However, such strategies do not bring northern research into the academic mainstream.

COLLABORATIVE RESEARCH

A framework of collaboration imposes specific structural requirements on research. Collaboration necessarily involves more than one conscious investigator. Instead of a social scientist asking questions in order to acquire raw data, the design and implementation of such research inevitably requires a great deal of attention to insider interpretations. On the surface, at least, collaborative research often seems to move us away from questions about social structure and social behaviour and toward questions of symbol and meaning.

Much of the research now ongoing in the western subarctic seems consistent with a growing interest in communication and language in anthropology – in the ways individuals mobilize symbolic resources to talk about their experience. This is a reflection of several factors: a continuing scholarly tradition of attention to northern Athapaskan world views by linguists and ethnographers like Sapir (1949), McClellan (1975), Ridington (1982), and others; the concentrated focus on documentation of Native languages and narrative texts in Alaska and Canada; and the increasing attention paid by Northern Athapaskans to documenting their own history and culture during the last decade.

A growing number of northern researchers have benefited from both this long tradition of scholarship and from a perspective on local research goals gained from living in the North. Some brief examples of locally based collaborative research in the Yukon may illustrate its overall continuity with traditions of subarctic ethnography.

The most striking change during the last decade has been the growing interest of both elders and younger people in documenting their own cultures in their own voices. Initially, such documentation involved production of booklets of stories, place names, and genealogies as they were recorded with specific elder storytellers (Sidney, Smith, and Dawson 1977; Sidney 1980, 1982, 1983; Smith 1982; Ned 1984). Their interest in this work at least partly reflects their understanding of how instructional techniques have changed during the last decade. Each of these elders received her education either from her own direct experience or from verbal descriptions or instructions from others. An ultimate value of oral tradition was the ability to recreate a situation for someone who had not experienced it so that the listener could benefit directly from the narrator's experience[3]. Elders' faith in oral tradition has to do both with their own experience of its effectiveness and with the direct relationship of teacher and listener. But they understand that in contemporary educational institutions power rests with the written word, and they want to devise ways to translate their knowledge into other forms of presentation.

More recently, Native researchers interested in and trained to do their own cultural documentation have done so in a variety of genres. Gertie Tom, for example, is a Tutchone language specialist who worked with linguists and anthropologists to produce a bilingual booklet about tanning moosehides (Tom 1981) and an extensive study of place names in the eastern Yukon Territory as well as narratives associated with those toponyms (Tom 1987). Daniel Tlen, a Southern Tutchone linguist, undertook a Yukon-wide survey of Native language programs and produced a comprehensive assessment of future program requirements (Tlen 1986). Mary Easterson, a Southern Tutchone woman who combined anthropology and education for her university degree, has regularly written articles about culture history in the North (e.g., Easterson 1987). Carol Geddes, an accomplished film director of Tlingit and Tutchone ancestry, has received national recognition for her work (Geddes 1987) and has recently directed a film documenting storytelling traditions in the Yukon (Geddes 1986). Louise Profeit LeBlanc is making an ongoing contribution to the revival of storytelling by younger Yukon women. Lu Johns-Penikett worked with a broadly based group to organize a potlatch conference in the southern Yukon and has documented the variety of potlatch traditions discussed at that conference (Penikett 1986). These are only a few of the Athapaskan and Tlingit women and men actively involved in such documentation, and in many cases their work has been part of collaborative research made possible through locally based associations like the Council for Yukon Indians, the Yukon Native Language Centre, or the Yukon Historical and Museums Association.

Some of the very detailed documentation of place names occurring throughout the North (Muller-Wille 1984; Ritter 1976, 1977; Kari and Kari 1982; Sidney 1980; Cruikshank 1984) originated from collaborative efforts among elders, linguists, ethnographers, geographers, and archaeologists to document Native land use. This research has generated interest in the ways people *use* place names to talk about the past. Renato Rosaldo's work on place names in the Philippines (1980b), Keith Basso's research on Apache place names (1984), and Frances Harwood's research in the Trobriands (1976) all suggest that place names are complex mnemonic devices. Research involving Athapaskan speakers in the subarctic indicates that they, too, use named landscape features to talk about the passage of time.

There is also considerable local interest in reconstructing genealogies in the Yukon. The major reason Athapaskan people give for initiating this work is their desire to assemble a pool of personal family names which may be given to children in appropriate ways. Much of this seems related to notions of self, whereby individuals share qualities with others who have been given the same names. In the course of compiling extensive genealogies, considerable information is becoming available about movement and marriage patterns within and across local groups, and about ways people manipulate their genealogies to claim simultaneous membership in different groups. This local initiative may contribute to our understanding of the nature and composition of local groups (Sidney 1983; Tom 1987).

Text collection, translation, and analysis have particular importance for studies of symbol and meaning. The detailed narrative texts already recorded at the Alaska Native Language Center and the Yukon Native Language Centre by Athapaskan speakers trained to write their own languages offer insights into the workings of Athapaskan language. They also illustrate how narrative, and metaphors derived from narrative, are used to talk about everyday life. The relationship between stories and social life is not a simple one: stories with a range of plots and outcomes provide narrators with a way to use the traditional dimension of culture to discuss troubling contemporary issues – the relationship of an individual to his or her social group, the ambiguities involved in a marriage to a distant group, the efforts to retain strong family ties. As well, stories provide narrators with ways to talk about and interpret their own actions on various occasions in the past. A striking example of this is the way women narrators may have acted with autonomy at critical points in their lives but use oral tradition to characterize their innovations as essentially conservative, stressing that they were really behaving in an old-fashioned way.

Collaborative research may actually alter the direction of specific research projects, blurring any clear line between investigator and the person being interviewed. One of my continuing interests during the years I have lived in the North has been recording life histories with elderly Athapaskan women I have known for more than a decade. A central feature of their accounts has been the women's insistence on including long passages of traditional narrative to explain certain aspects of their lives. When I asked them to talk about events that I knew had affected them, they would begin by doing so, then shift to a traditional narrative they wanted me to record. While these accounts initially seemed archaic and closer to our definition of myth than to personal accounts of a life, I came to see them as embodying a culturally distinct interpretation of everyday events. They also provide the necessary context for understanding the metaphors narrators use to reflect on their lives (Cruikshank 1987). These collaborative accounts bring two different perspectives to the documentation of personal experience and may, in turn, make some contribution to anthropological studies of life history.

CONCLUSION

From a northern perspective, then, ethnographic research is continuing as intensely as ever in the Arctic and subarctic, though under different circumstances. If that work is often invisible in the academic community, it may be because there are very few mechanisms to connect individuals living and working in the North with universities having northern research interests. It also says more about the way knowledge is circulated within the profession of anthropology than it does about the quantity or quality of work occurring in the North.

A growing number of anthropologists see involvement in public policy or in advocacy as a way to repay their hosts for the education and friendships they have acquired while living with them (Paine 1985). Even when researchers are divided in their views about how to respond to direction from local communities, they recognize that they can no longer claim the role of giving voice to or speaking on behalf of other cultural perspectives. To recognize the tremendous urgency with which self-definitions are being proclaimed within communities engulfed by nation-states is not to support uncritically the view that insiders have a privileged view of culture. The anthropological project focuses on more than cultural *uniqueness* and is concerned with understanding *similarities* in human cultural life. However, those similarities may be addressed most clearly by situating local, seemingly unique issues in the wider sphere of social relations – the interface at which public policy issues are negotiated.

Increasingly, anthropologists recognize that they produce enduring objects – texts – and that their statements always have potential, if not immediate, political consequences. The challenge remains one of bridging diverging traditions of knowledge so that locally based projects can achieve some broader visibility, and anthropologists can provide some perspective on the institutional, social formations within which those cultural expressions occur.

NOTES

1 This is a revised version of a paper presented at the 1986 meetings of the American Anthropological Association, Philadelphia, in the session "The Oblivion of an Ethnographic Area: Hunter-Gatherer Studies in the Arctic and Subarctic" organized by Fred Myers and Asen Balikci.

An earlier version, entitled "Telling About Culture: Changing Traditions in Subarctic Anthropology," was published in *The Northern Review*, (1988, 1[1]).

2 These comments are based on my attendance during the cross examination of expert witnesses between 21 February and 11 April 1989.

3 See McClellan (1975:66–7) and Ridington (1982) for a discussion of this.

BIBLIOGRAPHY

Asch, Michael. 1982. "Dene Self-determination and the Study of Hunter Gatherers in the Modern World." In *Politics and History in Band Societies*, eds. Eleanor Leacock and Richard Lee, 347–71. Cambridge: Cambridge University Press.

Balikci, Asen. 1963. "Vunta Kutchin Social Change: A Study of the People of Old Crow, Northern Yukon Territory." Ottawa: Northern Coordination and Research Centre, Department of Northern Affairs and National Resources.

–, and F. Myers. 1987. "The Oblivion of an Ethnographic Area: Hunter Gatherer Studies in the Arctic and Subarctic." Session at the American Anthropological Association Meetings, Philadelphia.

Basso, Keith. 1984. "Stalking with Stories: Names, Places and Moral Narratives Among the Western Apache." In *Text, Play and Story: The Construction and Reconstruction of Self and Society*, ed. Stuart Plattner, 19–55. Washington: Proceedings of the American Ethnological Society.

Berger, Thomas, 1977. *Northern Frontier, Northern Homeland: The Report of the Mackenzie Valley Pipeline Inquiry*. 2 vols. Ottawa: Minister of Supply and Services.

Chance, Norman. 1963. "Social Organization, Acculturation and Integration Among the Eskimo and the Cree: A Comparative Study." *Anthropologica*, n.s. 5(1):47–56.

Clifford, James. 1988. *The Predicament of Culture*. Cambridge, MA: Harvard University Press.

–, and G.E. Marcus. 1986. *Writing Culture*. Berkeley and Los Angeles: University of California Press

Cruikshank, Julie. 1984. "Tagish and Tlingit Place Names in the Southern Lakes Region, Yukon Territory." *Canoma* 10(1):30–5.

– 1987. "Life Lived Like a Story: Cultural Construction of Life History by Tagish and Tutchone Women." Ph.D. diss., Department of Anthropology, University of British Columbia.

Damas, David. 1969. "Contributions to Anthropology: Band Societies." *Proceedings of the Conference on Band Organization*. Anthropological Series, no. 84, National Museum of Canada Bulletin 228. Ottawa: Department of Secretary of State.

Easterson, Mary. 1987. "Traditional Ways Preserve Indian Culture." 2 parts. *Dan Sha* 14(1):15, (2):14.

Ellen, R.F., ed. 1984. *Ethnographic Research: A Guide to General Conduct.* London: Academic Press.

Feit, Harvey. 1982. "The Future of Hunters within Nation States: Anthropology and the James Bay Cree." In *Politics and History in Band Societies*, eds. Eleanor Leacock and Richard Lee, 373–411. Cambridge: Cambridge University Press.

Geddes, Carol. 1986. *Three Elder Storytellers.* 16 mm. film footage. Whitehorse, Yukon.

– 1987. *Doctor, Lawyer, Indian Chief.* Ottawa: National Film Board of Canada.

Harwood, Frances. 1976. "Myth, Memory and Oral Tradition: Cicero in the Trobriands." *American Anthropologist* 78(4):783–96.

Helm, June. 1965. "Bilaterality in the Socio-territorial Organization of the Arctic Drainage Dene." *Ethnology* 4:316–85.

–, ed. 1981. *Handbook of North American Indians*, vol. 6, *Subarctic.* Washington: Smithsonian Institution.

Honigmann, John. 1954. *The Kaska Indians: An Ethnographic Reconstruction.* New Haven: Yale University Publications in Anthropology, no. 51.

– 1966. "Social Disintegration in Five Northern Canadian Communities." *Canadian Review of Sociology and Anthropology* 2(4):199–214.

Hoseley, Edward H. 1966. "Factionalism and Acculturation in an Alaskan Athapaskan Community." Ph.D. diss., Department of Anthropology, University of California, Los Angeles.

Kari, James, and P. Kari. 1982. *Dena'ina Elnena: Tanaina Country.* Fairbanks: Alaska Native Language Center, University of Alaska.

Knight, Rolf. 1965. "A Re-examination of Hunting, Trapping and Territoriality among the Northeastern Algonkian Indians." In *Man, Culture and Animals: the Role of Animals in Human Ecological Adjustment*, eds. Anthony Leeds and Andrew P. Vayda, 27–42. Washington: American Association for the Advancement of Science.

Leacock, Eleanor. 1954. "The Montagnais 'Hunting Territory' and the Fur Trade." American Anthropological Association Memoir no. 78. Menasha, Wisconsin: American Anthropological Association.

Lee, Richard, and I. Devore. 1968. *Man the Hunter.* New York: Aldine.

Lysyk, Kenneth M., E. Bohmer, and W. Phelps. 1977. *Alaska Highway Pipeline Inquiry.* Ottawa: Minister of Supply and Services.

McCandless, Robert. 1985. *Yukon Wildlife: A Social History.* Edmonton: University of Alberta Press.

McClellan, Catharine. 1975. *My Old People Say: An Ethnographic Survey of*

Southern Yukon Territory. 2 vols. Publications in Ethnology 6 (1 and 2). Ottawa: National Museums of Canada.

McKennan, Robert. 1959. *The Upper Tanana Indians*. Yale University Publications in Anthropology, no. 55. New Haven: Yale.

Marcus, George E., and M.M.J. Fisher. 1986. *Anthropology as Cultural Critique*. Chicago and London: University of Chicago Press.

Muller-Wille, Ludger. 1984. "The Legacy of Native Toponyms: Towards Establishing the Inuit Place Name Inventory of the Kativik Region (Quebec)." *Onomastica Canadiana* no. 65:2–19.

Murphy, Robert, and J. Steward. 1956. "Tappers and Trappers: Parallel Processes in Acculturation." *Economic Development and Cultural Change* 4:393–408.

Ned, Annie. 1984. *Old People In Those Days, They Told They Story All The Time*. Compiled by J. Cruikshank. Whitehorse: Yukon Native Languages Project.

Osgood, Cornelius. 1936. "The Distribution of Northern Athapaskan Indians." Yale University Publications in Anthropology, no. 7:1–23. New Haven: Yale.

– 1971. *The Han Indians: A Compilation of Ethnographic and Historical Data on the Alaska Yukon Boundary Area*. Yale University Publications in Anthropology, no. 74. New Haven: Yale.

Paine, Robert, ed. 1985. *Advocacy and Anthropology: First Encounters*. St John's: Institute of Social and Economic Research, Memorial University of Newfoundland.

Penikett, Lu Johns. 1986. *Potlatch Conference Report*. Whitehorse: Yukon Historical and Museums Association and the Champagne-Aishihik Band.

Rabinow, Paul. 1977. *Reflections on Fieldwork in Morocco*. Berkeley and Los Angeles: University of California Press.

Ray, Arthur. 1986. Review of *Handbook of North American Indians*, vol 6, *Subarctic*, ed. J. Helm. *Ethnohistory* 32 (3):270–80.

Ridington, Robin. 1982. "Technology, World View and Adaptive Strategy in a Northern Hunting Society." *Canadian Review of Sociology and Anthropology* 19(4):460–7.

Ritter, John T. 1976. *Gwich'in (Loucheaux) Athapaskan Noun Dictionary: Fort MacPherson Dialects*. Whitehorse: Government of the Yukon.

– 1977. *Mayo Indian Language: Dictionary*. Whitehorse: Department of Education, Government of the Yukon.

–, T. McGinty, and J. Edwards. 1977. *The Selkirk Indian Language Noun Dictionary (Northern Tutchone Athapaaskan)*. Whitehorse: Yukon Native Languages Project.

Rosaldo, Renato. 1980a. "Doing Oral History." *Social Analysis* 4:39–99.

– 1980b. *Ilongot Headhunting 1883–1974: A Study in Society and History*. Stanford: Stanford University Press.

Said, Edward. 1979. *Orientalism*. New York: Pantheon.

Sapir, Edward. 1949. *Selected Writings of Edward Sapir*, ed. David Mandelbaum. Berkeley and Los Angeles: University of California Press.

Sidney, Angela. 1980. *Place Names of the Tagish Region, Southern Yukon*. Whitehorse: Yukon Native Languages Project.

– 1982. *Tagish Tlaagu: Tagish Stories*. Recorded by J. Cruikshank. Whitehorse: Council for Yukon Indians and Government of Yukon.

– 1983. *Haa Shagoon: Our Family History*. Compiled by J. Cruikshank. Whitehorse: Yukon Native Languages Project.

–, K. Smith, and R. Dawson. 1977. *My Stories are my Wealth*. Recorded by J. Cruikshank. Whitehorse: Council for Yukon Indians.

Smith, Kitty. 1982. *Nindal Kwadindur: I'm Going to Tell You a Story*. Recorded by J. Cruikshank. Whitehorse: Council for Yukon Indians and Government of Yukon.

Speck, Frank. 1915. "The Family Hunting Band as the Basis of Algonkian Social Organization." *American Antrhopologist* 17 (2):289–305.

Steward, Julian. 1955. *Theory of Culture Change: The Methodology of Multilinear Evolution*. Urbana: University of Illinois Press.

Tlen, Daniel. 1986. *Speaking Out: Consultations and Survey of Yukon Native Languages Planning, Visibility and Growth*. Whitehorse: Yukon Native Language Centre.

Tom, Gertie. 1981. *Duts'um Edho Ts'etsi Yu Dan K'i: How to Tan Hides in the Native Way*. Whitehorse: Yukon Native Languages Project.

– 1987. *Ekeyi: Gyo Cho Chu, My Country: Big Salmon*. Whitehorse: Yukon Native Languages Project.

Van Stone, James. 1965. "The Changing Culture of Snowdrift Chipewyan." Anthropological Series, no. 74, *National Museums of Canada Bulletin*, no. 209.

Yukon Native Languages Project. 1984. *Northern Tutchone Literacy Workshop*. Whitehorse: Yukon Native Languages Project.

– 1984. *Southern Tutchone Literacy Workshop*. Whitehorse: Yukon Native Languages Project.

– 1984. *Tlingit Literacy Workshop*. Whitehorse: Yukon Native Languages Project.

6 The Summer Meddler: The Image of the Anthropologist as Tool for Indigenous Formulations of Culture

PEGGY MARTIN BRIZINSKI

In a recent paper, Nancy Lurie (1988) has described the evolution of relationships between North American Indian hosts and the anthropologists who have worked with them. The collegial relationships of anthropologists with "key informants" in the late nineteenth and early twentieth centuries gave way in some areas after mid-century to many tense episodes between visiting anthropologists and the revisited communities they had studied. Public attention to this relationship increased in 1969, when Indian writer Vine Deloria, Jr. published scathing criticisms of the role of anthropologists in Native American communities, followed by further indigenous response both in print and in the field. Over the past twenty years the discipline of anthropology has been consumed with the need to understand and take account of these changes. Much of anthropologists' recent intervention in public policy is predicated upon a perceived need to restructure relationships between scientists and host communities; social scientists have attempted to demonstrate their worth to the Indian and non-Indian public.[1]

The cultivation of good relationships remains essential to good anthropology. I began the odyssey of my doctoral research in 1979 with a visit to Inuvik, Northwest Territories to explore a thesis topic dealing with women and employment. I arrived to find myself in the company of several other anthropologists, a contingent of athletes visiting for the Northern Summer Games, and the media, as well as the resident Native (Indian, Inuit, and Metis) and non-Native population. Although I stayed at the Inuvik Research

Laboratory, a facility built to provide logistical assistance to northern scientists, I carried on much like the other tourists and visitors and conducted a few informal interviews, accompanied by what I hoped was astute observation.

As it became known that I was a budding anthropologist, the tenor of my acquaintanceships changed. When, after a productive and enjoyable lunch with a non-Native woman who was a local leader in service organizations, my hostess inquired into my background, she told me, "I feel like I have been stabbed in the back." Another prominent non-Native woman admired my "bush" shoes and commented that they seemed like what an anthropologist would wear to come north and "trample," or exploit, their Native people. I witnessed a young Native woman at a party launch an emotion-charged attack on an archaeologist for the damage that anthropologists had done. Further, I was aware that the other anthropologists present that summer were watching my behaviour closely, offering advice, and testing my rapport-building skills.

I have since found that these types of encounter are not unusual in field work among Native people in the North, although they by no means typify the experience of all social scientists. At the time, however, I was consumed by a graduate student despair: Why did some Native people distrust anthropologists so much? Why did non-Native people see it as their job to protect Native residents from anthropologists? There was already a growing field of literature on the association of anthropology with the colonial experience, and some of it came from the perspective of the "studied" (see for example Brislin and Holwill 1979; Nash and Wintrob 1972; Morauta 1979; Powell 1974; Diamond 1974; Hymes 1974; Weaver 1973). But these explanations did not entirely satisfy me. The literature on anthropologist-host relationships was (and is) still written primarily from the anthropologists' point of view. Thus was born a longer-term research project to "study the studiers," as it became known. I went back to the Mackenzie Delta, one of the most studied regions of Canada, to ask people what they thought about researchers, particularly anthropologists.

My focus came to be on participant-observation methodology and the theory underlying it. The more accounts of fieldwork I perused, the more I realized the extent of variation in how the method is actually applied (see for example Goode and Hatt 1952:102–24; Cassell 1980; Denzin 1978; Gold 1969). This is in part a matter of practice: adapting the parameters of the method to local situations and research agendas. But it also derives in some measure from the assumptions which define those parameters, and the theoretical movements which influence the assumptions. In order to answer the questions posed above, I needed to know whether there was something about the nature of participant-observation as practised in this region of the NWT which had stimulated a wary response from northerners. Was this "something" derived from the personal relationships with the anthropologist, or was it derived from the political context which influenced those relationships? And, in turn, were the assumptions about participant-observation as culled from theoretical evolution of the discipline a factor in either the relationships or their context?

The ensuing research, which involved both a study of the literature of participant-observation and fieldwork back in the Inuvik/ Mackenzie Delta region, will not be described in full here. The research does not allow me to comment on the manifestations of participant-observation elsewhere, although some patterns of endeavour show clearly in northern Canada. Nor can I "prove" a relationship between theory and practice, but by comparing how anthropologists are taught to do participant-observation with what northerners expect about how it is done, one can observe some interesting comparisons. These comparisons, I believe, can illuminate some of the episodes of fieldworker/host interaction I encountered, and the subsequent reaction to them.

The fieldwork for the case study was carried out over two trips to the Mackenzie Delta, NWT, in 1981.[2] For the most part this involved structured interviews which took unstructured directions. My "sample" of respondents included Native and non-Native residents, permanent and transient citizens, people with research and science experience, and people with none. Although I was advised that I would be more successful in getting gossip about anthropologists if I posed as a biologist or even as a civil servant, I discerned a certain value in acting out my role. Not only was I not (I hoped) perpetuating the use of false roles which was repeatedly described to me, but I learned how people reacted to me – the very oddest of anthropologists, the one who had come to study the studiers because there were no more Native people left to study.

Thus there was a reason not to inquire too closely about the personal affairs of my predecessors, but to listen closely to what people chose to tell me, and to pose my questions at a certain level of generality. I tested people's response to reciprocity and to various statements and actions about participant-observation. Episodic encounters periodically evoked a series of hypotheses for further inquiry; a remark made about how an earlier investigator was consistently fooled by people, for instance, led to further probes about how anthropologists were deceived by hosts. Finally, my northern field-work was followed by a cross-country search to find out what many of the social scientists who had worked in the region had done, and by a search of archival records for more information on research sponsorship and utilization. This additional work was of use in discovering the policy and science contexts which determined both how participant-observation was practised and local response to it.

MODELS OF PARTICIPATION

By looking at the history of research done in the Mackenzie Delta and adjacent coastal and subarctic regions, one can discern a pattern in the way social science was conducted. It should be noted that not all social scientists were anthropologists, and not all intended to employ participant-observation. But, from a local perspective, those who came were visitors who "participated" to varying degrees in local life, just as have other temporary visitors, from tourists to transient government workers. Although the mode of research was chosen for political and scientific reasons largely external to the North, northerners began to formulate reactions to the studiers in response to changing patterns as they experienced them.

At the risk of considerable generalization, some aspects of this pattern can be identified. Prior to 1950, much of the research done in the Delta and adjacent coastal areas was done by solitary explorers and ethnographers, such as Vilhajumur Stefansson, Diamond Jenness, and later Cornelius Osgood and Richard Slobodin. Anthropological training and ethos at the beginning of the century were undergoing a shift from investigation by excursion to research via intensive long-term relationships. Stefansson regarded himself as a pioneer of the latter method, and by the time of Osgood and Slobodin the Boasian influence on participant-observation was clearly felt. Oral history from both researchers and northerners supports the idea that these early researchers were regarded as occasionally eccentric but not usually threatening. There was some mutual testing, as both Stefansson and Jenness have reported (Stefansson 1913–9–10; Jenness 1959–101, 127–8), but there seems to have been an optimism from Native people that the scientists would report useful things back to their sponsors. Perhaps, as Lurie (1988:550) hypothesizes, Native residents in the North as elsewhere in North America regarded social scientists as inadvertent allies against the other Euro-Canadians who were imposing a new economic and social regime. They were friendly and sympathetic, perhaps a potential source of help and influence.

Although some civil servants did short-term surveys for the government before 1950 (see for example Moran 1923; Moore 1945), this method was used more frequently after 1950 when national attention increasingly focused on the strategic value of the North for defense and for resource development. Social research became a way to ostensibly conduct social planning exercises – or, as it often appears in retrospect, as a way to rationalize economic and social policies, such as urban relocation, through science. Research objectives provided a mix of the utilitarian and the academic. Social scientists were sent by the government, along with engineers, surveyors, biologists, and other professionals, to facilitate the transition of northern Native people from the fur trade to the modern wage economy.

The relocation of Aklavik provides an example of this. Aklavik was a flourishing fur trade community established in 1912. By 1950, when the fur trade was in decline, the town had a permanent population of about 650, with two residential schools, a day school, several churches, a sub-district administrator, a medical officer, several trading posts, and two hospitals. In addition, five government departments had regional offices located there (W. Black 1969; H. Black 1975; Wolforth 1971). By 1953, the federal government, via the Advisory Committee on Northern Development (ACND), began to evaluate Aklavik's future as a government service centre. They perceived problems with flooding, the lack of a suitable airstrip site, the lack of sewage facilities, and the lack of gravel for landfill. They began to make plans to "relocate" Aklavik to a new site which would serve as an enhanced regional service centre.

In the summer of 1953, scientists were sent to Aklavik to do studies of local sanitation problems, but their research purposes were not made known to residents. The official decision to move the community was then made and approved by Cabinet. The people of Aklavik heard it on the radio (Wolforth 1971:68–72; H. Black 1975; *Aklavik Journal* May 1956; NA, RG85, v. 302, file 1009-3-6).

The ACND immediately sent a project manager to Aklavik to act as a liaison between the community and the committee. A local advisory council of three people was also set up to represent Aklavik, but its purpose was not so much to seek advice as to channel information and persuade the people to move. There was much local resistance, in fact, over the poor resources in the new site, over compensation and relocation expenses, and over the poor planning and high costs (triple the initial estimate). Some people never did attempt the move, and others went to Inuvik for jobs in construction and then returned to Aklavik. By 1959, 285 Native people had resettled in Inuvik, half of them from Aklavik (H. Black 1975;68). This represents about 20 percent of the population from that community.

One of the greatest overall causes of resentment, however, was the tendency of the government to make decisions without any real local involvement. Part of this resentment came to focus on scientists, surveyors, and other transient personnel who came in to do studies and surveys. Two researchers who were in Aklavik and Inuvik in 1959 remarked that one particular civil servant, doing a regional economic study, had made an extremely negative impression on local people because of his clearly derogatory attitude toward them (NA, RG85, v. 1656, file 2/3-24, pt. 1). A government official in Aklavik in 1963 also noted a general cynicism about the viability of any government-initiated projects (NA, RG85, v. 1415, file 251-1-4). Several northern scientists with whom I spoke in 1981–82 noted the importance of the Aklavik relocation for the Delta region in significantly changing attitudes toward scientists, and in reinforcing the perceived links between scientists and government. Neither the local advisors nor the advice given to scientists and surveyors from a community perspective had much positive impact on relocation plans; indeed, the arrival of scientists could be seen to presage some new government scheme.[3]

The period surrounding, and subsequent to, the creation of Inuvik was the beginning of the "fluorescence" of research in the Delta and environs. The 12 July 1966 edition of the *Inuvik Drum* listed twelve researchers, most of whom were social scientists, working in town on seven projects, primarily in the social sciences. By the late 1950s and early 1960s participant-observation was a widely accepted method in anthropology, and to some extent in sociology, and many social scientists who came north practised what I term "summer participant-observation." This combined many of the rules and strategies for long-term participant-observation with the technical limitations of a short summer season. Key informant interviews and observations were cross-checked using questionnaires, censuses, administrative records, and participation in community events (see for example Boek and Boek 1960; Lotz 1962; Clairmont 1963).

Some of those student and independent academic investigators who went North were on government contracts. The major Mackenzie Delta Research Project of the late 1960s and early 1970s provided some of those contracts. Its purpose was to identify and analyse social and economic factors thought to be inhibiting Native adaptation to an industrializing economy (e.g., Mailhot 1967; Ervin

1968; Lubart 1969; Parsons 1970; Wolforth 1971; Smith 1975).[4] The Inuvik Scientific Resource Centre (the "Research Lab") opened in 1964, designed as a logistical and support facility for northern science. Administered by both Northern Affairs and the Advisory Committee on Northern Development, the lab served as a funnel for researchers going to all parts of the western subarctic and Beaufort Sea region, and many scientists used it as a home base for local research.

Residents responded in different ways to this "invasion." Wariness increased, and apparently many social scientists were thought to be working for the Research Lab. Thus the association of social research with the government was increasingly made. In 1981 some residents recalled some of the research during this period as having been "bar" investigation, as researchers sought and informally interviewed Native people through the hotels – thereby opening themselves to the accusation that they were bribing and exploiting informants. Although a check of researchers during the 1960s and 1970s shows that some were sociologists, geographers, or psychologists, the designation "anthropologist" is applied broadly in retrospect.

In 1981 Native people criticized short summer visits, lack of cultural knowledge and preparation, and failed intimacy. A very few anthropologists, however, did stay longer than a summer. They did "classic" participant-observation, and were remembered fondly for extended stays in the bush and for their willingness to learn the language and bend to the culture.[5] Comments about these individuals inevitably led to discussions about how research should ideally be conducted, a topic to which I will return below.

This period of "fluorescence," from the late 1950s through the 1970s, was also a period in which non-Native reaction to research was shaped. The types of remarks I encountered in 1979 on my first trip North were reinforced in 1981 when I discussed social science with non-Native residents. I received both direct and indirect reports from non-Native northerners about the harm anthropologists had done to Native people, and occasional heartfelt counsel about how to "treat" Native people. Civil servants made limited use of social science, arguing that the research was "soft" and produced little that could not be better understood through their own experience. Non-Native response goes beyond a statement of science credibility, however, to a protectionist stance toward Native people and toward what is understood about Native culture. While this cannot be fully explored here, several researchers commented on the instructions they received from non-Native administrators in the North during this period: not to get too socially involved with Native informants, not to attempt to "go Native," and not to turn attention on non-Native transient government workers. There was an apparent fear of having criticism turned on Native development policy, but also an expression of the researchers' own role as "developers" and teachers of Native northerners. Since fears of anthropologists were often expressed in very public forums, including the media, the influence of these pronouncements across the North in creating images of anthropologists must be considered. An episode from 1961 illustrates these points.[6]

A young student researcher went to one of the Delta communities in the summer of 1961 to do a study of social organization and adaptation. This was part of a multi-community comparative study being run out of the University of Toronto and sponsored by the Department of Northern Affairs and National Resources (DNANR). A correspondence file regarding that study reveals that the researcher began by making key contacts in the community and establishing himself as a "student" looking at social change. He also began to attend social events, including drinking parties. After he held such a gathering in his own cabin, the local non-Indian population began to protest, claiming that the young man was corrupting the local people, and the researcher was charged by the RCMP with supplying liquor to minors. Eventually letters were also written by non-Native residents to the government, prompting further concern.

The researcher, supported by his academic sponsor, responded to government inquiries by saying that he felt he was being "set up" by local non-Natives, and that he had the support of the local people, including the chief of the band. The researcher was nonetheless advised by his academic sponsors to pay the proposed fine and smooth things over with the non-Native sector, including administrators, clergy, and the RCMP. This did indeed occur, to some extent, but the researcher asserted that it was necessary to continue to drink with the people to get data from them, although he also paid for time with a key informant. His academic sponsor supported these techniques as part of basic participant-observation methodology. Government sponsors also suggested that the researcher had become a pawn in local power games, but felt that the negative experience would create problems for any future investigations. The young researcher's report was never published (NA, RG85, v. 1656, file NR2/3-3, pt. 1 and 2).

In this instance the non-Native residents took active steps to discredit the anthropologist, calling attention to their role as teachers and protectors ("advocates") for Native people. The researcher as advocate then becomes a direct threat to them. In the period after the "fluorescence" of research described above, the amount of social science being conducted in the area decreased (by the late 1970s the Research Lab was only rarely being used to support social scientists), but the involvement of social scientists like Hugh Brody and Peter Usher as "advocates" for Native people in public controversy increased, particularly with the advent of environmental and other community hearings. The number of hearings had multiplied in the years after the Mackenzie Valley Pipeline Inquiry (the Berger Inquiry) of 1975–76, and by 1981 many northern residents had come to regard them as a form of intrusive investigation. "Key informants" attended as spokespeople for the views of the community, and both Native and non-Native residents complained that once again outsiders were coming in to get quick opinions for exercises that were largely based outside the North. Once again the investigators were walking away with a false sense of truth and insight, and once again no one was listening.

INTIMATE POLITICS

The recurrent theme of my discussions with both Native and non-Native northerners was one of betrayal. One cloudy early winter afternoon in Inuvik, anxious to make myself visible and perhaps meet some people who might answer questions for me, I attended a fundraiser being held by one of the Native organizations. Bingo and other games were played, and there was a cash bar for beer drinkers. Soon after my arrival a Metis man began to tell me stories of his life, and to introduce me to others present. Some jokes were made about my being one of the "anthropologists who return each summer like the geese." During the course of the afternoon I met an Indian man from a small community near Inuvik. At first he thought I was a nurse, but when I told him what I was doing, his response changed. He introduced me to his nephew, and more jokes were made about my work. The man then asked me if I thought he was prehistoric, and I made a joking response, hoping to keep the conversation light. He responded vehemently, calling me a phony who dared to come North and tell him who he is. People from the outside with a little education should not, he suggested, think they know more than the people who live there.

I left the room, stunned, to stand outside. A non-Native resident who had witnessed the encounter soon joined me, and assured me that, essentially, I need not feel guilty. In balance, non-Native people had "paid their dues," and provided so much help to Native people, he suggested, that they "couldn't get along without us." This kind of paternalism was a striking finale to the encounter, and went a long way to convince me that there was substantial truth to what the northern man had said.

This was the most emotional response I encountered; most people were tolerant and kindly, if they agreed to speak with me. I found that northern Native people would more likely avoid than confront someone to whom they did not want to talk. When a conversation or interview took place, the respondent might be guarded but the relationship would appear well intentioned. A degree of friendship and intimacy was desired by both sides and sometimes achieved. Other researchers I interviewed reported the same range of experiences: a few conflicts amidst overall co-operation and some good friendships.

Nonetheless, a theme recurred in my own fieldwork, and in that of others who had recently been North, often in quietly spoken comments but also in openly political statements: "We feel that our intimacy has been betrayed, that information given in trust has been taken out of context and used by outsiders for their own purposes, not ours." According to this view, anthropologists, generically, could not be trusted. If the link were not being made between particular acts of anthropologists and their outcomes, it was being made with government "spies," with tourists, and with authors of popular books who were cited as having betrayed friendships to write damaging items about northern people. The image of the anthropologist, seemingly a product of the intensity of social science in the post-war period, had by 1981 divorced itself from private relationships with individual social scientists and had taken on a purpose of its own. Why had the image become autonomous? I increasingly realized that one must look in some depth at the reasons for the sense of betrayal.

SEARCHING

The search for the reasons for the sense of betrayal, and the dichotomy of response, led in several directions. Although people were not able to pinpoint examples of anthropological betrayal, they did cite fear of government sponsorship as a reason for distrust: "It's not you we dislike, it's the government. People think of the government when they talk about anthropologists." Further interviews and archival work helped recreate the context of sponsorship and utilization of research by the government in the North in general, and in the 1950s and 1960s in particular.

To generalize, both archival documentation and interviews with civil servants and social scientists who had worked in that era supported a conclusion that social science had had little overall impact in shaping social and economic policy from Northern Affairs or other government departments responsible for the North. At the same time, little feedback had ever been provided to northern residents, so the link was uncertain, as noted in the above example of the Aklavik relocation. Few northerners I interviewed, apart from civil servants, had read studies about their communities, or knew where to get them. Rarely had social scientists or bureaucrats returned to the community to explain results.

Although this is a very cursory presentation of an enormous amount of data, this point is particularly relevant here. Clearly the political context had an effect on images, and the control of data sponsorship and utilization by government, academics, and other outsiders was understood to varying degrees by all northerners. The more that Native and non-Native residents came to experience and understand the link between science and government, the more they realized that the studies were rarely utilized in any effective manner. Rather, as was observed in the Aklavik incident, the appearance of social scientists and other types of investigators was merely the harbinger of some policy thinking elsewhere. Most residents had little or no control over the policy context of science, and the only influence they did have was on the nature of participation in research itself. The image of the anthropologist seemed to be a political critique of the way in which "participation" did (or did not) happen.

Insofar as a difference is perceived between the intimate student/teacher relationship valued in the North and the public ideology of anthropology as conveyed in images, is the betrayal to be found in the nature of participant-observation practice itself? The theoretical literature about participant-observation as a method provided some insights to me in 1981, and these have been supported since by a burgeoning literature on ethnographic practice and the relationship of practice to text construction.

Once again, then, a substantial body of literature is reduced here to some pertinent generalities.[7] The development of a model of participant-observation in anthropology can be traced back to any number of reference points: the thoughtful but ethnocentric observations of other cultures by the Greeks and the Arabic nations, the collections of missionary writings, the first European fieldwork guides of the early nineteenth century, or the popular endorsement of participation by Bronislaw Malinowski. Like tourism, participant-observation is a particularly western phenomenon, and as it "came into its own" from the 1920s to the 1970s in English and American variants, it was most often practised in colonized areas undergoing change. Initially taught by "experience," some general rules of practice began to emerge as anthropologists finally began to write (covertly at first) about how they actually performed fieldwork. At the most fundamental level, these rules specify that:

- One must spend substantial amounts of time in the field, at least one to two years.
- One must establish rapport.
- One must gain acceptance from key community members.
- One should learn the language spoken by one's teachers.
- One must immerse oneself to the greatest extent practicable in the daily lives of the people, to learn the rules of behaviour that make the lifestyle possible for group members.
- One should employ reciprocity as locally defined.
- One should play one or more roles viable in the society.
- One should also maintain objectivity from the situation and people being investigated.

As noted at the beginning of the paper, there is enormous variation, much of it locally exacted, in how these rules are put into practice. The rules are there to assist ultimately in the learning and comprehension of culture, and they are backed by assumptions about the "natural context" of culture and how it can be translated into objective knowledge subjectively understood. The difference between the anthropologist and the tourist is that the tourist never attempts to become like an insider, and filters what he or she sees only through his or her own culture. The anthropologist does try to straddle the line between insider and outsider, and to understand culture in such a way that she or he can write an "objective" account about the insider's knowledge. The method of participant-observation is shored by a series of assumptions about science and culture taken from both positivist and humanist theoretical orientations. The potential contradictions in what the ethnographer can achieve in both practice and textual translation have been explored extensively in recent literature (see for example Marcus and Fisher 1986; Clifford and Marcus 1986; Geertz 1988; Van Maanen 1988; Atkinson 1990).

The northern Native people whom I interviewed in 1981 communicated some of their expectations to me about the learning of culture. As noted above, these were often communicated in relation to the praise of an adept fieldworker, but were balanced by generalized criticism of method. As my personal knowledge of the depths of northern Athapaskan and Inuvialuit culture is limited, I can only surmise the extent to which these expectations derive from indigenous formulation of learning and from experience with researchers and other visitors. Certainly the people who spoke to me emphasized that there was never any aboriginal version of the "anthropologist," but there were individuals who were better able than others to retain, analyse, and communicate "truthful" versions of cultural knowledge. Therefore the people with whom I had contact expected that anthropologists should learn in similar ways.

As does the academic version of participant-observation, northern people expressed concern that extended stays are vital. Daily participation in routine is necessary, particularly experience with bush life. Language learning, rapport, and acceptance are important, as is the ability to learn "like a child," without the impediments of adult expectations, and with the patience to observe and imitate. Talking to learned and reliable teachers is vital. One of the most frequent questions asked of me in fieldwork concerned those with whom I had spoken. Only by learning in acceptable ways can one understand the critical values by which to assess accuracy. One man who had witnessed encounters with anthropologists in the small community in which he had been raised said, in paraphrase, "I could look at any of the studies and tell who told the anthropologist what. Often we told them 'bull' in order to see if they wrote it down."

Parallels between anthropologists and tourists were remarked upon, since both were thought to come in the summer, look around, and leave. But tourists were not the ones with the bad images; they were not the ones who attempted some level of understanding and intimacy during their visit, and they were not the ones who wrote about it. Expectations about anthropologists as experts were higher. Again, some social scientists were esteemed as learned and worthy individuals on a personal level. In general, the Native residents tended to evaluate people by their behaviour and character, not training, but they expected people to use training well.[8] If one looks at the last "rule" of participant-observation above, that the researcher maintain an objective stance, one sees the largest departure between Native and anthropological versions of learning. People rejected anyone who was not "being him- or herself" or who was adopting the mantle of a role which hid true motives. Expertise should not be a role to be played, but a culled wisdom born of experience and learning and appropriately used. The tourist was not playing a false role, but many anthropologists (and social scientists under the same label) were thought to be doing so.[9]

The betrayal comes, then, when expertise is falsely used, in local estimation, and the false use is linked to the political factors of outside control. This accusation thus came from political, not personal experience; political factors were in some measure responsible for "betrayed" expectations of expertise and intimacy. The dichotomy between private relationships and public ideology, between intimacy and image, is enhanced by this imposition.

CONTEXT AND CONTROL

The problem of "betrayal" of information given to investigators has of course been endemic to anthropology since its beginning, and in itself is not "news." Yet it had obviously become a problem in this region and has hampered the productive continuation of social science. On the most fundamental level the problem as manifested here and elsewhere appears to be one of control over cultural imaging and the political use of these images. The image of the anthropologist could represent almost any social scientist, but not any particular one. It is an image of an individual who:

1 may not give an accurate portrayal of data provided to him or her; and who
2 may not understand or practice "participation" as competent learning of culture, given local expectations;
3 fails in this because he or she is using his or her expertise falsely, playing an "objective" role;
4 may use expertise falsely because of external political influences, such as transience, on the sponsorship, conduct, and use of science.

Many of these factors are beyond the control of northerners, particularly the failure to make effective use of results for northern goals and objectives.

The value of cultural knowledge construed as *information* is determined not only by its use and perpetuation internally, but in this instance (when the information goes to the investigator) by the use of it outside the local community. Once it goes on the "market" of textual analysis, followed by print communication and dissemination, the originators lose further control over it. To my northern teachers, these internal and external processes were linked. External factors prevent effective participation and effective representation of culture and identity in "anthropological" works. The rule of "objectivity" and insider/outsider duality in participant-observation, conditioned by theoretical assumptions from the discipline, is not only seen as academically outside the control of hosts and teachers, but as influenced by a politicized milieu in which roles impose false expectations.

The remedy to the problem of betrayal is gradually under way. The advocacy role of social scientists in northern environmental and comprehensive claims issues has been noted, and represents a marked step toward exploring the parameters of role by all parties involved in the research.[10] Communities are also exerting their lawful power to grant or deny permissions to researchers. These steps in themselves are not the solution, since these decisions need to be taken seriously as a result of informed discussion from all parties. The link between production and use (textual and political) of data must be made, and for this to happen communities need to be involved in the research at all stages, from planning to feedback and utilization. Examples of this are appearing not only in the North but across North America, as researchers and their hosts experiment with new models of participation (see for example Guyette 1982; Lockhart and McCaskill 1986; Hedley 1986; St Denis 1989; Cruikshank this volume). Projects like the Dene Gondie study were designed to test new collaborative relationships (see Rees 1986).

Native people are demanding accountability in research, and this means, for many of them, that the criteria of validity of cultural knowledge be mutually acceptable to hosts and investigators. Although there is caution within the professional social science community about the prejudicial effects of this on the rule of "objectivity," accountability need not preclude a process by which the criteria of cultural interpretation can be jointly derived. Perhaps this means a return to the basic model of participation espoused by both anthropologists and many of their northern teachers (including a reduced reliance on the "quick" road to truth through short-term consultations and hearings).

The primary power of the anthropologist properly lies in the production of data. The use of these data in constructive ways in public policy is critical, my northern teachers told me, but the use should not effectively be separated from the production of adequate data. The accountability of good science should be rooted in cultural learning, which means that hosts should have a continuing part in the control of both production and use.

The value of information is enhanced by recreating the link between production and use with the help of our teachers, with renewed emphasis on how to best bring indigenous knowledge into the public realm. As Criukshank (this volume) reminds us, by paying attention to Native interpretations of culture and cultural learning, we return to the fundamental purpose of anthropological fieldwork. By participating in the interpreting process through collaboration and the regulation of method, we as anthropologists can recreate our own image as we assist our teachers in creating and disseminating their own cultural images.

NOTES

1 The term "host" is used here to refer to those people who allow researchers to go among them to study and to learn. They are the "informants" of anthropology, the teachers of anthropologists. The use of a generic term is not meant to imply disrespect for the complexity of relationship between the researcher and those who are being researched.

2 Funding for the research was provided by the President's Committee on Northern Studies, McMaster University. The summary of research results which follows was generalized from data obtained over five months from observation and through fifty-five interviews with Delta residents and twenty-five interviews with social scientists and civil servants who had worked in the North.

3 This point was reinforced through discussions with R.G. Williamson, Graham Rowley, A.J. Kerr, and Peter Usher.

4 Other researchers included Don Bissett, doing an Area Economic Survey; geographer Peter Usher, doing research on Banks Island; anthropologists John and Irma Honigmann, studying urban adaptation in Inuvik; and sociologist Charles Hobart, researching health and education in Inuvik.

5 S. Krech (1974), D. Smith (1975), the Honigmanns (1970), and Slobodin (1966) were among those who used aspects of the classic, long-term approach to participant-observation in Delta communities.

6 The details are provided here only in sketchy form to provide some protection for the identity of those involved. The incidents are, however, archivally documented and on public record at the National Archives.

7 An extensive portion of my thesis (Brizinski 1989) is devoted to the exploration of theoretical perspectives in relation to participant-observation, and the reader should consult this, the bibliography below, and other recent treatments of ethnographic method for more extensive treatment of this (for example, Atkinson 1990 for sociology; Agar 1980 and Marcus and Fischer 1986 in anthropology). I particularly focused on the concepts of objectivity, relativity, and culture as they cross positivist and interpretive bodies of theory and thence influence the creation of "ethnography."

8 The evaluation of competence through individual behaviour and

character rather than through one's job, role, or formal education is a pattern which appeared in the responses from the Native northerners to whom I spoke. Although I could find little published analysis which commented on this pattern in this type of context for any of the northern indigenous cultures, it may be linked to the individualism and self-reliance noted for northern Athapaskans and, to some degree, for Inuit. Each person is evaluated on personal rather than universal criteria. See Rushforth (1988) and Scollon and Scollon (1979:177–208) for summaries of the literature on this point. This characteristic may also be related to criteria for selection of leadership. Brody (1981) describes extensively the development of hunting competence and knowledge among Beaver Indians, and Nelson (1973) comments upon it to some extent among the Kutchin of Alaska. Brody (1975) also comments on Inuit reaction to white outsiders.

9 Although no researchers claimed to have deliberately deceived their hosts, there was a feeling among northerners that researchers used information given in trust for personal or political gain, thus betraying the original purpose. There was also, researchers reported, some confusion in the early years about what an anthropologist was, so that it was more productive to be a "teacher" or even a "student," more familiar roles. For those who are interested, there is a broad spectrum of literature in anthropology and sociology on the dimensions of research roles, including the advisability of covert role-playing as access to information. (See for example McCall and Simmons 1969; Wax 1971; Agar 1980; Georges and Jones 1980; Emerson 1983; Kimmel 1988).

10 The use of advocacy roles in anthropology is controversial. While it is taken as a fundamental ethical tenet that anthropological research must not do harm to the community of study, there are dangers of the anthropologist's becoming a "protector" in the same way that northern administrators once were, and of having to make critical decisions between science results and the use of scientific information in advocacy forums. The recent controversies over British Columbia Chief Justice Allan McEachern's comments about the use of anthropological evidence in the Gitskan Wet'sewet'en case illuminate this. Ideally, concerned involvement of the community in all phases of a study could help to alleviate contradictions between science and its use, but this remains to be fully tested and accredited by all parties.

REFERENCES

Agar, Michael. 1980. *The Professional Stranger: An Informal Introduction to Ethnography*. New York: Academic Press.

Aklavik Journal. 1956. May.

Atkinson, Paul. 1990. *The Ethnographic Imagination: Textual Constructions of Reality*. London: Routledge.

Berger, Thomas. 1977. *Northern Frontier, Northern Homeland: The Report of the Mackenzie Valley Pipeline Inquiry*. 2 vols. Ottawa: Supply and Services Canada.

Bissett, Don. 1967. *The Lower Mackenzie Region: An Area Economic Survey*. Ottawa: Economic Staff Group, Department of Indian Affairs and Northern Development (DIAND).

Black, Heather. 1975. *Aklavik, NWT: A Geographic Study of the Settlement's Viability*. Master's thesis, University of Alberta.

Black, W.A. 1959. *A Suggested Program of Economic Rehabilitation in the Mackenzie Delta Area*. Ottawa: Department of Mines and Technical Surveys.

Boek, W.E., and J. Boek. 1960. "A Report on Fieldwork in Aklavik and Inuvik, NWT." Ottawa: DIAND.

Brislin, Richard W., and F. Holwill. 1979. "Indigenous Views of the Writings of Behavioural Social Scientists: Toward Increased Cross-Cultural Understanding." In *Bonds without Bondage: Explorations in Trans-Cultural Interactions*, ed. A. Krishna, Honolulu: University of Hawaii East-West Center.

Brizinski, Peggy Martin. 1989. *Participation as Social Science Method and Theory: Indigenous Response in the Mackenzie Delta*. Ph.D. diss., McMaster University.

Brody, Hugh. 1975. *The People's Land*. New York: Penguin Books.

– 1981. *Maps and Dreams*. New York: Penguin Books.

Cassell, Joan. 1980. "Ethical Principles for Conducting Fieldwork." *American Anthropologist* 82 (1): 28–41.

Clairmont, D.H. 1963. *Deviance among Indians and Eskimos in Aklavik, NWT*, 63–9. Ottawa: Northern Co-ordination and Research Centre, DIAND.

Clifford, James, and G.E. Marcus, eds. 1986. *Writing Culture: The Poetics and Politics of Ethnography*. Berkeley: University of California Press.

Deloria, Vine, Jr. 1969. *Custer Died for Your Sins*. New York: Macmillan.

Denzin, Norman. 1978. *The Research Act: A Theoretical Introduction to Sociological Methods*. 2d ed. New York: McGraw-Hill.

Diamond, Stanley. 1974. *In Search of the Primitive*. New Brunswick, NJ: Transaction Books.

Emerson, Robert M. 1983. "Introduction." In *Contemporary Field Research: A Collection of Readings*, ed. R.M. Emerson, 1–16. Boston: Little, Brown.

Ervin, A.M. 1968. *New Northern Townsmen in Inuvik*. Mackenzie Delta Research Project no. 5. Ottawa: DIAND.

Fried, Jacob. 1963. "White-Dominant Settlements in the Canadian Northwest Territories." *Anthropologica* 5 (1): 57–63.

Geertz, Clifford. 1988. *Works and Lives: The Anthropologist as Author*. Cambridge: Polity Press.

Georges, Robert, and M.O. Jones. 1980. *People Studying People: The Human Element in Fieldwork*. Berkeley: University of California Press.

Gold, Raymond L. 1969. "Roles in Sociological Field Observations." In *Issues in Participant-Observation: A Text and Reader*, eds. G. McCall and J. Simmons, 30–8. Reading, MA: Addison-Wesley.

Goode, William, and P.K. Hatt. 1952. *Methods in Social Research*. New York: McGraw-Hill.

Guyette, S. 1982. *Community-Based Research*. Los Angeles: University of California American Indian Studies Center.

Hedley, M.J. 1986. "Community-Based Research: The Dilemma of Contract." *The Canadian Journal of Native Studies* 6(2): 91–103.

Honigmann, John, and I. Honigmann. 1970. *Arctic Townsmen*. Ottawa: Canadian Research Centre for Anthropology.

Hymes, Dell, ed. 1974. *Reinventing Anthropology*. New York: Random House Vintage Books.

Inuvik Drum. July 12, 1966.

Jenness, Diamond. 1959. *The People of the Twilight*. Chicago: University of Chicago Press.

Kimmel, Allan J. 1988. *Ethics and Values in Applied Social Research*. Applied Social Research Methods Series, no. 12. Newbury Park, CA: Sage.

Krech, Shepard, III. 1974. *Changing Trapping Patterns in Fort McPherson, NWT*. Ph.D. diss., Harvard University.

Lockhart, Alexander, and D. McCaskill. 1986. "Toward an Integrated, Community-Based Partnership Model of Native Development and Training: a Case Study in Process." *The Canadian Journal of Native Studies* 6(2): 159–72.

Lotz, J.R. 1962. *Inuvik, NWT*. Ottawa: DIAND.

Lubart, J.M. 1969. *Psychodynamic Problems of Adaptation in Mackenzie Delta Eskimos*. Mackenzie Delta Research Project no. 7. Ottawa: DIAND.

Lurie, Nancy O. 1988. "Relations between Indians and Anthropologists." In *History of Indian-White Relations*, ed. W. Washburn, 548–56. Handbook of North American Indians 5. Washington, DC: Smithsonian Institution.

Mailhot, Jose. 1967. *Inuvik Community Structure – Summer 1965*. Mackenzie Delta Research Project no. 4. Ottawa: DIAND.

McCall, George, and J. Simmons. 1969. "The Nature of Participant-Observation, Field Relations, etc." in *Issues in Participant-Observation*, ed. G. McCall and J. Simmons, 1–4. Reading, MA: Addison-Wesley.

Marcus, G.E., and D. Cushman. 1982. "Ethnographies as Texts." *Annual Review of Anthropology* 11:25–69.

– and M. Fischer. 1986. *Anthropology as Cultural Critique: An Experimental Moment in the Human Sciences*. Chicago: University of Chicago Press.

Moore, Andrew. 1945. "Survey of Education in the Mackenzie District." *The Canadian Journal of Economics and Political Science* 11:61–82.

Moran, J.R. 1923. *Local Conditions in the Mackenzie District*. Ottawa: NWT and Yukon Branch, Department of the Interior.

Morauta, Louise. 1979. "Indigenous Anthropology in Papua New Guinea." *Current Anthropology* 20(3): 561–76.

Nash, Dennison, and R. Wintrob. 1972. "The Emergence of Self-Consciousness in Anthropology." *Current Anthropology* 13(5): 527–42.

National Archives of Canada. RG85, v. 302, file 1009-3-6; v. 1415, file 251-1-4; v. 1656, file 2/3-24, pt. 1, file 2/3-3 pt. 1, 2.

Nelson, Richard K. 1973. *Hunters of the Northern Forest*. Chicago: University of Chicago Press.

Parsons, George. 1970. *Arctic Suburbs: A Look at the North's Newcomers*. Mackenzie Delta Research Project no. 8. Ottawa: DIAND.

Powell, J.P. 1974. "Attitudes of Melanesian Students to Fieldwork and Research in the Social Sciences." *Mankind* 9: 218–24.

Rees, William. 1986. "The Genesis and Structure of the 'Dene Gondie' Study: What the People Say about the Norman Wells Project." *The Canadian Journal of Native Studies* 6(1):141–57.

Rushforth, Scott. 1988. "Autonomy and Community among the Bear Lake Athapaskans." In *Native North American Interaction Patterns*, eds. R. Darnell and M.K. Foster, 112–42. Ottawa: Canadian Museum of Civilization.

St Denis, Verna. 1989. *A Process of Community-Based Participatory Research: A Case Study*. Master's thesis, University of Alaska.

Scollon, Ronald, and S. Scollon. 1979. *Linguistic Convergence: An Ethnography of Speaking at Fort Chipewyan, Alberta*. New York: Academic Press.

Slobodin, Richard. 1966. *Metis of the Mackenzie District*. Ottawa: Canadian Research Centre for Anthropology.

Smith, Derek. 1975. *Natives and Outsiders: Pluralism in the Mackenzie River Delta, NWT*. Mackenzie Delta Research Project 12. Ottawa: DIAND.

Spradley, James P. 1980. *Participant-Observation*. New York: Holt, Rinehart, and Winston.

Stefansson, Vilhjamur. 1913. *My Life with the Eskimo*. New York: Collier Books.

Sykes, Richard E. 1978. "Toward a Theory of Observer Effect in Systematic Field Observation." *Human Organization* 37(2):148–56.

Van Maanen, John. 1988. *Tales of the Field: On Writing Ethnography*. Chicago: University of Chicago Press.

Wax, Rosalie. 1971. *Doing Fieldwork: Warnings and Advice*. Chicago: University of Chicago Press.

Weaver, Thomas, ed. 1973. *To See Ourselves*. Glenview, IL: Scott, Foresman.

Wolforth, John. 1971. *The Evolution and Economy of the Delta Community*. Mackenzie Delta Research Project 11. Ottawa: DIAND.

7 Some Native Perspectives on Anthropology and Public Policy

RON IGNACE, GEORGE SPECK,
and RENEE TAYLOR
(As interviewed by Noel Dyck)

Note: In order to take into account some Native perspectives on the issues dealt with in this volume, Noel Dyck sought interviews with three members of Indian bands in British Columbia – Ron Ignace, George Speck, and Renee Taylor – who have encountered anthropology both through university training and by having worked with anthropologists at the community level. The arrangement agreed upon was that the interviews would be tape recorded, transcribed, and then jointly edited.

Since it was not possible for all four of us to meet at the same time, two separate interviews were held a couple of weeks apart in March 1989, one with Ron Ignace, the other with George Speck and Renee Taylor. Edited versions of the transcript of interviews are presented here.

AN INTERVIEW WITH RON IGNACE

Dyck: What do people at the reserve level feel about the activities of anthropologists? What are the issues that we should be concerning ourselves with? How does someone like yourself, who knows both anthropology and the reserve perspective, see anthropology developing?

Ignace: I guess, looking at the academic anthropologist or ethnographer, we've had a lot of difficulty with those types of people because they have an attitude that they define their work and insist that they should have the freedom to do whatever they feel academic individuals should do – that no one should curtail their activities. We have no way of monitoring the accuracy of the information that they collect; they may get a narrow perspective of a very complex situation in Native communities. They take that narrow perspective, and it's put on the world's stage; they may sell it to the provincial government and become experts for the provincial government in land claims struggles against Native peoples. Or they may sell it to various corporations, like the Canadian National Railway, and use that against us. Even the federal government hires anthropologists to define Native policies. That's happened historically. That kind of anthropology and ethnography has created problems for us that we've had to confront and deal with.

On the other hand, you have those applied anthropologists or ethnographers that come to the communities. The working relationship and perception of them has to be nurtured and developed because of the experiences that we've had with these other people. But once they've made a breakthrough and demonstrated their sincerity and their willingness to recognize the direction of their work as coming under Native leadership, then Native people welcome them. They welcome them because they see them as an important component of being able to interpret what's in the communities that can be used to defend ourselves against this other kind of anthropology. They become experts and we need them because they know the court system or the bureaucracy or whatever it is that we have to confront in order to make our points known.

It assists us because we can use that to give what we're saying credence through their becoming expert witnesses on our behalf who will legitimize what we're saying. The Gitksan-Wet'suwet'en have had that experience in their court case in which their elders got up and gave a history. Because it was not a written history, the courts initially refused to acknowledge it as legitimate history. You have that dilemma.

Then there are those "traditionalist" Native people who have lost their roots and lost contact with their elder generations and have come back and developed a quasi-understanding of themselves. They've become alienated from their history, their culture, their language, and have come back and been reborn as Native people. They call themselves the "traditionalists." They take a very puritanical, hard-line approach. They say that anthropologists and white people, period, should stay out of our lives and that we shouldn't have any dealings with them. A lot of the elders say that they understand these people and say, "They're lost right now, but they'll find their way home one day and they'll understand."

Dyck: When you look at the sort of work that's being done by anthropologists in these different settings, how accurate a picture of
the real life of Native communities today, in terms of the economic
and the political and the administrative situation of those communities, is given by these different anthropological works?
Ignace: In a general sense, the picture that is presented is a very
superficial one from what I can understand and see, because these
types of anthropologists replicate other anthropologists' work and
draw conclusions from it. In doing that, they replicate the shortcomings of others and maybe even compound these. We found this
to be the case in a lot of areas we've looked into in terms of the
work of anthropologists.

You take an ethnographer like James Teit in the Shuswap
country. I guess he was very radical in his approach in that he
married into the Indian community and lived among the people,
but even then, he had his own shortcomings, his own twists of
understanding of the Shuswap that we're finding that we have to
correct ourselves. Nonetheless, his work was very influential in
preserving a lot of cultural information that the younger generation
have lost contact with. What we're trying to do now is look at his
works and say to the elders, "How accurate a picture is this?" We're
trying to reassess that and determine the accuracy of that kind of
information. Hopefully we can revive our culture in that fashion.
Dyck: What do you think are the strengths and weaknesses of those
anthropological writings with respect to the everyday current
situation in Native communities? Let me explain why I ask that. It
seems to me that a lot of anthropological writing overlooks the way
in which governments have entered into people's lives. Anthropological writing sometimes tends to be a bit like the photographs of
E.S. Curtis who, when he went around in the early part of the
century to photograph Native people, tried to remove any reference
to the fact that it was the early twentieth century rather than some
other time. So he moved people away from telephone poles and
anything that would show that these people also lived in the twentieth century.
Ignace: Yes. Not only anthropologists behave in that way, but also
museums. They have similar views that really upset me. They don't
seem to understand that we still exist as a people, that we adapt and
change and we have that right to adapt and change, while still
maintaining some of our principles that were tried and true over
the years. Particularly principles that are necessary for survival as a
people. A lot of anthropological work reads as though we're dead
wood that anthropologists looked at and our culture is long gone

and past. As though it no longer exists today. That's a very sad thing when I see that.

When I walk into a museum, I get the same message. Using that as an analogy, you see a little aspect of Shuswap culture here and a little bit of it over there, but you never get the social dynamism of the culture and how that culture has grown and changed and adapted over the years.

One other obsession about academic anthropologists – I wish I could find a clearer designation for them – is to prove that indigenous people have come from somewhere else and are descendants of some other people. A lot of Native people find this very irritating because when we look back at our stories and our philosophy and our world view, we know that we are the products of the soil, descendants of this country, and a people of this land. We haven't come from anywhere else. I find that, because of this ever-growing attempt to try and prove that we've come from somewhere else, over some land bridge or whatever the case may be, that unfortunately, until recently, little effort has been made to focus on what actually happened *here*. How did the people evolve here on this continent?

The way I look at it, in 1810 we used bones to make our fishing spears. In 1989, we use iron to make spears. But the principles involved in spearing salmon are still the same. And the whole social process of distributing salmon ... the same principles are still there; we are still applying the same principles. Just because we may have once used bone, and today we're using metal, doesn't necessarily mean we're not living by our traditional principles. Because we live as a colonized people within the country of Canada, originally colonized by Great Britain and now by Canada, our rights are denied. You have two cultures. There is the open western culture that Native people live by, but there's also an underground Native culture that is not spoken about and not displayed. It's like an underground movement. Unless you get out and get to know the Indian people, you don't see that. I think this is where a lot of academic anthropologists miss the boat. They see only the surface lifestyles of a people and they don't get to understand the deeper ways and means of a people's techniques of survival under trying conditions.

Dyck: What are the things that anthropologists can do that would be of use both to Indian communities and to Canadian society in general?

Ignace: In this day and age, we have to realize that because of the whole history of colonization that we've had to live under – I am speaking of us as Shuswaps in particular – we've gone through a lot of trying times. It's estimated that between 1811, when we saw the first white man (other than Simon Fraser on the Fraser River) in the Williams Lake area, and the 1870s, we lost two thirds of our population. Then again, we lost some more population in the early 1900s and we were hit again in 1919 when we lost a lot of people. As a matter of fact, my community was once down to something like sixty-two people. We're back up to 300 now.

What that means is that you lose a lot of your elders who have a lot of knowledge about what it is to be a Shuswap person. We have suffered the residential school system where our young people were taken away and alienated from the few remaining elders. We're talking about a system of education that lasted until the 1960s. The children were separated from the elders, were divided up and didn't have the opportunity to learn from our elders what it is to be Shuswap, to learn the language from our elders, to understand our cultural history, our political history, our history of struggle. If you look at our population statistics, the majority of our population is under the age of twenty-five, maybe with a handful of elders left. This is representative of all the communities in the Shuswap country.

There is a sense of urgency. There are not enough elders to be able to teach the younger generation, who are impatient to learn, about what it is to be Shuswap. But there are those of us who are concerned, basically because we are concerned for the ongoing defence of our rights. We need that information to defend ourselves.

I use the analogy that today we are like a cup that's broken. Anthropologists who are responsible to the communities and to Native leadership can assist us in putting that cup together by going around and interviewing the elders and being able to do it systematically and scientifically, putting that cup together for us – the younger generation – who don't always have the opportunity or the skills to learn from our elders because we've been alienated. Anthropologists can do that for us. In that sense, the elders will speak openly and freely to them once they've gained the confidence of the elders, because they see that as important. They don't want the knowledge that they have to be lost, and they feel confident in this person, who is like themselves. I think the elders feel they are on the same level as a person with a master's degree or doctorate degree, because they, too, are masters and doctors in their own right in terms of botany or zoology or understanding the salmon, forestry, game, and traditional land use management.

I view the elders as having that level of expertise, and all they are doing is using the anthropologist as a collecting vessel to put this picture together for them in a way that they couldn't otherwise do. That preserves their knowledge in a contemporary way, so that it's not lost to the grave and eternity. They say that one day "the young people are going to wake up and they will be wondering who they are, where they've come from and where they should be going. How are they going to do this when they wake up?" The only way they can do this is through the information that the individual anthropologist has taken, collected from the elders, and has preserved. This is the function that we see our Secwepemc Cultural Education Society playing in Shuswap country.

Dyck: What about for the non-Indian society? What job do you think the anthropologist should be doing there?

Ignace: That, again, is connected to and not separate from what the elders also think. They see their information as providing as true a picture as possible – through the anthropologist in whom they have faith and trust. One of the litmus tests that we present to an anthropologist or whoever wishes to come to work for us, is, "Are you prepared to forego all copyrights except for the purposes of academic publication?" If they say no, then they're turned away with no more discussion after that. This is the position that the Shuswap bands and communities have taken. If they say yes, then we go through other tests and then we determine whether, yes, this is the type of person with whom we can entrust this information. We trust them because we want a true picture of Shuswap to be presented to the world, for we want to be understood for who we are, and what our hopes and aspirations are. We hope to be recognized as a people with collective rights, with a history, a language, and a culture that are just as rich and as valuable as those of any other people. When we go forward and stand up for what we feel is an injustice that needs to be corrected, whether it is in the form of reaffirmation of our rights to our traditional territory, we want non-Indians to understand that we are not necessarily attacking them, that we are not aliens or monsters that are out to throw them back into the river or ocean. We are just looking to have our rights recognized and to have the wrongs that have been done against us rectified. We want them to know and understand who we are, that we are human beings just like anyone else, and that our real struggle is with the Crown in the form of the Canadian government, and not so much with the ordinary man on the street.

Dyck: What do you think anthropologists have to offer to other disciplines: law, sociology, history and so on?

Ignace: Basically what anthropologists have to teach other disciplines is, number one, to be able to be principled in their approach and to respect indigenous peoples for who and what they proclaim themselves to be. We proclaim ourselves to be a nation of people known as the Shuswap. I guess it would be only fair and just for anthropologists not to interpret that, or to try to play that down, but to pass that information on. And how and why we perceive ourselves that way. That we have our own laws, our own customs, our own political systems that have to be understood, recognized, and respected. That would be of importance, because lawyers are constantly saying, "You're not a nation of people. If you were, you are no longer because Confederation did away with that." As a matter of fact, we're in court arguing this very issue today. The Crown's lawyers are saying we're just a minority, we've become assimilated and we've acquiesced because we've accepted driver's licenses, that we are no longer Indians. This is pervasive in other schools of thought such as law and political science, and appears in their interpretation of indigenous ways.

Dyck: What do you think anthropologists ought to be learning from other disciplines? What should we learn to do better as anthropologists? Or, maybe, what are the things that we shouldn't be doing at all?

Ignace: One thing that anthropologists shouldn't be doing is going around imposing themselves on people. I don't know whether I can prescribe what anthropologists could be learning from other disciplines. I guess, maybe, the capacity not to look at the life of a people on a piecemeal approach, but to learn from a legal perspective, from a political perspective, from an ethnographic perspective, from the archaeological perspective. These are things they could look at so that when they come into a community, they don't come in with a narrow view pertaining only to their own field, so that they can understand the political systems, the social interactions, the demography, and the economy of Native people, so that they could develop a well-rounded perspective. If you look at these factors in isolation, there might be dynamics there that you don't understand because of influences from other areas – the political leadership within the Native community, the political economy of the Native community. These types of things could give the anthropologist a better opportunity to gain a well-rounded view of what the Native society they're looking at is all about.

Dyck: If you had your way, if you could take over the training of anthropologists at Simon Fraser and UBC and other universities, what tasks would you like to set for them, whether they were non-Native anthropologists or Native students who decided to pursue a career in anthropology?

Ignace: I would see them playing more of an assistant's role rather than a leadership role in working within Native communities or within non-Native communities. Many Native communities are losing a lot in the way of culture and anthropologists could play a very positive role in preserving what little there is and piecing it all together. I have some vague recollections of what my elders have told me. Sometimes some of those recollections I feel are just dreams that I've had. As busy as I am, I don't have the opportunity to go out and confirm the notion that I have about a particular area of Shuswap values or lifestyle. When I read what they're doing, I realize it's not a dream that I've had, but that it is a part of our way of life and it confirms for me the notion that I've had. It helps strengthen me as a leader in my community, and I feel confident in myself and what I understood because we have very few elders left. Some of them can't hear or can't speak so you can't go and talk to them. Anthropologists can help us in that way.

There are some specific ways we can suggest in which the training of anthropologists can be more effective to deal with these concerns. First, because of the nature of the work that we most urgently require, that is, working with our elders in salvaging our language and culture, it would be useful for us if more students and graduate students were trained in the fieldwork methods to undertake such tasks. Secondly, anthropology students and anthropologists need to be sensitized more to the political and cultural contexts that Native communities and organizations are living in. Finally, with the help of non-Native anthropologists who have worked in Indian communities and understand our needs and our position, we could work on training our own Native people to become anthropologists and carry on some of this work ourselves.

[Anthropologists can help us] rebuild our nations, redefine our values that have become intertwined with colonial values, decolonize our minds to have an understanding of what our Native values are. Getting back to the basics. They could play a helpful role, providing that the work they do is based on the confidence of the elders who give them this information and they freely go under the leadership and guidance of Native people.

On the outside, anthropologists could play a very valuable role in teaching non-Native people that Native people have a very valuable contribution to make to world culture and can play a valuable role on the world stage, whether it's political, cultural, or economic. I think that's an aspect of the role they could play.

Dyck: That's a very intimate relationship and I can see why you'd want to be careful about knowing who you would have playing that sort of role which involves a lot of trust from the community. I can imagine that you would want to be very careful about how that trust is extended.

Ignace: If you read the *Memorial to Sir Wilfred Laurier* [a publication of the Shuswap Nation], it lays out a political prospectus about how we related to non-Native peoples. We invited them in freely and openly as guests into our house – we view the Shuswap country and Shuswap people traditionally as living in one house, one nation, one language, one culture. We felt that when a person came into our house, we treated them very specially. This is laid out in the *Memorial*, and we shared with them our riches, whether in the form of our cultural riches or the riches that come from our land. It's stated in there that we are a wealthy people, though we are not talking wealth in terms of dollars. Non-Natives were free to come in and share what we have. You can live on half of our land base, providing that you recognize whose house you are living in and respect that relationship. We will equally respect you and freely share our wealth. To come in and live with us and develop friendships and ties, just as countries develop treaties with other nations and other countries. That's one fashion in which we would do that.

This is why we're very cautious because when we originally did that, somehow we wound up being kicked out of our house and being placed into the woodshed. We lost control over our house. Now we live in the woodshed while other people live in our house, and live well in our house.

Dyck: Is there anything else that you would like to mention?

Ignace: Anthropologists have to respect the copyright issue because that's the way we maintain control. We're trying to move into an era in which we begin to control and manage our own destiny. That's one way to do it. There are other ways, but if we can develop working relationships based along those lines, I think we can go along with it.

I know I've made this from primarily a Shuswap perspective rather than a general or theoretical discussion, but I hope it's been helpful.

AN INTERVIEW WITH GEORGE SPECK AND RENEE TAYLOR

Dyck: The practice of anthropology spans a range of activities that reaches from traditional university teaching and academic research, museum work, and public education programs to consulting, contract research, and land claims research. Some anthropologists are employed either by government or by tribal or band councils. As a way of starting, would you indicate your experience with anthropology in any of these areas?

Speck: I have an undergraduate degree in anthropology and history and I spent a couple of years as a graduate student at Simon Fraser University. I did my fieldwork and then I went fishing.

Before I started university I was on the band council and occasionally we would get letters from anthropologists who wanted to come and do studies in Alert Bay. We dealt with whether or not we were going to allow them to do that and discussed the kinds of conditions we would like to impose on them and some of the concerns we had about the things they were going to look at and how they were going to present them.

Taylor: I've known a number of anthropologists in recent years who are working specifically on land claims and developing "expertise" in giving evidence. If I had to give one general comment on my perception of anthropology, which has not essentially changed in fifteen years of some involvement with anthropology in a more informal way initially, and certainly now in a more formal way, it is that there is a real tendency on the part of anthropologists to want to encapsulate the "Indian point of view" even if the source is just from one particular Indian. This leads to an inaccurate extrapolation of what people feel about things. Literally, on at least five occasions, I have had to say to anthropologists, "Look, this is what *I* think about something, this is *my* view of the world. I don't believe that it's shared by every member of my band and I don't believe that this is necessarily reflective of the community. It's a view that *I* have and that people I know may share."

I had an unfortunate experience about five years ago with an anthropologist I really liked and admired as an academic. But it developed into a very uncomfortable relationship for me because, essentially, she had decided that I was someone she could talk to; so come hell or high water, she was going to do a number of articles and possibly a book. The dynamic of the relationship changed because I went from really admiring some of her insights to resenting that kind of relationship, to consciously cutting the personal friendship and making it very formal and being circumspect about what I said because I doubted that there would be any honest reflection of the context that I was trying to put things in.

So, if you want a general comment from me on anthropology, I have a great deal of resentment towards anthropology and anthropologists from personal experience. That's aside from the last 100 years of stuff that's been written. This is my own personal experience. I think it's part of a bigger question. Anthropologists have an authority that comes from a place within the establishment, the state, and the polity of Canada as a whole. Yet, there's consistently, on the part of anthropologists that I've had a relationship with, a denial of that place, so that what twenty Indians would say gains credence when one anthropologist acknowledges that to be a truism. If one anthropologist says, "No, these people are mistaken," that has more credibility than 100 Indians saying otherwise.

I have made a conscious decision; I have no more time for anthropologists. This interview is an exception because I like the concept. I've got lots of time for Indians, I've got lots of time to discuss things that are relevant.

Dyck: How adequately does anthropology reflect and deal with the political and economic realities facing Native communities and their members today?

Speck: My focus has been on the Northwest Coast, but I've also done a lot of general work. Anthropology is just starting to deal with these issues of how it has looked at people, how anthropology has represented Indian communities, Indian society. I think anthropology as it's practised still reflects a lot of nineteenth-century assumptions. There is still a real focus on the "Culture" as I would define this focus on traditional culture. I'm not saying that's not important, but I think in 1989, the "traditional culture" is only a small aspect of a total culture.

Indian people are faced with – it becomes a tired refrain – poverty, alcoholism, issues of land claims, band councils dealing with the courts, the fishing issues, etc., and I don't think anthropologists have really touched on these issues. There are only a few examples that I can think of and even there, there are problems: Shkilnyk's book [*A Poison Stronger Than Love*, 1985] on Grassy Narrows, some work on James Bay. But on the whole, I think anthropology as a discipline still continues to look to the Indians for "real culture," and that is, in the case of the coast, the potlatch and traditions of the past and searching for the continued existence of "real culture." There is a problem with that kind of definition of culture. I believe culture is something that is constantly changing and growing, and anthropology doesn't see it that way. Or at least anthropology on the Northwest Coast. In North America generally culture is seen as something that is static or fixed. It's something that was given down to us sometime long ago in the dark past, and anthropologists are still looking for that culture and the untouched savage so that they can market it for the rest of their career. That's kind of a crass way of putting it, but that's how I see it.

Dyck: I've heard that expressed in terms of that type of anthropology which is always looking backwards, always trying to figure out what people were and telling them what they are today in terms of what they were supposed to have been in the past.

Speck: Yes. I see that as a real problem in terms of a lot of the political, economic, and social issues that Indian people have to deal with. For instance, with the land claims issues that are beginning to come out, Indian people are being forced into a position of proving that they still have a culture. That puts us in a really dangerous and tenuous position because the other side, the state, the courts, and things like that, can easily trot out – as they did in James Bay – the fact that Renee and I are sitting here in jogging shorts and blue jeans and that she smokes cigarettes, while I drink Coca Cola. They did exactly that during the James Bay court cases. The prosecutor would come out and say, "I can show you many examples of Indians leading a non-traditional life."

It is dangerous for Indian people to have our culture seen in that way. I'm not an advocate of the idea of acculturation because that is not possible. We've had a different history, we have a different social life, a different economic relationship to the Canadian state. All of these things make us a distinct culture of distinct people and will continue to do so as long as we live in the kind of society we live in. It will be the same for any other group of people who come to this country and are singled out and become a visible group of people within this kind of society. They will continue to have a distinct culture. Anthropologists and lawyers that present Indian people purely in terms of traditional ways of life are setting us up for a kick in the ass.

Taylor: Exactly. A case in point is the Bear Island criteria, which is now being touted as the definition of an Indian band as a definable people with a definable land base and a continuity of culture from time immemorial. All these little check lists of what makes an Indian an Indian totally miss the core values that people still share; it misses the reality of kinship ties; it misses the choices that people make. I define myself in terms of being a Kwakiutl. It doesn't matter whether I'm here in Vancouver, or Paris, or New Mexico, or if I happen to be in my community. It's not a romantic notion. It's simply the way that I view the world. I know that I've gone through periods of my life where I've had a period of estrangement from that community, and those are the times when my dreams are the most graphic and my thoughts the most graphic about who I am. I know then that I have to touch home base again.

All those ties of kinship and things that keep people who they are, I think non-Indian people are not seeing them. Anthropologists certainly aren't seeing them, the white community doesn't see them, because they're looking at external factors, things that are visible and skin deep.

In the legal precedents that are coming down in the last decade, in every major case, the pivotal point is that there is a relationship to the "people's culture." Well, culture is what you're doing every day. Culture is getting in my battered up old Honda to drive here in Vancouver and worrying about getting to my tax law course on time today. Culture is also that I'm going to be meeting one of my brothers and that's probably going to be touching home. We're talking about having a potlatch next year. It's all of that. It's what I do every day. That's culture.

Speck: I think when you said that what anthropologists study is only skin deep, I think it's worse than that. There is a presumption that they know what they're going to look at. If you were a traveller from Germany and you went to anthropologists and said, "Could you tell me about the Kwakiutl, I want to go and visit them," and they told you about the Kwakiutl and you went up there and it wasn't June when we have our potlatches, they wouldn't be able to find us.

They would go to Alert Bay and walk the streets and ask, "Where are the Indians?" We're the people down at the dock fixing our nets, we're the people walking down the streets drinking Coke and Slushies, we're the guys in the bar, we're the guys working at the band office or as teacher aids, we're social workers, but we're living in a community that is not recognizable in terms of long houses, button blankets, and masks. Our beaches aren't lined with canoes, they're lined with aluminum skiffs that we use for fishing, and logs that we still use in our stoves, but so do all the white people at the other end of the settlement, and lots of hippies. There is very little on the surface that distinguishes us from other people. It has far more to do with our history, our social and economic relations to the outside, and how white people and Indian people see each other and interact together. The white people in our community know who we are, they know we're Indians, they treat us as Indians. The other people in the area, from Sointula and Port Mac-Neil, know who we are. We not only define ourselves, but are defined by other people as Indians. That's what makes us Indians, as well as our traditions and our past.

Dyck: How adequately is this reflected in anthropological writings of the sort that you've seen as students?

Taylor: It's not. I used to fantasize a great deal when I was taking courses on the history of the Northwest Coast and cultural ecology. One professor was talking about the Ba'Xu Bakwalcnvxu Si'Wee as a metaphor for an epiphany, a great catastrophe that had happened in aboriginal times. People had to see this as the great monster at the end of the world. I remember sitting in class and thinking, "What absolute utter crap!" Why is there this tendency to mythologize everything, so that true history gets lost in the writing?

I'm talking about my grandmother telling me, and I believe it to be the absolute truth, that she's seen a snake that was as big as a tree around, piled up forty feet high. There are all kinds of natural phenomena in the world that I know of in my own time that are not made up. My grandmother did not go out and have a nip one morning when Gumpa was out trapping or somehow have this aboriginal flashback. What they saw is what is real. The point I'm making is why isn't it some kind of prehistoric creature? There may not be any evidence of it at this point, but there was, through time. Why are our symbols and our art and the stories that we have not an accurate reflection of our history, rather than anthropologists believing that everything is symbolic of something else? Why can't it be just what it is? People have very different explanations of what happens.

What I was learning in school and church, any time I stepped out of the influence of my community, that we had incredible imaginations, that we're somehow a naïve and simple people, that basically everything I was learning from the older people in my family as a child was really not quite true: at school I was learning the truth and at church I was learning the truth and when I sat around with educated people I was learning the truth, and essentially what I was learning in my own community was not really a lie, but an interesting "creation of reality." At about nineteen or twenty, when I moved out to a remote ancestral village for a while, I learned more truth about how the world really works and what people are like and what social relations are about from my own people than I ever learned outside. I decided, at that point, that that was true. The myths are in this larger institution, this place that's called "true knowledge."

Speck: I think a lot of the stuff that Renee has just said reflects what I said about how culture changes. You talk about how the old people like your grandmother saw these things and understood these things in these ways. Then you went to school and church and learned a different way of seeing it. And then you went back home and started living at Ectsukin and began seeing things differently again. That's exactly right. I don't have a problem with this because

I think world view is relative and these people were growing up in a time where these things were real from their point of view. Then you went to school and church and something else became real. And then you went back home and something else again became real because your understanding of the world is constantly changing, your culture is constantly developing and changing. Some things you've passed off and other things you hang onto, other things later you reintegrate again. Culture is incredibly adaptive and constantly in motion and change. I don't think people stay in one place.

Politics changed my world view and how I saw things, and continues to do so. Anthropology also contributes now to how I see the world and how I see Native people's relations to the Canadian state and the state's relations to Native people. My involvement in the potlatch has also had a role in those sets of relations and understandings. I'm involved in a number of roles – as my father's son, my brother's brother, as a dancer in the potlatch, as well as a graduate student in a university. I don't know what it's going to be like three years from now. Maybe I'll become a born-again Christian and renounce it all. Well, maybe a little longer than that, it would be a major conversion. That's the point I'm trying to make in terms of my understanding of culture and how culture changes and how people integrate different understandings into their whole way of life.

What anthropology misses is a people's whole way of life. What makes their informant an ideal informant? If you go to Alert Bay, an ideal informant is someone who is old, who will talk to you, and who is involved in the potlatch. If you're wearing blue jeans and working on your net on the dock, you are left to the sociologists, who want to know about fishing. Anthropologists don't talk to people.

Dyck: What do you see when you visit museums, when you pick up ethnographies?

Speck: To be fair, there have been ethnographies where the social system and "modern life" have been looked at. But modern life is always looked at in terms of how it's influenced by "the traditional culture." You're drunk because you've lost your culture or you're not a drunk because you're a traditionalist. It's all related back to this fixed thing, "the culture." These things are not integrated and understood as an active part of life, including tradition. It's always a one-way street, straight from "the culture" to all of these different aspects of an Indian's life, which I think is an a priori supposition.

Taylor: I firmly believe there are core values in terms of how people decide what's right and what's wrong. From my place, they are particularly Kwakiutl values and there is no way that I can describe these adequately. I have had some friends who have stepped into the Kwakiutl world for long periods of time and it takes so many years for them to understand, for example, sharing, the way that it is done, and that it's not a "tit for tat" thing.

This is not to say that there aren't appropriate insights that come from anthropology. There are a few things that I've read that I think have been significant in my own development, but most of what I've read in anthropological literature I personally consider to be irrelevant.

Speck: My focus has been on the Northwest Coast and the work that I've had to deal with has been primarily on the potlatch. That's interesting material for first- and second-year courses, but it gets tiresome after a long time. I found that a lot of the later stuff I've gotten from political and economic anthropology is really useful, but that work has been done in Africa, not North America. People are interested in how the African tribes are developing and how their culture is changing. I can see how political and economic anthropology would be really useful as an approach to Native communities and the problems of Native people with the Canadian state, how we got where we are now, why we do what we do. All of those things *could* be approached by anthropology. Anthropology could have a useful place in helping me to understand what was going on in terms of Indian people and public policy. And in some cases it has.

Taylor: There is an incredible displacement from the Department of Indian Affairs to the band council level, so that in many communities the band council is the biggest continuing employer in the community. With the inevitable settlement of land claims and the possible inclusion of some "sovereignty institutions," whether it be the courts or whatever else, Indian people are going to be asking for, or just deciding to set up their own institutions.

Last week I spent the better part of the week trying to find one place in all the legal literature where the relationship between the band council and band membership was defined. Was it a fiduciary relationship, was it one that fit into classic trust law, or what was the relationship, what was the responsibility, where is the accountability? There are no dispute mechanisms set up in the Indian Act. There is no allowance made for organized opposition, there is no way you have anything that parallels the Canadian state where you have the "majority" view and the "minority" view both having equal access to public expression.

I looked at some recent cases where band members have taken their band council to court. There are relatively few cases. In total, I could find about ten cases in the last five years where Indian band members have taken their band councils to court, either for misappropriation of band funds or perceived discrimination of one kind or another. Nowhere has the relationship between the band council and band membership ever been defined.

What I'm saying is that there is all this lip service given to democracy and sovereignty, but there is no substance or content to it. If it's a concern of anthropologists to become relevant, they had better hurry up because the stakes are getting bigger all the time and the new sultans, in some ways, are the band and tribal council administrators, the internal bureaucracy. Neocolonialism as a study is probably more relevant than anything else at this point.

The resolution of these problems is placed on *the chief* and *council*, whether or not that truly reflects the internal band power structure or the shakers and movers or how things really happen in an Indian community in terms of how people actually organize themselves. Little attention has been given to how communities actually organize themselves. Because the band council is the only thing that fits into the Canadian government's body politic, that's where the attention is paid. I think the state is coming to a point where it is going to legitimize and entrench band councils even more, whether or not they are democratic, or even rudimentarily fair.

Speck: It seems to me that although there are all these "banana republics" seemingly springing up, at the same time band members themselves are more and more making appeals to the state through the courts to settle these internal disputes. Whether that's a good or bad thing, from reading newspapers and talking to people involved in disputes within their communities, it is obvious that people are making appeals through the courts to settle disputes in terms of the rules and regulations of the state as opposed to anything coming from the community itself.

Taylor: When you say band members are going outside the community and the court system to try and get some measure of accountability at a local level, I'm sure that would be happening a lot more if band members generally knew that they could do this. You're not going to find that looking at Indian newspapers. The reason you're not going to find it is because everybody is so dependent on the main funding source of the state. Everybody plays the numbers game, whether it's the Union of B.C. Indian Chiefs, or the non-status Indians, or the Assembly of First Nations. It's who is supporting them, how many bands are giving them support. You can't shit in your own back yard. You could have 100 people writing in to Indian newspapers about irregularities happening in their communities, wanting to be heard, and you're not going to find one of them printed.

Dyck: Is there a sense of vulnerability that holds people back?

Speck: I've felt it at times. I've been in situations where I haven't wanted to say, "That's not the way it is, it's a lot uglier than that." You feel like you're giving aid to the enemy. At the same time, I've started to feel there is a real danger in that, as well as a similarity to what anthropologists have done. You have to reflect on the history of Indian people. They have been fighting this fight in B.C. since the 1880s and we're still here, so why should I make the assumption that we're not going to still be here in 2010 because I happen to say things are really ugly on my reserve for this and that reason. Or why shouldn't other people be able to say that? Why are we so afraid? There is always going to be someone who will stand up and say, "That's wrong, let's change it." I think there is more strength there than we give ourselves credit for. By not saying it, we allow it to continue.

Dyck: Of what use can anthropology be, and how would it have to go about reorganizing itself as a discipline to be of greater use?

Speck: Of what use can anthropology be? As an anthropologist, I assume that we are all advocating something, whether it be for the state, for Indians as a land claims worker, or as an anthropologist with a particular ideological point of view, which has a lot to do with our own history and where we come from. Of what use can it be? I tend to see things from the point of view of intervention to make life better. Knowledge for what? Knowledge for political action! That's from my own point of view and I'm advocating a political point of view for anthropology.

If you just look at the relationship of Indian people to the Canadian state, it's obvious that the relationship has been one of Indians getting screwed. Understanding that process and telling people about it, and helping Indians to understand that process, will move us to do something about it – understanding the Canadian state and its nature. I don't think a lot of people really understand how Indians have arrived where they are now as a result of public policy in relation to Indians.

If people understood the history of these processes I think they would be angry about it. Anybody with any little bit of morality would care. That's a relative term but I think there is a general morality in Canada that expects justice and democracy. If you show people that the Canadian state has been immoral, the Canadian state has been unjust, and here are examples in British Columbia that date back from day one to 1989 in a continuum, maybe then something will change. That's what I see anthropology doing. It has the tools to do it if anybody has the courage to take them up. I think the problem is the lack of courage – being afraid to step off the ship because the savages might get them.

Taylor: The best witness you can get for a land claims case is an anthropologist who is preferably tied to a university because there is a perception that there is an ongoing diversity and exchange of information in universities, so they are perceived as being an independent witness. It's preferable that they are not either a witness for the Crown or for the band, but a witness for the court, a judicial witness whom the judge has called as an independent party to come and give evidence. They come in with all the legitimacy presupposed, and ultimately their evidence has the greatest weight. This is all done under the guise that they can see both sides of the question and don't have any value judgments. They are just telling you what is true. That's just such utter crap. Everybody has a point of view just by deciding what to leave in and what to leave out.

The anthropologists who say, "Okay, like it or leave it, this is what I think about the world, this is what Indians are trying to say," who are very honest about their own biases, are easy to dismiss because they've taken a stand. But all these other anthropologists who "aren't taking a position" are said to be the more credible people. I think for anthropologists to become relevant, they must be honest. Anthropologists could take direction from communities. Anthropologists could be told what to do and what not to do. They could be real true employees. They can decide to be advocates openly, not silently.

If anthropologists want to be relevant, then there is a place for them. They should just come out and say who they are rather than pretend they don't have any views on things. That might limit them in terms of their own professional careers, in terms of what work they can do. Working with Indian groups, unless they are already into some specific claims or comprehensive claims money or something like that is not a lucrative affair. But being with tribal councils that already have that economic infrastructure can be lucrative. There are a few people, both anthropologists and lawyers, running around right now, the Indian experts and consultants, who do one piece of good work for one community and then can duplicate it twenty times and charge the same rate for it.

Speck: What I find really interesting is the assumption that because you're an advocate of any particular position, what you're saying is necessarily inaccurate. It would seem to me that that decision would be the job of the people who are reading this stuff. If anthropologists presented enough of themselves and enough of their understanding of what they were doing, as well as what they were studying, then somebody reading it would be allowed to make a judgment about that research.

Dyck: What can anthropologists learn from or teach to other disciplines and other professions? What is it that anthropology has to offer, not necessarily as it has been practised badly, but as it ideally might be practised? And what, more centrally maybe, does it have to learn if there is still time to learn it?

Speck: The thing you learn in a first-year anthropology course is that what anthropologists do is fieldwork. It started the march forward and I don't think it's finished. I think that's what anthropology has to offer – its involvement in communities. Somebody went and lived in an Indian community and saw a whole way of life. That's what it has to offer. Anthropologists have this tradition of going into communities and being the observer and trying to understand a way of life that's essentially different from that of the anthropologist. If they understood culture the way I understand culture, that's what they would study and have to offer other disciplines.

What can anthropology get from other disciplines? My present understanding of culture was, in part, taken from the work of Raymond Williams, somebody involved in literary criticism. Linguistics, all sorts of disciplines, are doing work in terms of the culture of language, the nature of the changes that occur. I think anthropologists are starting to look toward those kinds of things. I've read people who have talked about that. So these are the things that anthropology can take from other disciplines.

What can anthropology give to them? Again, what it's done all along – it's understanding of what needs to be known about a community. It just needs to do it.

Taylor: I think that what anthropology can offer is what we've been talking about. It was answered in part in the last question in the sense that anthropologists have to look at the very issues we've been discussing. They need to look at the internal dynamics of communities, at what the stated aspirations of people are, and maybe at bringing comparisons from other societies of things that may be relevant. In the whole area of land claims and settlements, we've got the American Indian Settlement Act and fifty years of work that's already been done by a whole host of academics, anthropologists, sociologists, and lawyers in the United States. There's been almost no effort made in Canada to talk about what happened in those communities, about the types of settlements that were made, not only where the pitfalls were and where the boons have been. One of the ways that anthropologists could be relevant is by looking at what it is people say they are going to do, finding out if it's been done anywhere else before, and what the consequences were so that there can be some real long-term planning.

We have obviously decided as a people that we want to be who we are. People talk about the last great orator, the last great carver, and the last great basket maker. I've heard my whole life that when one particular old lady on my reserve dies, we've lost all our baskets. Yet there are half a dozen young people doing that now. By simply being much more engaged with people, anthropology can find out not only who people say they are, but also what they say they want.

Dyck: That's one tendency within anthropology. The other would be to ignore all those questions and deal primarily with the romantic past.

Speck: That's how it started with Boas. Boas was going to capture the real culture before it disappeared. They have been predicting the demise of the Indian people for a long, long time. Unfortunately for them, we keep going on, except that now they start explaining it in terms of we're disappearing in terms of our culture. We're not. People are still making, for whatever reasons – which probably have far more to do with what's going on in these people's lives now than it has to do with their traditional past – people are now practising traditional activities like making baskets or dancing in the potlatch or commercial fishing, like I've been doing for the past nine months. I don't plan on going anywhere and I still plan on being here next year and ten years from now. I imagine my community will be too. I think that's really funny, the disappearing savage. It's an old refrain that never seems to go away.

Dyck: It's a very interesting notion that what anthropologists should be doing is writing better ethnography, doing a more adequate job of accounting for where people are and what they're dealing with and where they've come from. I think this would amaze most anthropologists who reckon they're already doing that quite adequately.

Speck: That's what I was saying about anthropologists who come to Alert Bay. The time of the year for an anthropologist to come to Alert Bay is in June. Why June? Because that's when the potlatches happen. Then they go away and start explaining.

Taylor: I think there are all kinds of phenomena happening and the only people I hear discussing them are Indians. An interesting phenomenon, for example, some anthropologist might want to take on, is that of the number of "educated" Indians, Indians who simply have gone on and done a classic liberal education. There's always been an assumption in anthropology, at least this is where I've seen it, that what's happened is that there's an estrangement of those individuals from the community because they've become acculturated. That's starting with a certain premise. I see it, and other people I've been relating it to see it as an estrangement from the power structure of the community, but not from the community itself. These people threaten the existing power structure. That's a completely different thing.

Speck: Yes, I've heard that same statement from anthropologists or other people about Indians who have become educated. What's not recognized is that we have family in that community – aunts, uncles, cousins – who still see us as being educated. In my case, it's being another source of getting that dig in: "What are you doing with that education, you're still fishing. You had to spend nine years to become a gill netter." It's not a vicious thing, it's more in the line of a joke. It's not like they can't talk to me any more. They're people I've grown up with all my life. For a lot of them, it's a source of pride that I've done this, not an estrangement.

I think Renee's really right, when you want to find out the direction the estrangement comes from, it has to do more with the internal politics of a community than it has to do with a cultural estrangement.

Dyck: But if we anthropologists approach communities and ask for their permission to look at the internal organization of the community and how problems and difficulties occur, living within this political system in this context, in this particular time and under these forces, then the communities and bands and band councils might be a little less than enthusiastic about granting us permission to conduct research.

Speck: But isn't that a problem that anthropologists run into all over the world? How do they deal with it there? You have to write for permission from some African government that has just had a revolution, and they want to know that you're politically correct and not going to be or do anything that will, in fact, incite the rebels to a greater effort. Right, it is a problem, but so what? Deal with it. You have to approach the band councils. You have to present a proposal that the band council is going to look at and make a judgment on. They are going to do that, but that's their right.

Taylor: That acute sensitivity or self-consciousness on the part of anthropology is what is certain to ensure its demise. Ponting and Gibbins, who wrote *Out of Irrelevance*, I don't know that they asked anybody's permission to do that. They talked about internal politics and the way that the dynamics of communities changed in terms of where government funding went. You're talking about public policy; a lot of *Out of Irrelevance* was about that.

At some point it seems to me that as an anthropologist you write to the band council because you are assuming they're the most relevant part of the whole picture anyway and you tell them you'd like to do this. There are certain large portions of the community that aren't always represented on council and may be interested in this. I think anthropologists have to take it upon themselves where they have an invitation or where they have some credibility. If people don't respect an anthropologist as a person, that person won't ever get any information that's worth a hang. But if anthropologists made a conscious decision that they were going to reflect and record what was happening, describe the community in ethnographic terms, or focus in on particular problems, well if they're waiting for permission to come, it is never going to come in that way. There's some point where people just start doing it. You may say that's a contradiction in terms, because you might say, how dare anthropologists, that's what the resentment has been about for so many years. They just went into the community, wrote what they wanted, had no responsibility to the community, and left. The difference in the model that I'm describing is that they are responsible to the community. They are responsible in terms of feedback, they're responsible in terms of whether their agreement is with the council or whether it is with a particular group. There are so many different groups in any one community. There are community clubs, women's groups, all kinds of groups. Women, I should say at some point, were almost totally ignored by anthropologists because of the "chief" fetish. In terms of local dynamics of how people relate to each other, there are all kinds of legitimate groups within the community – people associated with the big house, people associated with fishing.

If people understood that an anthropological study was to look at a particular concern of specific Indian people, then that group would be the constituency that would be recording the responsibility. This session you're doing here, the letter expressly stated that we would have some sort of editorial control over what we were going to publish and what we weren't going to publish. That's a precondition to my participating in this. That could be done elsewhere.

Speck: There shouldn't be an automatic assumption that people are not going to want to deal with painful topics. That doesn't necessarily follow. A good example is Dara's [Culhane Speck] book, *An Error in Judgement*. That was a painful period for our community. The book touches on topics that are sensitive, but she did exactly what you did with this interview. She gave people who were directly involved in the events of the book the option of reading it and going over it and judging its accuracy. And it still ended up being a powerful book that dealt with very sensitive issues. There shouldn't be an automatic assumption that "no, it isn't going to make us look good because it tells the stuff that's bad about our lives." Most people would want to make their lives better. I think that through participation in these kinds of things, people would feel that they need to know these kinds of things and to have other people know them so that our lives can get better.

The other thing is that there are other groups. How would an anthropologist approach a community in a non-Indian situation? Would you go to the city of Vancouver to ask permission to study the downtown east side?

Taylor: This soul searching has to happen among professional anthropologists' organizations. But in the meantime, we still had PHD students going off trying to figure out whether or not the Sisuitl are reflective of anal retentive phenomena. There are still people approving of these projects from the culture vulture trend. It's self-perpetuating.

Dyck: There is a whole series of nagging questions, I would say, that some people put right out of their minds. What is the future of Indian communities which lack an economic base, which are articulated into the Canadian state as dependent entities?

Taylor: I think there's a whole bunch of work that can be done there. I don't think there's any end to what could be done, it's whether or not anthropology as a science and anthropologists as people are going to have the courage to say we have a responsibility here, using our tools to give something back to communities, or carrying on, as many anthropologists do, enhancing their reputation, anthropologist qua anthropologist. Last week the Kwakiutl, this week off to look at the land tenure system in Australia. *Adios amigo*.

Speck: It's June, it's time to go to the potlatch. It's July, it's time to go ...

Taylor: It's National Geographic anthropology.

Dyck: What do you think we've missed in our discussion?

Taylor: I think the only part that's been left out that we sort of touched on is some "brown washing" that's been going on. There's a real tendency in all spheres right now, in education, in law, in anthropology, trying to rehabilitate institutions, and there's not really a sense of looking at the fundamental foundations of things. That's possibly more of an internal concern than an external one in the sense that it's something that Indians are going to be approaching more.

Speck: I've seen that as well. When I was doing my work on alcohol for my thesis, a lot of comments came from Indian people working in alcohol treatment; you get a sense from them that they are getting sick and tired of the Indian politicians and that we've got to look at our immediate problem, which is alcohol. "This is the big issue, alcohol. We're going to deal with alcohol now."

I think that that attitude is really dangerous. Yes, there are immediate problems like the alcohol problem, there's poverty, that's a problem. But in order for an Indian community to get better, you need an economic base, you need institutions that are relevant to their communities, and these have to come from the communities. Economic development requires resources that these Indian politicians are after. If we continue to depend on the state for our funding, the dance will continue and the problems will get worse and are getting worse. I think one of the biggest problems is our dependence, that we are dependants.

Taylor: I think earlier, when we were talking about participating in a forum like this, there was a real sense, even as educated Indians, of being conscious about our role and our responsibilities.

At university I went to a couple of the women's committee meetings and I decided in short order that I didn't have a lot that I could either give to or draw from that community because the kinds of things they were talking about were day care, equal pay for equal work, so-called bread and butter women's issues. As an Indian woman, I determined that there were more vital concerns for me. It happens to give most of my female peers who are not Indians a great deal of personal satisfaction that they need to be the individual and be the woman litigator and that they are going to address women's concerns.

For me, that doesn't do a lot because of the way I was raised. I don't believe so much in individuation or that my individual beliefs and feelings are the most important thing. I think I identify myself as part of a community; my kinship ties and the kin keepers are the ones I still have the highest respect for as a woman and as an Indian. It's very important for me to be an aunty, it's very important for me to be a sister, it's very important for me to be a niece. Those are my definitions of self. They are so tied together, I couldn't separate myself from it.

Dyck: That's culture.

Taylor: I'm a Kwakiutl first, foremost in this world, and that's what I choose to be. I realize that a lot of the social issues that are taking up other people's energy really don't have a lot of relevance for me at this point in my life. They're of secondary or tertiary importance because for me there are other more important things.

Speck: Just to show the variability of opinions in the Indian community, I'm not a nationalist, but in fact tend to see things in other terms: yes, there's poverty, all kinds of social problems like alcoholism and drugs. These are the issues that need to be dealt with, not only in the Indian community. I'm interested in them in the Indian community because I'm an Indian and that's where I live and those are my relatives, friends, and the people I've grown up with. That would be my primary interest. But only because it's a community, not because it's Kwakiutl. I am Kwakiutl because that's who I am, I've grown up that way. How you define a community where you live and grow up and where your family is and what your connections are.

That's who I am, but I don't see "being Kwakiutl" as my primary definition. I'm perfectly willing to fight and argue against poverty and social injustice anywhere they occur and I have within non-Indian groups. There is great variability within the Indian community, and people tend to see things in different ways. In the end, I think we're both saying the same thing anyway.

Taylor: Yes. It's just from a different base.

Speck: We have the same concerns and want better things for our community, which is what we're talking about, our community.

8 "Telling it like it is": Some Dilemmas of Fourth World Ethnography and Advocacy

NOEL DYCK

INTRODUCTION

The days when one might have lamented a lack of writing about the situation of Native peoples within Canadian society have long since disappeared. Indeed, during the past two decades a seemingly inexhaustible supply of government reports, popular and journalistic accounts, academic journal articles, monographs, and volumes of collected essays dealing with virtually all aspects of Native cultures and issues, past and present, has appeared. Anthropologists working in institutional settings ranging from university departments and museums to consultancy firms, government agencies, and tribal and band governments are prolific contributors to this rising tide of literature on Native issues.

Yet, notwithstanding the sheer volume and apparently all-inclusive scope of anthropological writings on Native issues, there are some significant matters about which anthropologists – along with others working in this field – generally prefer not to write. This essay seeks to elucidate factors that restrain our inclination to "tell it like it is." Beginning with an identification of sensitive topics that are, for the most part, conspicuous in their absence from contemporary anthropological accounts, the paper examines conditions which prompt self-censorship and considers some implications of this problematic practice. The concerns dealt with here have surfaced in private conversations shared over a number of years with a range of Native friends, several of whom are band leaders, and anthropological colleagues, including faculty members, consultants, land claims researchers, band and tribal council employees, and government officials. Those conversations and this essay have proceeded from the observation that advocacy – in either active or passive forms – is often a feature of contemporary anthropological endeavour (Van Esterik 1985). Careers that at different times accommodate both ethnographic research and applied or advocacy activities are especially common among anthropologists working with minority indigenous or "fourth world" (Dyck 1985) peoples. The object of this essay is to promote open and responsible discussion as an essential first step toward addressing the dilemmas that constrain the work of individual ethnographers and anthropological advocates as well as the intellectual advancement of anthropology as a social science.

THE SOURCES OF HESITATION

A recent example of informally shared anthropological musings serves to focus the discussion. In the course of a wide-ranging conversation conducted over lunch with a colleague from another province, discussion eventually turned to the current state of affairs in two Indian communities which one of us had read about in the anthropological literature but which the other knew personally through his activities as an advocate. We spoke at length about how the latter's observations of life in the communities today differed from accounts of both their "traditional" form (as reported more than a decade ago) and from the image of the communities now being propagated by their leaders in representations to governments and the Canadian public.

Two conditions deeply trouble these communities: (a) the existence of appalling and, arguably, worsening social conditions associated with poverty, including widespread alcoholism, child neglect, and intra-community violence, and (b) difficulties experienced at the community level due to the system of local government administration and band leadership that has developed during the past two decades. Of particular concern were several incidents which suggested that officials of one of these bands were making fundamental political decisions covertly on behalf of other band members, who are treated as if they are incapable of knowing what is best for them. This, of course, has been the credo of the form of coercive tutelage to which Indians were traditionally subjected by the Canadian state (Dyck 1991). It is scarcely in keeping with the ideal of consensual decision making celebrated in most anthropological accounts of aboriginal political organization.

The identification of these general conditions was, I hasten to add, not the starting point but the end product of a conversation that reluctantly recounted instances of drinking sprees that resulted in serious injuries and even death, and of individual leaders' apparent misuse of band funds and other resources[1] – practices which are sometimes temporarily "overlooked" by government officials. From gossip emerged comparisons with and contrasts between the situations in these and other Native communities, some spontaneous but limited attempts at generalization, and a tangible sense of distress mixed with an awkwardness in talking about these sensitive matters. While feelings of anguish for the misfortunes suffered by a people are understandable, the uneasiness encountered in discussing such matters and the associated tendency within the discipline not to deal with them except in off-the-record discussions[2] or in disembodied, statistical summaries requires explanation.

First, however, it is necessary to recognize some exceptions to this tendency. Perhaps the best known is Shkilnyk's (1985) controversial account of the impact of relocation and mercury poisoning upon the Grassy Narrows Band in Ontario, a study which purports to document the social destruction of an Ojibwa community. Responses to Shkilnyk's book have ranged from generally positive reviews in the popular press – one of which pronounced it to be "classic of the social sciences in Canada" (Fulford 1985:15) – to a number of extremely critical reviews by anthropologists and other social scientists.[3] The chief of the Grassy Narrows Band characterized the book as "garbage" in a radio interview.[4] Although not an anthropologist by training, Shkilnyk has been taken to task not only for what are identified as fundamental analytical deficiencies within her study, but also for having publicized intimate community problems against the wishes of band members; her justification for doing so was that "it is the price that they have to pay to make us [non-Indians] understand their case for social justice" (Shkilnyk 1985:10). Suffice it to say that while this book has received substantial attention, it does not provide an unproblematic example of whether or how anthropologists ought to write about the so-called "social pathologies" that afflict some Native communities.

A few authors have also criticized certain aspects of the system of political representation that today links Native communities to the agencies and institutions of the Canadian state. Pungent, though clearly partisan, non-anthropological critiques of the operations of provincial Indian organizations have been mounted by Wuttunee (1971), Burke (1976), Cardinal (1977), and Goldstick (1987), but these sources seem to be ignored in most social scientists' writings on Native politics in Canada. Less passionate but nonetheless searching assessments of the strategies and tactics of Native political representatives and of their dependency upon government funding and recognition have also been presented by Mortimore (1975), Dunning (1976), Elias (1976), La Rusic et al. (1979), Dyck (1983), and Daniels (1986). Overall, however, anthropologists have not written much about problematic developments in the unfolding relationships among Native communities, Native leaders, and the nation-state, despite the fact that a significant number of us have been in a position to observe these developments at close hand through our work as researchers, consultants, and advocates.

This hesitation to identify and analyse how these social and political problems are connected to the administrative and funding arrangements that have underwritten the operations of Native organizations and band and tribal councils at the local, regional, and national levels amounts to a form of self-censorship. In not exploring or writing about matters we know to be important – and not merely to us, but also to members of Native communities – anthropologists give short shrift to awkward but pressing social and political problems at the reserve or settlement level. This is a situation that most intellectuals would, in principle, be unwilling to tolerate in any other context. Why, then, is it accepted in this one?

One possibility is simple self-interest: to deal with unpleasant and controversial topics might jeopardize future prospects for research permission, lucrative contracts, or employment opportunities.[5] Without wishing to engage in special pleading on behalf of the discipline, I doubt that anthropologists have been simply "bought out." Anthropologists are located in far too broad a range of employment situations to make it likely that such a degree of conformity as exists within the anthropological literature has been orchestrated merely by means of bribes – in one form or another – or of coercion.[6]

A more likely explanation is that anthropologists abstain from writing about these topics primarily because we feel ourselves bound by moral and ethical constraints.[7] Specifically, we are inclined to respect the view held by many Native people that talking and writing about unpleasant aspects of their lives serves only to focus attention upon matters better forgotten or ignored.[8] This sentiment merits careful consideration, for it is clear that the commonplace negative and stereotyped perceptions of the situation of Native peoples do in practice furnish a negative public identity with which

Native people must contend both as individuals and as members of a social category.

These ethical concerns may not be unique to anthropology but are particularly potent in a discipline which relies upon participant-observation as one of its primary research methods. Unlike survey researchers for whom "research subjects" may, in experiential terms, be voices on the end of a telephone or tick-marks on a questionnaire, anthropologists tend to deal with "whole" persons and known communities on a recurring basis. The potential discomfort that anthropological publications or pronouncements might cause to the persons and groups with whom we work is, therefore, not an abstract matter but a tangible prospect. Exceptions to an underlying expectation that anthropologists should identify personally with the people they study and that they ought to protect their "subjects' " interests (i.e., Barrett 1984) serve to strengthen rather than subvert this ethical imperative, however clumsily it may sometimes be observed in practice.

Anthropologists are also cognizant of the vulnerability of the political gains registered by Native peoples in Canada during the past two decades. Victories ranging from the repudiation of the federal government's 1969 White Paper (Weaver 1981) to the recognition of aboriginal rights in the Constitution Act of 1982 (Sanders 1985) have been won through skilful mobilization of public support by Native leaders who have become astute practitioners of a "politics of embarrassment" (Dyck 1985) which is prosecuted through tactics of symbolic opposition. Recognizing the reliance of Native leaders upon the continued support of public opinion and, thus, upon maintaining an appropriate image of themselves and of their communities' needs in the mass media (Jhappan 1990), anthropologists exercise great caution when treading near matters that might easily contradict the public impressions that Native leaders nurture as one of their principal political resources.[9]

THE IMPLICATIONS OF OMISSION

But what are the implications of anthropologists' adopting this practice of self-censorship?[10] By choosing mostly not to deal with difficult and controversial issues we are, first and foremost, removing ourselves from the field of public debate, a territory which is increasingly occupied by the ill-informed and those who are far from sympathetic to the aspirations of Native peoples. In stating this, I do not wish to imply in any sense that anthropologists possess a unique capacity or responsibility to speak on behalf of Native peoples. The days when we might even have supposed ourselves to be encumbered by some sort of "anthropologist's burden" to represent the interests of those who were presumed to be incapable of doing so for themselves have, I trust, long since passed.

Nevertheless, we need to recognize that the issues on which anthropologists circumspectly abstain from commenting in our journals, monographs, and reports are today being dragged across the front pages of newspapers, television news broadcasts, and public hearings by those with less tender sensibilities.[11] For instance, local non-Indian supporters of the NATO air base proposed for Labrador have responded to the Innu campaign to prevent low-level flight training over their hunting territories by aggressively questioning the integrity of Innu culture (Armitage and Kennedy 1989). How can anthropologists – or, for that matter, anyone – respond to the partisan brandishing of evidence of serious social problems within a given Native community unless we can offer an informed explanation of the nature and source of these problems? In similar fashion, the internal political problems of the Westbank Band in British Columbia have prompted a series of public inquiries and, most recently, law suits between band members, all of which have received extensive coverage in local and national newspapers.[12] What are the implications of media coverage of these types of disputes for land claims cases in British Columbia and elsewhere that seek to demonstrate the continued existence of traditional consensually based forms of governance within Native nations?

And what are the implications of such disclosures for the credibility and integrity of anthropology as a discipline and of anthropologists as reliable interpreters of Native issues? I fear that our tendency to avoid writing about these sensitive matters might eventually place us in a position not unlike that of western intellectuals who visited China during the Cultural Revolution but who did not – for a variety of reasons – report the turmoil that later became all too apparent to the rest of the world. However meritorious or convenient the motives which inspire anthropological silence on these issues, we run the risk of producing diminished, analytically atrophied, and thus misleading ethnography[13] and advocacy which in the end will be of little use to Native communities, the Canadian public, or the discipline.

Anthropologists, in consequence, confront a dilemma. Should we simply proceed as we have done, skirting questions about acute social and political problems, and await the defrocking of anthropology, the rejection of Native claims, and the blaming of aboriginal peoples for the problems that may be lurking in their future? Or should we declare it to be our "duty" to unburden ourselves of our insights, fears, and misapprehensions and "tell it like it is," or at least as we think it is, letting the chips fall where they may? Viewed in these terms, it is an awful choice. While self-censorship is in the long run an untenable option, taking it upon ourselves to shore up our professional reputations by serving as self-appointed whistle-blowers – whatever the rationales that could be mounted to justify such behaviour – smacks of an unconscionable form of disciplinary opportunism.

THE ROOTS OF OUR DILEMMA

In a situation such as this one it may be best to step back for a moment and take a long, hard look at the conditions that shape our apparent dilemma. Upon closer inspection it would seem that much of our predicament is located in the intersection of two different fields of concern, both of which revolve around processes of representation.

On the one hand, we are buffeted by concerns connected with the so-called "crisis of representation" currently raging within the social sciences in general and anthropology in particular (cf. Marcus and Fischer 1986). In bidding for acceptance within the social scientific community, anthropologists since the time of Malinowski have traded upon the notion that our ethnographies comprise comprehensive and objective representations of the social and cultural realities of our subjects. Basking in the warm glow of what Marcus and Fischer have termed the "myth of the omniscient fieldworker," anthropologists have produced "closed" and simplified ethnographic accounts which have been supported by and suppor-tive of our claims to possess a privileged, "expert" ability to com-prehend the inner workings of aboriginal cultures and societies.

By operating on the premise that anthropology is ultimately capable of providing definitive accounts of what are, in practice, exceedingly complex, variable, and confusing phenomena, we have to some extent fallen victim to our own claim of "ethnographic authority." The question of whether or not anthropologists ought to "tell" about these situations presumes, in the first instance, that we "know" them in a manner that enables us to make comprehensive, definitive statements. Having cast ourselves in the role of the expert, we are now haunted by the possibility that we – like a friendly giant who does not know his own strength – might inadver-tently misuse our powerful knowledge.

The other side of this dilemma is shaped by the liberal-democratic ideology which is engrained within the political process in Canada. According to this perspective, the realization of Native peoples' political aspirations depends upon the acceptance of certain pragmatic truths: that public opinion, in the end, shapes public policy, that "playing the game" within the established political arena offers Native peoples the best – and, perhaps, the only – way to rectify their situation, and that to jeopardize the currently "favourable" image of Native cultures and claims held by Canadians[14] by publicizing the social and political problems suffered by Native communities would be to threaten their future. To the extent to which ethnographers and advocates observe these tenets in deciding how they should write about Native issues, they implicitly endorse the liberal-democratic perspective as providing the most "realistic" definition of the situation of Native peoples.[15]

Taken to an extreme this approach might subtly encourage anthropologists to package their "knowledge" in ways that would, at the very least, not contradict or criticize the positions taken by Native leaders and which might even help to support their claims. For instance, I have been told by some researchers that the struggle to win recognition of aboriginal land rights through court cases has obliged anthropologists (and others) working for Native communities to respond to predictably stereotyped and simplistic denials of the existence of distinctly aboriginal societies and ways of life. The temptation in these adversarial and less than scholarly settings may well be to fight fire with fire, to present equally stylized accounts which represent individual Native cultures and communities as virtually monolithic entities, and to gloss over historical particularities and internal differences that sometimes pit factions within communities against one another. While it may be argued that there is too much at stake in such court cases to allow for less than "definitive" submissions, the influence of such representations in guiding the design of subsequent ethnography and advocacy is problematic. Once started upon this course of representation, when will it be appropriate to recognize the complexity and the complications which in fact lie beneath these anthropological generalizations?

It has, of course, been flattering for anthropologists to be heard as expert witnesses in court cases and public inquiries, but we need to be mindful of the manner in which liberal-democratic institutions create both the demand for such expertise and the controls that govern it. During the past two decades there has been a willingness within these arenas to grant provisional recognition of anthropologists' special knowledge and expertise as cultural interpreters. This has not always been extended willingly, let alone on anything like a regular or permanent basis. That this has happened at all is because of the ability demonstrated by individual anthropologists in a number of key cases (notably the application of the James Bay Cree for a temporary injunction to halt construction of the hydro-electric project and the Mackenzie Valley Pipeline Inquiry) to provide detailed and reliable testimony concerning aboriginal subsistence patterns.[16] But when anthropologists begin to move beyond this relatively discrete and well-understood field of study, we need to be aware that liberal democracies prefer neatly wrapped definitions of the nature of public problems and uncomplicated and palatable "solutions."[17] To the extent that anthropologists are willing to offer "streamlined" depictions of the nature of Native communities and of the problems suffered by Native peoples within Canadian society, we may be enjoined to speak as experts in these settings.

But we should not be naïve about these arrangements. Anthropology's recent rise to prominence in this public, political field can just as quickly be reversed by exposure of telling gaps within our research and writing. Of more consequence than the embarrassment anthropologists will experience when this happens is the possibility that Native communities may be held primarily responsible for the shortcomings of the political arrangements that have been devised during the past twenty years to rectify their "situation." In the absence of any systematic critiques by anthropologists and other academics of these developments, Native people may one day be held accountable for the failure of this ostensibly well-intended and well-regarded system to solve the Native "problem." In short, Native people would be substantially identified as being in large measure the authors of their own misery – despite the best efforts of Canadian society to "help" them.

Hypothetically, such an argument might be stated thus: didn't Native leaders say that their peoples' problems would only be resolved by the granting of greater measures of Native autonomy and the funding of Native organizations and communities? And didn't anthropologists (and others) fully endorse these positions? And hasn't the Canadian state done as much as could be reasonably expected to satisfy Native demands, to increase self-determination, and to rectify past injustices? Is it not, therefore, the case that any "new" social and political problems "discovered" within Native communities today and in the coming years indicate not only the unreliability of anthropological evidence[18] and advice but also the incapacity of Native people to manage their own affairs?

ADDRESSING OUR DILEMMA

A useful way to address problems facing anthropologists working in "fourth world" settings is suggested by those who are endeavouring to deconstruct the myths of ethnographic expertise (e.g., Marcus and Fischer 1986; Clifford 1988) that our discipline has promoted and from which it has profited, but which now severely limit our work both as ethnographers and as advocates. What this will entail, in this context, is coming to terms with the inherent limitations of any ethnographic account of the complex situations Native people encounter as members of Canadian society. Even in depicting small-scale, local situations it is difficult for an ethnographer to obtain a comprehensive account of social, cultural, and political phenomena. To sustain the illusion that we might be able to do so in situations that are vastly more diverse, particular, and complex – that is, political and administrative relations that reach from remote reserves to Ottawa and back – is to engage in self-deception. We must, therefore, resist the strong temptation to satisfy seductive and unrelenting demands for simplistic definitions of the social and political circumstances of Native communities, however insistently these demands are made by the mass media and institutions of the nation-state or even by Native politicians.

What is needed is acknowledgment within our articles, monographs, and reports of the complexity of interests within Native communities, of the serious social difficulties that plague some, but not all Native people, and of the manner in which the representational and administrative arrangements entered into by Native leaders during the past twenty years and the resulting political positions have been shaped as much by the ideological assumptions and objectives of governments as by the wishes of the residents of these communities. There is not a single, "correct" Native voice but a diversity of perspectives on a wide range of issues. If anthropology purports to interpret the lives and aspirations of Native peoples, then it must endeavour to discover ways in which these diverging and sometimes contradictory viewpoints can be given voice in our accounts.

This will not be easy. Talking about discarding the pose of ethnographic authority is one thing, but writing accounts that will recognize, for instance, the nature of dissidents' disagreements with the stands taken by incumbents of leadership positions is quite another matter. It may be especially difficult for newly qualified anthropologists (some of whom work for Native organizations, band or tribal councils, while others take positions within government agencies) to pursue such courses of action without risking their employment. Perhaps anthropologists ensconced within universities might take the lead – and, quite possibly, some flak – in determining by experiment how best to incorporate these sensitive matters into anthropological writings.

This will require that anthropologists present for professional and public consideration written accounts which are more modestly framed than has often been the case in the past. Our writing will have to dispense with any lingering depiction of the anthropologist as the "omniscient fieldworker" while at the same time listening more attentively to Native peoples' frequently diverse understandings of the troubling problems within their communities. These ethnographies must also take note of the subtle but culturally significant ways in which these concerns are articulated by members of Native communities, for herein lie important directions for comprehending the ways in which Native communities seek to recognize and respond to these divisive but not insurmountable social and political problems.

A useful way to put these problems into perspective may be to compare the situation of aboriginal peoples in Canada with those of "fourth world" peoples in other liberal democracies (cf Dyck 1985). As well as affording a comparative dimension, which has traditionally been one of the principal strengths of anthropology, this tack will help us to appreciate that the dilemmas confronting anthropologists in Canada today are certainly not unique to this country or time. By examining the manner in which anthropologists working in other settings have dealt with similar and related concerns,[19] we can take a large step toward developing an analytical framework suited for our purposes.

Anthropologists might, it has been suggested,[20] also wish to reconsider who makes up the presumed audience for ethnographic accounts. Often this audience is implicitly envisioned as consisting primarily of non-Natives who tend to be sympathetic to Native interests. But what about another equally important, although traditionally neglected, audience – the Native groups about which anthropologists write? Might we not be obliged, both ethically *and* intellectually, to present our findings to them before publication? The right of subject communities and informants to protect themselves from misrepresentation or endangerment comprises the ethical consideration. Engagement in dialogue and multivocality would ideally enrich our final, published accounts. What this would require is the development of new processes for conducting field research and for writing up our findings that would permit the subjects of our research greater knowledge of the focus of our investigations and analyses. Anthropologists would, then, continue to write ethnographies but would include and/or take account of subjects' reactions to these anthropological interpretations as part of the final, published ethnography. Although the politics and logistics of this mode of consultation would likely be demanding, the finished accounts produced by means of it might well be both exciting and informative, perhaps revealing similarities and differences between anthropological and folk models of reality.

Coming to terms with the myths of ethnography should facilitate unveiling and freeing ourselves from the grip of the abiding ideological assumptions which underpin Native peoples' relations with the nation-state. It will permit us to pose some long overdue questions concerning the representational system constructed since the 1960s in order to link Native communities more directly to the federal and provincial governments. How can the overall political apparatus of band and tribal governments and provincial, territorial, and national Indian, Metis, non-status Indian, and Inuit organizations maintain its independence when there is such marked reliance upon government funding? Granted that this system is supposed to foster improved political representation and community services, is it possible that it serves the interests and purposes of the nation-state at least as well as or, perhaps, even better than it does those of the vast majority of Native people? Are recent endorsements by Canadian authorities of the existence of aboriginal rights and the need for aboriginal government essentially rhetorical in nature and largely intended to shift the burden of responsibility for resolving Native peoples' problems to recently constructed aboriginal political structures – structures which, more often than not, lack the power and/or the resources to do much more than sustain their own existence? What have been the social and economic ramifications of the creation of a paid Native political elite? What roles do non-Native consultants play within band and tribal councils and Native organizations? Is it possible that in limiting the scope and critical capacity of our work as ethnographers and advocates we may unwittingly bow to assumptions and preferences which may not be so much originated by Native communities as transmitted by Native representatives? These and other questions can be pursued with openness, tact, and impartiality once anthropologists face up to the factors that constrain our ethnography and advocacy from being as socially and politically aware as they ought to be.[21]

And that is what anthropologists have to gain by refurbishing our approach along these lines: a more modest but also more sophisticated mode of investigation and explanation in all our anthropological endeavours. In taking the time and the trouble to discover sensitive but effective ways to recognize and write about dissenting voices and complicated instances of local malaise – Brody (1981) and Culhane Speck (1987) provide excellent, but by no means the only, examples of how this can be done – we stand a far better chance of improving the quality of anthropological research and analysis and, correspondingly, its utility to all Canadians.[22] Anthropologists need to identify themselves as intellectuals who seek to comprehend the complex but crucial situation of Native communities and issues rather than as non-Natives who imagine themselves to be charged with a classificatory, status-based obligation to "protect" Native peoples.[23]

The media coverage and public support that aboriginal leaders have enjoyed in recent years has been a valuable resource, but, as an Indian friend remarks, Native communities cannot afford to become politically dependent upon it. Native peoples have had to work without such assistance in the past and may well have to do so again unless they are prepared to abandon their campaign to defend the identity and well-being of their communities, objectives which for more than a century have guided aboriginal peoples' politics and struggles to survive *as* aboriginal peoples. Native communities and anthropologists alike need to reflect carefully upon the long-term consequences of compromising the integrity of their respective purposes to the shifting premises and fickle sentiments that garb the political process within a liberal-democratic state.[24]

The ethnographic precedent we might usefully ponder is that offered by late nineteenth- and early twentieth-century ethnologists who, like photographer E.S. Curtis, sought to record the traditional ways of life of aboriginal peoples before these disappeared. In order to compose culturally "authentic" portraits Curtis insisted that his Indian subjects be suitably dressed and located away from any background which would have revealed that they were already engulfed in a rapidly changing social, economic, and cultural milieu.[25] Similarly, ethnologists of that period tended to ignore the far-reaching and fundamental transformations then occurring within Native communities in favour of capturing a retrospective and decidedly romantic vision[26] of the nature of aboriginal cultures and societies (Trigger 1985).

The limitations of this selectively focused approach to ethnography have become painfully obvious to later generations of readers who search in vain through our predecessors' writings for descriptions and analyses of what was actually happening within and to Native communities when this fieldwork was being conducted. But we might also contemplate whether the knowingly self-imposed constraints on anthropological writings on Native issues in the latter part of the twentieth century may not soon seem as contrived and misleading to future generations as Curtis's photographs appear to us.

In the end the only lasting resource anthropologists can hope to possess and share with others is a continuing commitment to examine and to seek to understand social relationships and cultural phenomena as perceptively as we can. To curtail or compromise this approach to our discipline – however seductive or compelling the arguments to do so – betrays anthropology's fundamental purposes and possibilities. Whatever the short-term motives for censoring or limiting our accounts, the inevitable result will be the production of work that is not what it purports to be. The demands inherent in attempting to satisfy the aim of "telling it like it is" have always been and will probably always be methodologically and analytically just beyond our grasp in any case, for that is the fate of social science. We cannot, in consequence, afford to confuse ourselves and mislead our readers, whoever they may be, by suppressing or ignoring the difficult epistemological and practical questions raised by our disciplinary "knowledge," whatever its current state and however it may complicate our lives as anthropologists.

NOTES

I wish to acknowledge the helpful comments and searching criticisms of different versions of this paper provided by Peter Armitage, Julie Cruikshank, Dara Culhane, Beverly Gartrell, Peter Harries-Jones, Cathy Livingstone, Krystyna Sieciechowicz, George Speck, and Jim Waldram.

1 Similar instances are being reported with increasing frequency in newspapers. See, for instance, the following two news stories: "Liquor flown into Davis Inlet on band council flights" (*The Labradorian* 27 March 1990, 3); "RCMP examining affairs of Manitoba native band" (Toronto *Globe and Mail*, 3 June 1991, A-5).

2 As Rabinow (1985:11) puts it, matters that are not written about are not necessarily trivial in nature; "corridor talk" may, instead, provide an informal means for informally exploring matters that are thought to be too sensitive to write about.

3 Academic reviews of the book have not, however, been consistently

negative: while Waldram (1985:112–19) and Usher (1987:40–4) find much to criticize in Shkilnyk's work, Ryan (1988:99–100) assesses it in generally favourable terms. Nevertheless, the sentiments of many of the anthropologists with whom I have discussed the book were aptly summarized by the following unpublished comment: "One cannot minimize the fact that it is an effort to state the hardest reality in the poorest way."

4 As cited by Usher (1987:43–4).

5 See Richer (1988) for an interesting argument that political involvement by anthropologists on behalf of the Native communities in which they conduct their research may, in effect, be a condition of fieldwork imposed by these communities. Although Richer does not address the particular concerns dealt with in this essay, his analysis is not incompatible with the one developed here.

6 This is not, however, to underestimate the impact within the discipline of occasional public criticism which has been levelled at individual anthropologists by Native communities with whom they have worked either recently or in the past. See, for example, "A revival in the wilderness" (Globe and Mail, Toronto, Features Page, 23 August 1986, 10) for a denunciation by contemporary Indian spokespersons of the ethnographic research conducted by James VanStone with the Snowdrift Chipewyan Band in the late 1950s and early 1960s. VanStone is quoted in the article as suggesting that members of the band may have been offended by "my descriptions of their drinking behaviour." Another example, which involved Mary-Lee Stearns's temporary ban by the Haida Nation, is discussed by Ames (1986:43–4).

7 The Social Sciences and Humanities Research Council of Canada's ethics guidelines for research with human subjects provides a set of general recommendations for the conduct of social science research. Whether the subsection "Research on Other Cultures, Countries, and Ethnic Groups" within these guidelines is intended to pertain to research conducted on aboriginal peoples in Canada is not entirely clear since a number of the assumptions contained in this subsection are not pertinent to the situation of most (or, perhaps, any) aboriginal communities in Canada.

8 This position was expressed nicely by Krystyna Sieciechowicz in a personal communication (9 November 1989): "This then brings up the thorny issue of white-washing or omitting any discussion of events and conditions which comment negatively on what goes on in Native communities. There is a code amongst us which states that we – the anthropologists – should not write the negative and damning as it is a question of invasion of personal and communal privacy and much more ... However, the point of why we have not spoken about the

dramas unfolding in the communities in which we have worked is not something we should feel guilty about; rather, I take it as a point of individual honour on the part of the researcher and of respect for the people with whom one has worked. I do [not] think that just because we do not write about some aspect of Indian cultural existence, regardless of how critical that aspect is, that we should be considered inexpert on that topic. There is a world of difference between knowingly obfuscating an issue to present some tortured notions of traditionalism – *this is* faulty ethnography – and delicately skirting one, wherein the subject is gently mentioned and diplomatically dropped.

9 This is also related to the decolonization of anthropology which Trigger (1988) identifies as being an essential step towards providing Canada's Native people with an opportunity to regain control over their own cultural heritage.

10 Jim Waldram (personal communication 15 October 1989) suggested that the term "self-censorship" may be somewhat misleading since it seems to imply that the anthropologist is entirely free to choose what and how she or he will study and write about. The politics of contemporary field research are, he observes, far more complicated than this and it is seldom the case that the individual anthropologist is wholly in control of the research process.

11 See, for instance, the following articles which have appeared in Canadian newspapers in recent years: "Probed band loses management reins" (*Vancouver Sun*, 21 November 1986, A-12); "Band office occupied as Indians question self-government move" (*Vancouver Sun*, 16 October 1986, A-19); "Terror blankets Manitoba Indian reserve: Gang brawls and beatings common" (*Globe and Mail*, 24 October 1988, A-1); and "B.C. Indian band grapples with patronage question" (*Vancouver Sun*, 30 June 1989, A-10).

12 See, for instance, the announcement of the convening of the Commission of Inquiry Concerning Certain Matters Associated with the Westbank Indian Band (*Vancouver Sun*, 26 September 1986) and an article entitled "Ex-chief wheels in style, but his style is questioned" (*Vancouver Sun*, 27 November 1986, B-1) for but two of the many articles dealing with the Westbank affair that have appeared in this and in other newspapers and magazines during recent years.

13 Robert Paine (forthcoming) discusses how anthropologists can also produce inadequate and misleading ethnography by giving insufficient attention to the positions held even by those members of a "fourth world" community whose views contradict anthropological interpretations of their "real" culture.

14 For a recent statement of public opinion on aboriginal peoples' issues in Canada see Ponting (1988).

15 See Weaver (1985) for a perceptive examination of the manner in which the assumptions of a liberal democracy with respect to "representivity" influence the fashion in which Native organizations and leaders interact with the agencies and institutions of the nation-state.

16 See Asch (1982, 1983), Feit (1982), and Salisbury (1986) for discussions of the valuable contributions of anthropologists in these settings.

17 Gusfield (1981) provides a powerful model for penetrating what he aptly depicts as the "culture" of public problems. I follow his approach here.

18 See McEachern (1991) for a recent example of this type of criticism.

19 See, for instance, Howard (1982) and Von Sturmer (1982) for accounts from Australia which share some of the concerns expressed in this essay. See also Harries-Jones (1991) for an excellent collection of essays on the overall relationship between advocacy and social science.

20 I am indebted to Peter Armitage (personal communication, 10 April 1990) for the observations and suggestions offered in this paragraph.

21 Salisbury (1976:257–9) provides an eloquent statement of the need for these qualities by anthropologists engaged in applied or advocacy activities. These qualities are also required for preparing perceptive yet responsible ethnographic accounts for academic audiences. In short, while there must be an openness in communicating the content of a community's concerns, tact should be exercised in identifying sources of information and in finding accurate but nonsensational terms for expressing the nature of these concerns.

22 Nor is this necessarily a one-way process which invariably results in the "discovery" and critical exposure of the shortcomings of Native political structures. For instance, Feit (1985) provides an apt example of how an open and comprehensive ethnographic account can serve to refute criticisms made by other social scientists of the procedures practised by Native communities.

23 I am indebted to Dara Culhane (personal communication, 18 December 1989) for bringing this way of stating the matter to my attention. She also suggests that a necessary precondition for "telling it like it is" is for the anthropologist to exercise self-reflexivity and locate him- or herself within the ethnographic account. Taking this approach, a more accurate way of characterizing the ethnographic act might be "calling it like I (or we) see it." This, of course, raises questions concerning the basis of anthropological sensitivities and preoccupations: why do we "see it" the way "we see it"? What gender, class, ethnic, and political biases influence anthropological accounts and analyses? Which aspects of our activities as fieldworkers and our lives as anthropologists would we prefer to have dealt with circumspectly?

24 In a personal communication (5 February 1990) Peter Harries-Jones noted the existence of differing anthropological and mass media understandings of what is significant. "There is a definite selection within anthropology about what to comment upon; there is an alternate selection within the mass media. Because anthropology is not sensitive to mass media, the two frameworks for selection are rarely contrasted in systematic order."

25 It is interesting to speculate about whether the photographing of the then current situation and conditions of Indians would have been as acceptable to Curtis's sponsors – J. Pierpoint Morgan and President Theodore Roosevelt – as was his mission to capture the aboriginal heritage before it disappeared in the wake of American settlement and industrialization.

26 See Deloria (1969) for a critique of the continuation of this romantic tendency within anthropological writing at the neglect of less culturally exotic but nonetheless pressing issues within the lives of contemporary Indian communities.

BIBLIOGRAPHY

Ames, Michael M. 1986. *Museums, the Public and Anthropology: A Study of the Anthropology of Anthropology*. Vancouver: University of British Columbia Press; New Delhi: Concept Publishing Company.

Armitage, Peter, and J.C. Kennedy. 1989. "Redbaiting and Racism on Our Frontier: Military Expansion in Labrador and Quebec." *Canadian Review of Sociology and Anthropology* 26(5):798–817.

Asch, Michael I. 1982. "Dene Self-Determination and the Study of Hunter Gatherers in the Modern World." In *Politics and History in Band Societies*, eds. E. Leacock and R. Lee, 347–71. Cambridge: Cambridge University Press.

– 1983. "Native Research and the Public Forum: Implications for Ethnological Theory." In *Consciousness and Enquiry: Ethnology and Canadian Realities*, ed. F. Manning, 201–10. Ottawa: National Museums of Canada.

Barrett, Stanley R. 1984. "Racism, Ethics and the Subversive Nature of Anthropological Inquiry." *Philosophy of the Social Sciences* 14:1–25.

Brody, Hugh. 1981. *Maps and Dreams: Indians and the British Columbia Frontier*. Vancouver: Douglas & McIntyre.

Burke, James. 1976. *Paper Tomahawks: From Red Tape to Red Power*. Winnipeg: Queenston House.

Cardinal, Harold. 1977. *The Rebirth of Canada's Indians*. Edmonton: Hurtig.

Clifford, James. 1988. *The Predicament of Culture: Twentieth Century Ethnography, Literature and Art*. Cambridge: Cambridge University Press.

Culhane Speck, Dara. 1987. *An Error in Judgement: The Politics of Medical Care in an Indian/White Community*. Vancouver: Talonbooks.

Deloria, Vine. 1969. *Custer Died for Your Sins: An Indian Manifesto*. New York: Macmillan.

Daniels, Douglas. 1986. "The Coming Crisis in the Aboriginal Rights Movement: From Colonialism to Neo-Colonialism." *Native Studies Review* 2(2):97–115.

Dunning, R.W. 1976. "Some Speculations on the Canadian Indian Socio-political Reality." In *The Patterns of Amerindian Identity*, ed. M.A. Tremblay, 107–24. Laval: University of Laval Press.

Dyck, Noel. 1983. "Representation and Leadership of a Provincial Indian Association." In *The Politics of Indianness in Canadian Society*, ed. A. Tanner, 197–305. St John's: Institute of Social and Economic Research, Memorial University of Newfoundland.

– 1985. "Aboriginal Peoples and Nation-States: An Introduction to the Issues." In *Indigenous Peoples and the Nation-State: Fourth World Politics and Canada, Australia and Norway*, ed. N. Dyck, 1–26. St John's: Institute of Social and Economic Research, Memorial University of Newfoundland.

– 1991. *What is the Indian "Problem": Tutelage and Resistance in Canadian Indian Administration*. St John's: Institute of Social and Economic Research, Memorial University of Newfoundland.

Elias, Doug. 1976. "Indian Politics in the Canadian Political System." In *The Patterns of Amerindian Identity*, ed. M.A. Tremblay, 35–57. Laval: University of Laval Press.

Feit, Harvey. 1982. "The Future of Hunters Within Nation-States: Anthropology and the James Bay Cree." In *Politics and History in Band Societies*, eds., E. Leacock and R. Lee, 373–411. Cambridge: Cambridge University Press.

– 1985. "Legitimation and Autonomy in James Bay Cree Responses to Hydro-electric Development." In *Indigenous Peoples and the Nation-State: Fourth World Politics in Canada, Australia and Norway*, ed. N. Dyck, 27–65. St John's: Institute of Social and Economic Research, Memorial University of Newfoundland.

Fulford, Robert. 1985. "Displaced Persons." *Saturday Night* 100(5):9–15.

Goldstick, Miles. 1987. *Wollaston: People Resisting Genocide*. Montreal: Black Rose.

Gusfield, Joseph R. 1981. *The Culture of Public Problems: Drinking-Driving and the Symbolic Order*. Chicago: University of Chicago Press.

Harries-Jones, Peter, ed. 1991. *Making Knowledge Count: Advocacy and Social Science*. Montreal and Kingston: McGill-Queen's University Press.

Howard, Michael. 1982. "Australian Aboriginal Politics and the Perpetuation of Inequality." *Oceania* 53(1):82–101.

Jhappan, C. Radha. 1990. "Indian Symbolic Politics: The Double-Edged Sword of Publicity." *Canadian Ethnic Studies* 22(3):19–39.

LaRusic, Ignatius E., S. Bouchard, et al. 1979. *Negotiating a Way of Life: Initial Cree Experience With the Administrative Structure Arising from the James Bay Agreement.* Ottawa: Research Division, Department of Indian and Northern Affairs.

McEachern, Allan. 1991. *Reasons For Judgement: Delgamuukw v A.G. Smithers Registry (B.C.).* No. 0843.

Marcus, George E., and M.M.J. Fischer. 1986. *Anthropology as Cultural Critique: An Experimental Moment in the Social Sciences.* Chicago: University of Chicago Press.

Mortimore, G.E. 1975. "Colonial Transfer: Abandonment or Disguised Domination?" *Anthropologica* 17(2):187–203.

Paine, Robert. Forthcoming. "The Claim of Aboriginality: Saami in Norway." In *Festskrift to Fredrik Barth.* eds. R. Gronhaug, et al. Oslo: Norwegian University Press.

Ponting, J. Rick. 1988. "Public Opinion on Aboriginal Peoples' Issues in Canada." *Canadian Social Trends* (Winter):9–17.

Rabinow, Paul. 1985. "Discourse and Power: The Limits of Ethnographic Texts." *Dialectical Anthropology* 10:1–13.

Richer, Stephen. 1988. "Fieldwork and the Commodification of Culture: Why the Natives are Restless." *Canadian Review of Sociology and Anthropology* 25(3):406–20.

Ryan, Joan. 1988. Review of *A Poison Stronger Than Love*, by Anastasia M. Shkilynk. *Culture* 8(2):99–100.

Salisbury, Richard F. 1976. "The Anthropologist as Societal Ombudsman." In *Development From Below: Anthropologists and Development Situations*, ed. D.C. Pitt, 255–65. The Hague: Mouton.

– 1986. *Homeland for the Cree: Regional Development in James Bay, 1971–1981.* Kingston and Montreal: McGill-Queen's University Press.

Sanders, Douglas. 1985. "The Indian Lobby and the Canadian Constitution, 1979–81." In *Indigenous Peoples and the Nation-State: Fourth World Politics in Canada, Australia and Norway*, ed. N. Dyck, 151–89. St John's: Institute of Social and Economic Research, Memorial University of Newfoundland.

Shkilnyk, Anastasia M. 1985. *A Poison Stronger Than Love: The Destruction of an Ojibwa Community.* New Haven and London: Yale University Press.

Social Sciences and Humanities Research Council of Canada (SSHRC). 1988. *Research Grants: A Guide for Applicants.* Ottawa: Minister of Supply and Services.

Trigger, Bruce. 1985. "The Past as Power: Anthropology and the North American Indian." In *Who Owns the Past*, ed. I. McBryde, 11–40. Melbourne: Oxford University Press.

– 1988. "A Present of Their Past?: Anthropologists, Native People and Their Heritage." *Culture* 8(1):71–9.

Usher, Peter. 1987. "Choosing Your Poison: Differences of Opinion About the Destruction of a Native Community." *This Magazine* 20(5):40–4.

Van Esterik, Penny. 1985. "Confronting Advocacy Confronting Anthropology." In *Advocacy and Anthropology, First Encounters*, ed. R. Paine, 59–77. St John's: Institute of Social and Economic Research, Memorial University of Newfoundland.

Von Sturmer, John. 1982. "Aborigines in the Uranium Industry: Toward Self-Management in the Alligator River Region?" In *Aboriginal Sites, Rights and Development*, ed. R.M. Berndt, 69–116. Perth: University of Western Australia Press.

Waldram, James B. 1985. Review of *A Poison Stronger Than Love*, by Anastasia M. Shkilynk. *Native Studies Review* 1(2):112–19.

Weaver, Sally M. 1981. *Making Canadian Indian Policy: The Hidden Agenda, 1968–70*. Toronto: University of Toronto Press.

– 1985. "Political Representivity and Indigenous Minorities in Canada and Australia." In *Indigenous Peoples and the Nation-State: Fourth World Politics in Canada, Australia and Norway*, ed. N. Dyck, 113–50. St John's: Institute of Social and Economic Research, Memorial University of Newfoundland.

Wuttunee, W.I.C. 1971. *Ruffled Feathers: Indians in Canadian Society*. Calgary: Bell Books.

PART THREE

Anthropological Involvement in Native Policy Issues

This section contains six case studies and methodological analyses which examine different facets of anthropological involvement in public policy issues. The papers by John O'Neil and his colleagues and by Douglas Elias are particularly relevant in outlining methodological approaches useful in tackling pertinent public policy issues. The former describes a process of participatory research in various health care projects, the latter describes the various technical approaches useful in land claims research. Explicit in both is the need for a collaborative relationship between anthropological researcher and population being researched to ensure the production of data that both meets the exigencies of the public policy process and involves community residents in a meaningful, not token, manner.

Essays by Joe Sawchuk and Jim Waldram offer personal reflections of what can be involved in working directly for Native organizations and communities. In Sawchuk's case, the many barriers and confines placed on his role as land claims researcher meant that he needed to develop skills in dealing with the internal politics of Native groups while attempting to conduct policy-relevant research. Accounts of these matters are relatively rare, and represent an effort supportive of Dyck's call in the previous section to "tell it like it is." In contrast, Waldram's paper highlights a case in which the anthropologist had the relatively uncritical support of a Native community in his efforts to represent their interests to government. In this case, it was the lack of guidance by the community, rather than intervention by it (as in Sawchuck's case), that affected the process of anthropological involvement.

The next paper, by Colin Scott, returns us to the macro level by examining the manner in which both Native and non-Native politicians manipulate definitions of "custom" and "tradition" in their policy formulations and strategies. The role anthropologists have played, sometimes, inadvertently, in such a process is delineated. The final paper in the volume, by Julia Harrison, describes one of the more difficult issues to face Canadian anthropologists in many years. Harrison, as curator of the Glenbow Museum's *The Spirit Sings* exhibition during the 1988 Calgary Winter Olympics, faced an attempted boycott and protest by members of the Lubicon Lake Band and its supporters. The Canadian anthropology community became galvanized around the issue: some strongly supported the protests, others were opposed. What was at stake was more than the Lubicon issue: the very nature of the relationship between anthropology and Native peoples was scrutinized. Insofar as the controversy sparked debate within the anthropological community in Canada, it served a valuable function. The question that naturally flows from the issue is one that this volume has, in general, attempted to address: what, exactly, is the role that anthropology should play in the public policy issues faced by Native Canadians today and in the future?

9 Political Considerations in Health-Related Participatory Research in Northern Canada

JOHN D. O'NEIL, JOSEPH M. KAUFERT,
PATRICIA LEYLAND KAUFERT, and
WILLIAM W. KOOLAGE

This paper[1] examines the role of anthropology in relation to two northern Canadian realities. First, the health status of northern people is significantly lower than that of the general population in Canada (Postl 1987; Young, 1989). At the same time, "northern medicine" has evolved into one of the most powerful institutional forces at the community level (O'Neil 1986, 1989).[2]

These realities are a product of the internal colonialism that characterizes northern history. Northern aboriginal people have been subjected to successive epidemics of infectious disease, chronic disease, and social and mental disorders. Mortality and morbidity rates are consistently much higher than comparable rates for the general population. Ironically, the primary health care system in northern communities has become one of the best clinical systems in a remote area anywhere in the world. Per capita expenditures in the Northwest Territories are nearly three times the Canadian average. Clinical primary health care facilities in most northern communities are modern and well equipped, and the "provider-patient" ratio is, again, above Canadian standards.[3]

The tragedy of this paradox may not be immediately apparent. The health problems that affect northern communities are clearly a reflection of the economic and social conditions of life, and require culturally embedded, holistic, and community-based solutions (Young 1989). Northern medicine on the other hand has been for the most part indistinguishable from western medicine generally, and has been largely oriented to a biomedical and individualistic approach to health. The greatest tragedy occurs when, for example, children die from contaminated water or teenagers kill themselves out of frustration and hopelessness, and the medical system can do little except send their bodies south for a postmortem investigation. A further tragedy occurs when Native families interpret the autopsy as having a racist motivation and subsequently lose respect and confidence in the medical system (Kaufert and O'Neil 1990).

Although these medical realities have been increasingly a part of the Native experience since European contact, anthropologists have been largely uninvolved in advocating for change (cf. Weaver 1972; O'Neil 1981, 1988; Hodgson 1982; Kaufert and Koolage 1984; Culhane Speck 1987; and Kaufert, Kaufert, et al. 1985 for exceptions). Anthropologists have achieved influential advocacy roles in relation to some institutions which affect the lives of northern peoples, such as education, economic development and the judiciary. While anthropological influence in these areas is the result of complex and sometimes fragile relationships with both Native clients and institutional sponsors, there is little doubt that the discipline has affected policy development and institutional change in virtually every sector of northern community life except medicine. This lack of involvement is particularly notable given the increasing importance of health issues on the political agenda of most Native groups over the past decade (Bruyère 1988).

This paper reports the experiences of a group of medical anthropologists/sociologists on the medical faculty of the University of Manitoba who have attempted to establish a collaborative and participatory research program with Native communities and organizations. This group has established a research agenda which relies on the structured participation of Indian and Inuit representatives in the development, design, implementation, and analysis of research projects dealing with community–based health policy. Our approach also involves collaboration with medical colleagues in an attempt to ensure that an anthropological perspective informs medical policy development in the area of northern health.

We present here a retrospective examination of our collective experience in attempting to operationalise this research agenda. It is a reflective and critical examination of the process of participatory research, identifying areas where we feel our efforts have been successful, but also discussing situations where our goals have not been realized. The discussion will be based on a series of research projects developed over the past nine years.

EVALUATION, ADVOCACY OR EMPOWERMENT: THE HOSPITAL INTERPRETERS PROJECT[4]

This project has been reported on extensively in the literature (Kaufert and Koolage, 1984; Kaufert, Koolage, et al. 1984; Kaufert, O'Neil, et al. 1985; O'Neil 1988a; J. Kaufert and O'Neil 1990). In the late 1970s, when Native interpreters were hired in the two Winnipeg tertiary hospitals to provide language services to the large Native patient population, Joseph Kaufert and Skip Koolage were approached to evaluate the programs. However, a review of the literature revealed that most evaluations of medical interpreters were critical of their "filtering" effect on medical communication. It was also implicit in the literature that medical interpreters represented a threat to professional control over medical encounters (Bloom, Hansin, et al. 1966; Gerver 1974; Launer 1978). Discussions with the Native interpreters themselves also indicated that they did not appreciate the idea that non-Native academics should "evaluate" their work.

The research protocol that emerged adopted an advocacy perspective instead. A case study approach was developed where the researchers used videotape and interviews to document the activities of Native hospital interpreters in problem situations or "trouble cases" (Kaufert, Koolage, et al. 1984). The methodology allowed the interpreters to provide the sampling frame by notifying us when they encountered difficult cases. Our research staff would then document the interpreters' attempts to mediate these situations using videotape and interviews with all participants. In addition to the principal investigators, two Native research associates were hired. One of these people had recently completed her B.Ed. degree and was interested in a year of research prior to beginning her teaching career. In addition to fluency in her native Cree, she was also conversant in Ojibwa and Island Lake dialects. The second associate was mid-way through her degree in Native studies.

The first research associate was rapidly adopted by the interpreters' group, and not only observed their activities but participated as an interpreter-advocate for patients, and advocated with hospital staff on the interpreters' behalf. Her fieldnotes were rich with the dilemma of such a participatory role as the following excerpt illustrates.

Mrs A. was transferred from Norway House Hospital on May 4. I was going to check on Mrs A. today to see how she was coming along. When I arrived on the ward, she was not there, so I went to ask the nurse where Mrs A.

was. She asked if I was a relative, and I told her no, that I was doing research work with the interpreters.

I spoke with the daughter, Maggie, and asked her when they had decided to do the surgery on her mother.

She said she had spoken to her brothers in Norway House, and that she had indicated to them that she had not signed the consent for the amputation, because she did not want to be blamed for it. I asked her who signed the consent, and she said that probably her mother had. I asked her if she felt her mother knew enough English to understand fully about the consent, and she said that her mother knew some English, but that she didn't think enough to fully understand.

As we were talking, Dr F. came to speak with her telling her that the surgery was completed and that all had gone well. I asked Dr F. if he had given her a general anaesthetic, he said no, a local. I asked if there was an interpreter present, he said no, Mrs A. understands English. I asked if she understood the consent, he said yes. After he walked away, the daughter said that she was sure if her mother knows that they might have to cut her leg further, she would not give her consent.

I told Maggie that this was the type of case that we were watching out for, because one of our concerns in this research was to find out if patients are made to fully understand the details of their diagnosis and treatment, especially when they sign a form consenting to some type of treatment.

I spoke to the interpreter this morning re: Mrs A. when she told me that she had been up to see her yesterday morning and she had asked the nurse, who is in charge of her care, how Mrs A. was doing. She said the nurse, who was in the room with Mrs A., very abruptly said: "I don't know, I just came on!"

When the interpreter had told me this, she said she was going up to see how Mrs A. was doing today, so I went with her. The nurse entered the room just as we entered. She went over to Mrs A. and began fixing up the I.V. She looked at the people there and said: "I'm sorry, but you'll have to leave! At least some of you, anyway. She is only allowed two visitors at a time!" Everyone just got up immediately and started leaving. I just stood there looking at this nurse, very surprised at the way she spoke to these people. I stood and looked at her after everyone had left the room, appalled at the tone of voice and the implications of her words, as if reproaching the family for visiting their mother. She looked at me and read my name tag. I walked out and I found Illa speaking to her daughter in the hallway. Maggie was very upset. As they were speaking the other daughter came and expressed a need for something to be done to improve the attitude of the people around [here]. Illa told them that she could speak to the head nurse for them, and they agreed that Illa should do this. I went with Illa to ask for the head nurse. One of the things that I said to the acting head nurse during our conversation was that the family was gathering at their mother's bedside because they were seeing her as not being able to pull out of this and that this was a form of tradition, for the whole family to gather at the bedside of a very ill person, as a type of support for that person.

The second research associate brought a more cultural approach to her work and was particularly sensitive to actions which she felt were contrary to traditional cultural principles. Indeed, she was critical of the behaviour of some of the interpreters in their relations with elders, and expressed these feelings openly. Although probably the result of a misunderstanding, her attitude threatened the interpreters and she was unable to continue as a participant-observer.

We also hired a non-Native media consultant with a background in anthropology. The media consultant worked closely with the first research associate to videotape hospital interactions and also produced several videotapes that have been used in medical and community education.

Research activities often required the principal investigators to investigate clinical situations where an Indian patient was unhappy with the care she or he was receiving. These cases were increasingly brought to our attention by either the first research associate, who became the confidant for the interpreter staff, or by the director of the interpreter services once she recognized that we would support the Native interpretation of a problematic clinical situation. For example, in a case where hospital rules about limiting the number of visitors clashed with Native values concerning family support of the terminally ill, we were asked by the interpreting staff to interview and advise the hospital staff.

As the project continued, the research focused increasingly on the ways in which hospital procedures and the behaviour and attitudes of medical and nursing staff compelled the interpreters to adopt strong advocacy roles in order to protect the rights and interests of Native patients. This change in focus from a study of medical interpreters' activities came about largely because both our Native collaborators and research associates were more interested in studying the medical institution and professions.

The product of this research has been the documentation of the Native hospital interpreter's advocacy functions for Native patients. Both publications and videotapes report on issues such as informed consent, child protection, community liaison, access to traditional healers, and health promotion. Other collaborative ventures have included presentations at both medical and anthropological professional meetings, workshops, or rounds in the medical school, and sessions with medical students at various levels.

CHANGING THE DEFINITION OF THE "RESEARCH ASSOCIATE": THE HEALTH COMMUNICATION STUDY[5]

This second study emerged from consultations with community organizations in the Keewatin region, Northwest Territories where loss of patient confidence in health services was identified as a significant community concern (O'Neil 1989).

In the winter of 1984, John O'Neil met with hamlet councils, health committees, and other concerned parties involved in providing health services to the region. These meetings were open ended and were intended to elicit community concerns about health care service problems. In virtually every community, communication difficulties with health care staff were mentioned as a significant problem.

Several methodological options were available to us to study this issue. These ranged from a household survey of people's opinions of health services, through an intermediate methodology of indepth open-ended interviews with people after a visit to the nursing station, to an observational study of clinical interactions. Although the most difficult and time-consuming, our experience in the urban interpreter study had indicated that an observational study was the most likely method to empower our Inuit research associates to become advocates in the health care system.

After a lengthy period of consultation with Inuit communities and health care providers and administrators, the study began in May 1985. The first task was to identify two Inuit research associates who could assume the responsibilities that an observational study of clinical encounters would require. Negotiating access to any field setting for participant-observation has a political dimension; negotiating access to medical encounters is particularly problematic.

The process requires general support for the research at a systemic level (e.g., medical and nursing supervisors), but more important, individual consents must be obtained from clinicians, patients and interpreters for each encounter observed. These encounters are relatively unpredictable in northern communities because patients do not make appointments. The researcher is confronted with the delicate problem of obtaining consent immediately prior to a medical encounter with people who may already be emotionally stressed due to the nature of their illness. Clearly, fieldwork of this nature requires above average interpersonal skills, sensitivity, and an awareness of the background of concerns of all the parties about being observed.

A further complication to this problem was that Inuit research associates would be observing (and by definition evaluating) non-Inuit nurses and physicians. Although these people supported our study in principle, we knew that inter-ethnic politics in northern communities might inhibit our research staff from achieving observational access to clinical encounters, particularly when there was conflict between patients and providers. We were determined to develop a collegial relationship with our northern staff and designed these positions to attract suitable candidates.

The selection process began with the distribution of a job description in all Keewatin communities through local employment services, and in regional and national newspapers. The text of this advertisement is reproduced below.

The Health Communication Study is a two-year project beginning approximately May 1985 funded by Health and Welfare, Canada. The study will broadly investigate social and cultural factors which hinder effective communication between Inuit in the Keewatin Region, N.W.T. and health care services. Research will be conducted in several Keewatin communities and preliminary training and some data analysis will take place in Winnipeg. The project will be based in Eskimo Point and Rankin Inlet and the Research Associates will be expected to travel frequently between these communities.

The Research Associates will work closely with the Project director to conduct a series of interviews with Inuit and Medical Services staff in Keewatin communities. Videotape techniques will also be used to observe and record activities in health care settings. Research Associates will become skilled in the use of microcomputers for managing and analyzing research data. Occasional travel between Winnipeg and the Keewatin region will be necessary.

All travel expenses and a northern accommodation allowance will be provided. Incumbents will also be eligible for all University of Manitoba employee benefits. Although these positions are presently funded for two years only, the incumbents will also be affiliated with other research projects carried out by the members of the Northern Medical Unit and the Department of Social and Preventive Medicine at the University of Manitoba and there is a strong possibility of continued employment in the health research field after the project terminates. Arrangements can also be made if a successful candidate wishes to pursue post-secondary studies on a part-time basis at the University of Manitoba.

Qualification for this position includes fluency in English and Inuktitut, demonstrated administrative ability, previous experience in research and/or health care setting, and willingness to travel. The salary is approximately $30,000 per annum.

Two people were selected from fifteen applications. One research associate had worked previously as the Inuktitut language co-ordinator with the Inuit Cultural Institute. He had also worked as a research assistant in the Ottawa offices of Inuit Tapirisat and the Nunatsiaq member of Parliament. The second research associate had recently completed her first year of law school at the University of Manitoba and had worked previously as a medical interpreter in Churchill and Baker Lake. She had decided to take a year off from school to live back in her home community.

We brought our research associates to Winnipeg where they underwent an extensive two-month training program. Our "urban medical interpreter" project was still under way, and we were able to attach our Inuit research associates to that project. In fact, our Cree research associate assumed some of the responsibility for introducing the Inuit associates to hospital routines. Several Inuit patients were observed and videotaped by our staff during their admission and subsequent diagnostic investigations. Both research associates were provided with office space in the department and introduced to faculty members as research colleagues. They were included in various formal and informal departmental activities including colloquia, seminars, and social occasions. Our overall objective was to ensure that they were confident working in medical environments and interacting with medical professionals.

Once back in their home communities, O'Neil and the research associates held extensive meetings with Nursing station personnel and other local organizations. The hamlet council in one community provided office space and a work area was provided in the nursing station of another community. Not only did these arrangements provide appropriate work environments they also provided our research associates with an identity that assisted in their negotiation with patients and clinical staff for access to medical encounters.

The research associates set up video tape equipment in their respective nursing station examining rooms, and with each patient's and health worker's permission began videotaping up to five encounters per week involving Inuit patients, medical interpreters, and nurses and doctors. O'Neil visited these communities an average of two weeks out of every six over the ensuing year. During these visits, videotapes were reviewed and interviews conducted with various participants. Further field trips were conducted to other Keewatin communities where the principal investigators and research associates recorded community health meetings, interviewed past and present medical interpreters, and discussed communication problems with local health care staff.

Research associates were also provided with portable computers. Telecommunication links facilitated transfer of fieldnote files to Winnipeg on a daily basis. Comments and inquiries related to these files were sent back to the research associates immediately.

A third community was added to the study in August, 1987 when another research associate was hired and trained to replace one of our associates who left to take another job. Our third research associate was a member of and highly recommended by the health committee.

REPRESENTING DISPARATE IDEOLOGIES: THE OBSTETRIC EVACUATION STUDY[6]

This project was initiated in 1986, also in response to concerns expressed by Inuit in the Keewatin region of the Northwest Territories. A component of the communication study described above was to observe meetings between health service providers and community representatives. It was apparent during these meetings that a primary concern was that obstetric policy had shifted over time to a point where all Keewatin Inuit babies were being born in Manitoba (P. Kaufert and O'Neil 1990). Inuit women no longer had the option of giving birth in their home communities (O'Neil and Kaufert 1990).

It was also clear that health care providers shared these concerns. Medical Services Branch (MSB) staff were concerned over the loss of qualified nurse-midwives in the nursing stations and the resulting general deterioration in the primary care qualifications of nurses at the community level. Several pediatricians were worried that the current policy might be contributing to an increase in pediatric morbidity among young children left behind during their mother's confinement in Manitoba hospitals. Both general practitioners and obstetricians indicated that the emotional stress of evacuation might be contributing to birth complications.

We obtained a formulation grant from Health and Welfare to initiate a collaborative project which would systematically evaluate the impact of current obstetric practices in the region. The grant allowed us to integrate the various points of view of the groups identified above into the design of the project. Foremost among these groups was Pauktuutit (Inuit Women's Association or IWA) who represented Inuit women across the North. The IWA wanted to re-evaluate the traditional birthing system and had identified traditional Inuit midwives as a potential human resource for primary care services at the community level.

The Keewatin Inuit Association (KIA) presented a second perspective. The KIA had indicated that their priority in the health field was the construction of a birthing centre for Inuit in the Keewatin region; the cultural implications of entire generations of Inuit being born with Manitoba birth certificates constituted their primary concern. The Medical Services Branch perspective required information regarding staffing and training if community deliveries were to be reinstated, while a fourth perspective, that of the medical staff at the two Manitoba hospitals (Churchill and the Health Sciences Centre), gave priority to determining the reliability of risk scoring and saw the problem of effectively identifying low risk women as a primary consideration.

We therefore developed a protocol which would structurally provide for the integration of these various research interests. The first departure from a standard health research protocol was to identify the chief executive officers of the two Inuit associations (Eva Voisey, IWA and Peter Ernerk, KIA) as co-investigators on the project. Our other co-investigators represented MSB and the medical staff of both the Churchill and Winnipeg hospitals.

The formulation grant allowed us to travel to each of the communities in the Keewatin in order to discuss our research questions. Each co-investigator presented her or his case to the communities. This strategy generated considerable information about differences between medical and Inuit beliefs when, for example, medical perspectives clashed with the views of the Inuit Women's Association.

The community response to this initiative indicated three broad areas for evaluating the overall impact of childbirth policy in the region. These areas of concern included (1) the experience of women in childbirth; (2) stress on the family created by the mother's extended absence; and (3) loss to the community of traditional knowledge, human resources, and empowerment.

This consultative process broadened our study beyond the initial question of whether or not it would be possible for some low-risk women to deliver babies in their communities. Our research questions had grown to include issues related to cultural identity, cultural history, family integrity, and human resource development.

The scientific review of our research proposal was quite positive but raised questions about potential bias in the direction of birthing options at the community level. The reviewers felt that the political context should be separated from the scientific objectives of the study. Our response was direct. We felt that the structure of the research team included all possible biases. We argued that if the participatory objectives of the project were to be more than token, the ideological goals of all of our co-investigators must be represented.

In this project, our Inuit associates have functioned as co-investigators, research co-ordinators, and research assistants. Although Eva Voisey was no longer with IWA when data collection began, she assumed the role of field co-ordinator and was active discussing the study on northern radio and in community meetings. Her expertise was recognized by Native and non-Native northerners through invitations to speak about the study at several conferences.

The other Inuit co-investigator, Peter Ernerk, became the region's political representative in the territorial legislature in 1987. During his election campaign health concerns, and particularly the construction of a birthing centre for the region, were important issues. Because the construction of a birthing centre is in the political arena, we were expected to provide ongoing analysis and interpretation of our preliminary data in support of Ernerk's political activities.

The other research co-ordinator continued to work with us after fieldwork was complete on the Inuit Health Communication Study. Research assistants were hired in each of the other Keewatin communities on the recommendation of the local health committees and/or hamlet councils.

The study proceeded along three dimensions:

1 Inuit research assistants and co-ordinators administered a series of questionnaires to all women who became pregnant over a one-year period. Different questionnaires were administered beginning three months prior to delivery, immediately prior to, and after delivery, and one month after the birth. Questionnaires were also administered to family members during the mother's

absence. Research assistants consulted with nursing station staff in order to recruit participants and to secure each participant's written consent to be interviewed.

2 Our research staff in Winnipeg reviewed the obstetric records for all women during the period 1980–88. This very detailed audit will provide us with obstetric histories for nearly a thousand births.

3 John O'Neil and Patricia Kaufert conducted open-ended interviews with doctors, nurses, older Inuit women, Inuit midwives, and others involved in health care throughout the region. Inuit research co-ordinators have assisted with these interviews wherever possible.

In November 1988 we also organized a workshop to discuss the interim results of our study with providers and consumers of obstetric care in the Keewatin (O'Neil and Gilbert 1990). Our Inuit research co-ordinators and co-investigators and others working in this area in other northern regions participated.

A MODEL FOR PARTICIPATORY HEALTH RESEARCH IN NATIVE COMMUNITIES

Our experience has taught us that the success of participatory health research in Native communities depends on factors largely extraneous to specific methods for data collection and analysis.

We have found that the formulation phase is critical to the ultimate success of the project. The participatory research idea in the health sector is new to many Native communities; they are more accustomed to biomedical research where research questions are highly technical and data collection is controlled externally. An extended consultation period is necessary both to ensure informed collaboration and to refine research questions, data collection instruments, and frames for analysis.

For medical anthropologists to have impact on health policy in northern communities, the participatory research framework should include a multidisciplinary focus; it is insufficient to merely conduct studies and then present reports to health care practitioners and administrators. In the medical interpreter study, collaboration with senior nurses and physicians in the two hospitals had both formal and informal dimensions. The interpreter programs had advisory boards consisting of physicians and nurses with administrative responsibility for both the programs and medical and nursing services in the hospitals. Regular research reports at the board meetings not only kept hospital staff informed of research plans and progress, but also provided opportunities for "trouble-case" discussions. These discussions sometimes had immediate policy impact in areas such as limitations on visitors or arrangements for traditional healers. Formal seminars on specific topics such as informed consent and death rituals were organized in the authors' home departments and included medical and nursing representatives from other hospital departments.

In the Inuit Health Communication Study, senior nursing and medical officials assisted in the planning of the project and were consulted regularly. Local nursing station personnel were actively involved in identifying "trouble cases" and opportunities for case discussion with the Inuit research associates were encouraged. In some instances case management was positively influenced by these discussions.

Multidisciplinary collaboration was perhaps best achieved in the Inuit Childbirth Study. Co-investigators actively represented relevant medical disciplines but these representatives have become, or continue to be, advocates for the wider cultural framework the study addresses. Clearly, a culturally informed obstetrician is likely to have more direct impact on obstetric policy than a medically informed social scientist.

Redefining the status and role of research assistants is also critical to successful participatory research. The goal is to create a structure parallel to the academic research enterprise in the client community. Inuit organizations and their representatives provide the equivalent of university departments and co-investigators. Inuit research associates were defined as the equivalent to senior technical experts or graduate students. This is a departure from the traditional use of local assistants as translators or questionnaire administrators, and requires a significant commitment of both resources and time for training. It also requires attention to the social and political structure of research relations to avoid status and role problems.

Achieving this objective required innovation on several levels. First, new technologies made possible the long-distance supervision of an Inuit ethnographer. Our field staff were provided with portable video tape equipment to record all clinical encounters. Providing portable computers with telecommunication capabilities also meant that we could review cases and analytical notes in Winnipeg immediately, rather than wait for periodic field trips by the principal investigator.

We sought the participation of hamlet councils and health committees in Keewatin communities to assist us to select appropriate individuals. This required extensive consultation regarding our expectations of the research associates. We emphasized that they would gain an understanding of health service structures and could make their insights available during negotiations for health resource allocations.

In order to attract individuals to operationalise these goals, we had to convince funders that appropriate salary scales were necessary (e.g., $25–35,000 per year) in 1985. Although project continuity does not guarantee low turnover of field staff, our priority has been to facilitate the transfer of field staff from one project to another without lay-offs.

From the outset, our research associates were identified as professional colleagues. During preparatory visits to the communities to be studied, we ensured that they participated in meetings and social gatherings with the resident health professionals. Discussions during these occasions often have much to do with the health and illness behaviour of the client population. We felt it was important to include our Inuit research staff in these discussions to orient them to the ways in which health professionals conceptualized the beliefs and behaviour of their people. We encouraged our research staff to challenge assumptions that they felt were stereotypic. These experiences both helped to demystify the aura of power that sometimes accrues to health professionals in northern communities, and also increased the confidence of our research staff that they could interact with local health workers on a professional basis.

As the study progressed, our research associates became increasingly significant commentators on the health care system. Nurses consulted them when they experienced communication difficulties, and some became active members of their local health committees. One of our research associates continued to work with us on subsequent studies while the other has become active in both regional and national political affairs, working to ensure that health is given serious consideration in land claim and constitutional negotiations.

Creating this parallel research structure has not meant the reproduction of "academics" in the client community. Our Inuit research associates have social, economic, and political responsibilities in their home communities that are vastly different from those of university-based researchers. This means that unanticipated changes in priorities and objectives will sometimes occur in response to the different agendas held by community-based co-investigators. For example, Peter Ernerk's election to the N.W.T. Legislative Assembly meant that we felt a responsibility to provide him with data to support his political initiatives.

Participatory research also requires a demystification of research methods. Qualitative methodology may be more appropriate because it is closer to the experiential approach that client communities use to identify and resolve local problems. Interpretive frameworks for quantitative methods must allow for the construction of culturally relevant variables.

This experience suggests several important principles for anthropologists involved in northern health research and northern research in general. First, definitions of health and determining which social and environmental variables are related to health are set by dominant social institutions whose interests are generally sustained if these definitions and boundaries are narrowly conceived. Investigators entering the field often have their perspective of the problem shaped by the institutional mandate. Given constraints in funding and career pressures on researchers, transformation of an advocacy issue into an academic product often means the researcher must adopt the dominant institutional framework.

Second, despite the image of a value-free scientific approach, epidemiological research, and indeed all research, is implicitly political. Research protocols which openly address political issues are sometimes resisted by the medical research establishment and government funding agencies (which is of course a conservative political act in and of itself). Research questions are favoured which limit the responsibility of political and economic structures in the production of health problems. Wider environmental studies are more difficult to design, and research review panels can critique them ostensibly on the basis of confounded variables or lack of reliability.

By recognizing these principles, anthropologists should adopt a participatory approach to research and advocacy in Native health which ensures that the Native client's agenda is empowered. Although this strategy is explicitly political, it ensures that both the research process and products are linked structurally to community change. In the health sector, it is often a developmental process where Native and institutional definitions of health and health care are deliberately contrasted and scrutinized for the mutual improvement of both.

Research protocols must also encourage bilateral surveillance. We must provide equal opportunity for client communities to investigate the health service system while the system studies them. Indeed, our experiences indicate that when collaboration truly occurs, we may have little choice but to facilitate the study of the medical system. This was particularly true in the urban interpreter

study where the solidarity that emerged between the medical interpreters and our research associate determined which questions
should be asked, and of whom.

Finally, we must recognize that the knowledge/power relationship
has a profound effect on our research. If Inuit communities are to
negotiate effectively for changes in health or other policy that meets
local needs, they must not only have access to the same data but
also the ability to interpret that data to their own ends. Just as self-
determination in health policy and programs is an important new
direction in Native public health, so must the health research enterprise be guided by the same principles.

NOTES

We are most grateful to our collaborators on the various projects de-
scribed here, Ellen Haroun, Suzanna Iyago, Andy Koster, Nellie Kusugak,
Marie Mason, John Patterk and Charlotte St. John, and to our northern
co-investigators, Rosemary Brown, Patrick Brown, Peter Ernerk and Eva
Voisey. We would also like to thank our University-based co-investigators,
Bernie Binns, Michael Moffatt, and Brian Postl. Finally, our research staff
in Winnipeg, Charlene Ball, Eileen Bowden, Penny Gilbert, and Jackie
Linklater provided unfailing support throughout these projects. The
research was supported by NHRDP grants 6607-1441-57, 6607-1364-46,
6607-1305-49, and Health Scholar Awards to J. O'Neil (6607-1379-48) and
P. Kaufert (6607-1213-48).

1 This is a revision of a paper originally prepared for presentation at the
  Canadian Ethnology Society Annual General Meeting, Saskatoon,
  11–15 May 1988.

2 For the purposes of this paper, northern nursing services, physician
  services, and the bureaucracies that administer these services are
  considered together as "northern medicine."

3 Providers include physicians and nurse-practitioners.

4 J. Kaufert, W. Koolage and J. O'Neil, Principal Investigators.

5 J. O'Neil, J. Kaufert, and W. Koolage, Principal Investigators.

6 J. O'Neil, P. Kaufert, and Brian Postl, Principal Investigators.

BIBLIOGRAPHY

Bloom, M., H. Hansin, G. Fries, and V. South. 1966. "The Use of Interpreters in Interviewing." *Mental Hygiene* 50(1):214–21.
Bruyère, C.R. 1988. "Special Report on the National Indian Health

Transfer Conference." Assembly of First Nations/National Indian Brotherhood, Ottawa.

Culhane Speck, D. 1987. *An Error in Judgement: The Politics of Medical Care in an Indian/White Community*. Vancouver: Talonbooks.

Gerver, D. 1974. "The Effects of Noise on the Performance of Simultaneous Interpreters: Accuracy of Performance." *Acta Psychologica* 38:1659–67.

Hodgson, C. 1982. "The Social and Political Implications of Tuberculosis among Native Canadians." *Canadian Review of Sociology and Anthropology* 19(4):502–12.

Kaufert, J., and W. Koolage. 1984. "Role Conflict Among Culture Brokers: The Expereince of Native Canadian Medical Interpreters." *Social Science and Medicine* 8(1):6–45.

–, W. Koolage, P. Kaufert, and J. O'Neil. 1984. "The Use of 'Trouble Case' Examples in Teaching the Impact of Sociocultural and Political Factors in Clinical Communication." *Medical Anthropology* 8(1):6–45.

–, J. O'Neil, and W. Koolage. 1985. "Cultural Brokerage and Advocacy in Urban Hospitals: The Impact of Native Language Interpreters." *Sante, Culture, Health* 3(2):2–9.

–, P. Kaufert, et al. 1985. "Advocacy, Media and Native Interpreters." In *Advocacy and Anthropology: First Encounters*, ed. R. Paine, 98–115. St John's: Institute of Social and Economic Research, Memorial University of Newfoundland.

–, and J. O'Neil. 1990. "Biomedical Rituals and Informed Consent: Native Canadians and the Negotiation of Clinical Trust." In *Social Science Perspectives on Medical Ethics*. Dordrecht: Kluwer Academic Publishers, ed. G. Weisz, 41–63.

Kaufert, P., and J. O'Neil. 1990. "Cooptation and Control: The Reconstruction of Inuit Birth." *Medical Anthropology Quarterly* 4(4):427–42.

Launer, J. 1978. "Taking Medical Histories through Interpreters: Practice in a Nigerian Outpatient Department." *British Medical Journal* 2:934–5.

O'Neil, J. 1981. "Health Care in the Central Canadian Arctic: Continuities and Change." In *Health and Canadian Society: A Sociological Perspective*, eds. D. Coburn et al., 141–58. Toronto: Fitzhenry and Whiteside.

– 1986. "The Politics of Health in the Fourth World: A Northern Canadian Example." *Human Organization* 45(2):119–28.

– 1988a. "Referrals to Traditional Healers: The Role of Medical Interpreters." In *Health Care Issues in the Canadian North*, ed. D. Young, 29–38. Edmonton: Boreal Institute Press.

– 1988b. "Self-Determination, Medical Ideology and Health Services in Inuit Communities." In *Northern Communities: The Prospects for Power*, ed. G. Dacks, 33–50. Edmonton: Boreal Institute Press.

– 1989. "The Cultural and Political Context of Patient Dissatisfaction in

Cross-Cultural Clinical Encounters: A Canadian Inuit Study." *Medical Anthropology Quarterly* 3(4):325–44.

–, and P. Gilbert. 1990. "Childbirth in the Canadian North: Epidemiological, Clinical and Cultural Perspectives." Northern Health Research Unit, Department of Community Health Sciences, Faculty of Medicine, University of Manitoba, Monograph Series no. 2.

–, and P. Kaufert. 1990. "The Politics of Obstetric Care: The Inuit Experience." In *Births and Power: Social Change and the Politics of Reproduction*, ed. P. Handwerker, 53–68. Boulder, Colorado: Westview Press.

Postl, B. 1987. "Native Health – A Continuing Concern." *Canadian Journal of Public Health* 77 (July/August):253–4.

Weaver, S. 1972. *Medicine and Politics Among the Grand River Iroquois: A Study of the Non-Conservatives*. National Museum of Man Publications in Ethnology, no. 4. Ottawa: National Museums of Canada.

Young, T.K. 1989. *Health Care and Cultural Change: The Indian Experience in the Central Subarctic*. Toronto: University of Toronto Press.

10 Anthropology and Aboriginal Claims Research

PETER DOUGLAS ELIAS

INTRODUCTION

In Canada 1969 marks the beginning of the contemporary era of law and policy pertaining to aboriginal rights and title. In that year the White Paper on Indian Policy was published, proposing the repeal of the Indian Act and extensive dismantling of the Department of Indian Affairs. All programs were to be transferred to the provinces, and the special federal status of Indian and Inuit people eliminated. Finally, the White Paper served notice that the Government of Canada considered any unique rights once possessed by aboriginal people to have long since been submerged in the flow of history. These views were so forcefully rejected by Indians, Inuit, and Metis that two years later the government suspended any plans for implementation, and instead began to consult aboriginal people on changes being contemplated for federal policy (Boldt and Long 1985:3–14; Ponting 1986:32–41).

Since 1969 there has been a vigorous reconsideration of the legal, political, and cultural life of Indians, Inuit, and Metis, in turn fuelling advances in defining and protecting the rights of aboriginal people in Canada. In 1973 Calder et al. v. Attorney General of British Columbia, decided by the Supreme Court of Canada, affirmed that aboriginal people acquired rights by virtue of ancient possession of their lands, independent of any legislative enactment, executive order, or treaty.[1] Immediately following the Calder decision, the Government of Canada established the Office of Native

Claims to negotiate settlement of interests in land derived from the aboriginal rights confirmed by the Supreme Court. Finally, the Constitution Act (1982) guaranteed the protection of aboriginal rights. These advances represent three fronts on which issues of aboriginal rights have been approached in Canada – litigation, negotiation, and legislation.

Aboriginal leaders, members of the federal parliament and provincial legislatures, and legal scholars generally agree that negotiation is the most satisfactory way to settle conflicts of aboriginal and non-aboriginal rights and interests (Sanders 1983). However, the series of first ministers conferences, convened under the provisions of the Constitution Act to define the nature of aboriginal rights, ended in 1987 without any substantial conclusion. The Meech Lake Accord was intended to finalize the content of Canada's constitution, but aboriginal people were disallowed any role in shaping the accord. As result, they viewed the constitutional process as little more than a betrayal of themselves and their interests. When in 1990 Elijah Harper had the opportunity to stall ratification of the accord in the Manitoba legislature, he was accorded the widespread, almost unanimous support of aboriginal people to do so. The Office of Native Claims, given the mandate to negotiate land rights, held considerable promise in 1973, but has since settled few of the many outstanding claims (Canada 1985). By the late 1980s, there were announcements that claims in Yukon, the Western Arctic, and the Eastern Arctic were about to be settled, but by the early 1990s, the Western Arctic settlement had all but collapsed and the Council for Yukon Indians was cautioning that important issues had yet to be resolved in their claims.[2] Litigation appears to be the remaining course left open for resolving many issues involving aboriginal rights. This is an opinion shared by some aboriginal people in Canada.

In 1983, less than a year after the passage of the Constitution Act, the Restigouche Band told the Special Committee on Indian Self-Government that their land claims had been stymied by bureaucrats. Policies and procedures had been manipulated, in the band's opinion, by the government for the purpose of its own self-protection. In their case, they said, "It would be best to go to court in order to ensure fair treatment" (Canada 1983:114). Five years later, in July 1988, the Prairie Treaty Nations Alliance sponsored an assembly at Beardy's and Okemasis Reserve to discuss future actions they might take to secure their treaty and unsurrendered aboriginal rights. The federal government was accused of foot-dragging, failing to adhere to its own policies, and attempting to coerce Indian nations into submission. David Ahenekew, past chief of both the Federation of Saskatchewan Indian Nations and the Assembly of First Nations, concluded that the courts were the only route left for the resolution of Indians' claims to lands and protection of hunting rights.[3] Even more recently, the Government of Canada also seemed to agree that litigation is the route for settling land claims. In January of 1989 the government terminated negotiations with the Lubicon Cree in Alberta. A final offer was made, and a government spokesperson suggested that if the Cree were dissatisfied, then they should take the matter before the courts.[4]

A significant trend may be seen in all this. The direction of federal and provincial policy including aboriginal rights and aboriginal title is now largely being steered by the courts; as questions of law are settled by the courts, their determinations are reluctantly incorporated into government policy. This should occasion little surprise. As Kenneth Tyler pointed out some years ago, federal policy on the resolution of land claims only commits the government to meeting its legal obligations (Tyler 1981:27; Canada 1981:12).

There is as well another, less apparent trend. As important questions of law are resolved, especially by the Supreme Court of Canada, questions of fact become increasingly important. Since the Calder and Guerin v. The Crown cases[5] (the latter decided by the Supreme Court in 1984), there is no longer a serious question as to the source of aboriginal rights – in common law those rights are derived from an ancient and continuous occupation of lands and use of resources. But there are still abundant opportunities to challenge any claim of aboriginal right. Claimants may be individually required to show that their particular history and culture qualify them as common law possessors of the right. A group of claimants must be able to bear a considerable burden of proof. They must show the courts that they are aboriginal people with a line of history grounded in the lands and resources claimed, and with a culture geared to the occupation and use of particular lands and resources; they must show a current and ongoing involvement in those lands and resources; and they must show that the way they now use those resources is consistent with tradition.

In "the old days," when aboriginal rights were argued primarily as questions of law, making these proofs was relatively simple. As Chief Justice McEachern of the British Columbia Supreme Court has pointed out, the landmark Calder case took only four days at trial, Kruger and Manuel v. The Queen[6] was an appeal from a decision made in a trial which lasted less than one day, and Baker Lake (Hamlet) et al. v. Minister of Indian Affairs and Northern

Development[7] took twelve days. The trial of The Attorney General for the Province of Ontario v. The Bear Island Foundation et al.[8] holds the record as the longest civil trial in Ontario history, almost 300 days over three years, while that of Delgamuukw et al. v. The Queen in Right of British Columbia and Attorney General of Canada[9] lasted 374 days over four years.[10] In earlier, related hearings, Chief Justice McEachern attributed the brevity of the precedent trials to admissions into evidence "that permitted legal issues to be argued without exhausting and exhaustive evidence."[11]

Those days, however, are over. Now it seems that nothing is admitted in the courts about the identity, history, or culture of a claimant group, nor can anything be admitted without conceding major points to the claimants. Legal scholars have recognized as much. In 1980 Elliot wrote, "If aboriginal rights are to be cognizable in the courts of law, there must be some means of proving their existence to the courts of law in the first place" (Elliot 1980:657). More specifically, Bartlett has suggested that "the primary question for analysis [is] not the existence of the concept of aboriginal title, but rather its proof" (Bartlett 1984:15). Recently, Hurley commented that Guerin did not establish the content of Indian land title as a matter of settled law. Rather, he suggests, "The content of Indian land title may have to be determined on an individual basis" (Hurley 1985a:571).

In the end, these developments have meant that claimants of aboriginal rights must be prepared to marshal vast data in support of their claims. Much of these data will, of course, come in the form of testimony by members of the claimant population itself. Other data will come from expert witnesses who are often social scientists of one kind or another and frequently anthropologists. This present paper is intended to examine the capabilities of the social sciences viewed from the perspective of a legal or legalistic strategy for arguing a claim of aboriginal rights.

ABORIGINAL RIGHTS AND TITLE

Since 1973 considerable literature dealing with legal questions about aboriginal rights and title has developed, as a reading of the extensive bibliographies contained in recent theses dealing with these matters shows (Hurley 1985b; McNeil 1987). Little of this literature, however, does more than mention the role of social sciences as a source of information in court decision-making processes. Legal scholars have made virtually no attempt to show how social science data have been or might be integrated into an overall legal strategy for addressing these questions.

The law itself has received considerable airing in the learned journals, the result of which has been a sophisticated discussion of legal aspects of these questions. On the other hand, the technical and intellectual position of the social sciences in this arena seems to have developed in an undisciplined, *ad hoc* manner. This situation has not been good for either the social sciences or for the causes in which they are involved. Indeed, if Chief Justice McEachern's words are taken as indicative the courts seem to be on the verge of losing patience with the volumes of data that are adduced as evidence:

While the primary function of a trial judge is to hearken to the evidence, which is what I have been doing for three weeks, and what I expect to do for many further weeks into the future, I reject the notion that a trial judge must be a sponge soaking up everything that is tendered in evidence. There are limits to how much evidence a party may adduce, and a trial must always be confined within reasonable limits.[12]

This sentiment was reflected in Mr Justice Addy's comments in Apsassin et al. v. Canada, heard in 1987 by the Federal Court, Trial Division:

The issues, although complex to some extent, were, in my view, unnecessarily further complicated by the adducing of a substantial amount of evidence with little or no relevancy or probative value.

The tendering of massive details on the assumption that this might help the court to more fully understand the background of the case, more often than not, serves to confuse the real issues and, far from facilitating the court's task, merely complicates it unnecessarily.[13]

At the very least, we can see in these comments an appeal for more sparing use of evidence. A re-examination of the history of court-oriented land claims shows how this efficiency might be achieved.

While in Canada the contemporary legal history of aboriginal rights and aboriginal title begins with Calder, the antecedents of this and subsequent decisions extends far back into Canadian, United States, and English traditions. In the course of this history, there has evolved a set of tests that claimants of aboriginal rights must meet in order to make their case. These tests have been stated by judges in a number of ways, but the most succinct expression of them was provided by Justice Mahoney of the Federal Court in the Baker Lake decision:

The elements which the plaintiffs must prove to establish an aboriginal title cognizable at common law are:

1 That [the claimants] and their ancestors were members of an organized society.
2 That the organized society occupied the specific territory over which they assert the aboriginal title.
3 That the occupation was to the exclusion of other organized societies.
4 That the occupation was an established fact at the time sovereignty was asserted by England.[14]

Since 1980, these tests have been embellished, expanded, and contracted, depending upon the particular matter being heard, and the interpretations of law provided by the trial judges. Mr Justice Steele of the Ontario Supreme Court, in Bear Island Foundation rephrased the tests and asserted that

The onus is on the defendants to adduce evidence to prove on a balance of probabilities:

1 the nature of aboriginal rights enjoyed at the relevant dates (1763 or at the coming of settlement);
2 the existence of an organized society or social organization and the fact that it exercised exclusive occupation of the Land Claim Area. Included would be proof that there was an organized system of land holding and a system of social rules and customs distinct to the band;
3 the continuity of the exclusive occupation to the date of the commencement of the action.[15]

In 1991 Mr Justice McEachern accepted the tests set out by Mahoney J. in Baker Lake, but added a fifth test. In Delgamuukw, he required the Gitksan and Wet'suwet'en claimants to show that aboriginal activities are the same as those that "were carried on by [their] ancestors at the time of contact or European influence and which were still being carried on at the date of sovereignty, although by then with modern techniques."[16]

The tests, then, are subject to change. It may not be possible at present to identify a standard and universal statement of what must be proved in order to make good a claim of aboriginal rights or title. However, it is possible to derive a set of questions containing the elements of what is demanded by the courts.

In this paper, I will formulate the tests as questions that might be put to social scientists, and then to show how the answers are framed. For this demonstration, I will rely on data generated by the Kaska Dena Tribal Council of Lower Post, British Columbia, in the course of their program of research conducted as a part of their land claims. These data were generated with both negotiations and litigation in mind, and are offered here in a greatly abbreviated form only as examples of the methodology employed. As well, the social science data presented in this paper are too general and detached from the actual contents of Kaska Dena culture. However, since the present work is only an attempt to suggest a model useful in the construction of proof of aboriginal rights, such ethnographic detail is not necessary. Indeed, much of the data presented in this paper are purposely generalized to the point of anonymity. What is considered here are the methods and techniques used by anthropologists and other social scientists to provide precise and efficient answers to the kinds of questions asked by the courts, not the actual answers themselves.

Test One: What is the specific territory in which an existing aboriginal interest is claimed?

This question is consistent with federal land claims policies and court decisions which assert that claims and interests are expressed in respect of specific lands, namely lands currently used and occupied by the claimants.

The federal government's statement of policy, *In All Fairness*, puts the matter in general terms.

Comprehensive land claims relate to the traditional use and occupancy and the special relationships that Native people have had with the land since time immemorial.

By negotiating comprehensive land claims settlements with Native people, the government intends that all aspects of aboriginal land rights are addressed on a local and regional basis. (Canada 1981:7)

Once a claim has been settled in principle, "Lands selected by Natives for their continuing use should be traditional land that they currently use and occupy" (Canada 1981:23). These statements have been interpreted to mean that a claimant group must be able to clearly identify and describe the lands in which they claim to have an interest.

As for the courts, Mr Justice Mahoney of the Federal Court said in Baker Lake that to prove a common law aboriginal title, claimants must be able to show that they have "occupied the specific territory over which they assert the aboriginal title."[17] In formulating this test, reference was made to Kruger and Manuel, in which Mr Justice Dickson of the Supreme Court of Canada said

Claims to aboriginal title are woven with history, legend, politics and moral obligations. If the claim of any Band in respect of any particular land is to be decided as a justiciable issue and not a political issue, it should be so considered on the facts pertinent to that Band and to that land, and not on any global basis.[18]

The relationship between aboriginal rights and territory has been restated in several recent decisions. In 1988, the British Columbia Provincial Court heard evidence that members of the Fountain Band had always fished at identified locations on the Fraser River. The court decided in The Queen v. Adolph and Adolph that the aboriginal right to fish in those "specific spots" persisted.[19] In 1981, Mr Justice Griffiths of the Ontario Supreme Court had to decide whether one Tennisco, charged with a breach of the Game and Fish Act, was entitled to exercise his aboriginal right to fish. In his findings Griffiths tied rights to specific lands, namely, "lands over which ... the Algonkian Indian tribe had originally acquired aboriginal fishing and hunting rights."[20] In The Queen v. Bigstone, decided the same year, the Saskatchewan Court of Appeal related the exercise of the right to hunt for food to specific lands – "an area which is part of the traditional hunting area of [the accused's] band."[21] These last two cases had to do with lands and rights covered by treaties, thus the particulars of the situations and their resolution differ from what is usually involved in a land claim. However, the cases do emphasize and operationalize the principle of connecting the existence and exercise of rights to specific lands. Indeed, the treaties themselves were made with direct reference to specific lands to which Indian interests were attached, as a reading of any of the numbered treaties will show (Morris 1880).

The linkage of rights and specific lands permeates traditions of law and policy. Courts and governments say that if any aboriginal right with respect to land is intact, the claimants of the right must currently occupy the specified lands. If the claimants cannot show current occupation of the lands, this may be interpreted as their having abandoned possession of them. Abandonment of lands, in English common law, may result in termination of any rights with respect to them (McNeil 1987:62–71). At least three recent decisions have taken this approach – Bear Island,[22] Ominyak et al. v. Norcen Energy Resources Ltd. et al.,[23] and MacMillan Bloedel Ltd. v.

Mullin et al.[24] In Delgamuukw the court decided abandonment, as a principle of law, could be neither objectively determined nor administered on the ground. Mr Justice McEachern did, however, conclude that much of the claimed land was only sparsely used by the Gitksan and Wet'suwet'en – "very close to the line" of abandonment. This, he suggested, must be taken into account when negotiating future relationships between the Gitksan and Wet'suwet'en, the Crown, and the land.[25] Since the Sparrow decision in 1990, courts have been urging negotiated settlement of aboriginal claims, and this seems to be a trend in federal and provincial policies as well. Thus in both litigation and negotiation strategies for settling claims, facts must show that current use of specific lands is sufficient to maintain rights of use and occupation.

The "map biography" is the technique used to identify lands in which there is an aboriginal interest. Detailed mapping of aboriginal land use began in the early 1970s with the Inuit Land Use and Occupancy Project, directed by anthropologist Milton Freeman (Freeman 1976). In that project Inuit populations of Canada's Arctic prepared maps explicitly setting out the ways in which they used their resources and occupied their territories. Since then many populations, from the Inuit of Labrador to the Haida of British Columbia, have gone through similar exercises. Most have used very similar techniques of collecting map biographies, and they have been described by Brody (1981) for the Beaver Indians of north eastern British Columbia, Brice-Bennett (1977) for the Labrador Inuit, Freeman (1976) for the Arctic Inuit, and by Ballantyne et al. (1976) for the Cree of the eastern Churchill River Basin in Saskatchewan. These studies proceed from a common conceptual base and have yielded comparable results; anthropological research skills are central in this kind of work.

In each instance, the object was to prepare a set of maps illustrating land occupation and use by an aboriginal population. The technique involves having members of the population mark on a National Topographic Survey map all locations where they have hunted, fished, trapped, travelled, dwelt, or in other ways occupied lands and used resources over the course of their lifetimes. Respondent biographers' information is subsequently aggregated to yield maps of increasing generalization. The final product is a closed line embracing territory used by respondents in the claimant population. In the instance of the Kaska Dena land claim, for example, the final perimeter line defines the territory in which the Kaska Dena claim an aboriginal interest by virtue of continuing use and occupation.

The basic technique can be adapted to unique circumstances.

The researchers contributing to the Inuit Land Use and Occupancy Project say in their reports that data could best be collected on an areal rather than a point basis because activities involved in the harvest of certain resources were in fact conducted over fairly large, compact, and contiguous geographic areas. These areas could be adequately and accurately identified by a closed line marking an area used by a respondent as a muskrat hunting area, or caribou hunting area, and so on. The specific mapping technique reflected the environmental reality confronted by both the Inuit hunters and the researchers.

For the Kaska Dena, however, this approach was not appropriate. The mountainous topography of much of the territory occupied by the Kaska Dena results in sharp environmental gradients and localized distribution of resources. Thus, with some exceptions it is almost impossible to circumscribe harvest areas in a meaningful way. Accordingly, respondents were asked to mark use sites as points, with each point located on the map showing where a specified activity or harvest of resources took place. A map of data collected from several respondents, such as one aggregating the use sites identified by many men and women into a single sheet, is a generalization. To some extent, it will obscure the brute facts of evidence each respondent provided. Thus, for both legal and scientific purposes, it is imperative to be able to return generalized data to the source.

In the Kaska Dena map biography project, each respondent was asked to mark his or her land use sites on a clear acetate sheet overlaying topographic mapsheets at a scale of 1:250,000, the most detailed scale of maps available for the area in the mid-1980s. While the respondent was marking out use sites, a tape recording was made of all comments and conversation between the respondent and the project mapper. These tapes contain considerable information about the characteristics of sites being marked on the map, the features of the resource harvested, the circumstances under which harvest took place, who accompanied the respondent, and much other useful information. Immediately after each map biography was completed, the data on the overlays were prepared for computer entry, and the tape recordings transcribed. Preparation of site data consisted simply of completing a number of "primary data key" forms indicating the longitude and latitude location of each use site identified by each respondent, the activity that took place at the site, the name of a nearby landmark named on the topographic map, and a number identifying the respondent. In turn, all of these data were entered into computer files for subsequent manipulation.

Once the data were computer accessible, they were laid into a computer-generated map. These maps are printed with the base map showing landmarks on paper, and the maps showing use sites on clear plastic. To use them, the base map is overlaid with the plastic sheets containing site information. Any number of the clear sheets may be added to the base map to show any one or any combination of use sites. The maps may also be produced so that one plotting contains all site information, distinguishable through the use of different symbols for each resource, or they may be produced in colour, with each resource distinguished by its particular colour. Finally, all maps and site information can be viewed on the computer screen for rapid visual analysis.

Each point showing on the map is keyed to a number identifying the respondent who provided the site-specific information. This information may be plotted along with the site markers. The identification numbers may be stripped out of the computer map as required and passed to a data base manager, allowing an immediate tracking of all data – overlays, tape recordings, transcripts, data keys, field notes, computer files – directly back to the source respondent. After all individual map biographies are aggregated into mapsheets, and all mapsheets joined to form a single large map, the exact boundary of the territory currently used and occupied by the Kaska Dena claimants can be plainly seen.

Because of the way in which the data are organized and managed, maps of tremendous variety and utility can be rendered. For instance, maps can be generated showing use sites for each resource (moose, caribou, berries, firewood, etc.), with the use sites identified by all map biographers marked in. It is equally possible to map the use sites of selected individuals, or any combination of individuals, with regard to any single resource or any combination of resources. In matters where aboriginal people might be seeking an injunction against what are perceived to be harmful activities, such maps will assist quick identification of the individuals suffering the alleged harm, and the resource vectors by which the harm is transmitted to the human population. As well, such maps are useful in selecting lands described in the terms of land claims agreements, should the matter come to that. Such maps would then be useful in managing conflict between competing users. Finally, the maps could be useful to aboriginal managers should their communities acquire expanded and protected rights to lands and resources.

Courts and bureaucracies approve orthodox ways of doing things, and map biographies are the result of what are now standard anthropological techniques and practices. All data contained in the maps may be readily returned to the source, that is, the hands and mouths of the individual respondents. Common sense can grasp the essential information once the techniques are understood.

Test Two: What is the significance to the claimants of the current occupation of lands and use of resources?

This question is consistent with legal traditions requiring a demonstration of the extent to which resources contribute to the claimants' economy. Injunctions in particular require a measure of the extent and locus of injury resulting when competing interests interfere with aboriginal peoples' use of resources and occupation of lands. More generally, courts have seen the level of economic benefit derived from use activities as an indication of the strength of continuing ties between a claimant population and the lands and resources in which they claim an interest.[26]

The technique used to show the economic importance of land and resource use is derived from techniques used in harvest surveys and the preparation of household budgets. The final product of this work is an accounting of the absolute value of resources used, and the relative value of those resources within the domestic economy of the claimant population. Harvest surveys and household budgets have been used in the study of northern aboriginal community economies for at least the past two decades (Knight 1968; Usher 1971; Elberg, Hyman, and Salisbury 1972; Ballantyne et al. 1976), and these techniques have become standardized at a high level of sophistication (Wolfe and Ellanna 1983; Wolfe, Gross, Langdon, et al. 1984). Together, the two techniques clearly reveal the importance of resource use and land occupation in the local economies of aboriginal populations.

The Kaska Dena Tribal Council's research program was designed to gather detailed information from as many households as possible as often as possible. Much of this data collection was done by resident research assistants in each of three community centres. In mid-April 1984, just as the research was starting up, five assistant researchers were taken to Lower Post for training in collecting map biographies, conducting oral history interviews, and administering the household economy schedules. They were also introduced to the techniques of data management used in the program, and instructed in how to label, store, and control data. Three of the five assistant researchers were enrolled in an off-campus university credit course in introductory computer science. The research program was structured so that I reviewed all information obtained in the field and then deposited it in the council's archives. The final result of the data collection phase of the research is several sub-sets of data that together depict the household economies of the Kaska Dena – the "detailed interview data set," the "annual interview data set," and the "ethnographic data set."

The core of data describing household economies was collected as the detailed interview data set. (The lists in Figure One inventory the categories of data collected through the Detailed Interview instrument.) The data in this set were collected by administering a bi-weekly interview to an adult member of most households in Lower Post. A household was defined as one or more persons living under one roof. The first intention was to include all of Lower Post's households in this data gathering program, and all were approached and asked to participate. Not all households agreed to do so; thus, the sample was from the beginning an opportunistic sample, rather than a random one. The interviews were conducted by a research assistant who asked a designated household member a number of questions contained in a standard instrument. A calendar was on hand, and respondents were reminded when the past two weeks had begun. This was done to help assure that all responses referred to the past two weeks only, and not to days that fell beyond the prescribed time. The research assistant wrote the responses onto the interview forms.

This bi-weekly timetable of interviews was flexible, allowing on-the-spot fine tuning to accommodate the household respondent's personal activities. This regime was continued for a calendar year plus one month, starting in April and May 1984, and ending in early June 1985. As the completed interview forms were returned from the field, they were given identification codes, and all quantifiable data were converted to a computer-accessible format. At the same time, a text file was generated for each household, recording non-quantifiable data from the interview sheets. Examples of non-quantifiable include routes of gift giving, specifics of income generation and expenditure, sharing of labour, and records of travel. The interview schedules included questions requiring a response in the form of a count, weight, or measure of some material or time – meat, fish, firewood, hours of work, moose skins, moccasins, and so on. The respondent's answer to such a question was usually taken at face value. If someone said they received so many pounds of moose meat as a gift, that was the weight used to make calculations of value. Often it was possible for me to have a look at the resource claimed to have been harvested or used, and to make my own estimate of weight or volume. I could not flatly contradict any measures cited in the interviews.

CASH INCOME
Wages
Sale of Fur
Sale of Commodities/Crafts
Social Services
Unemployment Insurance
Canada Pension Plan/
  Guaranteed Income Supplement
Family Allowance
Gift
Loan
Other

HUNTING INCOME
Moose
Caribou
Elk
Grouse
Rabbit
Beaver
Porcupine
Sheep
Goat
Ducks
Geese
Groundhog
Bear

TRAPPING INCOME (FOOD)
Martin
Lynx
Coyote
Fox
Beaver
Squirrel
Weasel
Wolverine
Wolf

FISHING INCOME
Grayling
Trout

Jackfish
Whitefish

OTHER RESOURCE INCOME
Firewood
Building Material
Water
Topsoil
Berries
Other

OTHER DOMESTIC PRODUCTION
Housing
Transportation
Clothing
Household Maintenance
Services
Garden
Tools

CASH COSTS OF PRODUCTION
Cost of Hunting
Cost of Trapping
Cost of Fishing
Cost of Other Resources
Cost of Other Domestic Production

SUBSISTENCE CASH COSTS
Housing
Rent
Heating Fuel
Utilities
Services
Transportation
Clothing
Tools
Food

NON-CASH GIFTS GIVEN

NON-CASH GIFTS RECEIVED

Figure 1
Categories of Data Collected through the Detailed Interviews

As data were entered into the computer file format, each quantifiable item of response was assigned a dollar value. Thus what appears in the computer file is a dollar value representation of the real or equivalent value of a number of things that are classified together. For example, the category in the interview instrument that is described as "sale of commodities/crafts" embraces a variety of items. The total inventory included in the category is a list of items actually reported on the interview schedules. Under sale of commodities/crafts respondents reported the sale of moccasins, mukluks, mitts, hats, gloves, belts, jackets, snowshoes, cloth clothing, babiche (shaved rawhide), firewood, gravel, beadwork, river boats, tanned skins, semi-processed fur, quillwork, and wood, antler, horn, and beartooth carvings.

In assigning dollar values to each of the variables, wherever possible actual costs and incomes were used as reported by the respondent. In most instances, this was fully adequate. However for a number of variables, figures were assigned to reflect market equivalent values. Income reported in the form of meat, fish, and fowl was generally in the form of numbers of animals taken. This was then converted into the amount of edible meat available from each animal. (The figures used to make this conversion are those reported by Dimitrov and Weinstein (1984) for their research at Ross River in Yukon.) This figure was then multiplied by $6.60 per kilogram, the lowest price at which store-bought meat of any kind (pork neck-bones and chicken backs) could be purchased at Watson Lake in 1984–5. For other items, retail cost equivalents at Watson Lake were used. Labour was valued at $5.00 per hour where it was appropriate to assign a dollar value based upon the hours of work involved in a specific form of production.

At this point, the complete body of interview data recovered for each household occupied its own computer file. The task then was to prepare all this information for analysis, resulting in a set of figures representing specific economic activities for a full year in the life of the households in the sample. From this, projections could be made to describe the annual economic activities of the entire population. The data were first ordered so that the economic activities of each household were represented by comparable time periods. This was done by dividing the year from 1 May 1984 to 30 April 1985, into thirteen twenty-eight day "date classes."

Data recovered in an interview were simply divided so that reported values were allocated proportionately to the date classes spanned by the two weeks actually covered by the interview dates. As an example, let us say that a given interview covered the two weeks from 12 to 25 October. This straddles date classes 6 and 7, including 3 days in date class 6 and 11 days in date class 7. Therefore, 3/14 of the value for each datum was assigned to date class 6 and 11/14 to date class 7. Each interview for each household was subjected to this treatment. The result is a second set of computer files, one file for each household, converting raw data into date class data.

No household yielded a full year of bi-weekly interviews. It was therefore necessary to inflate recovered data to a full year of representation. Three approaches were used in this task. First, each item of data in each date class was simply multiplied by a factor that would inflate the recorded value to a full fourteen days of activity. This approach was barely useful; simple mathematical extrapolation tends to grossly overestimate or underestimate a variety of data items. For example, extrapolating the results of two days of moose hunting to a full fourteen days makes it appear that a household took a great number of moose in one date class; in most instances, this was known not to be true. This approach, used very sparingly, was most useful for extrapolating only those items that are very regular in occurrence – pay for full-time employment, transfer payment receipts, utilities payments, rent, and so on.

Second, use was made of the annual interview data set. In May 1985, a single interview designed to elicit information about economic activities was administered in most Kaska Dena households in all community centres. The instrument used for these interviews was a shortened and simplified version of the one used for the detailed interview data set. Its purpose was to gain data from the recall of the past calendar year of economic activities. All data recovered from each community centre through use of this instrument were consolidated in one computer file. Most of the Lower Post households retained in the detailed interview data set also completed annual interviews. Data contained in the annual interviews were then used to guide extrapolating an incomplete set of detailed interviews into data representing a full year of activity.

Finally, the ethnographic data set was applied to the problem. The ethnographic data set includes detailed information about household composition, age and gender of household members, and employment history. From these data, observations could be made about the regularity of Family Allowance, Canada Pension Plan and Guaranteed Income Supplement, and Social Services and Unemployment Insurance incomes. These data were also used to evaluate patterns and levels of expenditure on subsistence items such as food and clothing. Detailed descriptions of kinship networks in each community allowed an evaluation of figures related to sharing and reciprocity.

Also included in the ethnographic data set are notes and comments gleaned from living in Lower Post. Many matters of economic interest are discussed freely and in detail in the course of daily life, and this information built up in each household's file. As well, the research assistants were perfectly fluent in the economic activities of their people, and it was quite easy to find out how long some person had been working for an employer, or how much was spent on child care, or how many moose a certain hunter took in a year, and so on. Finally, I had access to records detailing transfer payments, wages, rent and utility payments, income from sale of furs, etc. This ethnographic information was supplemented with the observations of Douglas Leonard of the Manitoba Museum of Man and Nature, who conducted ethnographic fieldwork outside Lower Post. The procedure for using all these data involved loading a household file of date class data into the computer, and then, item by item, inflating the data so as to fill a full fourteen-day period. In general, the most reliable data were those figures taken directly from the detailed interviews. Next, the annual interview and ethnographic data set returns were consulted to determine an appropriate figure for inflation.

To arrive at a set of figures representing all households in Lower Post, not just those in the sample, a technique known by Statistics Canada as "donor records" was used.[27] The files of ethnographic data and annual interview data for households not included in the bi-weekly schedule of interviews were compared with those that were part of the sample in terms of numbers and gender of adults, children and other dependents, employment history, known sources of cash income, known patterns of hunting, fishing, and trapping, access to productive technology, and so on. Appropriate figures were borrowed from those households about which specific data were available, and donated to those for which data were lacking. In this manner figures for all households in Lower Post were derived from the empirical data collected in the sample. The end result is a complete set of figures representing a full year of economic activities for all households in Lower Post.

The household economics data may be presented in a number of ways to reveal more or less detail according to the requirements involved in a particular explanatory or evidentiary strategy. Any level of aggregation, including complete disaggregation, may be necessary, and so it is essential that complete integrity of the data be maintained (Figure 2). Here, the data are presented in the most

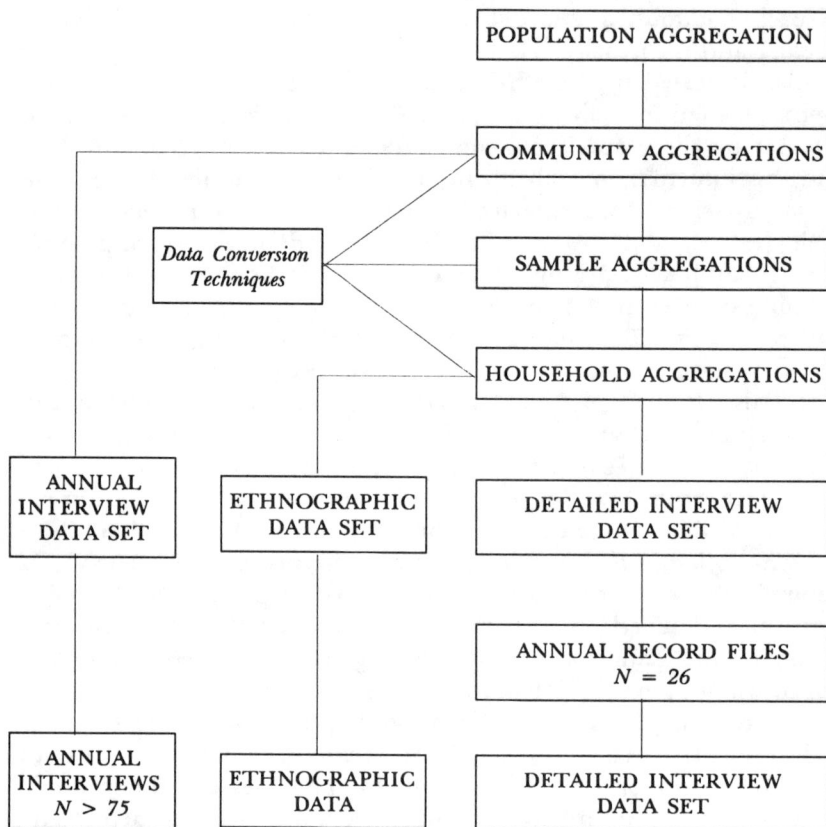

Figure 2
Integrity of Economics Data

general terms (Figure 3). All results for all communities are laid into a single table, giving a set of figures revealing the economic significance of resource use to the Kaska Dena currently occupying lands in which they claim to have an aboriginal interest. In this example, the dollar value equivalent of all resources used (net total resource income = $635,500) is shown to be 41.6 percent of the value of all income derived from all sources (total income: cash and resource = $1,526,600), and the value of all cash income not derived from resource use (all other cash income = $891,100) is shown to be 58.4 percent of all income.

While these data are not amenable to common-sense appreciation directly from the raw form of interview schedules, the organization of data does not involve anything novel or innovative. The

Level of Aggregation: Kaska Dena Population, 1984–85
Level of Detail: Summary

GROSS DOLLAR-VALUE EQUIVALENT DERIVED FROM RESOURCE USE

Sale of Commodities/Crafts	9,100.00
Hunting	403,100.00
Trapping	241,700.00
Fishing	19,300.00
Other Resources	104,300.00
Other Domestic Production	47,100.00
Gross Total Resource Income	**$824,600.00**

CASH COSTS OF PRODUCTION

Cost of Hunting	70,100.00
Cost of Trapping	83,200.00
Cost of Fishing	17,500.00
Cost of Other Resources	5,800.00
Cost of Other Domestic Produciton	12,500.00
Total Cash Costs of Produciotn	**$189,100.00**

NET DOLLAR-VALUE EQUIVALENT DERIVED FROM RESOURCE USE

Sale of Commodities/Crafts	9,100.00
Hunting	333,000.00
Trapping	158,500.00
Fishing	1,800.00
Other Resources	98,500.00
Other Domestic Production	34,600.00
Net Total Resource Income	**$635,500.00**
All Other Cash Income	**$891,100.00**
Total Income: Cash and Resource	**$1,526,600.00**

Figure 3
Comparison of Income Derived from Resource Use, Income Derived from Other Sources, and Income Derived from All Sources

techniques are fully in compliance with the standards recommended by Usher, Delancy, and Wenzel (Usher, Delancy, and Wenzel 1985; Usher and Wenzel 1987) for an aboriginal harvest survey, and by Wolfe, Gross, Langdon, et al. (1984) for compiling a household budget. That is:

1 The human population is clearly specified on a name-by-name basis.
2 The area of resource harvest and use is specified as coincidental with the area described by the map biographies.

3 The harvest is defined in terms of economic production and consumption.

4 Each resource is identified by kind as closely as possible and all categories representing economic behaviour have an empirical case-by-case definition.

5 All time variables are specified.

6 All data-gathering methods are documented.

7 Nonresponse and response bias are accounted for by standard practices of ethnography conducted by two independently operating ethnographers.

8 Recall failure and veracity are checked and controlled through the use of overlapping data-gathering devices.

9 Interviewer-induced error and bias is controlled by training, use of single-format instruments, and hierarchical examination of results.

10 The integrity of the data is such that each and all statements made in the final research product can be returned to a named individual claimant.

11 The raw data, or any stage of its organization, may be subjected to the closest independent scrutiny.

Test Three: On what grounds may the claimants be said to constitute an organized society?

This question is consistent with the legal tradition of attributing aboriginal rights to groups, rather than individuals; aboriginal rights to lands are vested in a human population integrated as the bearers of a distinct social construct.

In Baker Lake, the plaintiffs were required to prove "that they and their ancestors were members of an organized society."[28] In designing this test, the court referred to Calder, in which Mr Justice Judson said, "The fact is that when the settlers came, the Indians were there, organized in societies and occupying the land as their forefathers had done for centuries. This is what Indian title means."[29] In the same case, Mr Justice Hall referred to the Amodu Tijani v. Secretary, Southern Nigeria case, in which aboriginal title is described as being based "not on such individual ownership as English law has made familiar, but on a communal usufructuary occupation ... The original native right was a communal right."[30] The principle that aboriginal rights may be associated only with organized societies has been upheld in more recent decisions, including Delgamuukw, decided in 1991.[31]

The courts in Canada (and the United States) have accepted a variety of indicia to show that a specified claimant population forms a distinct society. These include a common language, reciprocal recognition of identity by other such populations, and general components of lifestyle (Bartlett 1984:30). In matters relating to land claims or the exercise of aboriginal rights with respect to resources, the over-riding focus is on the claimant population's interest in lands and resources. I suggest that a potent demonstration of social organization may be based on evidence simultaneously implicating the territory, the resources, and the fundamental social relationships among the claimants. Such a demonstration may be made employing techniques that are, and long have been, at the very bedrock of anthropology, namely, techniques of kinship study. Kinship is a principal factor in the social organization of hunting and trapping peoples. I assume here that a population forms a distinct society if the individuals of that population are mutually involved in kin relations and if there are significant ways in which kinship materializes relationships between the claimant population and the lands and resources in which they claim to have an aboriginal interest. This assumption is reinforced by legal traditions that insist that a current, living population acquires whatever aboriginal rights it might possess to lands and resources as a result of descent from persons who occupied the same lands since times immemorial.

For purposes of this paper, I take it that there has now been a sufficient demonstration of a specific territory currently occupied by the claimant population of Kaska Dena. I further take it as proven that the territory provides the claimant population with identifiable resources to the extent that those resources are of significant economic importance to the claimant population. For now it remains to be shown that the claimants are mutually involved in relations of kinship, and that those relations of kinship are significant in the population's occupation of territory and use of resources. For the Kaska Dena claimants, this demonstration may be done through the use of a compiled genealogy in the form of a kinship chart such that each individual claimant may be located within it.

The sources for the data used in this exercise include statements by contemporary Kaska Dena, government and church documents, historic records, and enrolment files compiled by the Kaska Dena Tribal Council and the Council for Yukon Indians. All genealogical data were compiled by computer into a single kinship chart, a small part of which is reproduced here for demonstration purposes (Figure 4). Ties of kinship can be identified and described with precision, and it can be shown that each and every claimant is included within a real web of kin ties.

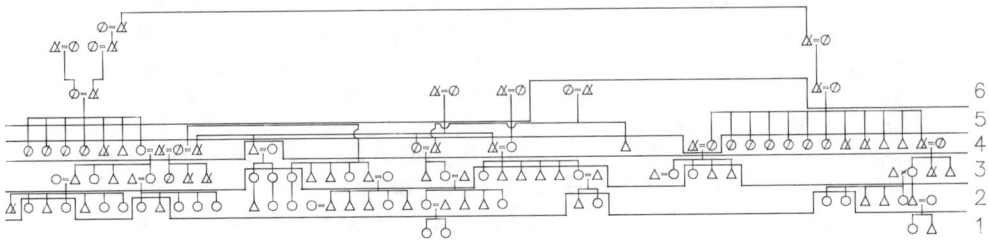

Generation 1: born 0–20 YBP
2: born 21–40 YBP
3: born 41–60 YBP
4: born 61–80 YBP
5: born 81–100 YBP
6: born >100 YBP

Figure 4
Partial Charting of Kin Relationships

As part of both the detailed and annual interviews, respondents were asked to name persons with whom they and other members of their household went hunting, fishing, trapping, berrying, wood-cutting, and in other ways occupied lands and used resources. They were also asked to identify persons with whom they shared the labour of non-harvesting productive tasks, such as construction of housing, maintenance of the means of transportation, garden preparation, hide tanning, boat building, and so on. Finally, they were asked to identify persons with whom they shared the products of resource use through giving and receiving gifts of products. Simply by referring to the complete kinship chart or the computer-accessible genealogical data base, it is possible to state the relationship, if any, between the respondent and any other person named by the respondent. By doing so for all respondents and all persons named as those with whom productive effort is shared, a model of kin relations implicating a fundamental level of social organization can be derived. The model will show social relations of production as these relate to the occupation of specific lands and the use of specific resources.

For the Kaska Dena, the generalized model of co-operative labour appears as Figure 5. This is a very generalized diagram, in which each square represents a person of either gender. The square marked "R" represents the individual from whose perspective the diagram should be interpreted. The numbers in other squares represent the percent of all occasions that the individual "R" received assistance in productive tasks from each of the other indicated indi-

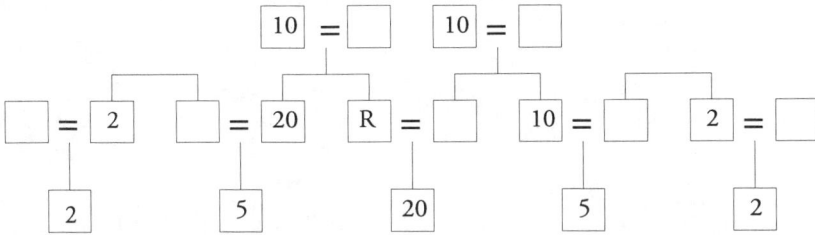

R = Respondent beyond these kin = 5%
Non-kin = 7%

Figure 5
Generalized Model of Cooperative Labour

viduals. Clearly, there is a quality of more or less here. That is, any given Kaska Dena individual will tend to share productive effort more frequently with close kin than with distant kin. The numbers in the squares total 88 percent; of the remaining instances of effort sharing, approximately 5 percent involved kin beyond the limits described in the diagram, and 7 percent involved non-kin. An individual who may be distant kin for one particular "R" will be close kin for another. Thus, the radii of kin involvement in productive effort overlap to link all the claimants into a distinct, identifiable social construct. The extent of cohesion may be clearly demonstrated simply by plotting the reported instances of effort sharing as an overlay of the total kinship chart, thus returning all data to the identifiable, individual respondents who were the sources of the data.

Production is, as it were, only one side of the coin. Distribution and consumption of the results of production is the other. Again, as part of both the detailed and annual interviews, respondents were asked to identify those with whom they shared the results of production, that is, those to whom they gave or from whom they received meat, fish, fowl, berries, firewood, and any other product of resource use. The same technique is used to organize these data as was just described for data relating to the sharing of productive effort. Again, the result is a generalized model (Figure 6).

Differences in the patterns of effort sharing and product sharing are evident. Individuals tend to call on labour more frequently from members of their own generation or the descending generation than they do from the ascending generation. On the other hand, individuals tend to give products as gifts more frequently to the ascending generation than to the descending generation. The joint

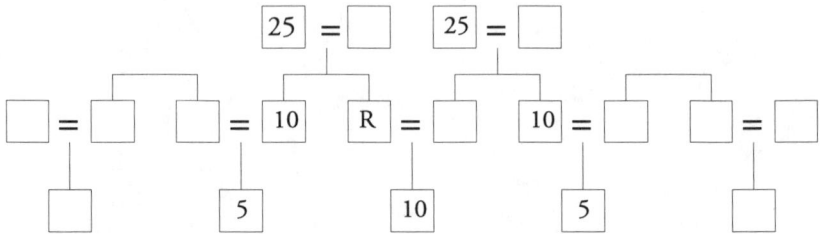

R = Respondent beyond these kin = 5%
Non-kin = 5%

Figure 6
Generalized Model of Distribution

pattern of sharing of effort and sharing of products thus binds three generations into a single construct. Of course, with the passing of time the relationships between particular individuals will change: a young and vigorous person who calls upon juniors for assistance and in turn instructs juniors in productive tasks will in time be the person to whom those juniors will give gifts of products. The operative model, as experienced by the Kaska Dena, is derived from an assumption of continuity through time which binds one generation to the next, relative to the same territory and inventory of resources.

This, I believe, is a clear demonstration of the social integrity of the claimant population. The techniques of demonstration are ultraorthodox in the field of anthropology, and the finished evidence of social integrity needs little explanation beyond what is necessary to define the conventions of kinship studies. The generalized form of the evidence is as fully accessible to common sense as are the individuated items of data.

Test Four: What is the historic relationship between the claimants and those who in the past occupied the lands in which an interest is presently claimed?

This question is consistent with the legal tradition that says that those who claim a present interest in lands and resources must be descendants of those people who used the resources and occupied the lands since times immemorial or at least since a long time ago. This paraphrasing of the question is virtually identical with its statement by the court in the Sparrow case: "It is clear that the Musqueam have a history as an organized society going back long before the coming of the whitemen [*sic*]; and that the taking of salmon from the Fraser River was an integral part of their life and has continued to be so to this day."[32] This principle has been stated and restated by many other courts.[33] The Kaska Dena contend that in their legal history, a long time ago is signified by the year 1870 and the British Columbia Terms of Union (1870) and the Rupert's Land and North-Western Territory Order (1870). To meet the test, they must demonstrate continuity of use and occupation extending from the current claimants to persons alive since before 1870. This requires both kinship study and ethnohistorical inquiry.

Historical black boxes – areas of unknown facts – become apparent here, as has been acknowledged by the courts in the past. In Simon v. The Queen (1985), for example, it was found that to insist upon a line of documented historic facts connecting a living population to a population alive in a previous century would impose an impossible burden of proof upon people with traditions of oral rather than written history.[34] In the case of the Kaska Dena, no more than a handful of literate people was known ever to have visited their lands prior to 1870 (Karamanski 1983). While it is not possible to simply will the facts into existence, it is possible to set out whatever data there are so as to make the black boxes as small as possible.

For this exercise, the chart of kin relations (as described under Test Three, above) among the Kaska Dena and their ancestors was used to establish known paths of kin connections. All available sources of historic data were then searched to locate any references to named individuals that also included information about the person's age. Taking the kinship chart in Figure 4 as an illustration, one can see at least six generations represented, terminating with a child who was under age ten in 1985. The most remote confirmed ancestor is the man in the sixth ascending generation. He is mentioned by name in five separate places in the Hudson's Bay Company records between 1904 and 1908. His son is mentioned by name in eight separate locations in the Company records between 1906 and 1917. All subsequent generations are thoroughly documented in official records of vital statistics. The Hudson's Bay Company agent at Lower Post reported the oldest man in the sixth ascending generation to have died on 28 April 1908, at what the agent estimated to be an age of about 100 years. Even allowing for gross inaccuracy in the agent's estimate, the man would have been born well before 1870, which was only thirty-eight years prior to his reported death. Even if he were, let us say, only seventy years of age, the oldest man in the chart would have been born in the year 1838 or thereabouts. Completion of this exercise involves locating such historic references to names and ages and attaching them to the genealogical records and kinship chart of the claimants.

This exercise, of course, only says that the living generations of Kaska Dena did in fact have ancestors, which is scarcely to be doubted. It now remains to be shown that those ancestors who were alive a long time ago occupied the same lands as the present generation. Various Hudson's Bay Company records, government documents, and oral history records, including those collected in conjunction with the map biography program, mention known geographic locations where named individuals known to be ancestors of the claimants were active within the claimed territory. It is a matter, then, of compiling a list of historic records correlating named individuals and named geographic locations. The cut-off date for this correlation exercise is arbitrarily set at 1930, since it is assumed that matters of land use and occupancy since 1930 are comprehended in the map biographies. For the Kaska Dena, the result is a listing from over sixty sources containing approximately 700 correlations of named individuals known to be ancestors of the Kaska Dena claimants and named geographic sites within the territory currently used and claimed by the Kaska Dena. Even this demonstration may be too broad a generalization: it says no more than that all of the present Kaska Dena occupy the lands previously occupied by all of their known ancestors. It may be informative to examine the finer grain of the matter.

In some instances, map biographies were collected from representatives of two and even three generations of living individuals who are related through ties of kinship. Where the map biographies are available, it is relatively simple to specify the lands occupied by each generation. For those earlier generations where there are no map biographies, historic sources are available which help define traditions of land use and occupancy. One example will be developed here as a demonstration.

The horizontal lines running through the chart shown in Figure 4 divide the population subset into six generations – long periods according to the number of years before 1985 of each member's birth. For the second and third generations, the data collected in the map biographies may be used to identify the lands currently used and occupied by the members in those generations. The members in the first generation are all too young to have been included in the map biography project. For the fourth, fifth, and sixth generations, historic resources are available to allow at least a partial identification of the lands used and occupied by those generations.

Figure 7 shows all the site-specific data accumulated into a single schematic map tracing the territory used and occupied by each of the six generations shown in Figure 4. The total area shown in this schematic map is the area contained within the limits of eighteen National Topographic Survey maps at a scale of 1:250,000. The area covered by the map sheets, between 124'00" and 132'00" longitude and between 57'00" and 62'00" latitude, includes all the lands in which the Kaska Dena claim to have an aboriginal interest. For purposes of this demonstration, each map sheet is divided into eight sections, and each section is hatched to document occupation by the pertinent generation of Kaska Dena people. As can be clearly seen, each succeeding generation has tended to occupy much of the land occupied by preceding generations. Some of these lands (between 59'00" and 60'00" by 124'00" and 126'00" and between 59'30" and 60'30" by 127'00" and 128'00") have been occupied continuously by the full six generations, that is from well before 1870 until the present.

Together, these data constitute firm evidence that the present claimants are the direct descendants of those people who have occupied the claimed territory since before 1870. All data may be easily returned to their source, and virtually no explanation or interpretation is required for their understanding.

Test Five: Are the practices currently claimed as recognized and protected rights consistent with traditional practices?

This test is implicit in much of what has to do with the consideration of the content of aboriginal rights. In the introduction to *In All Fairness*, for example, comprehensive land claims are described as relating to "traditional use and occupancy and the special relationships that Native people have had with the land since time immemorial" (Canada 1981:7). The concept of tradition has become central in the adjudication of matters of aboriginal rights. Thus there is reference in decisions to "their traditional use of the lands,"[35] "the traditional ... way of life of their ancestors,"[36] "lands traditionally reserved ... for purposes of hunting and fishing,"[37] "their traditional and historic right to hunt and fish for food,"[38] "the traditional hunting grounds of the ... band,"[39] "the traditional Indian fishery,"[40] and "fishing in the traditional Indian way."[41] Finally, there is legislation invoking tradition, as in the Northwest Territories Fisheries Regulations, Section 22 of which allows an aboriginal person to "fish without a licence by his [sic] traditional methods for food for himself, his family or his dogs."[42]

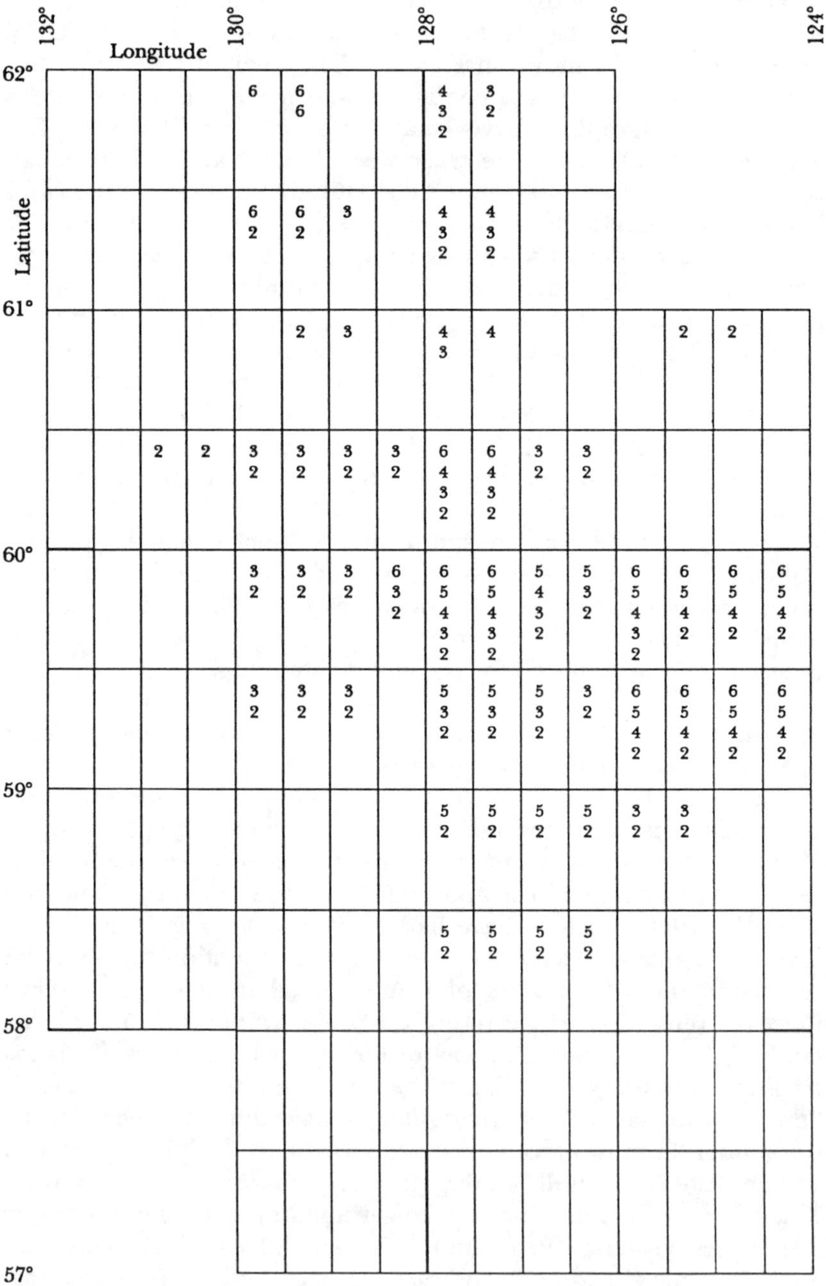

Figure 7
Succesion of Use Territory
(Numbers indicate generations)

Longitude headings (left to right): 132° · 130° · 128° · 126° · 124°
Latitude headings (top to bottom): 62° · 61° · 60° · 59° · 58° · 57°

Latitude band	c1	c2	c3 (≈130°)	c4	c5	c6	c7 (≈128°)	c8	c9	c10	c11 (≈126°)	c12	c13	c14 (≈124°)
62°			6	6 6			4 3 2	3 2						
(61–62°)			6 2	6 2	3		4 3 2	4 3 2						
61°				2	3		4 3	4				2	2	
(60–61°)	2	2	3 2	3 2	3 2	3 2	6 4 3 2	6 4 3 2	3 2	3 2				
60°			3 2	3 2	3 2	6 3 2	6 5 4 3 2	6 5 4 3 2	5 4 3 2	5 3 2	6 5 4 3 2	6 5 4 2	6 5 4 2	6 5 4 2
(59–60°)			3 2	3 2	3		5 3 2	5 3 2	5 3 2	3 2	6 5 4 2	6 5 4 2	6 5 4 2	6 5 4 2
59°							5 2	5 2	5 2	5 2	3 2	3 2		
(58–59°)							5 2	5 2	5 2	5 2				
58°														
57°														

The assumption on the part of policy makers and judges seems to be that current practice consistent with past practice materializes legal continuity from "time immemorial" to the present. Tradition thus becomes a measure and test of legal continuity. Using the Kaska Dena Tribal Council's data, a strategy for meeting this test may be proposed.

It is first possible to identify the resources currently used by the Kaska Dena and harvested within the boundaries of the territory they claim. The map biographies provide detailed information as to the particular varieties of resources used by the individual respondents. Thus the inventory of resources used, and the identification of the purposes for which the resources are used, come in part from the same body of data as forms the base of data for demonstrating the territory currently occupied by the claimants. Data collected to provide an assessment of the population's household and local economies confirms the inventory drawn from the map biography data, which have been discussed as the detailed interview data set and the annual interview data sets. Together, these sources yield an exhaustive inventory of resources important in Kaska Dena culture (Figure 8). The inventory has the same evidential characteristics as the map biographies, since they are both part and parcel of the same process – standard techniques of data generation, integrity, and common-sense appeal (Figure 9).

This, of course, says nothing about whether the ways in which those resources are used are traditional. For this demonstration, it is necessary to examine the particulars of the sociocultural system of the Kaska Dena. The important question is whether the identified resources play a role in Kaska Dena society consistent with their role in the past.

The data pertaining to the Kaska Dena show that gross equivalent income derived from the use of resources contained within the claimed territory accounts for 54 percent of all income of Kaska Dena. In the very least of economic terms, the Kaska Dena land claim is an attempt to secure a significant part of their livelihood. Without attempting here to marshal the historic material in support, it can be said that there are no data whatever to suggest that the local economy of the Kaska Dena has ever had anything less than a significant use-based component. Still, it remains that about half of the Kaska Dena total income is in the form of cash. Does this cash, or any particular part of it, represent a break with tradition?

Cash is derived from several sources. Wages contribute about 55 percent of all cash in the local economy, or about 34 percent of the total value of all income from all sources. Income derived from

BERRIES	roundfish	sheep
bearberries	sucker	otter
lowbush cranberries	lake trout	grizzly bear
highbush cranberries	whitefish	beaver
saskatoons		wolverine
huckleberries	MAMMALS	gopher
blackberries	marten	grouse
soapberries	bear	goose
roseberries	caribou	
mossberries	fisher	OTHER RESOURCES
blueberries	mule deer	gravel
	goat	sand
FISH	groundhog	top soil
brown trout	mink	firewood
carp	squirrel	construction wood
Dolly Varden	porcupine	water
grayling	lynx	other minerals
lingfish	moose	
salmon	weasel	DWELLING SITES
char	rabbit	
rainbow trout	duck	BURIAL SITES
pike	fox	
jackfish	muskrat	

Figure 8
Inventory of Resources Used by the Kaska Dena

resource-based sources accounts for about 37 percent of the total value of all income from all sources. Clearly, wages are no more important in the local Kaska Dena economy than is the use of resources. Regression analysis of the economic data shows that as cash income rises, so too does income from hunting, fishing, and other forms of resource use and domestic production. A mere increase in the number of available dollars, however, does not itself result in increased harvests of game, firewood, fish, construction materials, and so on. Regression analysis also shows that as cash income rises, so too do expenditures on productive tools such as guns, vehicles, motors, and chainsaws. Dollars are spent on tools used to harvest resources. Improved technology, in turn, increases the gross value of resources harvested. Again in strictly economic terms, it is clear that increased investment of cash in productive technology is a sound practice. The data show that for each dollar invested in technology associated with resource use, there is a net return of $3.36. The implication is that wages (and other sources of

```
        ┌─────────────────────────────────────┐
        │   INVENTORY OF RESOURCES USED       │
        └─────────────────────────────────────┘
```

MAP BIOGRAPHY DATA

DETAILED INTERVIEW
DATA SET

ANNUAL INTERVIEW
DATA SET

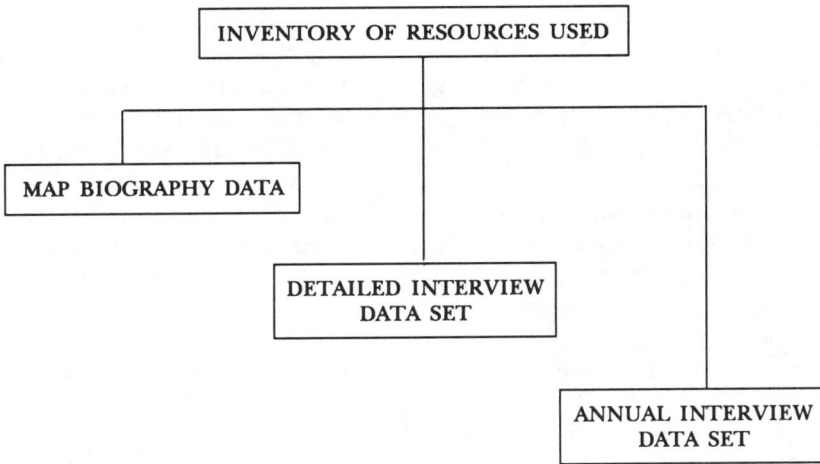

Figure 9
Integrity of Resource Inventory Data

cash income) are used to underwrite the cost of resource production. There can be no suggestion that hunting, fishing, trapping,
and other uses of resources are simply supplements to an essentially
wage-based economy. There is nothing remarkable about this
observation; even the most recent research in northern regions has
reached the same conclusion (Wenzel 1986; Petterson 1987; Wolfe
and Walker 1987; Bone 1989; Smith and Wright 1989; Hopper and
Power 1991; Kruse 1991; Nutall 1991). If hunting, fishing, trapping,
and other use of resources constitutes the core of tradition in the
exercise of aboriginal rights, then it may be concluded that the
Kaska Dena enjoy a fundamentally traditional economy. That is to
say, the Kaska Dena have adapted to changes in their environment
(including their social and political environment) in ways that are
entirely consistent with the practices of past generations.

Perhaps, though, the younger generations of Kaska Dena are just
now in the process of abandoning their traditions. As has already
been shown (under Test Four above), successive generations of
Kaska Dena have occupied approximately the same lands for as far
back in their history as it is possible to say with any level of confidence. As well, as has been shown (under Test Three above), all
generations of Kaska Dena participate in obtaining and consuming
resources, and these processes are materialized within the kinship
structure of Kaska Dena society. Finally, regression analysis demon-

strates that old and young all maintain similar levels of use-based production. In other words, there is little to distinguish the economic habits and characteristics of one generation from those of another, with the exception that younger people are obliged to spend cash in order to build up an appropriate tool kit the likes of which their elders already possess. Today's elders were once required to do the same. Given that lands occupied, resource use patterns, modes of production, and modes of consumption are indistinguishable on a generational basis, one can only conclude that traditions are persisting, not waning. Again, none of this will surprise researchers familiar with the field.

Test Six: Has the claimant group retained exclusive occupation of the territory claimed?

It would seem that meeting this test relies on no more than the contents of the historic record: either there is documentary and oral history to support an assertion of exclusive occupation or there is not. The question is not quite so clear as that, however.

In general, exclusive use refers to the territory claimed, not the manner in which the territory was used. Thus the Inuit claim of aboriginal title in the Baker Lake case was partially defeated when evidence showed that the Inuit and the neighbouring Dene both made use of some of the same lands, although at different seasons and in pursuit of different resources.[43] Apparently, whatever conflict might have arisen as a result of this joint use was a conflict expressible only in English legal terms, not in terms of local Inuit or Dene culture. In Bear Island Foundation, it was found that the claimants had to show exclusive occupation until the time they started their claims action. This would require the claimant group to show that they have excluded not only other groups of Indians, but well-armed non-Indian explorers, miners, traders, settlers, and police as well.[44]

Since demonstrating exclusive occupation relies completely on the quality and quantity of relevant historic data in any particular situation, I will not attempt here to generalize an approach to meet this last test.

CONCLUSION

It does seem possible to meet the tests set by court traditions dealing with questions of aboriginal title and aboriginal rights, but it is obviously a monumental task to do so. Furthermore, the tests are becoming increasingly particular, to the point that if they are elaborated much further, it would not be possible to meet them with any amount of research and data-gathering. The tests set out by Mr Justice Steele in Bear Island Foundation, discussed above, for example, may have crossed the line of social science comprehension. It is difficult to imagine what resources are available that could be used to reconstruct aboriginal practices at the time of the Royal Proclamation of 1763, and then to show that those practices were unique to the Temagami people, especially at the level of definition and detail demanded by the court.

Courts have been reluctant to accept cultural or historical gene-ralizations; whatever data are tendered as evidence must pertain to the principals involved in the matter. Thus Mr Justice Steele was reluctant to accept the opinions of James V. Wright and the late Edward S. Rogers, pre-eminent Canadian scholars of aboriginal culture and history, because they had conducted research in areas adjacent to the Temagami but not among the Temagami them-selves.[45] Where hard data are lacking, social scientists in the role of expert witnesses are asked for opinions, and it has been easy for the courts to view these opinions as somewhat less than professionally scientific submissions. In Baker Lake, for example, Peter Usher's testimony was much discounted by Justice Mahoney, who described his words as having "more the ring of a convinced advocate than a dispassionate professional."[46] Similarly, Hugh Brody was described by Mr Justice Addy of the Federal Court, Trial Division, in Apsassin as "an informed champion and an enthusiastic supporter of the aboriginal peoples' cause generally and of the Dunne-za Cree in particular but, by the same token, as a person who conspicuously lacked the objectivity required of an expert witness."[47] In Del-gamuukw, Mr Justice McEachern characterized anthropologist Daly as "more an advocate than a witness."[48]

There may well be some substance in these complaints, and if so, remedies must be provided so that similar errors will not be re-peated. The solution, however, does not ultimately lie in producing more or better data so as to obviate opinion. In some instances, there are no more data to be found no matter how diligent the re-searchers and analysts. In all instances, greater volumes of data must be equated with increased costs, and the costs of running a fully developed program of research are already obscenely high. In the last analysis, the solution lies with parliament, which alone has the capacity to form constitutional protections of aboriginal rights that need not and cannot be undermined in the courts. Until that is done, however, the courts remain central in any discussion of these matters.

In the interim, I would suggest that aboriginal people, legal scholars, legal practitioners, and social scientists take steps to establish ways for thoughts and ideas to flow among them. At present, it would seem that each of these actors knows very little about what constitutes the roles played by the others. Those involved in these matters already have knowledge-sharing institutions in place – conferences, journals, newspapers, and classrooms – but they tend to share information among their own kind, and all too rarely involve others in parallel fields. As an example, the 1983 Anthropology and Advocacy Conference at Memorial University of Newfoundland did not include a single Canadian lawyer as a participant (Paine 1985). This mutual isolation cannot be helpful.

Aboriginal claims research, negotiation, and litigation require of anthropologists a great variety of skills and knowledge. Knowledge of computers, data management and analysis, and cartography; ethnohistorical and oral tradition methods and techniques; and techniques of genealogical reconstruction and participant-observation must also be combined with a working knowledge of the law on aboriginal claims and the manner in which expert testimony is received by the courts. This is a tall order for any anthropologist, and in most cases a team approach is most appropriate.

All too often, though, claimants of aboriginal rights are unable to fund teams of researchers. They are usually fortunate if they can afford to retain a lawyer and a single cultural expert to mount their claim. In many respects, anthropologists' tradition of multidisciplinary training and interests best suits them for the role of cultural expert. The questions involved in land claims work, however, are largely questions of law rather than science, and cultural experts must be as aware as possible of the legal culture shaping the field. Similarly, in circumstances where an anthropologist embodies all the technical assistance available to a lawyer, it is in the lawyer's interest to know what anthropologists are capable of doing. I hope this paper will help inform lawyers about some relevant aspects of the social sciences, and social scientists about some aspects of law. If it generates discussion and criticism in either camp, then its objectives will have been met.

NOTES

I would like to thank the Kaska Dena Tribal Council for permission to use data derived from their land claims research. From early 1984 until 1987 I was the council's director of research. Thanks are also due to the Social

Sciences and Humanities Research Council of Canada, who funded research in 1987 and 1988, and to the Scott Polar Research Institute at the University of Cambridge, England, whose generous hospitality provided the opportunity to study these matters from an international perspective. Several scholars and practitioners have read various drafts of this paper and offered well-considered criticism, including Kent McNeil, Wallis Smith, Allan Pratt, Ignatius LaRusic, Roger MacDonnell, Paul McHugh, Jennie Abell, Steve Walsh, and Julie Cruikshank; any remaining weaknesses are, of course, no fault of theirs.

This paper is an updated and edited version of one published in the *Canadian Native Law Reporter* 1 [1989]: 1–43 under the title "Rights and Research: The Role of the Social Sciences in the Legal and Political Resolution of Land Claims and Questions of Aboriginal Rights." Some elements of methodology have been omitted in this version, and the reader is directed to the original for a full methodological discussion.

1 [1973] *S.C.R.* 313, [1973] 4 *W.W.R.* 1, 34 *D.L.R.* (3d) 145.

2 *Globe and Mail* 23/07/88.

3 *Star Phoenix* (Saskatoon) 20/07/88, 21/07/88, 22/07/88.

4 *Herald* (Lethbridge) 27/01/89; *Windspeaker* 04/12/91.

5 [1984] 2 *S.C.R.* 335, [1984] 4 *W.W.R.* 481, [1985] 1 *C.N.L.R.* 120.

6 (1977), [1978] 1 *S.C.R.* 104, [1977] 4 *W.W.R.* 300.

7 (1979), [1980] 1 *F.C.* 518, [1980] 5 *W.W.R.* 193, [1979] 3 *C.N.L.R.* 17 (F.C.T.D.).

8 (1984), [1985] 1 *C.N.L.R.* 1 (Ont. S.C.).

9 Delgamuukw et al. v. The Queen in Right of British Columbia and Attorney General of Canada [1991] unreported.

10 Ibid. on Registry cover.

11 (1987), [1987] 6 *W.W.R.* 155, [1988] 1 *C.N.L.R.* 188 at 201.

12 Delgamuukw, *supra*, note 11 at 201.

13 [1988] 1 *C.N.L.R.* 73 at 80.

14 Baker Lake, *supra*, note 7 at 45 *C.N.L.R.*

15 Bear Island, *supra*, note 8 at 16.

16 Delgamuukw, *supra*, note 12 at 227.

17 Baker Lake, *supra*, note 7 at 45 *C.N.L.R.*

18 Kruger and Manuel, *supra*, note 6 at 303.

19 [1988] 2 *C.N.L.R.* 70 at 72–3.

20 R v. Tennisco, [1981] 4 *C.N.L.R.* 138 at 140.

21 R v. Bigstone, [1981] 3 *C.N.L.R.* 103 at 104.

22 (1984), [1985] 1 *C.N.L.R.* 1 (Ont. S.C.).

23 [1985] 3 *C.N.L.R.* 111 at 114–15 (Alta. C.A.).

24 [1985] 2 *C.N.L.R.* 26 at 50–2 (B.C.S.C.).

25 Delgamuukw, *supra*, note 9 at 291–2.

26 Calder, *supra*, note 1 at 26–8 *W.W.R.*

27 P. White, Statistics Canada. Personal communication, December, 1987.

28 Baker Lake, *supra*, note 7 at 45 *C.N.L.R.*

29 Calder, *supra*, note 1 at 11 *W.W.R.*

30 Amodu Tijani v. Secretary, Southern Nigeria (1921), 2 A.C. 399 at 409–10, quoted by Hall, J. in Calder, *supra*, note 1 at 70–1 *W.W.R.*

31 Joe et al. v. Findlay and the Attorney General of Canada (1981), 3 *W.W.R.* 60, [1981] 3 *C.N.L.R.* 58 at 60 (B.C.C.A.); R v. Curley (1982), 2 *C.N.L.R.* 171 at 174 (N.W.T.T.C.); Bear Island *supra*, note 8 at 15–16; Sparrow v. R, [1987] 2 *W.W.R.* 577, [1987] 1 *C.N.L.R.* 145 at 151 (B.C.C.A.), Delgamuukw, *supra*, note 12 at 208.

32 Sparrow, *supra*, note 31 at 152 *C.N.L.R.*

33 Calder, *supra*, note 1; Re Paulette et al. and Registrar of Titles (No. 2) (1974), 42 *D.L.R.* (3rd) 8; Baker Lake, *supra*, note 12; Paul v. R. (1981), 2 *C.N.L.R.* 83; R v. Taylor and Williams (1981), 34 *O.R.* (2nd) 360, (1981) 3 *C.N.L.R.* 114; Dick v. Attorney General of Canada and Attorney General of Nova Scotia (1985) 62 *N.R.* 1, 23 *D.L.R.* (4th) 35, [1985] 4 *C.N.L.R.* 55; Adolph and Adolph, *supra*, note 19; Delgamuukw, *supra*, note 12.

34 (1985), 24 *D.L.R.* (4th) 390, [1986] 1 *C.N.L.R.* 153 at 171–2.

35 Re Paulette, *supra*, note 33 at 33.

36 Baker Lake, *supra*, note 7 at 30 *C.N.L.R.*

37 Tennisco, *supra*, note 20 at 142.

38 Taylor and Williams, *supra*, note 33 at 124 *C.N.L.R.*

39 Dick, *supra*, note 33 at 57 *C.N.L.R.*

40 Sparrow, *supra*, note 31 at 169 *C.N.L.R.*

41 R. v. Wilson, [1988] 2 *C.N.L.R.* 167 at 168.

42 Northwest Territories Fisheries Regulations, *C.R.C.* 1978, c. 847 made pursuant to Fisheries Act, *R.S.C.* 1970, c.F-14.

43 Baker Lake, *supra*, note 7 at 48–50 *C.N.L.R.*

44 Bear Island, *supra*, note 8.

45 Bear Island, *supra*, note 8.

46 Baker Lake, *supra*, note 7.

47 Apsassin, *supra*, note 13 at 123.

48 Delgamuukw, *supra*, note 11 at 50.

REFERENCES

Ballantyne, Phillip, P. Brook, P. Burns et al. 1976. *Aski-Puko – The Land Alone*. Saskatoon: Federation of Saskatchewan Indians.

Bartlett, Richard. 1984. *Aboriginal Land Claims at Common Law*. Saskatoon: University of Saskatchewan Native Law Centre.

Boldt, Menno, and J.A. Long. 1985. *The Quest For Justice: Aboriginal Peoples and Aboriginal Rights*. Toronto: University of Toronto Press.

Bone, Robert M. 1989. "Country Food Consumption During the Norman Wells Project, 1982–1985." *Polar Record* 25(154):235–8.

Brice-Bennett, Carol. 1977. *Our Footprints are Everywhere*. Nain: Labrador Inuit Association.

Brody, Hugh. 1981. *Maps and Dreams*. Vancouver: Douglas & McIntyre.

Canada. 1981. *In All Fairness: A Native Claims Policy*. Ottawa: Supply and Services Canada.

– 1983. *Report of the Special Committee on Indian Self-Government*. Ottawa: Supply and Services Canada.

– 1985. *Living Treaties: Lasting Agreements. Report of the Task Force to Review Comprehensive Claims Policy*. Ottawa: Supply and Services Canada.

– 1986. *Mackenzie Environmental Monitoring Project 1985–1986 Final Report*. Ottawa: Indian and Northern Affairs Canada.

Dimitrov, P., and M. Weinstein. 1984. *So That the Future Will Be Ours*. Ross River: Ross River Band.

Elberg, N., J. Hyman, and R.F. Salisbury. 1972. *Not By Bread Alone: The Use of Subsistence Resources Among James Bay Cree*. Montreal: Programme in the Anthropology of Development, McGill University.

Elliot, David W. 1980. "Baker Lake and the Concept of Aboriginal Title." *Osgoode Hall Law Journal* 18:653–69.

Freeman, Milton M.R., ed. 1976. *Report, Inuit Land Use and Occupancy Project*, 3 vols. Ottawa: Indian Affairs and Northern Development.

Hopper, M., and G. Power. 1991. "The Fisheries of an Ojibwa Community in Northern Ontario." *Arctic* 44 (4):267–74.

Hurley, John D. 1985a. "The Crown's Fiduciary Duty and Indian Title: *Guerin v. The Queen*."*McGill Law Journal* 30:559–602.

– 1985b. *Children or Brethren: Aboriginal Rights in Colonial Iroquoia*. Saskatoon: University of Saskatchewan Native Law Centre.

Karamanski, T.J. 1983. *Fur Trade and Exploration: Opening the Far Northwest 1821–1852*. Vancouver: University of British Columbia Press.

Knight, Rolf. 1968. *Ecological Factors in Changing Economy and Social Organization Among the Rupert House Cree*. Ottawa: National Museums of Canada.

Kruse, John A. 1991. "Alaska Inupiat Subsistence and Wage Employment Patterns: Understanding Individual Choice." *Human Organization* 50 (4):317–26.

McNeil, Kent. 1987. *Common Law Aboriginal Title: The Right of Indigenous People to Lands Occupied By Them at the Time a Territory is Annexed to the Crown's Dominions by Settlement*, Ph.D. diss., Oxford University.

Morris, Alexander. 1880. *The Treaties of Canada with the Indians of Manitoba and the North-West Territory.* Toronto: Bedfords Clarke and Company, reprinted by Coles Publishing Company, Toronto 1971.,

Nutall, Mark. 1991. "Sharing and the Ideology of Subsistence in a Greenlandic Sealing Community." *Polar Record* 27 (162):217–22.

Paine, Robert. ed. 1985. *Advocay and Anthropology.* St John's: Memorial University of Newfoundland.

Petterson, John S. 1987. "Subsistence Continuity and Economic Abundance in the North." In *Developing America's Northern Frontier,* ed. Theodore Lane, 91–106. Lanham: University Press of America.

Ponting, J.R. 1986. *Arduous Journey: Canadian Indians and Decolonization.* Toronto: McClelland & Stewart.

Sanders, Douglas. 1983. "The Rights of Aboriginal Peoples of Canada." *Canadian Bar Review* 61:314–38.

Smith, Thomas G., and H. Wright. 1989. "Economic Status and Role of Hunters in a Modern Inuit Village." *Polar Record* 25 (153):9–98.

Tyler, Kenneth J. 1981. "A Modest Proposal for Legislative Reform to Facilitate the Settlement of Specific Indian Claims." *Canadian Native Law Reporter* 3:27.

Usher, P.J. 1971. *The Bankslanders: Economy and Ecology of a Frontier Trapping Community,* 2 vols. Ottawa: Department of Indian Affairs and Northern Development.

– , and G. Wenzel, 1987. "Native Harvest Surveys and Statistics: A Critique of Their Construction and Use." *Arctic* 40 (2):145–60.

– , D. Delancy, G. Wenzel, et al. 1985. *An Evaluation of Native Harvest Survey Methodologies in Northern Canada.* Environmental Studies Revolving Funds Report no. 004. Ottawa: Environment Canada.

Wenzel, George W. 1986. "Resource Harvesting and the Social Structure of Native Communities." In *Native People and Renewable Resource Management.* Symposium of the Alberta Society of Professional Biologists, 29 April – 1 May Edmonton, Alberta.

Wolfe, Robert J., and L.J. Ellanna. 1983. *Resource Use and Socioeconomic Systems: Case Studies of Fishing and Hunting in Alaskan Communities.* Juneau: Division of Subsistence, Alaska Department of Fish and Game.

– , J.J. Gross, S.J. Langdon, et al. 1984. *Subsistence-Based Economies in Coastal Communities of Southwest Alaska.* Juneau: Division of Subsistence, Alaska Department of Fish and Game.

– , and Robert J. Walker. 1987. "Subsistence Economies in Alaska: Productivity, Geography, and Development Impacts." *Arctic Anthropology* 24 (2):56–81.

11 Anthropology and Canadian Native Political Organizations: Past and Future Trends

JOE SAWCHUK

INTRODUCTION

The last twenty years have seen the rise of some new and significant roles for anthropologists in Canada, including those of advisors and researchers for Native political organizations. I am fortunate enough to have spent a good part of my career working for several of these organizations, including the Metis Association of Alberta (MAA), the Manitoba Metis Federation (MMF) and the Manitoba Indian Brotherhood (MIB). While I occasionally acted as an independent part-time consultant on such issues as education, housing, and land claims, the vast majority of my work was as a full-time, salaried employee – a very different proposition from being an outside consultant. This is an experience which has remained fairly unique for anthropologists in Canada, whereas consulting has become quite common. Generally I have found the experience to be an exciting and challenging one, even though I have encountered more than a few problems and frustrations. This chapter describes some of the experiences and pressures one can expect to find working within Native political organizations in Canada and considers the future of the partnership between anthropology and these organizations.[1]

Much of the chapter deals with the questions, doubts, and contradictory feelings I experienced as a full-time employee for one particular political organization involved in land claims research.[2] I came to see a real gap between many of the assumptions and ideals of anthropological work, as they were expressed in the academic and applied field, and the realities I experienced while working within Native politics in Canada. Part of this gap derived from the differing expectations and perceptions of the value of anthropological research held by anthropologists and non-anthropologists, particulary Native politicians; part derived from the state of anthropological knowledge at the time regarding the penetration of organizations and bureaucracies and the design and analysis of public policy. At first, this caused me to question the relevance of my anthropological training, although I eventually came to value it greatly as I realized that it provided me not only with basic skills and knowledge I needed to pursue the land claims research, but also gave me a unique and insightful perspective into the ongoing political relationships both within the organization and between the organization and the federal government. This anthropological perspective allowed me to step back and analyse some of the distractions which continually plagued me in my work, such as being pressured to become involved in the internal political struggles of the organization, or facing attempted manipulations from government officials who wished me to serve their own narrow objectives.

NATIVE POLITICAL ORGANIZATIONS
IN CANADA

Within anthropology there has been a growing recognition of the problems and actions of indigenous peoples as they interact with the state governments which now rule their former territories. This situation is generally referred to as the "fourth world" (Graburn 1981), and there have already been several important Canadian studies on the subject (see for example Weaver 1981, 1983, 1986; Dyck 1983, 1985; Tanner 1983). This Canadian interest is no doubt due to the existence of a uniquely Canadian phenomenon: government-financed, but Native-designed and Native-run, political pressure organizations found on both the provincial and federal levels. It is true that Native pressure group organizations are found in other countries, most notably Australia and Norway, but Canadian organizations differ from those in several important ways. For the most part, the organizations in Canada were not created by the government, as they were in Australia, nor is there as much government opposition to their existence as is evidenced in Norway (Weaver 1983:4–6). The Canadian government has been reasonably supportive of these organizations, and it has provided almost all the finances necessary for their operation. Despite this heavy subsidization, the organizations have remained largely independent of the state government as far as being able to determine their own political directions and priorities. This independence is not absolute, of course; these groups are still subject to various pressures and constraints by the Canadian government, particularly the threat of discontinued funding.

Native political organizations have been part of the Canadian scene for many years. Some currently in existence originated in the early 1930s; others now defunct were in operation as early as the 1890s (Sawchuk 1982). Their general purpose has been to achieve public and governmental recognition of the unique rights and position that Indian, Metis, Inuit, and non-status Indians occupy in Canada by virtue of their aboriginal status, and to achieve a greater degree of self-determination and access to the country's resources and wealth for Native people. Each category of Native people in Canada has its own specific organization or organizations, usually represented by separate national and regional divisions roughly corresponding to Canada's political structure. Thus we find national or federal organizations such as the Assembly of First Nations (AFN) representing most of the status Indians across Canada, the Inuit Tapirisat of Canada (ITC) representing a major part of the Inuit (mostly from the Eastern Arctic), the Metis National Council (MNC) representing the national interests of the Metis (located mainly in the three prairie provinces and the Northwest Territories), and the Native Council of Canada (NCC) which at one time purported to represent the issues of both Metis and non-status Indians across Canada, but now exclusively represents non-status Indians.

Counterbalancing these national structures, and for the most part older than they, are organizations which represent Native people at a regional or provincial level. Examples of these would include provincially based organizations such as the Metis Association of Alberta, founded in 1932 and one of the oldest Native political organizations in Canada, and the Federation of Saskatchewan Indian Nations. There are also some narrower regional organizations, usually representing a particular political, cultural, or administrative grouping (such as the Nishnawbe-Aski Nation, which represents status Indians belonging to Treaty Number 9 and Treaty Number 3 in northern Ontario), tribal affiliations (such as the Gitksan-Wet'suwet'en Tribal Council in British Columbia), or the Mushkegowuk Chiefs Council of the Cree of James Bay.

Generally, the structures of all these organizations have been borrowed from the larger society, and often consist of a president and vice-presidents elected by the members at large (Sawchuk 1982). However, one organization, the AFN, has developed a new structure which more closely adheres to current Native sensibilities, if not actual tradition, by creating a federation of the elected chiefs of the local bands.³ But whatever the actual structure of the political organization, the important point is that the leaders of these groups are generally recognized as legitimate representatives of Native people by the public at large, by the various levels of government in Canada, and increasingly by Native people themselves, even if they don't necessarily support the individual leaders at all times.

The current surge in Native political movements began in the 1960s, when significant amounts of government funding were first made available to these organizations. A government's subsidizing its own opposition through protest groups might strike some as an anomaly, or even a distortion of democracy, but the reason for government funding of these organizations is not difficult to see. Pressure groups and special interest groups are a very efficient way to transmit the demands and views of groups whose interests cannot be adequately served by either the internal apparatus of the government or by political parties (Pross 1984:287), and they are fast becoming a permanent fixture in the Canadian political structure.

The importance of political pressure groups to Canadian aboriginal peoples is obvious. Their needs cannot be adequately served by conventional political parties, as Native peoples make up such a small percentage of the total Canadian population (approximately 3 percent) that they are of little interest to the general politician. Native political organizations can therefore fill an important gap in Native-government relations, especially since Native people often find themselves in a relationship to the government which is different from that of the average citizen. Those who possess Indian status find that they must look to the federal government for services other citizens routinely receive from provincial governments. Others, such as the Metis or Inuit, may find that their traditional territorial boundaries differ from those served by existing political divisions, such as provinces or territories. A good example is provided by the specific concerns of the Metis of western Canada, who have found that they have many common concerns which crosscut the borders of Manitoba, Saskatchewan, and Alberta, and therefore formed their umbrella organization, the Metis National Council.

For its part, the Canadian government needs the Native political organizations to exist almost as much as the Native people do. One of the most important of the government's tasks is to appear to be able to deal with the various sectors of the public, including Native people. It must be able to indicate that it knows what the various sectors of the public want and need, and to demonstrate that it can provide leadership for them. In recent years, public opinion has generally favoured several Native concerns, and editorial coverage of influential newspapers like the *Globe and Mail* has given qualified support to issues like settlement of Native land claims and the right to self-government. Given such a political climate, the government *needs* credible Native leaders who can demonstrate that they have the support of their people, support that can be seen through democratically recognized means such as election by secret ballot (even though these may not have been the traditional ways these leaders were chosen.) A democratic government needs democratically recognized Native leaders who are identified and accepted by the public as "genuine" leaders, qualified to speak for their constituents, and the Native organizations can provide such spokespersons.

Of course, the government may also see the groups as a useful shield for the deflection of criticism. Providing them with funds creates a ready-made scapegoat when government policies and initiatives fail. That is, the government's failure to overcome poverty or other problems can be blamed on political obstructionism, naïvete, or the incompetence of Native leaders and groups (Sawchuk 1980). Thus, the development of organizations such as the Assembly of First Nations, the Metis Association of Alberta, and others continues to serve many different, often conflicting needs for the Canadian government on the one hand, and the Native people on the other.

THE ROLE OF THE ANTHROPOLOGIST IN NATIVE ORGANIZATIONS

The day-to-day operations of Native political organizations require the use of many different kinds of consultants and specialists, who are usually brought in on an *ad hoc* basis to assist in such activities as land claims cases, economic and business development projects, environmental planning, engineering projects, government lobbying, legal actions, public relations, etc. Anthropology can contribute to many of these functions, and organizations such as Nishnawbe-Aski Nation, the Metis Association of Alberta, and others employ, or have employed, anthropologists permanently and full time, as well as some working on contractual short-term appointments. There are several ways an anthropologist can become involved with Native political organizations: as a consultant, either with a consulting firm or freelance, as a university-based researcher or consultant, as a full-time salaried employee of the Native organization, or as an employee of the government.

While there are problems and traps for the unwary associated with each of these functions, this paper is particularly concerned with the role of full-time employees in these organizations. This relatively new experience for anthropologists brings with it certain problems that might prove troublesome for someone accustomed to pursuing his or her own research interests independently, because one can no longer study just what is interesting from an anthropological perspective alone. This is a problem shared by those anthropologists working as part-time consultants or government advisors as well. The people doing the hiring determine the type and direction of the research – what is to be done, and what is not to be done. Often the information Native people may want or need is very different from that which would interest a traditional university-based anthropologist.

One major problem experienced by those anthropologists working as full-time employees for Native organizations is that they may no longer have the auspices of a university to fall back on. This is a support that is not always appreciated until it is missed. The lack of institutional support leaves one highly vulnerable to pressures and influences from both government officials and political factions within the organization. For example, government officials and civil servants will often attempt to influence and control researchers who are ostensibly under the direction of Native organizations by treating them as government employees one step removed, presumably because the money used to hire these researchers comes from government grants. Furthermore, Native politicians will often attempt to pressure researchers into forming alliances against other factions within the organization (both problems will be considered in some detail below). A university position gives the researcher some independence from these kinds of pressures, as his or her livelihood is not so threatened.

The full-time employee shares some problems with other anthropologists involved with Native organizations, including university-based ones. For example, the leaders of the organization may have a distorted idea of what anthropology is, or what anthropology can or cannot do for them. This can take the form of being asked to explain how "a study of old bones and arrowheads could possibly be of use to a modern political organization," or it can lead to unrealistic ideas of what can be achieved by research results, such as expectations of an instant resolution of land claims, or housing problems, or whatever else is being investigated. To counter this, the anthropologist has to be able to clearly isolate what it is the discipline can do for the association.

Anthropology can be useful in several areas. Weaver has pointed out three types of resources besides leadership and funding necessary for a Native political organization or pressure group to operate efficiently and to present its interests forcefully and clearly to government (1983:14). These are political cohesion, operational knowledge of government, and policy research capacity. Of these three areas, the anthropologist can most obviously make a contribution in policy research. A compelling example would be land use and occupancy studies such as those undertaken in the 1970s for certain areas of northern Ontario, the Arctic, and elsewhere, which gave the Native organizations the ability to make strong presentations to provincial and federal governments regarding the protection or establishment of their land base (for example, Rushforth 1976; Kayahna Tribal Area Council 1985). The second resource, operational knowledge of government, refers to understanding how policy is made, and a personal knowledge of the key players in government who institute that policy. Anthropologists can be useful here as well, although this sort of knowledge is not the exclusive possession of anthropologists. This comes from personal interaction with government employees and politicians during negotiations, and depends on developing a personal network of the key people in government as well as a knowledge of governmental procedures. The anthropologist is as likely to acquire that skill as anybody, but usually will not be in a position to offer that skill to an organization until he or she has worked for it for some time. The third area, political cohesion, is best developed by the political leaders and their constituents themselves, although some of the anthropological analyses of political processes and the strategies of leaders may be of use to the executives of the organizations.

RESEARCHERS AND NATIVE LEADERS AS POLITICAL RIVALS

The anthropologist working for a Native organization may face suspicion and sometimes outright obstructionism and interference from the various politicians running the organization he or she is ostensibly serving. It is common for politicians within the organizations to regard their own research staff (whether these people be anthropologists or not) with a certain amount of suspicion. This is because the advice offered may be seen as politically threatening. The board of directors or the executive may see the advice as usurping their own role of political decision making and policy determination. Furthermore, the politician may have a hidden agenda not obvious to the research staff. While the anthropologist is offering research or advice according to the manifest reason the work is being done, the politician may be evaluating it from a very different perspective. For example, the anthropologist may tell the politician, "This is the way this material can be used to pursue a land claims case." But the politician may be asking himself, "What effect will this have on my career; how can I use this information against my rival, or how can he use it against me?"[4] Finally, the politician may not see the value or need for policy research, and may dismiss the findings as "too academic" or irrelevant.

The role of researcher vis-à-vis politician within the Native organization, and the operation of a policy research department itself, requires an analysis of both the internal organizational decision-making process and the way Native political organizations react to outside influences like government political pressures and government funding. One has to understand the acquisition, control, and manipulation of power within the organization to describe the processes of its operation and the determination of the goals of the organization and its protagonists. This is best done by focusing on the struggle of power groups and individuals within the organization over two things: the *external* supply of resources (government funding in most cases) and the *internal* allocation of personnel, money, and facilities to accomplish organizational tasks. In this context, Native political organizations resemble other agencies dependent on outside funding (Zald 1970; Gummer 1978).

In theory, the typical Native organization is made up of two levels: one political, distinguished by the existence of an electoral system which determines the board of directors and the executive, the other administrative, consisting of paid employees. While there is supposed to be a distinct and recognized difference between elected officials and non-elected employees of the association, as demonstrated by their different duties and responsibilities, in reality the *entire association* can be regarded as a single political arena in which individuals or interest groups can compete for control of the organization's direction and goals. In other words, power struggles occur not just between the political leaders themselves but among *all* members of the association, including the politician and the researcher or policy advisor.

Also, a blurring of the lines between paid employee and elected official is often found because many of the Native employees are or have been politically active, often having held political positions (such as board member of the association) in the past. However, even if an employee is non-Native, and therefore by definition excluded from overtly political roles within the association, he or she often will indulge in political activity in another dimension, in attempting to secure or enhance his or her own position within the organization. For example, if a power struggle occurs between an anthropologist researcher and a politician, it is not likely this will involve a struggle for control of the direction of the association *per se*, but is more likely to be a struggle over control of the research project, or the direction of the research.

The association is thus manifested as a political arena in which interest groups and individuals compete for the control. They do this by trying to gain control of organizational resources which can be used to achieve the enhancement of their position within the organization. Several kinds of internal resources are available for this. The most obvious one is money in the form of grants from government and private granting agencies, but there are others as well: specific programs and departments such as land claims and economic development are very useful if control can be gained over them; technical knowledge (such as the operational knowledge of government or knowledge possessed by a lawyer or a constitutional expert) can also form a powerful political tool. Another scarce resource for which politicians compete anywhere is jobs for their followers in the organization (this tends to be extreme in Native organizations because of Native poverty). There are many other resources that could be mentioned as well. The major struggle in the association will be over the control of the resources which enable members to accomplish organizational purposes, which in turn enables those members to secure and enhance their own position within the organization.

How does establishing control over the resources coming into the organization help the members to achieve their ends and how would this influence the direction of research being undertaken there? It may be instructive to see how this could influence the direction and progress of research by referring to a particular case involving myself and the president of the organization and his attempts to control the land claims research project I was directing.

Although the president was not responsible for bringing the project into the association (it was initiated by the government), he attempted to ensure that all political credit the project might generate would accrue to him. He did this by immediately isolating the project from the control of any other person in the association, particularly the vice-president (his political rival), by personally taking charge of the project, and by not allowing the board of directors to have any input into the land claims department. For example, he went to elaborate lengths to prevent the board from interviewing me when I submitted the quarterly reports of the land claims department, or from meeting me face to face, even when I was first interviewed for the position of research director. He had the executive (president, vice-president, secretary, and treasurer) do this alone. By controlling all information flowing into and out of the land claims department, he was quite safe in referring to it as "his" project. It then became as much an asset to him as if he had brought it into the organization himself. It is extremely important for a politician to be able to demonstrate to the membership at large that he can successfully bring in government concessions and programs. He has to show success in "getting something for the people" (Bee 1979), or as Eidheim referred to it, being able to present relevant results (1968). For the president, control of "his" land claims project brought this kind of political recognition.

Despite his strategies on land claims, the president, along with his vice-president, was defeated in the next election (on matters that had little to do with land claims). The incoming vice-president attempted to gain control over the land claims department in much the same manner as had the former president. The new president did not offer much opposition to this attempt, since he was more interested in initiating some new economic development programs for the association. Thus his "presentation of relevant results" did not include much emphasis on land claims at first.

The new vice-president attempted to use the land claims issue to neutralize the political gains the president was making with economic development. But he was unsuccessful, because by interfering with the research in the land claims department, he precipitated a political struggle on another level – between the land claims staff and himself. At first he attempted to involve me in plotting against the president. When I refused to participate in this rivalry, hoping to keep myself and the land claims department free from internal organizational politics, he attempted to have me ousted by forming an alliance with several of the land claims research staff working under me. This forced me, however unwillingly, to enter the political arena myself by forming an alliance with the president, bringing him into direct involvement with land claims. As research director, I had to take this tack in order to maintain a certain amount of autonomy over the direction of the research, something that would not have been possible had the vice-president gained control of the department. Although I would have preferred to remain neutral in the rivalry between the president and vice-president, I was bloody-minded enough to decide that I was not going to be manoeuvered out of the association without a fight. And it was becoming obvious that if I did *not* get involved in the political process (at least to the extent of becoming an ally of one politician, and an opponent of another), I would be able neither to continue the research nor to protect my position within the organization as an employee. This was in direct opposition to my first instincts as an applied anthropologist or participant-observer to try to stay out of the internal politics of the organization.

I soon discovered that making alliances was not the only way I could strengthen my position within the association. Another useful tactic was gaining control over resources. This was demonstrated after I secured a grant from a private funding agency which allowed the land claims office to remain open after federal funding had been cut off. Under the terms of this new grant, I was one of the co-signers of all cheques issued by the land claims department. In this way I was able to re-establish my own position within the organization and to protect land claims finances from raids by the vice-president or other departments (the most common tactic involved the vice-president or a department head attempting to bill travel expenses or other debits incurred in their operations to land claims).

The special position of anthropologists working for Native political organizations (as opposed to working for the government or as independent researchers) makes them particularly susceptible to becoming involved in political factions within the association. They may find that whether they want it or not, they'll be dragged into a political struggle – forced into taking sides with one political rival or another – simply to be able to complete a research project or to maintain their position in the organization.

PRESSURES ON RESEARCHERS FROM GOVERNMENT OFFICIALS

The land claims research program which involved the Metis Association of Alberta was part of a Canada-wide investigation into the nature of both Metis land claims in the prairies and non-status Indian claims in Eastern Canada. The research was underwritten by the Department of Indian Affairs (the first time the department funded any sort of program for Metis or non-status Indians) and was undertaken to determine whether or not the Metis indeed had the basis for a land claims case. The program was structured so that every Metis and non-status Indian (MNSI) organization in each province involved would be responsible for gathering and analysing the data for its own area. The Native Council of Canada (which was the national MNSI organization at that time) was responsible for the over-all co-ordination of the program. The funding of the program lasted approximately two and a half years.

It is important to note that these funds were not in the form of a grant, but in the form of contract payments, a fairly common practice by which Native organizations can fund operations with government assistance. But this practice can have far-reaching effects for the organization and the researcher involved in delivering the contractually determined information. In the case of the Metis land claims investigation, each provincial MNSI association signed separate contracts agreeing to provide research information on Metis claims to the Department of Indian Affairs. The nature of the research was determined beforehand, but nevertheless a serious controversy arose between the government and the associations over what was "legitimate" information and what was not. As well, there were serious differences on both sides over the nature of the research and the problem.[5]

One specific problem of government contract work is the potential for government interference either in the operations of the organization or with the role of the researcher. Many civil servants attempt to treat researchers and consultants working for Native organizations as government employees one step removed. I first became aware of the "proprietary" feelings that government officials can exhibit toward consultants working for Native organizations shortly after I took over as director of land claims research. A few weeks after I had started (I had not been involved in the original meetings to determine the nature of the project), I was summoned to Ottawa to meet with the special inter-departmental committee that had been set up to evaluate and regulate the research from the various provinces. Before the meeting, I was taken aside by some officials of the Department of Indian Affairs, who wanted to "make a few things clear" to me. It was reiterated that the MAA had *not* been given a grant to do research: it had signed a contract to provide certain information on the status of Metis land claims to the government. The officials implied that as far as the Department of Indian Affairs was concerned, I *also* was under contract to the federal government, and if I did not fulfil the terms of the contract to the government's satisfaction, I could be dropped as director of research, and/or funding to the MAA would be discontinued.

This threat came as something of a surprise to me. After all, I had been approached by the Metis Association of Alberta, not the government, to take on the position of land claims director. I had been interviewed for the position by the president of the MAA; I signed a contract with the Metis association; I was being paid by the association. Therefore, it seemed logical to me that I was an employee of the association. It seemed like quite a leap in logic to classify me as a government employee, even one step removed. The officials tried to underscore my (and the MAA's) dependence on the government and the Department of Indian Affairs by closely questioning my salary and other financial arrangements I had made with the MAA. The officials and I all knew that they had no formal jurisdiction over these matters, but the fact that these threats were implied at all was significant: I was being warned that I was not invulnerable to government manipulation.

Once my supposedly dependent position was demonstrated to the officials' satisfaction, the reason for this separate meeting was revealed, and certain directions suggested. The Indian Affairs officials were particularly anxious that Metis in the remote areas of Alberta not be informed of the ongoing land claims research, because, "It would only raise the hopes of an imminent land claims settlement among the Native population." It also became clear in the course of this meeting that the officials had already concluded that there was little or no substance to Metis claims, and any claims the association did make would likely be rejected out of hand.[6]

The main concern seemed to be to prevent the MAA from making a political issue out of the land claims research, and to prevent any Metis leader from building a personal political base by promising a land claims settlement to his or her constituents. The Indian Affairs officials claimed that their major concern was the prevention of an even greater level of discontent among the Native population if land claims settlements failed to materialize from the research. While there may indeed have been such a danger, it is much more likely that these officials had a hidden agenda – a reluctance to give Metis leaders any sort of tool with which to politicize their constituents. Again I was warned that I should tread carefully or I might be dropped as research director. This incident illustrates the ambivalent attitude to pressure groups often held by government officials: while the organizations may be seen as a necessary means of communication with Native people, they are also seen as threats to democratic government, or at least to the smooth operation of government departments. Therefore, the researcher may find him- or herself the subject of some persistent attempts at being turned into an agent of control over these organizations.

As could be imagined, I found the attitude of these government officials most disturbing. I regarded myself as an employee of the Metis, and I did not welcome the suggestion that I was some sort of second-hand employee of the government, or one who could be bent to government demands. I regarded myself as an advocate anthropologist; I was there because I was "for the Metis." In one way, it was not difficult to sidestep the government pressures. The obvious tactic was to prepare the kind of research reports that would keep the government happy, while at the same time making every effort to undertake the sort of research desired by the Metis association. The problem with this, however, was that it took up a lot of extra time, money and effort. I estimate that at least 25 percent of the actual time spent by the MAA's land claims research department was devoted to preparing the required reports to the federal government. These reports were useless as far as furthering the Metis claims was concerned. The format of the reports was determined by federal requirements, giving very little emphasis to substantive research findings, and much emphasis to detailed descriptions of how each researcher spent his or her time. In addition to wasting time, it caused strife within the research department, as researchers chaffed under what they saw as unnecessary regulations and constrictions emanating from the research director, not realizing that these demands came from the government.

The government employed several other tactics to control the direction of research by the various MNSI associations across Canada during this project. One common device was to play one association off against the other. There were several meetings per year between the inter-departmental committee co-ordinating the research and the MNSI associations involved. At these meetings, one of the association's reports would invariably be praised to the denigration of others. Not surprisingly, this had the effect of sowing additional bitterness and misunderstanding among the various MNSI associations, weakening their co-operative ability, which had not been particularly great to begin with. There was a fair amount of distrust between the organizations on a regional basis, the western (predominantly Metis) associations distrusting the eastern (predominantly non-status Indian) groups.

The government also deliberately created uncertainty over the continuance of funding for the land claims research. Requirements for the research were never clearly spelled out (beyond the format of the reports themselves), but this did not prevent the government from routinely accusing research directors of not meeting these mythical requirements anyway. The withholding of funding was continually threatened for this alleged failure. All these efforts were made to force the directors of the land claims research to follow the government line rather than take instructions from their own associations.

THE RELEVANCE OF ANTHROPOLOGY FOR NATIVE ORGANIZATIONS

Much of my experience with Native organizations was gained while I was a graduate student. Long periods of working in the organizations (three years in one case) were interspersed with time spent attending graduate school or lecturing at universities. This dual experience often left me impatient with my university colleagues and professors and the impressions they had of working in a non-academic setting. Many of the concerns at the university, particularly the issue of advocacy anthropology and the roles anthropologists could play in Native organizations, seemed to be totally divorced from my experiences in the organizations themselves, and I felt my colleagues had an entirely unrealistic view of what, how, or when anthropology could be of use to aboriginal peoples in the particular setting with which I was familiar. Not surprisingly, this sometimes led to my questioning the value and relevance of the training I was receiving in anthropology.

By the time I began working full time for the Metis Association of Alberta in 1978, events in Canada had progressed to the point that anthropology was no longer needed in many of the ways my professors assumed it would be. For example, one of the roles traditionally suggested for anthropologists was as cultural translators or mediators in government-Native relations. This struck me as a particularly patronising, even offensive attitude. At the time Native leaders, especially the ones at the national and provincial levels, were routinely talking to government bureaucrats and politicians every day, and were more competent in the bureaucratic language, rhetoric, norms, and rules of the game than any academically trained anthropologist fresh out of graduate school was likely to be.[7] Cultural translators were not needed because government-Native relations had moved into a bureaucratic arena that largely transcended cultural differences. Within this system the two sides, government and Native, understood each other very well, and this had been true for quite some time. For example, Dyck's analysis of Native political leaders in Saskatchewan (1983) demonstrates that they were already consummately able to manipulate government officials in the 1960s and 1970s. And organizations that currently maintain full-time observers at the United Nations (such as the Indian Association of Alberta, or the Cree of Eastern James Bay) hardly need an anthropologist to give them pointers on the effective lobbying of governments.

That said, it does not follow that anthropology has nothing to offer. My own experience has convinced me that an anthropological approach can be particularly useful in penetrating bureaucratic structures and pursuing policy analysis and research, even though traditionally it has not often been used in this way. But anthropologists have to remember that in order to play a useful role within modern Native organizations, they must both accurately estimate the knowledge that both government and Natives already possess and, as my experience with the MAA indicates, be clear about the motives of all the players involved.

Some anthropologists like La Rusic (1985:25–26), have stated that while the holistic approach and intensive field-work common to the anthropological method gives us a better perspective on the local conditions of a group of people than most other researchers can afford, this perspective alone does not give us any particular capacity to design (or presumably analyse) public policy. La Rusic suggests that our ability to offer coherent advice is usually limited by our ignorance of the social reality of government – we may understand the Natives' culture nicely enough, but we don't know how the bureaucracy works. Our anthropological training leaves us with little understanding of the inside workings of the government or of the constraints on or the needs of policy makers. This is an old complaint, one that Cochrane made as long ago as 1971. There may be some justice to this statement, but what both La Rusic and Cochrane seem to be missing here is that our training *does* leave us in a position where we can learn that knowledge quickly and efficiently *if that is what we choose to study*. And it certainly is a subject worthy of study; in contemporary Canadian Native society, government-Native relations are as much of the cultural milieu as kinship, land-use patterns, or hunting techniques, and are just as amenable to anthropological investigation.

When I first began my work with the Metis Association of Alberta, I found that I had much to learn before I could make a significant contribution. While I was in a position to give advice to them on the nature of land claims and on other issues where I had special training, I had no real knowledge of the inside workings of the government or of the constraints on or needs of the policy makers at that time. However, these were things peculiar to the particular field work situation I found myself in, and my anthropological training had prepared me to *expect* that there would be things I could not know until I was in the field. This realization gave me a head start in learning the specific and esoteric knowledge I needed regarding government structures and Native organizations. As I began to learn the special environment of government-Native organizations, my value to the association increased dramatically. Eventually I learned how the government bureaucracy was working, at least as far as the specific issue of land claims was concerned, and I began to understand the relations among government departments such as Finance, Justice, and Indian Affairs in that particular context. I also began to learn the players and their personalities on both the government and Native sides. This was a useful resource and one I exploited daily. It may be true that a researcher in another discipline (history or political science, for example) working in the same context would have developed that same knowledge, but an anthropologist is in a particularly good position to "learn the ropes" quickly.[8]

After I was well established within the Metis Association, I became useful in other ways as well. For example, I was often asked to write speeches for the president, especially when he was speaking in a university setting, because as he said, I "knew what academics want to hear." That may have been true, but I also knew what other groups wanted to hear, including government officials, which helped the organization to develop strategies that could achieve organizational ends while satisfying government concerns. That didn't come from anthropology alone, but it did come from the flexibility and ability to adapt to the social structures around me, which *did* come from my anthropological perspective. So even though much of the ability we may have to offer useful advice either to Natives or policy makers is developed as a by-product of our research, the anthropological perspective is still useful. Despite the fact that I felt somewhat unprepared by my anthropological training when I first started working for the Metis association, I have come to the conclusion that it gave me an ability to cope better than I realized.

I suspect that most recent anthropology graduates would be as naive about Native organizations and government as I was when I first started, but that need not continue to be the case. Courses in policy review and practice in bureaucracy could easily be developed and would certainly be useful, given the contemporary nature of anthropology. There are many researchers and consultants who could help the next generation of anthropologists work with these organizations more efficiently, or at least prepare them to navigate their way through the maze of conflicting loyalties and duties that are part of working for such organizations. These people could also give graduates a realistic idea of their potential roles within such organizations. And we now have several anthropologists who are working full time for government bureaucracies (such as the Ontario Native Affairs Secretariat) as well as those working for Native groups. These people also have much to contribute to improving our knowledge about the Native organizations and government milieu.

It has often been suggested that anthropology can play an important role in resolving the fundamental conflicts of interest between aboriginal peoples and industrialized nation-states and economies (Asch 1982:366; Feit 1982:374.) Anthropology certainly may have such a role to play in the arena of Native political organizations in Canada, but one must bear in mind the caveat mentioned above: that Native politicians and government officials already are working together within a tightly defined political arena where the two sides understand each other quite well, and have little need for cultural translators. Dealing with such a sophisticated clientele means that anthropology will have to offer equally sophisticated answers and analyses before Native organizations will have much use for it.

One way to achieve this would be to pursue an extended effort into developing a body of theory and practice in public and private policy, in effect developing a new field in anthropology – the study of action (and inaction) within organizations. Anthropology, because of its unique approach and orientation, is admirably suited to penetrating bureaucratic structures: seeing, extracting, and explicating structures and relations in a wide variety of societies has defined the anthropological approach from its beginnings. I would suggest that this form of policy analysis may prove to be the wave of the future for anthropology, especially if we aim at going *beyond* Native structures to apply the same insights into organizations in general. We are already well under way as far as Native structures are concerned; Dyck's characterization of Indian perception of roles (1983) is a good example of the analysis of Native leadership strategies within organizations, and Weaver's analysis of Indian Affairs (1981, 1986) is an insightful look into the motivations, values, and principles behind government policies. As good as these works are, their primary value is to indicate the potential for future analyses.

However, there is a factor which may still limit the role anthropology can play in the future of these organizations. More and more Native associations are beginning to hire *Natives only* to do policy research. This is becoming easier for them to do as far as legal research is concerned, as there is a sizeable number of Native lawyers working today, and many more are being trained. However, the same cannot be said for anthropology. Many aboriginal peoples seem to consider anthropology irrelevant to their contemporary needs. This is demonstrated by the fact that while many Native students will take a few anthropology courses as undergraduates, not many go on to graduate school in order to pursue a career in anthropology. Since there are so few Native anthropologists in the making, it is possible that anthropology's interaction with the political organizations will diminish to that of arms-length observer. A few Native anthropologists are involved in the political organizations; one example is the current president of the Dene Nation in the Northwest Territories, who holds a degree in anthropology from the University of Alberta. However, unless we can demonstrate the relevance of anthropology to an even wider audience of Native people, the discipline may soon find itself limited to an observer status rather than a participant one.

Again, the development of policy research as a widely recognized sub-field of anthropology will do much to alleviate this problem by demonstrating that anthropology has much to offer, not only in the land use studies and land claims we've contributed to in the past, but in the ongoing academic analysis of the Native political structures and the government bureaucracies and regulations which affect them. The growing number of studies which elucidate the evolution of government policies toward Indians and the evolution of Indians' attitudes and strategies in dealing with government will surely prove useful to the organizations. I have already seen such works as Weaver (1986) being consulted in Native organizations, so I don't think it is overly optimistic to expect that anthropology will continue to have something to offer in the future. Anthropological analyses could prove to be eye opening to all politicians, not just Native ones; sometimes those closest to the action cannot see all the significant parameters, and our perspective may well prove to be a valuable one to those involved.

These studies should surely make anthropology seem more relevant to Native people as the role of these organizations changes and takes on even more significance in Canadian society. The 1990s are likely to be an era of expanded Native-government relations as self-government negotiations begin in many Indian communities, and the role of Native political associations changes to accommodate these developments. For example, the government's enthusiasm for its recent community-based negotiations for self-government can be seen in part as an attempt to defuse the larger regional and national political organizations. Thus, we may see a shift from an emphasis on national organizations to more regional and locally based ones. Anthropology is in a good position to monitor and interpret these changes. While this should attract more Native students to both undergraduate and graduate courses, it is also opening a new line of inquiry in anthropology that can have implications for fields far beyond that of Native concerns alone.

Even if the chances of our continuing an active role within the organizations themselves may be short lived, the encounter to date has been a mutually beneficial one. One of the significant aspects of the relationship between anthropologists and Native organizations is the way this coming together has changed anthropology. It is not simply the fact that anthropologists are now working *for* the Native people we used to study, we are also working *with* them, often to help change our own society, or at least change the way our society has been dealing with its Native peoples. True, this has not always been a completely harmonious relationship, nor is there any reason it should be; the anthropologist may not always agree with or approve of the organization's directions, and the Native politicians may not always agree with the anthropologist's viewpoint or find it useful. But it seems to be an improvement over the situation where someone like Vine Deloria (1969) could characterize the ongoing relationship between Natives and anthropologists as not only irrelevant, but harmful to Native people.

NOTES

1 I am grateful to Jim Waldram, Noel Dyck, Sam Corrigan, and some of the anonymous reviewers for their valuable criticisms and suggestions on earlier drafts of this paper.

2 For the most part, this chapter is based on my work as the Director of land claims research for the Metis Association of Alberta (MAA) from 1978 to 1981.

3 The local tradition of many aboriginal peoples never included elected chiefs, although these have been imposed almost universally by the federal government, and they have now become accepted as "traditional" leaders by many groups.

4 This is not to suggest that there is necessarily a conflict between the personal career strategies of the politician and the needs of the organization and client population. We can safely assume that in their actions, organizational members are attempting to promote their own interests, that is, securing and enhancing their own position within the association. However, one of the best ways to secure a position within the organization is to demonstrate that you are doing a good job in serving your people. This is especially true for elected positions (see Bee 1979).

5 The actual legal and historical nature of the Metis claim is discussed elsewhere (Sawchuk, Sawchuk, and Ferguson 1981).

6 This is what eventually happened; the government totally rejected the Metis claims. But this meeting, which took place *two years* before the final report was submitted or evaluated, revealed that as far as the government employees were concerned, the negative result of the claims investigation was a foregone conclusion.

7 I should point out that my comments regarding the familiarity of Native leaders with government bureaucracy apply only to the large, heavily funded provincial and national Native political organizations. This same level of bureaucratic and governmental sophistication is not always evident at lower levels, particularly in some of the smaller communities Hedican (1989) refers to as non-reserve Native communities. These communities are not considered reserves under the Indian Act, so they are not eligible for help from the federal government. Nor do they fit comfortably into the mandate of the provincial status Indian organizations, so they are unable to get much help from the provincial organization's leadership expertise.

8 This observation has also been made by academics outside anthropology. Historian David McNab, who works within the office of Indian Resource Policy of the Ontario provincial government, has commented on the fact that graduate students in anthropology, because of their training in field work, make particularly good researchers in land claims cases compared to those trained as historians (1986:133).

REFERENCES

Asch, Michael I. 1982. "Dene Self-determination and the Study of Hunter-gatherers in the Modern World." In *Politics and History in Band Societies*, eds. Eleanor Leacock and Richard Lee, 347–72. Cambridge: Cambridge University Press.

Bee, Robert. 1979. "To Get Something for the People: The Predicament of the American Indian Leader." *Human Organization* 38(3): 239–47.

Cochrane, Glynn. 1971. *Development Anthropology*. New York: Oxford University Press.

Deloria, Vine, Jr. 1969. *Custer Died For Your Sins*. London: Collier-Macmillan.

Dyck, Noel. 1983. "Representation and Leadership of a Provincial Indian Association." In *The Politics of Indianness: Case Studies of Ethnopolitics in Canada*, ed. Adrian Tanner, 197–305. St John's: Institute of Social and Economic Research, Memorial University of Newfoundland.

–, ed. 1985. *Indigenous Peoples and the Nation-State: Fourth World Politics in Canada, Australia and Norway*. St John's: Institute of Social and Economic Research, Memorial University of Newfoundland.

Eidheim, Harald. 1968. "The Lappish Movement: An Innovative Political Movement." In *Local Level Politics*, ed. Marc J. Swartz, 205–16. Chicago: Aldine.

Feit, Harvey A. 1982. "The Future of Hunters within Nation–States: Anthropology and the James Bay Cree." In *Politics and History in Band Societies*, eds. Eleanor Leacock and Richard Lee, 373–411. Cambridge: Cambridge University Press.

Graburn, Nelson H.H. 1981. "1,2,3,4...: Anthropology and the Fourth World." *Culture* 1(1): 66–70.

Gummer, Burton. 1978. "A Power-politics Approach to Social Welfare Organizations." *Social Service Review* 52(3):349–61.

Hedican, Edward J. 1989. "Policy Dilemma or Institutional Neglect? Non-reserve Native People in Canada." *Proactive* 8(2):18–22.

Kayahna Tribal Area Council. 1985. *The Kayahna Region Land Utilization and Occupancy Study*. Toronto: University of Toronto Press.

La Rusic, Ignatius. 1985. "Reinventing the Advocacy Wheel?" In *Advocacy and Anthropology, First Encounters*, ed. Robert Paine, 22–7. St John's: Institute of Social and Economic Research, Memorial University of Newfoundland.

McNab, David T. 1986. "Some Reflections on the Life and Hard Times of an Indian Land Claims Researcher." *The Canadian Journal of Native Studies* 6(1):129–39.

Pross, Paul A. 1984. "Pressure Groups: Talking Chameleons." In *Canadian Politics in the 1980's*, 2nd ed., ed. Michael S. Whittington and Glen Williams, 221–42. Toronto: Methuen.

Rushforth, Scott. 1976. "Recent Land Use by the Great Bear Lake Indians. Evidence Presented to the Mackenzie Valley Pipeline Inquiry." Yellow-knife. *Records of the Mackenzie Valley Pipeline Inquiry* 148:22632–72.

Sawchuk, Joe. 1980. "Development or Domination? The Metis and Government Funding." In *The Other Natives: The Metis*, vol. 3, eds. D.B. Sealey, A.S. Lussier, Winnipeg: Manitoba Metis Federation Press.

–, P. Sawchuk, and T. Ferguson. 1981. *Metis Land Rights in Alberta: A Political History*. Edmonton: Metis Association of Alberta.

– 1982. "Some Early Influences on Metis Political Organization." Culture 2(3):85–91.

Tanner, Adrian, ed. 1983. *The Politics of Indianness: Case Studies of Native Ethnopolitics in Canada*. St John's: Institute of Social and Economic Research, Memorial University of Newfoundland.

Weaver, Sally. 1981. *Making Canadian Indian Policy. The Hidden Agenda 1968–1970*. Toronto: University of Toronto Press.

– 1983. "Towards a Comparison of National Political Organizations of Indigenous Peoples: Australia, Canada and Norway." Lecture series presented 19–26 October, Institute of Social Sciences, University of Tromsø, Tromsø, Norway. Mimeo. Available from author, Department of Anthropology, University of Waterloo.

– 1986. "Indian Policy in the New Conservative Government, Part I: The Nielsen Task Force of 1985." *Native Studies Review* 2(1):1–43.

Zald, M.N. 1970. "Political economy: a Framework for Analysis." In *Power in Organizations*, ed. M.N. Zald, 221–61. Nashville: Vanderbilt University Press.

12 Some Limits to Advocacy Anthropology in the Native Canadian Context

JAMES B. WALDRAM

INTRODUCTION

The nature of anthropological research is such that the anthropologist is frequently brought into sustained, intimate contact with people who are, more often than not, members of a minority, and hence somewhat marginal or powerless within their nation-states. Through the research technique known as participant-observation, anthropologists come to know and be known by the people they study more than researchers of any other social science. The anthropologist is frequently seen as a "marginal native" (cf. Freilich 1970), an individual who knows both the host society and the powerful industrial and government bureaucracy systems that impact on that society. It is not surprising, therefore, that many anthropologists come to act as brokers between the minority group and the nation-state. According to Pelto and Pelto (1976:539–40), "The ethics of the complex exchange relationship of fieldwork require that researchers be prepared to use considerable amounts of their financial resources, skills, and information for the benefit of the people who supply them with data in the long hours and days of the fieldwork enterprise." Indeed, from time to time the anthropologist's role becomes even more subjective: he or she becomes an "advocate" for the host society.

The purpose of this paper is to explore some of the "limits" to which an anthropologist can go when acting as an advocate. My own experiences as an advocate for a northern Native community will be assessed in terms of current literature on advocacy in anthropology, and these limits delineated.

THE NATURE OF ADVOCACY ANTHROPOLOGY

It has been over a decade since Schensul and Schensul (1978) described the nature of advocacy anthropology in the context of urban research with minority groups in Chicago and Hartford. To them, the advocate anthropologist adopted primarily a research role, utilizing his or her research skills to produce the data that empower community groups to seek change according to their own agenda. As the Schensuls write, "In this perspective the professional is not a leader or a pleader but plays a background and supportive role. Courses of action, and decisions, are made by the indigenous lay advocates" (Schensul and Schensul 1978:122–3).

Van Willigen in a volume on American applied anthropology, has essentially accepted the Schensuls' view of the advocate anthropologist as one who works behind the scenes, providing research data which "is not intended to make a contribution to the generalized pool of scientific knowledge." He emphasizes that, in what he terms "community advocacy anthropology," the anthropologist "serves not as a direct change agent but as an auxilliary to community leaders" (Van Willigen 1986:111–13).

Perhaps the best-known examples of advocacy anthropology in the context of Native Canadian issues relate to the ongoing studies and activites of anthropologists in the James Bay region of Quebec. In the early 1970s, the late Richard Salisbury, then director of McGill University's programme in the Anthropology of Development, was invited by the Quebec Government to undertake a socio-economic impact assessment of the potential consequences of hydroelectric development on the Cree Indians in the northern part of the province. (Many of the anthropologists who worked on this study under Salisbury's direction subsequently went on to other related activities with the Cree.)

In their 1972 impact report, Salisbury, Filion et al. (1972) stated that the study would be neutral, that they would not take sides in the controversy, and that the data would be presented in such a manner as to allow the principal parties access to all available information from which to present their positions. Salisbury (1976) subsequently referred to the role of the anthropologist in this dispute as that of "societal ombudsman." His anthropological ombudsperson was essentially a broker, making "intelligible to people with a particular perspective the viewpoint of a different group," and using "the accumulated knowledge of the discipline to suggest possible courses of action TO BOTH SIDES" (1976:257; emphasis original). Salisbury argued against a partisan role for the anthropologist, stating that "when an anthropologist commits himself to one side only, he nullifies many of the benefits that his professional training could give to that side" (1976:257). Further, he stated his belief that "the anthropologist is only an information source, not an advocate of a particular policy" (1976:262).

In the opinion of journalist Boyce Richardson, Salisbury's 1972 report, guided by this philosophy, was potentially damaging for the Cree since, in his efforts to provide all the information he felt necessary to allow for public debate, Salisbury and his team effectively stated that Cree society was in serious trouble even without the hydroelectric project (Richardson 1975:245). Eventually, Salisbury himself seemed to reluctantly admit that simply providing all the relevant information to both sides of a dispute did not place the minority group on an equal footing with the government (Salisbury 1975, 1977), and the subsequent work of a handful of anthropologists directly for the Cree (Salisbury 1986:151–6) indicates clearly that the "societal ombudsman" role for many of them was jettisoned in favour of a more activist one.

Harvey Feit is one of these anthropologists who has worked directly for the Cree in a variety of activities. He has written, "Anthropologists are being called upon ... to play new roles, roles that often require them not only to criticize the societies in which their professional work is embedded, but to go beyond such critiques to evaluate/discover/create means by which other societies can achieve their own futures in the face of world political and economic interventions" (1982:374).

Feit describes four new "demands" upon anthropologists who work in Native Canadian contexts. The first is to "document the aboriginal and contemporary ways of life" of Canadian Native peoples (1982:377). This in itself does not represent a new role for anthropologists, but the purpose of the research is considerably different than before: "to provide evidence for use by the native peoples in their legal, para-legal and political confrontations." Here Feit is defining a role which departs considerably from that Salisbury describes. The second role is to "advise the native peoples on the detailed formulations of their goals and the means of attaining them in the light of present social-science theory and knowledge of the interactions, processes, and transformations of hunting societies and national and international institutions." The third role is essentially that of broker, "to help present and articulate such policy as is adopted by the native people to the public, to the government, and to the courts," and the fourth is "to do problem-oriented research on present conditions and ... help to implement the changes sought" (1982:377).

But for Feit and other anthropologists involved in various forms of advocacay anthropology with Native Canadians (such as Asch 1982), the link between applied work and anthropological theory remains important. As Feit (1982:378) writes, "There is therefore an opportunity both to be useful and to do theoretically significant research" in such situations. But what of anthropologists involved in advocacy work for its own sake, where anthropological theory neither directly guides the work, nor benefits from it?

The most salient discussion of attitudes toward advocacy anthropology in Canada, especially as it pertains to work with Native Canadians, is that found in the volume edited by Robert Paine (1985), *Advocacy and Anthropology*. This collection of presentations and commentaries from a workshop of invited anthropologists and others offers the most current thinking to date on this topic. Although there is some agreement with the previous comments by American and Canadian applied anthropologists, the tone of Paine's volume is considerably more activist. It would be prudent to use Paine's volume as a springboard for the present discussion.

According to Paine (1985:163), "Advocacy implies adversarial discourse." To this we can add Van Esterik's definition that "advocacy refers to the act of interceding or speaking on behalf of another person or group" (1985:60). The anthropologist who adopts this role automatically chooses sides, and invariably becomes both friend to one side of a dispute and foe to the other. Clearly, in doing so the anthropologist eschews any pretense of value-free, apolitical research or intervention. "Going native" is a frequently heard appellation when an anthropologist comes to identify with the struggles of the people with whom he or she works, and therefore violates one traditional "rule of thumb ... don't get involved" (Wallman 1985:14). But as Ryan (1985:213) notes, the decision to become an advocate is a personal one, and the simple fact that so many Canadian anthropologists working with Native peoples have become advocates in one form or another argues persuasively that this rule is terribly antiquated.

Van Esterik (1985) makes a very useful distinction between what she calls "small 'a' advocacy" and "large 'A' advocacy." Small "a" advocacy is relatively benign; it is the kind of advocacy that all anthropologists adopt when, for instance, they consciously decide to withhold data they feel might harm the people under study. This form of advocacy might also include helping a group apply for government grants or helping individuals appeal decisions to the Unemployment Insurance Commission. The main skill the anthropologist brings to this type of advocacy is simply a good knowledge of the larger society, its methods of communication, its legal system, and its "culture." But these are not skills anthropologists attain through training in anthropology; rather they are skills they bring with them as a result of their own process of enculturation. The anthropologist thus becomes a resource to the local people, one who seems to know relatively more about the power structures that affect local life, and who is accessible and seems willing to help. Indeed, for many anthropologists, precisely this kind of helping often facilitates entry into the community, allowing the actual research to proceed.

Large "A" advocacy involves being more active, more avowedly partisan, in the pursuit of a much narrower goal which nevertheless has implications for a larger group of local people. In this arena the public policy implications are considerably greater, and anthropological knowledge and skills may assume greater significance. An anthropologist who works on behalf of a Native group in land claims negotiations or litigation could, in its very crassest sense, contribute to the expenditure from public coffers of millions of dollars for the Native community, and in its most dramatic sense could contribute to a change in the political face of the country. As Van Esterik (1985:63) argues, "The image of large 'A' advocates as dragon-slayers, champions of a cause, and rabble rousers colours the public and professional evaluation of these activities." While this may be true, the real issue for the anthropologist considering an advocacy role involves defining his or her primary reference group: for many, this group constitutes the Native peoples themselves, and these anthropologists are willing therefore to accept criticism from the public, other anthropologists and even judges disturbed by their politicization.[1]

Paine's (1985) volume also provides some cautionary notes for advocacy anthropologists, and these are of particular relevance to this paper. Paine (1985:xiv) himself sets the tone in the preface when he asks, "How can we prevent our advocacy inducing (or maintaining) dependency among the client group?"

Georg Henriksen and David Maybury-Lewis tackle the issue more directly. Henriksen argues that it is very easy for anthropologists to create "clients" out of the people they study because "the authorities need to use anthropologists as a go-between or cultural translator or even as an advocate on behalf of the very subjects studied by anthropologists" (1985:121). He continues: "In dealing with indigenous peoples through experts or advocates who are competent in the majority's language, rhetoric, norms and 'rules of the game,' the authorities have practically ensured that their actions will be met by arguments (made by anthropologists on behalf of their clients) that they can then refute on their own terms" (Henriksen 1985:121–2). As a result, Native peoples at the community level may become alienated from the whole political process, becoming even more passive, and this, argues Henriksen, serves only to "further the colonial processes" which most advocate anthropologists abhor (1985:125). As Maybury-Lewis (1985:145) stresses, these anthropologists should really be assisting local groups to conduct their own advocacy effectively.

It is with these thoughts in mind that I now turn to one of my own experiences as an advocate anthropologist where, I believe, the limits of such a role were reached.

A CASE STUDY OF ANTHROPOLOGICAL ADVOCACY

Since 1979 I have been researching the political, economic, and social implications for Native peoples of hydroelectric development in western Canada. My research has demonstrated not only the serious socio-economic consequences of these hydroelectric projects for these peoples, but also the insensitivity of governments and power corporations to the Natives' needs for mitigation and compensation. What has happened to these northern Native peoples has violated my own sense of justice and human rights, and has led me down the path to advocacy anthropology. But I have always felt frustrated at my inability to move beyond the stage of researching and tendering reports of my findings, even though these reports have had some significant impacts on the policy process. I am indebted to these people for my academic success and wish to assist them in whatever manner possible when requested to do so. However, I have always refrained from intruding uninvited into an issue.

In the summer of 1985, a call for assistance came from one of the small northern communities I had studied.[2] They had been alerted by the provincial power corporation that there were to be some alterations to the method of operation of the hydroelectric project which had been built on their lake some years earlier. They were informed that the terms of the original licence granting the right to construct and operate the facility were, in essence, based on speculation. During the design phase, the engineers had been unsure how much water the project could safely handle, and therefore how much power could be produced once the project was completed. Since completion, the power corporation had requested permission, on an annual or semi-annual basis, to deviate from the terms of the original licence, altering even further the water levels in the lake adjacent to the community, to generate more power. The government had routinely given permission, and the community informed accordingly. The community had never before objected to this procedure, but in the spring of 1985 they did.

When I was contacted later that spring, the chief told me that the people were no longer willing to allow the province to simply rubber-stamp licence deviations because, they felt, these deviations were having a negative impact on the already damaged lake and local economy. They felt the water level fluctuations were excessive, and contributed to increased debris in the lake, which made open water travel difficult and played havoc with their fishing nets. Similarly, they believed that the operations of the project resulted in high ice ridges and slush in winter, which made snowmobile travel and the crossing of the winter ice road more difficult. The Natives were also concerned about the political process involved, wherein there occurred little consultation by the hydro corporation prior to decisions which could affect their community. I was asked if I would consider undertaking an impact study to determine exactly how these deviations were affecting the community. While tentatively agreeing, I made it clear that, in purely methodological terms, it might not be possible to separate the impacts of the original hydro-electric project from the incremental impacts of the licence deviations. I would investigate this and report back before launching any major research effort.

Over the ensuing months the community demanded action from the government on the issue, threatening to sue for damages if the current licence deviation request was approved without an impact study or compensation. The government's response was to offer to initiate discussions with the community on the question of impacts. If there were additional impacts caused by the deviations, the government would be prepared to discuss compensation. It was decided to convene a board to examine the whole question and to chart a course of action to resolve the issue.

The board was to consist of four members: one from the government, one from the power corporation, and two from the community. To my surprise, the local council asked me to be one of the community delegates, along with one of the council members. While I had lived in the community for about eighteen months while undertaking my research, I had not lived there for several years when this request was made. When I asked, "Why me?" council members said that I obviously knew a great deal about both hydro-electric dam impacts and the political process surrounding them. Implicit in the request, of course, was the indication that the people trusted me to represent their interests. I was overwhelmed by this show of confidence, and agreed to join the board.

Over the next two years, the board met on many occasions to develop and execute a plan of action. The course of these meetings must be presented to explain how, and why, I reached what I would consider to be the limits of my advocacy role on behalf of the community.

Just prior to the first board meeting, a minor controversy developed concerning my role and function. The community saw me as their representative, as if I were a community resident. The government, on the other hand, saw me as an external consultant retained by the community to represent them, a professional advocate if you will. The government insisted that I be paid a consulting fee. When I had agreed to represent the community, there was no discussion of a fee; I was to volunteer my time and "expertise" to aid the community, and we all assumed that the government would cover related expenses. The government decision that I should be paid clearly redefined my role into one with which they felt comfortable. Henriksen's (1985:121–2) cautionary note referred to above certainly applies here. I took the government's concerns back to the community leadership, and they saw no difficulty in my being paid if that was what the government wished. Their view was that we all should take advantage of government money when it was offered, including me. The government then decided that, to avoid the appearances of a conflict of interest on my part, the community should pay me directly, so I would appear to be working for them, and then the government would reimburse the community. Again, this was discussed with the leadership, who found the arrangement acceptable. I expressed my concerns that I wished not to be labelled the "expert," and that I felt strongly that the other community representative should likewise be paid by the government (via the community). This was discussed at length, and since the government had already offered this other member a fairly generous *per diem* allowance (based on normal consultation rates paid to northern Native representatives) which was perfectly acceptable to him, it was decided not to make an issue of it. Clearly, the government was establishing relative statuses within the board itself: I was the outside consultant, and should be treated as such, whereas the other community representative was to be viewed as simply doing his job as an elected official. Nevertheless, through a variety of means the two of us were able to more or less equalize the renumeration.

At the very first meeting of the board, a major issue erupted. The representative of the power corporation stated that they would only consider compensation for documentable impacts, and that most of the major impacts identified by the community were, in one way or another, already compensated for under existing agreements. Two major compensation agreements had been signed in the previous two years, one covering trapping and the other fishing. The power corporation was of the view that all problems even remotely related to these activities were beyond the scope of the board's mandate, including such things as travel problems connected with fishing and trapping. The licence deviations were considered to be part and parcel of the terms of these existing compensation packages. This latter point was a shock to me, as I had received no indication from the community that this was their understanding. This led to one of many dilemmas I would experience as a community advocate.

In investigating this issue, I discovered that the specifications for the water level and flow deviations were part of a five-year plan for the hydroelectric project being submitted for government approval. The plan was not submitted until after the fishing and trapping agreements had been signed. A reading of these agreements indicated that the power corporation would maintain lake levels within specific limits. These limits were not those of the original licence, but those indicated in the five-year plan and those represented by the various applications made to deviate from the licence. The fishermen and trappers were unaware of the significance of the elevation levels stipulated in the compensation agreements; to them, the figures were nearly meaningless numbers. The lawyer who had acted on behalf of the fishermen and trappers in negotiating these agreements, and whom they trusted implicitly, stated to me only that "all aspects [of the agreements] were negotiated." Feeling that the community had been inadequately informed of the meaning of these elevation figures, the other community representative and I on our own consulted another lawyer familiar with hydroelectric issues, and were informed that grounds did exist for demanding re-opening these agreements. Further, this lawyer opined that the whole licence deviation issue could be handled through the arbitration procedures extant in a wide-ranging mitigation and compensation pact which covered the northern part of the province.

We explored this option extensively, and informed the council of our findings. However, we did not feel comfortable advocating that the community consider either of these actions. We were extremely uncomfortable doing anything to criticize the lawyer involved, since the people had had some bad experiences in the past with lawyers, and this one had at least managed to get some form of compensation. Re-opening these agreements would be both time-consuming and potentially costly, and would be a clear repudiation of the leadership in the fishermen's and trappers' associations who had signed the agreements. A crisis in community leadership might have resulted.

In the end, the community took no action either to reopen the fishing and trapping compensation deals or to use the arbitration procedures. The council members were unsure of their mandate with respect to these agreements, which had been negotiated with the fishermen and trappers, and not with council.

Board meetings were often dominated by discussions of technical data on water flows and levels that neither representative could fully comprehend. It became apparent that both the government and power corporation representatives saw me as the primary target of their discussions. The other community representative was afforded less opportunity to talk or ask questions than I was, and his comments were often glossed over by the government representatives who interpreted them as being out of context. In some ways, the management of this issue affecting a Native community became a discussion among three non-Natives, despite my attempts to involve the other community representative. Indeed it was precisely my ability to talk to the government representatives and deal with them on their own terms which the community considered my greatest asset – and, as Henriksen (1985) noted, made me attractive to government. The community leadership expected me to do most of the talking. Although uncomfortable with this role, I accepted it as their wish. Nevertheless, the other community representative and I met extensively prior to board meetings to plan our strategy. In addition, I communicated extensively with the community leadership, including numerous conference calls with the entire council, to get direction. I did not want to be placed in the position where I could influence and perhaps even make decisions on behalf of the community. But this is precisely what happened.

The board ultimately decided to commission a feasibility study into the question of whether it was even possible to undertake an impact study of the type needed. We drew up terms of a contract, and interviewed firms that submitted tenders. When we finally selected one consulting firm, I expected to play a minimal role in the assessment process. But this was not the case. The firm relied heavily on my previous work, and especially on my contacts within the community. We were able to convince the engineers of the need to visit the community and interview residents, and we were also able to convince the government that the chief engineer and I should fly up to the community in advance to explain the research to the residents. This trip gave me ample opportunity to discuss with him the concerns of the people, and to precondition him to what he would see.

The other representative and I had developed a plan for the engineer to see the human side of the community before he undertook his scientific studies. I introduced him to many residents, took him on social visits and gave him the opportunity to experience elements of the Natives' lifestyle with which he was unfamiliar. (Indeed, he was a relatively new resident to the province, and had never been north or to a Native community. For him, it was almost like an exotic holiday!) But most important, he saw and heard from the people about the devastation caused by the hydroelectric project. In the end, he proved to be a very sensitive individual who appeared to feel guilty when he was forced to inform us that, scientifically, it was not possible to separate impacts caused by the dam overall from impacts caused by the deviation program. Nonetheless, in his final report to the board he stated very clearly that though there were probably some negative impacts, they could not really be measured.

The result of the engineering study was predictable for all members of the board. In an earlier meeting with the community council I had presented a variety of scenarios outlining the possible outcomes of the study. Political options were explained and discussed. In outlining each possible scenario, I presented at least two options, one of which was always the "no action" option. I personally believed that the community should fight for compensation, and that they could be successful, even if the engineering study proved inconclusive. But this was my personal opinion, and I kept it to myself until, after all the information was presented, one council member asked my view. At this point I felt the tension within me rise; the inevitable question had been asked. I felt at the time that I could, if I wished, direct the decision of the council to a great extent. Should I argue for legal action, or for more negotiations? Part of me was still so furious at the injustice inflicted on these people that, in some ways, I felt the government had to be punished. But the community's best interests were what mattered, and

I was able to explain quite calmly my firm belief that the engineering study would be inconclusive, and then more passively suggest that negotiations with the government regarding compensation should be considered. I made it clear, however, that the decision was for them alone to make, and that I would work to provide whatever information I possessed or could acquire to help them make that decision.

When the engineering report was finally tendered, the council contacted me about what the next step should be. I suggested releasing the report, with a press release, to put the government on the defensive. The council accepted my advice, and asked me to write the press release and then send it along with copies of the report to various news media. I consulted the council on the contents of the release, and what I believed would be its impact. I advised them to be ready to give interviews, since it would direct the media to them and not to me, and not to avoid the media as some past leaders had occasionally done. The whole hydroelectric issue was to go public once again.

Initial media response to the report and the press release was very good. The story was picked up by a variety of northern and southern newspapers and radio stations in the fall of 1987. The community leader gave an excellent interview to the major provincial newspaper, demanding compensation, and the paper published short excerpts from the report which supported the community's assertions that there was indeed a negative impact. The provincial energy minister was even quoted in the story as saying, "There is always room for discussion," and that he would be prepared to talk to community representatives regarding compensation. It seemed as though the whole exercise had moved positively in favour of the community, and while no compensation had been promised, at least the responsible minister was on record as being willing to open discussions.

At this crucial point the whole process ground to a halt. The government representatives on the board contacted me and asked what I felt we should do next. I probably could have moved the board in a new direction at this time, if I had wished, since these individuals never challenged my authority as a community representative. However, I insisted that I could not make a decision on behalf of the community, and could only act under their direction. But such direction was not forthcoming. Despite my repeated requests for guidance, the council seemed suddenly no longer interested in the issue.

In the midst of the licence deviation dispute there had been an election and a change in community leadership. Since the whole issue had been spearheaded by the former chief; the new chief (who had not been a member of council) knew little about it. He was also politically inexperienced, and more conservative in his approach to government than his predecessor. A variety of personal and political problems, unrelated to the hydro issue, increasingly paralyzed the council's ability to make decisions. As I have described elsewhere (Waldram 1984, 1988), this type of political inertia had caused problems for Native communities in the past as they grappled with the complex legal and political implications of hydroelectric development, and I have been critical of special interest groups that have inadvertently exploited this inertia in similar disputes by seizing the limelight. It was within this context that I reached the final and ultimate stage for me as an advocate: I believe I was, in effect, in a position to push for a decision by the community council, heavily influence that decision, and perhaps even make the decision myself. Indeed, in my view the government was prepared to accept *any* decision, even one I made, as the community's decision. Certainly the political climate was ripe; now was the time to move if the issue were to be resolved. What to do?

My decision was to do absolutely nothing without clear direction from the community council. I refused to make a decision on their behalf, even knowing that failure to move immediately might jeopardize the previous two years' work and the future chances for a settlement. There was a limit to the amount of prodding I could do, especially from a distance, and I informed both the council and the board that I was ready to re-enter the fray whenever called upon.

The controversy over the water licence deviations effectively died soon after the engineering report was tendered. The council did not move any further on the issue, for reasons I only partly understand. I believe there was no antagonism either to me personally or to my role in the matter. The new chief and I had become fairly good friends during my residency in the community, and many of the council members, including the other representative on the board, remained unchanged after the election. The change in leadership had not resulted in a rejection by the council of the role I had been playing. And, at first, the new leader seemed quite willing to pursue the issue that had been sparked by his predecessor. However, within two years, a new hydroelectric issue would arise (this time involving a demand for compensation for damages caused to the domestic fishery on the lake), with yet another leader at the helm. I was not active in this dispute, although I did provide data and methodological advice to the consulting firm hired to investigate the issue. The community leaders did not share my strong belief in the importance of settling the water licence deviation issue.

DEFINING THE LIMITS TO ADVOCACY ANTHROPOLOGY

Advocacy anthropologists often retain a deep commitment to the people with whom they have worked. They also have a strong desire to "help," to rectify injustice, and to ensure that the people are better off than before. In sum, they are emotional about the issues they have adopted and the people they represent, to the point where they are willing to place at risk professional relations with their colleagues and absorb public criticism if that be the price.[3] Under such circumstances, it can be difficult to recognize that there are indeed limits to the advocacy role, and to discern the nature of those limits. I wish to conclude this paper with some general remarks stemming from my own experiences which might help to define these limits.

To understand the limits of the advocacy role, one simple fact appropriate to most advocacy situations must be recognized: in the long run, how the issue is resolved will likely be of minimal, if any, consequence to the anthropologist, and any impact we might incur will pale in comparison to the impact on the peoples for whom we work or whom we temporarily represent. When asked by the council why I was not more forceful in guiding them through the dispute described above, I stated that it was not my community, I did not live there, and how the dispute was resolved did not affect me. It was not my issue, it was theirs. I was concerned, and I wanted to help, but they had to make the decisions precisely because they had to live with the consequences of those decisions.

With this in mind, I would like to set out my view of the principles which should guide advocacy anthropology in the Native Canadian context:

1 Anthropologists should generally wait to be invited to assist a community or people. Offering to help is acceptable, but intervening in a dispute requires the utmost caution and consideration for the ramifications of the action.
2 Anthropologists should operate only under direction from the people they purport to represent or for whom they are otherwise working. They should follow the lead of the people, not become leaders themselves. They should learn to be good team players and good employees.
3 Anthropologists must be accountable to the people they represent. This entails ongoing discussions, report writing, and whatever other forms of communication seem appropriate.

4 Anthropologists must allow the people to speak for themselves, and not steal the limelight from them. This is difficult to avoid, given the fact that both government and media tend to be attracted to culturally similar individuals to act as spokespersons.
5 Anthropologists must always provide a range of options to the people to help in the decision-making process. They must be as objective as possible and not unduly attempt to influence decisions.
6 Above all else, anthropologists must always be prepared to back off, to curtail their input and, ultimately, reduce their activity to a negligible level when appropriate. They must appreciate that they are outsiders, and will forever remain so, and that the leadership of Native communities are quite capable of acting in the best interests of their constituents.

In the case study presented in this paper, principles one, three and five were easily adhered to. The ultimate dilemma pertained more specifically to principles two and four. As the case progressed, I received less and less direction, to the point where I was forced to either continue on my own or cease my activitiy. Some potential existed to push for resolution, and the government representatives were willing to act, but I refrained, and the local leadership ultimately abandoned this particular issue in favour of others. An autonomous people's right to make decisions parallels their right not to make decisions, and of course their right to disagree with their advocates. It became necessary for me to invoke principle six, and back out of the issue.

The type of advocacy anthropology described in this paper represents a considerable departure from that suggested by Salisbury (1976) many years ago. The game of politics which shrouds all aspects of Native-government relations in Canada renders ineffective any attempts by anthropologists to remain neutral in disputes, to be ombudspersons. The kind of advocacy described here is more similar to that demonstrated by many of Salisbury's students who worked directly for the Cree in the capacities of researchers and policy advisors in a manner compatible with the model of advocacy anthropology delineated by Schensul and Schensul (1978).

But it is possible to move beyond the traditional roles of researcher and advisor without violating the principles I have presented above. One can become the adversary of government while supporting a Native cause, as Paine (1985:163) suggests, to the point of speaking or acting on behalf of the Native group, when you have been invited to do so, and only after extensive consultation with the group and its leaders. In rare circumstances, by virtue of research and related scholarship, the anthropologist may be in a position to positively affect an outcome by initially involving her- or himself in an issue uninvited; certainly anthropological ethics demand consideration of such an action if non-intervention and silence may harm the interests of a Native group or if the people are unaware of information the anthropologist possesses. I would suggest that large "A" advocacy (Van Esterik 1985) will continue to shape and define the relationship between Native peoples and anthropologists in the near future. Furthermore, this form of advocacy is not guided by a desire to advance anthropological theory, nor is it necessarily derived from such theory: it is advocacy for its own sake.

Immense satisfaction, both personal and professional, can be attained through assisting a group of people in their struggles for justice, fair play, health and welfare, and so on. But the corollary also holds: losing battles into which we have put so much intellectual and emotional energy can be crushing. In the case presented here, it was terribly difficult for me to watch the water licence deviation issue die. But stepping in and attempting to make decisions on behalf of the community, or unduly attempting to influence decisions, would only propagate the colonialism decried by Henriksen (1985), Ryan (1985) and others. When the advocate anthropologist is in a position to either make or influence decisions on behalf of a group of people of which he or she is not one, the limits of advocacy anthropology have been reached.

NOTES

1 The disdain for anthropologists expressed by Chief Justice Allan McEachern in the Gitksan-Wet'suwet'en land claim decision in March 1991 demonstrates the extent to which the discipline as a whole can be questioned, and not just those who act in an advocacy capacity. Nonetheless, the implications of the McEachern decision are clear: having an anthropologist as a researcher or to provide "expert" testimony in a land claim case may prove to be a liability to Native groups unless the fundamental errors and misconceptions of the McEachern decision are addressed. The 1991 Canadian Anthropology Society meetings at London, Ontario, saw a group of committed anthropologists come together to develop a strategy to counteract the McEachern decision.

2 I have chosen to keep the names of the community and specific residents anonymous, and have accordingly altered other aspects of the

story without sacrificing its basic integrity. In so doing, I am employing Van Esterik's (1985) small "a" advocacy.

3 My activities as an advocate anthropologist were not made known either to the public or to my colleagues. I avoided media attention as much as possible, and though there were a few occasions when I spoke to reporters, I always made sure they were directed to the council. At the time I did not inform my colleagues in the discipline because it was not my intent to turn my participation into an academic exercise. I have written this paper about my experiences because of the lessons I hope it imparts to others who find themselves in similar circumstances.

REFERENCES

Asch, Michael I. 1982. "Dene Self-Determination and the Study of Hunter-Gatherers in the Modern World." In *Politics and History in Band Societies*, eds. Eleanor Leacock and Richard Lee, 347–71. Cambridge: Cambridge University Press.

Feit, Harvey. 1982. "The Future of Hunters within Nation-States: Anthropology and the James Bay Cree." In *Politics and History in Band Societies*, eds. Eleanor Leacock and Richard Lee, 373–411. Cambridge: Cambridge University Press.

Freilich, Morris. 1970. *Marginal Natives: Anthropologists at Work*. New York: Harper and Row.

Henriksen, Georg. 1985. "Anthropologists as Advocates – Promoters of Pluralism or Makers of Clients?" In *Advocacy and Anthropology, First Encounters*, ed. R. Paine, 119–29. St John's: Institute of Social and Economic Research, Memorial University of Newfoundland.

Maybury-Lewis, David. 1985. "A Special Sort of Pleading: Anthropology at the Service of Ethnic Groups." In *Advocacy and Anthropology, First Encounters*, ed. R. Paine, 130–48. St John's: Institute of Social and Economic Research, Memorial University of Newfoundland.

Paine, Robert, ed. 1985. *Advocacy and Anthropology, First Encounters*. St John's: Institute of Social and Economic Research, Memorial University of Newfoundland.

Pelto, G., and P. Pelto. 1976. *The Human Adventure: An Introduction to Anthropology*. New York: Macmillan.

Richardson, Boyce. 1975. *Strangers Devour the Land*. New York: Knopf.

Ryan, Joan. 1985. "Decolonizing Anthropology." In *Advocacy and Anthropology, First Encounters*, ed. R. Paine, 208–14. St John's: Institute of Social and Economic Research, Memorial University of Newfoundland.

Salisbury, Richard F., F. Filion, F. Rawji, and D. Stewart. 1972. *Development and James Bay. Social Implications of the Proposals for the Hydroelectric Scheme.*

Montreal: Programme in the Anthropology of Development, McGill University.

- 1975. *Policy Regarding Native Peoples: An Academic Social Scientist's Perspective*. Communication Series, no. 37. Montreal: Programme in the Anthropology of Development, McGill University.
- 1976. "The Anthropologist as Societal Ombudsman." In *Development from Below: Anthropologists and Development Situations*, ed. David C. Pitt, 255–65. The Hague: Mouton.
- 1977. "A Prism of Perceptions: The James Bay Hydro-Electricity Project." In *Perceptions of Development*, ed. Sandra Wallman, 172–90. Cambridge: Cambridge University Press.
- 1986. *A Homeland for the Cree: Regional Development in James Bay 1971–1981*. Montreal and Kingston: McGill-Queen's University Press.
Schensul, Stephen L., and J.J. Schensul. 1978. "Advocacy and Anthropology." In *Social Scientists as Advocates: Views from the Applied Disciplines*, eds. George H. Weber and George J. McCall, 121–65. Beverly Hills: Sage.
Van Esterik, Penny. 1985. "Confronting Advocacy Confronting Anthropology." In *Advocacy and Anthropology, First Encounters*, ed. R. Paine, 59–77. St John's: Institute of Social and Economic Research, Memorial University of Newfoundland.
Van Willigen, John. 1986. *Applied Anthropology*. South Hadley, MA: Bergin and Garvey.
Waldram, James B. 1984. "Hydroelectric Development and the Process of Negotiation in Northern Manitoba." *Canadian Journal of Native Studies* 4(2):205–39.
- 1988. *As Long as the Rivers Run: Hydroelectric Development and Native Communities in Western Canada*. Winnipeg: University of Manitoba Press.
Wallman, Sandra. 1985. "Rules of Thumb." In *Advocacy and Anthropology, First Encounters*, ed. R. Paine, 13–15. St John's: Institute of Social and Economic Research, Memorial University of Newfoundland.

13 Custom, Tradition, and the Politics of Culture: Aboriginal Self-Government in Canada

COLIN H. SCOTT

Cultural distinctiveness is a key value and indispensable political resource for aboriginal peoples in Canada. During the past twenty years, as state policy makers have forsworn assimilationist objectives, demands for accommodation of indigenous "traditions" and "customs" have become increasingly potent. Nowhere is this more evident than in discourse on self-government, where aboriginal leaders routinely contrast indigenous values and institutions to those of the centralized, hierarchical state, arguing that the "sovereign" grip of the latter must be relaxed for the former to develop and flourish.

The ethnonational demands of aboriginal peoples are not unique; they reflect the politics of culture, culture as both means and end in the construction of relations between social groups (MacCannell 1979). It can be argued that the politics of culture are particularly consequential for encapsulated aboriginal peoples (Schwimmer 1972; Paine 1985). Implicit in these politics are issues about the rights of suppressed cultural collectivities, issues impassioned by hopes of equity in economic and jurisdictional terms. In the Canadian political arena, these issues are played out in multiple discourses on "First Nations," "distinct societies," the "multicultural mosaic," and "Canadian identity." Indeed, it is apparent that "culture" itself has become an "essentially contested concept" (Connolly 1974) in our political life.

This paper reviews and critiques some policy, legal, and constitutional perspectives on culture, custom, and tradition in aboriginal governance. The analysis is related to a report prepared by Scott,

Hutchins, et al. (1988) on policies needed to respond to aboriginal groups' proposals to structure self-government along the lines of customary and traditional institutions.[1]

The conclusions of this analysis were that indigenous cultural practices are institutionally extensive and profoundly embedded in collective life; that policies on aboriginal government must accommodate the reality of aboriginal culture as changing, adapting, and developing; that policy makers should reject the notion that these dynamic qualities signify cultural assimilation; and that municipal-style powers "delegated" by a "sovereign crown" are inconsistent with the political culture of aboriginal peoples. Attempts by central state authorities to regulate aboriginal governments through "positive law" regulation (i.e., legislative prescription) fail to recognize the institutional scope and depth of aboriginal culture, and provide insufficient flexibility for its autonomous development as historical circumstances change. Therefore, policy should recognize the inherent authority of customary and traditional forms of aboriginal government, and remove legislative or constitutional impediments to their free functioning and development.

HISTORICAL ACKNOWLEDGMENT OF CUSTOM AND TRADITION

The legal doctrine of aboriginal rights in Canada stems from early colonial experience, when commercial and military self-interest, if not love of justice, impelled Europeans to acknowledge the political and territorial integrity of indigenous nations. The issue for European monarchs was to assert sovereign claims against one another while preventing unacceptable levels of interference in the territories and affairs of their indigenous allies. Accordingly, the doctrine of aboriginal rights entails significant recognition of indigenous institutions and practices: "Except where modified by treaty or legislation ... Native peoples presumptively hold full rights to lands in their possession, and retain their accustomed laws and political institutions, including a measure of internal autonomy" (Slattery 1987:732).

During colonization, the Crown's claim of sovereignty involved a "notional" title to Indian territories, but Native property rights remained a burden on the Crown, and customary Native systems of land use and tenure "remained in force within the Native communities and governed the relations of their members *inter se*" (Slattery 1987:742). The doctrine of aboriginal rights "governs the title of a Native group considered as a collective unit," but subject to valid legislation members of the Native group are "governed by rules peculiar to the group, as laid down by custom or internal government organs" (Slattery 1987:745). Further, while these rules have a customary base, "they are not for that reason necessarily static. Except to the extent that they may be otherwise regulated by statute, they are open to both formal and informal change, in accordance with shifting group attitudes, needs and practices" (Slattery 1987:745).

After the early nineteenth century – when aboriginal nations ceased to be of significance as military allies – colonial and Canadian government policy became bluntly assimilationist. But even so, concessions to aboriginal custom and tradition were in some respects deemed expedient, and were included in pre- and post-Confederation treaties, and successive Indian acts. Although Indian Act legislation was an important vehicle for suppressing aboriginal political institutions,[2] certain customary aspects of leadership selection, band membership, and remedies for trespass were provided for. And to the extent that indigenous cultural practices were protected by treaty, Section 88 of the Indian Act shielded them against provincial laws of general application.

EMERGENCE OF ABORIGINAL CULTURE AS A PUBLIC POLICY VALUE

Aboriginal culture has gained prominence as a positive policy value only in the last twenty years. The watershed cited by many observers was the political failure of the 1969 White Paper policy of the Trudeau Liberal government, which had proposed to abolish the Indian Act and to do away once and for all with special Indian status (see Weaver 1981). Decisions in 1973 in the Supreme Court of Canada (Nishga) and in Quebec Superior Court (James Bay Cree) stimulated the development of policies recognizing the continued existence of special aboriginal rights. Between 1973 and 1978, federal comprehensive claims policy shifted from presenting claims settlements as a way of ameliorating problems caused by loss of way of life, to presenting them as a way of promoting the social, cultural, and economic continuity of aboriginal society (Asch 1984).

An intimate connection between cultural survival and self-government powers was recognized by the all-party Special Parliamentary Committee on Indian Self-Government, which reached its conclusions in 1983 following extensive consultation with Indian constituencies and leadership. The committee called for "First Nation government" powers that would include "virtually the entire range of law-making, policy, program delivery, law enforcement, and adjudication" within territories of First Nation governments (Canada 1983:63). The committee emphasized "the importance of Indian control in areas central to the cultures of the First Nations ... in some cases only Indian control of legislation and policy would ensure the survival and development of Indian communities" (Canada 1983:27), and reiterated, later in its report, that "there are matters that must be controlled by Indian communities to ensure their cultural survival ... By exercising control over these matters, Indian people could ensure that future generations were able to preserve and enjoy their culture and heritage" (Canada 1983:35).

The Government of Canada, in its response, promised self-government legislation that "would be based on a reaffirmation of the Government's commitment to the preservation and enhancement of Indian culture and heritage, including Indian institutions." Legislation, furthermore, "must be framed so as to allow Indian First Nations to evolve within Canada in a way that is consistent with their culture, history and philosophy" (Canada 1984a:4).

General framework legislation, designed to supplant the Indian Act, and to enable the establishment of First Nations governments, was drafted and passed by the Liberal cabinet (Canada 1984b). Passage through Parliament, however, was prevented by the election of a Conservative government.[3] Its demise notwithstanding (and aboriginal criticisms about their limited ability to participate in its drafting), the bill was significant as an indication of the potential for federal politicians to move in the direction of recognizing indigenous institutions. The definition of Indian nations was not restricted to bands, but could include any Indian communities with a common language, culture, and history, including any nation or tribe referred to in the Royal Proclamation of 1763. Structures of Indian nation governments were not legislatively prescribed, but were left to the constitutions of the First Nations. The legislative powers for First Nations went well beyond Indian Act provisions, and included areas where custom clearly could operate, such as administration of justice, family law, and property within the boundaries of the lands of the First Nation.

The Coolican Task Force on comprehensive claims policy (Canada 1985) affirmed the central importance of self-government in encouraging "the development of aboriginal communities as strong, confident, and *distinctive societies* within confederation" [my emphasis]. The report states: "Aboriginal peoples should exercise the greatest possible control over matters that directly affect the preservation and enhancement of their culture ... in principle, aboriginal people should be free to determine the form of government best suited to them; however, discussions between governments and the aboriginal people will be necessary to determine how the structure of aboriginal self-government would relate to the larger Canadian political system" (Canada 1985:71–2).

In 1987, the federal minister of Indian Affairs and Northern Development published an amended claims policy which replaced a former language of "blanket extinguishment" of aboriginal rights and claims with a language of specification and "certainty" in defining land rights (Canada 1987). This makes it possible, in theory, to convert contested aboriginal land rights into negotiated bundles of more defined rights, without prejudice to political or other rights which are presumed to continue except as explicitly modified. The amendment was logically coherent with the entrenchment of existing aboriginal and treaty rights in the Constitution Act (Canada 1982), and with the notion that any rights not explicitly altered by treaty flow through undiminished. In practice, however, aboriginal parties to comprehensive claims negotiations find the federal party still heavily committed to terms which amount to extinguishment of general and unspecified aboriginal rights.

CULTURE, CUSTOM, AND TRADITION IN THE DISCOURSE OF THE FIRST MINISTERS' CONFERENCES ON ABORIGINAL CONSTITUTIONAL MATTERS

In addition to legislation giving effect to First Nations governments, the Trudeau Liberal government undertook to negotiate constitutional recognition of the right to aboriginal self-government – a process inherited after 1984 by the new Conservative prime minister, Brian Mulroney. The forum for these negotiations was the series of four Canadian First Ministers' Conferences on Aboriginal Constitutional Matters (CFMCs 1983, 1984, 1985, 1987) held pursuant to patriation of the Canadian Constitution.

In Section 35 of the Constitution Act, "the existing aboriginal and treaty rights of the aboriginal peoples of Canada are ... recognized and affirmed," where aboriginal peoples include "the Indian, Inuit, and Metis peoples of Canada." Section 25 of the same act stipulates that the Charter of Rights and Freedoms in the Constitution

shall not be construed so as to abrogate or derogate from any aboriginal, treaty or other rights or freedoms that pertain to the aboriginal peoples of Canada including

(a) any rights or freedoms that have been recognized by the Royal Proclamation of October 7, 1763; and

(b) any rights or freedoms that may be acquired by the aboriginal peoples of Canada by way of land claims settlement.

The legal effect of these sections of the Constitution remain largely untested, but it might reasonably be supposed that the right to indigenous forms of government, insofar as they have not been surrendered or specifically abrogated by the Crown, are among "existing aboriginal rights." It was the explicit recognition of "inherent" rights of self-government that dominated the agendas of the CFMC's.

In their position speeches at the constitutional conferences, several federal and provincial first ministers endorsed the objective of aboriginal self-government on two principal grounds: cultural survival and the resolution of socio-economic problems besetting aboriginal people.[4] There was broad agreement among first ministers that aboriginal people suffer inequities. There was disagreement, however, on the extent to which inequities could be remedied within the framework of mainstream institutions, as opposed to constitutionally empowered aboriginal governments.

A key function of self-government, according to Premier James Lee of Prince Edward Island, would be that "such structures would enable Aboriginal People to protect their culture and traditions and to develop better social and economic conditions for their people" (CFMC 1985:65). Premier David Peterson of Ontario observed that "Canadians are deeply disturbed by the social and economic inequities that aboriginal peoples face ... In my view, these conditions can be alleviated only if we provide a framework under which aboriginal people will be able to develop their communities as centres of cultural integrity and economic opportunity. That is the goal of aboriginal self-government" (CFMC 1987:63–4). Even Brian Peckford of Newfoundland, one of the premiers to object most strenuously to constitutional entrenchment of an inherent right of aboriginal self-government, professed support for aboriginal culture: "We appreciate that Native peoples wish to be economically self-reliant and want the ability to preserve and enhance their unique culture, languages, and traditions. We are not fearful of these legitimate aspirations and will work closely with the aboriginal people of our province to shape the new institutions that can fulfill these functions" (CFMC 1987:117). Premier René Lévesque of Quebec claimed a special empathy for the objective of cultural self-determination: "Je comprends nos amis inuit et amérindiens quand ils parlent du maintien de leur culture, du maintien de leur identié, bien nous aussi [I understand our Inuit and Amerindian friends when they speak of upholding their culture, of upholding their identity, well us too]" (CFMC 1983:48).

The rhetoric of premiers who resisted the idea of an inherent right of aboriginal government – particularly those of British Columbia, Alberta, Saskatchewan, and Newfoundland – alleged continued support for aboriginal culture as a policy objective. But cultural survival could be met through municipal-type powers for aboriginal governments or sensitization of existing educational, social services, and provincial and federal community development programs. Other first ministers required constitutional recognition to protect the original authority and diverse functions of aboriginal governments. According to Premier Howard Pawley of Manitoba: "At the time of the European settlement in what is now Canada, our ancestors encountered aboriginal people who existed and who had long existed as distinct nations. These aboriginal peoples exercised the power of self-government over their religious, their cultural, their economic and their political life. They exercised control over their territory and over the living and the natural resources in the land that they inhabited" (CFMC 1983:59).

Prime Minister Brian Mulroney justified his support for constitutional entrenchment of self-government rights, in part, by reference to the *inferior* ability of aboriginal cultures to maintain their cultures under the status quo: "In Canada, we assume that our cultural and our linguistic backgrounds and traditions will be respected, even cherished and enhanced. Let somebody put a finger on them and see what happens. But Indian, Inuit and Metis peoples do not have this assurance ... nor the power to determine their own cultural development. In fact, there were times when aspects of their cultures were subject to legal sanctions and suppression" (CFMC 1985:10). This utterance put an intriguing spin on standard equality arguments. Universalist ideologies generally emphasize the equal rights of individuals before the state – but to enjoy equality of *cultural* development, Mulroney argues, aboriginal peoples need recognition of special collective rights of self-determination. The prime minister continued with the assertion that only the aboriginal people can "decide what mix of traditional and modern life they find appropriate to meet their needs ... they alone can strike that critical balance between the old and the new" (CFMC 1985:14).

Aboriginal leaders, for their part, tied cultural rights to the historical priority of aboriginal peoples, and to an institutionally comprehensive definition of cultural survival:

Our position is that aboriginal rights, aboriginal title to land, water and sea ice flows [sic] from aboriginal rights; and all rights to practise our customs and traditions, to retain and develop our languages and cultures, and the rights to self-government, all these things flow from the fact that we have aboriginal rights.

In our view, aboriginal rights can also be seen as human rights, because ... these are the things that we need to continue to survive as a distinct peoples [sic] in Canada. The right to cultural survival is a human right, and all these things, all these aboriginal rights that we are talking about ... shouldn't be seen as extraordinary rights or anything like that. *They are there because we were here first, we had certain customs and traditions and the way we did things before the Europeans came, and we have the right to continue to practise and retain these things.* (my emphasis; John Amagoalik, Co-chairperson of the Inuit Committee on National Issues; CFMC 1983:130)

According to Bill Wilson, vice-president, Native Council of Canada, the aboriginal right "is a right to self-government, a right to govern yourselves with your own institutions, whichever way you want those institutions to be or to run; the right to culture, to language, the right basically to practise your own religion and customs, the right to hunt, trap and fish and certainly gather ... and also the right to utilize the resources, exploit them ... in terms of what is happening in Canada today" (CFMC 1983:134).

Two features of cultural rights are highlighted in the statements of aboriginal leaders. First, the authority of customs, traditions, and institutions stems from the customs and traditions themselves and their historical precedence, not from any non-aboriginal government. Second, aboriginal custom can adapt to contemporary circumstances without loss of rights.

The aboriginal vision of Canada, a state comprised of a plurality of federated nations, was spelled out by Georges Erasmus, national chief of the Assembly of First Nations: "Canada must be truly reflective of the reality of the diversity of cultures and languages and traditions of which it is really made up; let us together build a genuine confederation or alliance of nations to be the soul of the nation-state Canada that will inspire future generations of all of its component nations and be a model of multilingual and multinational harmony that is second to none in this world" (CFMC 1987:25).

The series of first ministers' conferences which ended in 1987 failed to achieve a constitutional amendment on aboriginal self-government. With insufficient first minister support to recognize an inherent right of self-government, aboriginal leaders were offered a right of self-government that would be subject to approval by provincial and federal authorities prior to implementation – that is, self-government as a delegated or "contingent" right. Several first ministers, in other words, sought guarantees that the authority of aboriginal self-governing institutions would be constitutionally inferior to their own. Aboriginal leaders unanimously rejected this possibility. They argued that self-government as an inherent right is already implicit in Section 35 of the Constitution, and that it would be a step backward to accept entrenchment of a delegated self-government right.

THE LIMITS OF DELEGATED RIGHTS

Having abandoned the former Liberal government's objective of general legislation to enhance First Nations self-government, and with constitutional amendment at an impasse, the federal Conservative government decided to negotiate piecemeal what it terms "community-based self-government arrangements" with Indian bands. Its justification for this approach hinges on the sensitivity of case-by-case negotiations to diverse traditions and cultures:

The federal government's policy approach to self-government is to acknowledge the desire expressed by communities to exercise greater control and authority over the management of their affairs. This may result in the establishment of different types of institutions in different parts of the country which reflect the particular circumstances of each distinct aboriginal group or community. The objectives of the government's policy on community self-government are based on the principles that local control and decision-making must be substantially increased; that flexibility is needed to recognize diverse needs, traditions and cultures; and that greater accountability to community members must be achieved. Any particular approach to community self-government must respect existing constitutional principles and be consistent with government practice. (Canada 1987:17–18)

The language of the present policy indicates a reaction to the more aggressive reforms sought in the early 1980s. "First Nations" have been pruned back to "Indian communities," and "First Nation Governments" to "self-government arrangements." The authority of these latter is explicitly to be "*granted* to any new institutions or bodies" by federal legislation (my emphasis; Canada 1987:18). The piecemeal approach to negotiations also represents a serious logistical limitation on the rate of self-government development. Actual case-by-case negotiations involve only a small fraction of Indian groups in Canada.

Several of the groups developing proposals for these negotiations have explicitly structured self-government charters around customary and traditional institutions and values – the potlatch, clan-based territorial management, clan-based administrative jurisdictions, and consensus-style tribal and tribal confederate government. Notwithstanding the federal government's position that self-governing rights will be "granted," the proponents commonly stress the view that their "Supreme Law" is inherent in their own indigenous institutions and values – not delegated by federal or provincial governments.[5]

Federal and provincial governments are involved in a paradox. They seek in some measure to accommodate aboriginal culture without recognizing it as a source of authority in its own right. But what does it mean to "grant" authority to indigenous institutions that, in social practice, possess this authority by force of custom and tradition?

THE LIMITS OF THE STATE

Federal and provincial governments wish to interpret their own authority as final or absolute. The orthodox ideology of the state is that "its institutions alone can be the source of law. Laws are valid only in so far as they are acknowledged in some way by the organs of the state. The law is defined, in other words, as a set of consistent principles, valid for and binding upon the whole population and emanating from a single source. The written, rational state system is the only one which is 'properly law' " (Hooker 1975:1).

Is it possible to surpass this ideology? A first step is to recognize that it is not an accurate representation of state authority. The view of the state as a single authority emanating one law for *all* ignores the reality of "multiple systems of legal obligation" (Hooker 1975:2) that comprise the state and which arose in colonial contexts as the introduced law of colonizing powers came into contact with indigenous law and institutions. European "settler" states such as the U.S.A., Canada, Australia, New Zealand, and South Africa have attempted to impose "general laws" on aboriginal peoples. Yet all have found it necessary to adopt special legislation for aboriginal populations, legislation which has vacillated between "protection" and assimilation. Treaties with aboriginal nations, as sources of law in their own capacity, are further indication that the sovereignty of the state is less than absolute.

Faced with competing aboriginal institutions and practices, "settler" states have been inclined either to outlaw them or to define them as inferior to and dependent on central state institutions.[6] This tactic engenders social conflict and policy paralysis, due not only to the entrenched resistance of aboriginal people, but also to the intrinsic limitations of state law and institutions. As Falk Moore (1978: 2–3) has remarked, "Ordinary experience indicates that law and legal institutions can only effect a degree of intentional control of society, greater at some times and less at others, or more with regard to some matters than others ... the impossibility of durable full systematization has implications for the analysis of reglementation and for applied planning and administration." State policy makers might well question whether it is worth attempting "positive law" regulation of those arenas of aboriginal life where the state is experienced as intrusive and illegitimate, and where experience indicates that legislation will have effects quite other than the intended ones.

Constitutional *sharing* of "sovereign" powers – building on a history of treaty-making with First Nations, and on Sections 25 and 35 of the Constitution – seems unavoidable if policy is to break with the assimilationist premises of the past. It is not just that aboriginal governments have legitimate sovereign claims of their own, but that their institutional forms are largely inconsistent with Euro-Canadian forms. Aboriginal leaders and social analysts have argued that the vision of hierarchical, centralized authority pertaining to a "sovereign crown" is diametrically opposed to indigenous cultural premises in which authority is delegated by grassroots constituents to leaders (Boldt and Long 1984; Marule 1984; Porter 1984). A share of "sovereign" powers for aboriginal governments would create the space for aboriginal societies to explore the potential of indigenous premises in contemporary institutional development.

CUSTOM AND TRADITION AS EVOLVING PHENOMENA

It is sometimes argued, in policy circles and in public debate, that indigenous institutions have long since lost their relevance to decision-making and social regulation in modern aboriginal communities. Claims based on cultural distinctiveness are regarded as futile denials of the inevitable course of progress, or worse, as mere political opportunism.

Anthropological theory has challenged such views, but has also shaped them. On the one hand, evolutionist views contributed to the presumption that "earlier" societies were on a trajectory of inevitable acculturation and assimilation to the forms of the industrial nation-state. On the other hand, the doctrine of cultural relativism has promoted pluralistic accommodation of distinctive social systems. Yet relativist positions in the twentieth century ethnology have frequently been found in association with static and romanticized conceptions of culture, tending to reinforce the sentiment that cultural integrity is based on timeless beliefs and values. This sentiment in turn fosters a form of disillusionment when it is realized that aboriginal peoples, like any others, adapt their cultural repertoires to embrace contemporary circumstances.

For well over a decade, contemporary anthropology has involved itself in a thorough-going critique and rejection of static models of culture. We are now keenly aware of culture and traditions as "invented" (Wagner 1981; Hobsbawn and Ranger 1983), of cultural "objectification" in nationalist discourse as selective and never finished (Handler 1988), and of "custom" as a political resource for burgeoning national elites who are sometimes far removed from indigenous practices (Keesing and Tonkinson 1982; Philibert 1990).

But our disavowal of static views of culture may lead us to *under*-represent the extent to which processes of cultural innovation are conventionally constrained. To guard against this, it is useful to bear the full spectrum of cultural practices in mind. Culture is indeed involved in political means-end relations, and becomes as such an object and device of rhetoric; but it comprises, at the same time, the order of lived reality. This distinction corresponds to two levels of cultural practice: (1) social practice at the level of explicit discourse, the deliberate formulation of rules, values, norms, traditions, models, institutional charters, and (2) the unconscious conventions of everyday life, the compelling but largely implicit premises of cultural practice that, while tending to endure, are shaped by their encounter with historical circumstances – Bourdieu's (1977) "habitus." In all societies, there is an intimate and ongoing relationship between the two levels. Custom in the narrower legal sense of explicit "rule" (customary law) pertains to the first level. Custom in a broader sense also includes more deeply embedded, unreflective conventions of social action and experience.

In the European legal tradition, the relationship between general custom and the written law is well known; general custom has been a source of common law by judicial acceptance, and has often been legislatively codified. Although state codification and enforcement subverted the functional integrity of custom as it existed prior to state control (Diamond 1984), formal congruencies were at least sustained.

But laws and institutions imposed by colonial authorities have no such congruence with the cultural premises of aboriginal people.

This disjunction is a major factor in the loss of meaning experienced under colonial domination, and in the continuing inability of state authorities to make "good law" by aboriginal standards. Hence the alienation of aboriginal people and the special difficulties of centralist states in establishing legitimacy among them.

Tradition is a powerful rationale for both continuity and innovation in social practice, and an important source of legal reasons specifically. Appeals to tradition ostensibly maintain the social constitution. But maintenance of the social constitution also requires adaptation to novel historical circumstances, and profound innovations may be justified in the name of tradition (Leach 1977). When aboriginal peoples invoke tradition in modelling collective practice, as in constitutions or charters for self-government, they bring the authority of tradition to bear on current experience. This is a normal process in the history of societies, and it is a specious double standard that equates changes in custom with a loss of rights for aboriginal peoples (yet not for Europeans). As Elias (1988:3) has pointed out, when tradition is "taken to be absolutely static, invulnerable to change, and devoid of historic relativity," when any change in tradition is "disallowed as a form of behaviour qualifying as a right," then "tradition" is reduced to "traditionalism."

COMPARATIVE POLICY APPROACHES TO ABORIGINAL CUSTOM AND TRADITION

In "settler states" that have evolved as liberal democracies, there are three principal ways in which aboriginal custom and tradition have received some recognition. The first is "sensitization" of the general law of foreign majorities to aboriginal custom, achieved through concessions in state judicial process rather than through constitutional or statutory recognition. These concessions are allowed within the framework of the general law and constrained by human rights defined as "basic" by central authorities, who retain ultimate discretionary power (an approach favoured by the Law Reform Commission of Australia, see Australia 1986).

A second approach is statutory recognition of aboriginal custom and tradition, or elements of it. There have been measures to codify custom very extensively as a basis for general law in some emergent Third World states (Bennet and Vermuelen 1981). In a more specific vein, Australia's Aboriginal Land Rights (Northern Territory) Act (1976) has recognized land rights according to indigenous criteria of ownership/management – that is, the rights of descent groups who can demonstrate responsibility for sacred sites on a territory.

Statutory recognition of customary rights as a criterion for aboriginal land entitlements in Australia compares favourably with any system achieved in Canadian territories.

A third approach has been overt and tacit recognition of custom and tradition via treaties, which confer constitutional status. Here the effect is to recognize a locus of autonomy for custom without codifying it or insisting that its authority is "delegated" by the state. This approach marks the earlier constitutional histories of New Zealand, Canada, and the United States, and is undergoing "rediscovery" in the context of modern aboriginal and treaty claims (Hutchins n.d.; Frame 1981; McHugh 1985). In the United States the judicial doctrine of "domestic dependent sovereignty" stems from the historical autonomy of Indian nations, on which the treaty–making process was premised. The doctrine affords wide latitude for Indians to decide the extent to which custom and tradition will enter into tribal governments and courts (Collins, Johnson, and Perkins 1977; Sanders 1985).

TREATY AND LEGISLATIVE OPTIONS FOR RECOGNIZING ABORIGINAL GOVERNMENTS IN CANADA

Self-government via treaties between aboriginal groups and the federal government has the advantage of continuity with the doctrine of aboriginal rights as it has developed since early contact with Europeans. In contemporary jurisprudence, pre- and post-Confederation treaties are increasingly interpreted as either implicit or explicit acknowledgment that indigenous institutions, customs, and traditions remain in effect. Contemporary land claims agreements and treaties continue in this vein; like earlier treaties, they enjoy protection under Section 35 of the Constitution.

Treaty agreements between the Crown and aboriginal nations, as vehicles for self-government arrangements, do not preclude federal legislation adopted pursuant to treaties, as with the Cree-Naskapi (of Quebec) Act pursuant to the James Bay and Northern Quebec and Northeastern Quebec Agreements. To the extent that self-government arrangements are embodied in a treaty, Section 88 of the Indian Act can also operate.

Perhaps fearing the constitutional force of treaties, however, the federal government is now avoiding self-government negotiations in any context defined as treaty-making. Matters of governmental jurisdiction, for instance, are in principle excluded from comprehensive claims negotiations. Instead, as previously described, the federal government is negotiating with aboriginal communities self-government jurisdictions that will be "delegated" through legislation. This approach postpones constitutional resolution, and is clearly inferior to treaty-making as a guarantee of autonomy.

Treaty-making aside, options for legislation range from detailed *prescription* to general *recognition*. Prescriptive codification of custom would risk inhibiting the reality of its process. Codification lifts custom out of social context and may "fossilize" an inappropriate form – particularly when translation into a foreign cultural paradigm is involved. The practice of custom and tradition in band and tribal societies involves dynamic processes of political consensus and collective adaptation to specific historical circumstances. Codification and adjudication by the state would deny people the control, interpretation, and application of custom and tradition in the course of their face-to-face social practice (Maddock 1982, 1983; Gordon and Meggit 1985; Layton 1985; Sansom 1985).

The less intrusive route is for legislation to recognize in general principle that custom and tradition are present and can operate rather than to attempt detailed specification. Custom may then be legislatively enacted by aboriginal governments, but need not be. In some cases aboriginal groups have codified custom as they developed self-government charters and constitutions. Codification may serve a function of consensus-building in communities, so long as the choice whether to codify, and in what areas, remains in aboriginal hands. Any *obligation* upon an aboriginal government or nation to codify custom for the convenience of external agencies, however, would clearly be detrimental.

THE SURVIVAL AND "REVIVAL" OF INDIGENOUS INSTITUTIONS

The history of forced adaptation of aboriginal politics to a uniform system of administrative "bands," "band councils," and "chiefs" under the Indian Act might suggest that indigenous forms of decision making and social reglementation are largely defunct. It is remarkable how much of the voluminous literature devoted to policy, legal, and administrative aspects of aboriginal self-government in Canada fails even to mention the role of indigenous institutions (important exceptions, which include a number of aboriginal authors along with other social science and legal experts, are Feit 1979; Asch 1984; Boldt and Long 1984; Delisle 1984; Lyons 1984; Marule 1984; Porter 1984; Boyko-Wuerscher et al. 1985; Little Bear 1986; Salisbury 1986; Franks 1987).[7]

In fact, all forms of corporate organization referred to in late nineteenth- and early twentieth-century "classical" ethnography on aboriginal people in Canada – families, clans, bands, tribes, and tribal confederacies – are active in some capacity in the political life of aboriginal societies in Canada today. Until rather recently evolutionary premises coloured anthropological perception of these forms (Service 1962; Jenness 1967; Fried 1967). It was commonly assumed that most would be absorbed and dissolved by the "state." Despite adverse state policies, these forms have frequently *not* disappeared, and in the past fifteen to twenty years, anthropologists have become increasingly conscious of the importance of documenting and understanding this persistence (Leacock and Lee 1982).

Yet some erosion of indigenous institutions must be admitted. Aboriginal people themselves frequently speak of "restoring" institutions that have been weakened in the colonial encounter. They have nonetheless typically retained cultural practices that are significantly different from those of the mainstream. Even if some institutional forms of traditional government have been undermined, it remains the case that indigenous premises shape everyday life. It is likely, then, that given the opportunity, aboriginal communities will know how to reconstruct self-government institutions that are coherent with their cultural premises.

INSTITUTIONAL LINKAGES

Contemporary aboriginal governments are involved in complex linkages between indigenous and state institutions, due both to changes in the size and distribution of aboriginal polities and to the interdependence of aboriginal, provincial, and federal government jurisdictions. The adoption of formal electoral and bureaucratic practices is sometimes taken as evidence of one-way acculturation.[8] Yet it is clear that indigenous values and customs shape these "modern" practices, and are not simply replaced.

There are potential overlaps in the ways different political cultures implement values of democracy and individual autonomy. Societies which have emphasized consensus-style democracy may stress such participatory processes as general assemblies, *ad hoc* leadership review, and referenda, while eschewing such adversarial forms as party politics – as approaches taken by the Dene and Inuit of the Northwest Territories illustrate. The fact that some of these processes have counterparts in Euro-Canadian political life may facilitate accommodation of indigenous preferences.

There is internal conflict in some aboriginal polities over the appropriate roles of indigenous or introduced institutions. Traditional structures of government have become opposed to Indian Act structures as competing power bases, fostering chronic factionalism and dispute. It should not be assumed that redoubled intervention by state authorities will improve the situation. On the contrary, withdrawal of state presence could remove the key structural impediment to community consensus-building.

INDIVIDUAL RIGHTS AND FREEDOMS

One encounters a prevalent ethnocentrism among policy makers and many citizens that the state is a better guarantor of individual rights and freedoms than aboriginal institutions can be. This bias is sometimes compounded by superficial interpretation of aspects of aboriginal culture, not in terms of their own social context, but in terms of foreign categories and beliefs. Examples include fears that the customary authority of elders equals gerontocracy, or that the political influence of leaders with "hereditary" title is by definition undemocratic. Yet these institutions occur among the world's most democratic and egalitarian societies.

Clearly it would be unhelpful to idealize indigenous forms of authority – all human systems contain potential for injustice. But consensus-based polities, no less than other democracies, recognize the potential for abuse and possess various internal checks and balances. Indeed, because aboriginal societies are on a scale at which face-to-face politics prevail and consensus-building is feasible, they benefit from democratic processes that become unwieldy at the level of the nation-state.

Where individuals feel that their rights and interests have been poorly served by aboriginal governments, it will be argued that they must have the right to seek remedy from central state institutions. But such recourse is not always a reasonable option. Appeal to external authorities is clearly inappropriate, for example, when they lack the cultural knowledge of local authorities to decide matters of custom and community precedent.

CONCLUSIONS

The survival and development of indigenous institutions of government is crucially related to the degree of power they exercise. If the policy objective is to enlarge the scope of aboriginal culture and institutions, then there must be areas in which intervention by external legislative and juridical authorities is minimized if not eliminated. Constitutional sharing of powers among federal, provincial, and aboriginal levels of government advances this objective; delegation of powers by "senior" federal and provincial governments to "subordinate" aboriginal administrations ultimately contradicts it – even if new legislation were less intrusive than Indian Act rules.

Cultural distinctiveness has been integral to the history of exchange between aboriginal nations and the Euro-Canadian state. Assimilationists have sought to dissolve the exchange by eliminating or denying cultural distinctiveness or, failing this, by advancing restrictive concepts of culture that would subordinate indigenous institutions to those of the state. Advocates of self-determination, on the other hand, employ an institutionally holistic vision of cultural distinctiveness, a vision that relativises the premise of Euro-Canadian sovereignty, opening space for the inherent authority of aboriginal institutions.

The view that aboriginal cultures have surrendered their integrity and authenticity in adapting to modern circumstances, and that territorial, political, and other rights are thereby diminished, is a persistent manifestation of assimilationist double standards. Contemporary anthropology has largely abandoned the evolutionary and romantic premises that underwrote these assimilationist expectations. We recognize that indigenous cultures are neither static nor bound to assimilate to the dominant cultures of encapsulating states. But our currently fashionable accounts of tradition as "invented," of culture as fetishized in nationalist discourse, etc., contain pitfalls of their own. Current thought could be naïvely interpreted to mean that culture may be reducible to arbitrary or opportunistic artifice, and that social actors are capable of infinite adjustments without loss of meaning, without suffering. Space must be created for the unfettered operation of both convention and invention if violence to indigenous cultural realities is to be reversed.

NOTES

1 The assistance of Peter Hutchins, Cristina Scatolin, and Rick Cuciurean, through their collaboration on the 1988 report for Indian and Northern Affairs Canada, deserves special acknowledgement. Thanks also to Simon McInnes, Elizabeth Tromp, Phil Ross, and others at the Self-Government Sector, Department of Indian Affairs, for identifying important issues and for their generous and constructive commentary. Responsibility for the chapter in its present form rests entirely with me.

2 Indian Act legislation earlier in this century led to well-known cases of suppression of customary government (through enforced election provisions and the banning of "ceremonies"). Notorious instances are the jailing of leaders and adherents of the Six Nations Longhouse government, and of northwest coast potlatching. Both institutions are integral to self-government proposals that have received media exposure and are presently under discussion with the Department of Indian Affairs Self-Government Sector.

3 See Weaver (1986) for a detailed account of Indian policy in this government.

4 Beckett (1988) has argued that the principal value of aboriginal culture to the state is as a rationale to provide special welfare services to minorities who present intransigent policy dilemmas.

5 The emphasis on indigenous structures occurs in territorial as well as self-government claims. The opening address of the Gitksan-Wet'suwet'en in the British Columbia Supreme Court, for instance, built its evidence and argument around an ethnographically sophisticated account of systems of authority and ownership in Gitksan and Wet'suwet'en societies, and on an interpretation of contact history framed by the categories of those systems (Uukw et al. v. The Queen, etc. 1988). By insisting that the courts deal with feasting, clans, houses, chiefs, and territory stewardship in their own cultural terms, the Gitksan-Wet'suwet'en dramatize the cultural contingency of Canadian legal and political ideologies, while underscoring the equivalent claim to legitimacy and authority of their own.

6 Pluralist models of the state hold out greater promise for the kind of decentralized authority required to accommodate cultural self-determination: the consociational models of Switzerland and Belgium (Asch 1984), home rule in Greenland, and the autonomous status of the Isle of Man or the Faroes.

7 See Peters (1986) for an extensive bibliography.

8 See La Rusic, Bouchard, et al. (1979) and Salisbury (1986) for accounts of the James Bay Crees' experience with these structures.

REFERENCES

Asch, Michael. 1984. *Home and Native Land: Aboriginal Rights and the Canadian Constitution*. Toronto: Methuen.

Australia. Law Reform Commission. 1986. *The Recognition of Aboriginal Customary Laws*. Report no. 31. Summary Report. Canberra: Australian Government Publishing Service.

Beckett, Jeremy. 1988. "Cultural Constructions of Aboriginality." Paper presented to the Canadian Ethnology Annual Congress, University of Saskatchewan, Saskatoon, 11–15 May.

Bennet, T.W., and T. Vermeulen. 1981. "Codification of Customary Law." *Journal of African Law* 24(2):206–19.

Boisvert, David A. 1985. *Forms of Aboriginal Self-Government*. Background Paper number 2, Aboriginal Peoples and Constitutional Reform. Kingston: Institute of Intergovernmental Relations, Queen's University.

Boldt, Menno, and J. Anthony Long. 1984. "Tribal Traditions and European-Western Political Ideologies: The Dilemma of Canada's Native Indians." *Canadian Journal of Political Science* 17:537–53. Reprinted in Menno Boldt and J. Anthony Long, eds. 1985. *The Quest for Justice: Aboriginal Peoples and Aboriginal Rights*, 333–46. Toronto: University of Toronto Press.

Bourdieu, Pierre. 1977. *Outline of a Theory of Practice*, trans. Richard Nice. Cambridge: Cambridge University Press.

Boyko-Wuerscher, R., L. Héon, D. Kane, and K. Tyler. 1985. *Joint Canada–Saskatchewan–Federation of Saskatchewan Indian Studies of Certain Aspects of the Justice System as They Relate to Indians in Saskatchewan*. Vol. 1. Working Papers Prepared by the Working Group on Customary Law.

Canada. 1982. *The Constitution Act*. Ottawa: Supply and Services Canada.

– 1983. *Indian Self-Government in Canada: Report of the Special Parliamentary Committee*. Ottawa: Supply and Services Canada.

– 1984a. *Response of the Government to the Report of the Special Committee on Indian Self-Government*. Ottawa: Supply and Services Canada.

– 1984b. *Bill C-52: An Act Relating to Self-Government for Indian Nations*, first reading, 27 June 1984.

– 1985. *Living Treaties, Lasting Agreements: Report of the Task Force to Review Comprehensive Claims Policy* (Coolican Report). Ottawa: Department of Indian Affairs and Northern Development.

– 1987. *Comprehensive Land Claims Policy*. Ottawa: Supply and Services Canada.

Canadian First Ministers' Conferences on Aboriginal Constitutional Matters (CFMC). 1983, 1984, 1985, 1987. Unofficial and Unverified Verbatim Transcripts. 4 vols. 15–16 March 1983, 8–9 March 1984, 2–3 April 1985, 26–27 March 1987, Ottawa. Ottawa: Intergovernmental Document Centre, Canadian Intergovernmental Conference Secretariat.

Collins, Richard B., R.W. Johnson, and K. Imig Perkins. 1977. "American Indian Courts and Tribal Self-Government." *American Bar Association Journal* 63:808–15.

Connolly, William E. 1974. *The Terms of Political Discourse*. Princeton: Princeton University Press.

Delisle, Andrew. 1984. "How We Regained Control over Our Lives and

Territories: The Kahnawake Story." In *Pathways to Self-Determination: Canadian Indians and the Canadian State*, eds. L. Little Bear, M. Boldt, and J.A. Long, 141–7. Toronto: University of Toronto Press.

Diamond, Stanley. 1984. "The Rule of Law vs. the Order of Custom." *Social Research* 51:387–418.

Elias, Peter D. 1988. "Courts and Concepts: Defining Aboriginal Rights." Paper presented at the Annual Conference of the Canadian Ethnology Society, Saskatoon, 11–15 May.

Falk Moore, Sally. 1978. *Law as Process: An Anthropological Approach*. London: Routledge & Kegan Paul.

Feit, Harvey. 1979. "Political Articulations of Hunters to the State: Means of Resisting Threats to Subsistence Production in the James Bay and Northern Quebec Agreement." *Etudes/Inuit/Studies* 3(2):37–52.

Frame, Alex. 1981. "Maori Affairs. Colonizing Attitudes Towards Maori Custom." *New Zealand Law Journal* (March): 105–10.

Franks, C.E.S. 1987. *Public Administration Questions Relating to Aboriginal Self-Government*. Background Paper number 12, Aboriginal Peoples and Constitutional Reform. Kingston: Institute of Intergovernmental Relations, Queen's University.

Fried, Morton. 1967. *The Evolution of Political Society*. New York: Random House.

Gibbins, Roger. 1986. "Citizenship, Political and Intergovernmental Problems with Indian Self-Government." In *Arduous Journey: Canadian Indians and Decolonization*, ed. J. Rick Ponting, 369–77. Toronto: McClelland & Stewart.

Gordon, R.J., and M.J. Meggit. 1985. *Law and Order in the New Guinea Highlands: Encounters with Enga*. Hanover: University Press of New England.

Handler, Richard. 1988. *Nationalism and the Politics of Culture in Quebec*. Madison: University of Wisconsin Press.

Hobsbawm, E., and T. Ranger, eds. 1983. *The Invention of Tradition*. Cambridge: Cambridge University Press.

Hooker, M.B. 1975. *Legal Pluralism: An Introduction to Colonial and Neo-Colonial Laws*. Oxford: Clarendon Press.

Hutchins, Peter. n.d. Aboriginal People and the Law, Lecture notes, McGill University Law Faculty, Montreal, Quebec.

Jenness, Diamond. 1967. *Indians of Canada*. 7th ed. Ottawa: Queen's Printer.

Keesing, Roger, and R. Tonkinson, eds. 1982. *Reinventing Traditional Culture: The Politics of Kastom in Island Melanesia*. Special Issue, *Mankind* 13(4).

Keon-Cohen, B.A. 1982. "Native Justice in Australia, Canada and the USA: A Comparative Analysis." *Canadian Legal Aid Bulletin* 5:187–258.

La Rusic, Ignatius, S. Bouchard, A. Penn, T. Brelsford, and J.-G. Deschênes. 1979. *Negotiating a Way of Life. Initial Cree Experience with the Administrative Structure Arising from the James Bay Agreement*. Montreal: ssDcc.

Layton, Robert. 1985. "Anthropology and the Australian Aboriginal Land Rights Act in Northern Australia." In *Social Anthropology and Development Policy*, eds. Ralph Grillo and Alan Rew, 148–67. London and New York: Tavistock/Methuen.

Leach, Edmund. 1977. *Custom, Law and Terrorist Violence*. Edinburgh: Edinburgh University Press.

Leacock, Eleanor and R. Lee, eds. 1982. *Politics and History in Band Societies*. Cambridge: Cambridge University Press.

Little Bear, Leroy. 1986. "Aboriginal Rights and the Canadian 'Grundnorm.' " In *Arduous Journey: Canadian Indians and Decolonization*, ed. J. Rick Ponting, 243–59. Toronto: McClelland & Stewart.

Lyons, Oren. 1984. "Spirituality, Equality, and Natural Law." In *Pathways to Self-Determination: Canadian Indians and the Canadian State*, eds. L. Little Bear, M. Boldt, and J.A. Long, 5–13. Toronto: University of Toronto Press

MacCannell, Dean. 1979. "Ethnosemiotics." *Semiotica* 27:149–71.

McHugh, P.B. 1985. "The Constitutional Role of the Waitangi Tribunal." *New Zealand Law Journal* (July):224–5, 233.

Maddock, Kenneth. 1982. "Aboriginal Land Rights Traditionally and in Legislation: A Case Study." In *Aboriginal Power in Australian Society*, ed. Michael Howard, 55–78. Honolulu: University of Hawaii Press.

– 1983. "Owners, Managers and the Choice of Statutory Traditional Owners by Anthropologists and Lawyers." In *Aborigines, Land and Land Rights*, eds. Nicolas Peterson and Marcia Langton, 211–25. Canberra: Australian Institute of Aboriginal Studies.

Marule, Marie Smallface. 1984. "Traditional Indian Government: Of the People, by the People, for the People." In *Pathways to Self-Determination: Canadian Indians and the Canadian State*, eds. L. Little Bear, M. Boldt, and J.A. Long, 36–45. Toronto: University of Toronto Press.

Morse, Bradford. 1984. *Aboriginal Self-Government in Australia and Canada*. Background Paper number 4, Aboriginal Peoples and Constitutional Reform. Kingston: Institute of Intergovernmental Relations, Queen's University.

Paine, Robert. 1985. "The Claim of the Fourth World." In *Native Power: The Quest for Autonomy and Nationhood of Indigenous Peoples*, eds. Jens Brosted, Jens Dahl, Andrew Gray, et al., 49–66. Oslo: Universitetsforlaget.

Peters, Evelyn J. 1986. *Aboriginal Self-Government in Canada: A Bibliography 1986*. Kingston: Institute of Intergovernmental Relations, Queen's University.

Philibert, Jean-Marc. 1990. "The Politics of Tradition: Toward a Generic

Culture in Vanuatu." In *Customs in Conflict: The Anthropology of a Changing World*, eds. F. Manning and J.-M. Philibert, 251–73. Peterborough: Broadview Press.

Porter, Tom. 1984. "Traditions of the Constitution of the Six Nations." In *Pathways to Self-Determination: Canadian Indians and the Canadian State*, eds. L. Little Bear, M. Boldt, and J.A. Long, 15–21. Toronto: University of Toronto Press.

Salisbury, Richard F. 1986. *A Homeland for the Cree: Regional Development in James Bay 1971–1981*. Montreal and Kingston: McGill-Queen's University Press.

Sanders, Douglas. 1985. *Aboriginal Self-Government in the United States*. Background Paper number 5, Aboriginal Peoples and Constitutional Reform. Kingston: Institute of Intergovernmental Relations, Queen's University.

Sansom, Basil. 1985. "Aborigines, Anthropologists and Leviathan." In *Fourth World Politics in Canada, Australia and Norway*, ed. Noel Dyck, 67–94. St John's: Institute of Social and Economic Research, Memorial University of Newfoundland.

Schwimmer, Eric. 1972. "Symbolic Competition." *Anthropologica* 14(2): 117–55.

Scott, Colin, P. Hutchins, C. Scatolin, and R. Cuciurean. 1988. *Custom, Tradition and Aboriginal Self-Government Within the Context of Canadian Constitutional Principles and Federal Government Practice*. Report prepared for Indian and Northern Affairs Canada, Self-Government Sector, Contract No. 87-0146.

Service, Elman. 1962. *Primitive Social Organization*. New York: Random House.

Slattery, Brian. 1987. "Understanding Aboriginal Rights." *Canadian Bar Review* 66:727–83.

Uukw et al. v. The Queen in the Right of British Columbia and the Attorney General of Canada. 1988. "Gitksan-Wet'suwet'en land title action." *Canadian Native Law Review* 1:14–72.

Wagner, Roy. 1981. *The Invention of Culture*. Chicago: University of Chicago Press.

Weaver, Sally. 1981. *Making Canadian Indian Policy: The Hidden Agenda, 1968–1970*. Toronto: University of Toronto Press.

– 1986. "Indian Policy in the New Conservative Government." Parts 1, 2. *Native Studies Review* 2(1):1–43; 2(2):1–45.

14 Completing a Circle:
The Spirit Sings

JULIA D. HARRISON

MY SHADOW CELEBRATES

Though it was natural for me to create my leather dress
The beads and quill my ornamentation.
You call it art
It makes me feel wise with a sense of identity.

Though it was necessity I used bone, stone and wood to
carve my images
You call it art
It makes me feel wise and seer of beauty.

Though I created the mast for mystical purposes
The amulets my ritual objects.
You call it art
It makes me feel wise as my spirit flows with love.

My sketches have revealed the loneliness of fading away
The message passing the wind into all eternity.
You call it art
My shadow celebrates, you have found me.

Rita Joe,[1] written in response to
The Spirit Sings

INTRODUCTION

In a provocative article on racism, Shelby Steele, an English professor at San José State University in California, wrote: "The human animal almost never pursues power without first convincing himself that he is "entitled" to it. And this feeling of entitlement has its own precondition; to be entitled one must first believe in one's own innocence ... By innocence I mean a feeling of essential goodness in relation to others and, therefore superiority to others ... In this sense, *innocence is power*" (emphasis in the original). Steele goes on to describe the process of " 'seeing for innocence' – a form of seeing that has more to do with one's hidden need for innocence (and power) than with the person or group one is looking at ... '*Seeing for innocence' is ... [the] use of others as a means to our own goodness and superiority*" (emphasis added; Steele 1988:47–8).

At its worst "seeing for innocence" is the fuel of racism; at its least it nurtures misunderstanding and perpetuates falsehoods among groups which are not necessarily even separated by skin colour or physical type. In all cases – save the temporary position of aboriginal peoples worldwide, who are in the throes of cultural and political resurgence and need to rally their people to believe in themselves and their cultures again – it is destructive.

The Spirit Sings: Artistic Traditions of Canada's First Peoples, a major exhibition presented by the Ethnology Department of the Glenbow Museum in Calgary in 1988, became the focus of a boycott attempt by a group of Cree in northern Alberta to draw attention to their land claim struggle. Tragically the museum and its supporters on the one hand, and many Native individuals, organizations, and portions of the general public on the other hand, were seen to be in two warring camps. The academic community as represented by one of its professional associations (Canadian Ethnology Society/La société canadienne d'ethnologie [CESCE], now Canadian Anthropological Society/La société canadienne d'anthropologie [CASCA]) joined the Native peoples' camp and supported the boycott. While both sides viewed their actions as representing the principles of justice, equality, and fairness, it could be suggested that the Native community, the museum profession, and academic anthropologists were in fact "seeing for innocence," and in that process using others "as a means (to) their own goodness and superiority." Such a suggestion does not imply that this was the overt intention of any one group, but that it could be interpreted as the hidden, unconscious, and ultimately tragic root of their actions.

Canadian Native groups who are attempting to affirm their unique identity in the contemporary world through their land claim struggles and demands for self-government and cultural autonomy tend overtly to "see for innocence" to garner their own strength for the relentless battle with governments and their effort to gain acceptance with the public at large. In the context of this struggle there is justification for such a "vision" for Native people, but at what point can the museum community and the academic anthropological profession be seen to be justified in their own search for such "innocence?"

The work of these two groups will be strengthened because of the current self-analysis found in both the museum and the anthropological communities. Each group is working valiantly to shed the impression that its work is the dalliance of a culturally imperialistic elite, fuelled by the misguided sentiments of "bleeding heart" liberals, or simply actions of "fools of the fringe." But both communities must come to terms with the dangers of their tendency to claim innocence for themselves as a means to solicit power. Museums and academic anthropologists do good and valuable work. It is anthropologists, along with the writers, poets, and visual artists of our world, who can offer the social critique imperative to our continuance.

The following is an effort to put *The Spirit Sings*, the museum anthropologists, and other professionals who worked on it, in context. In addition, the different responses of four separate audiences to *The Spirit Sings* will be presented: museum professionals, the general public, academic anthropologists, and the Native community. What these responses say about the relations between museums and Native peoples, museums and academic anthropologists, and academic anthropologists, Native peoples, and the public draws attention to the self-destructive potential to "see for innocence" of any one group and consequently threaten its continuance. The question is critical. Unless all concerned gain a clear understanding of the motives and objectives that should prompt anthropological work and study, the future of museum anthropology and anthropology as a whole is in doubt.

THE EXHIBIT AND THE CONTROVERSY

In the nineteenth century it was the collections of many European museums which contributed to the development of anthropology. And it was these collections which inspired the idea for an exhibition eventually titled *The Spirit Sings: Artistic Traditions of Canada's*

First Peoples. The thousands of objects held in European ethnographic collections which were obtained as presentation pieces, war booty, plunder, curios, souvenirs, or objects for scientific study (the latter three groups were often purchased) from Canadian Native peoples in the early years of contact comprise an important part of the cultural heritage of Canada. Little of this material had ever been seen in Canada, let alone publicized in any comprehensive manner. Few Native people knew of its existence; fewer still had ever had the opportunity to see any of it. It seemed appropriate, if not imperative, that a selection of this material be brought together for an exhibition in Canada. Such an exhibition would have accompanying publications to document the history and location of these materials for reference and study (Harrison 1987:7–8; Whitehead 1987). It would then be up to Native peoples and museums around the world to determine who had the right to control this material.

The staging of the 1988 Winter Olympics in Calgary provided the opportunity to secure the necessary funds and co-operation for the city's Glenbow Museum to mount such an exhibition. Organized by the museum's ethnology department, of which I was the curator, and with the assistance of a group of six regional specialists who formed the Curatorial Committee,[3] *The Spirit Sings* included 650 objects drawn from nearly ninety national and international collections. Committee members were drawn from universities and museums across Canada and included specialists with backgrounds in anthropology, art history, philosophy, and English. In selecting the committee members, I was interested in researchers who were doing innovative research, were knowledgeable about European collections, were available, and were willing to work as part of a larger group.

The committee members travelled extensively to view museum collections from which to make selections to elucidate the three themes for the exhibition: diversity and complexity of Canada's Native cultures as they were witnessed in the early years of contact; the common threads that link these cultures together to create a distinctive worldview; and the adaptability and resilience of these cultures. The exhibition divided Canada's Native peoples into six geo-cultural groupings which followed relatively consistent breakdowns used by anthropologists: the east coast, the northern woodlands, the northern plains, the western subarctic, the Arctic, and the northwest coast. *The Spirit Sings* opened in Calgary on 14 January 1988, as part of the Olympic Arts Festival. After closing in early May, it moved to Ottawa where it ran for five months under the auspices of the Canadian Museum of Civilization (CMC).

To complement the historical focus of the exhibition and publications, a Celebration of Native Cultures[4] was organized while *The Spirit Sings* was in Calgary. In the celebration Native peoples presented a variety of contemporary cultural expressions to the public. These included dance performances, craft demonstrations (beadwork, quillwork, weaving, catlinite carving, food preparation, etc.), story telling, contemporary and traditional fashion shows, and readings by Native authors. The direction and focus of the celebration grew out of meetings of a liaison committee which consisted of representatives of a variety of interested Native groups and individuals. Glenbow forwarded approximately 300 letters to Native individuals and organizations on local and national levels. Those who responded constituted the Native Liaison Committee which advised Glenbow on several aspects of the project. The participation of the Native community was co-ordinated by Native peoples hired by both Glenbow and CMC during the project.

Preliminary work began in 1983, but it was not until April 1986 that a sponsor was found which ensured that it would become a reality. Shell Canada Limited contributed $1.1 million to the total estimated budget of $2.6 million, the largest single donation ever given to an arts project in Canada. The remainder of the funding came from the Olympic Organizing Committee, the federal government through the Canadian Museum of Civilization, and Glenbow.[5]

In mid-April 1986 the Lubicon Lake Cree in northern Alberta announced a boycott of the 1988 Winter Olympics to draw attention to their unresolved land claim. Shortly thereafter their boycott focused on *The Spirit Sings*. The exhibition was an appropriate target; it was about Native peoples, was sponsored by one of the oil companies which was drilling in the area claimed by the Lubicon as their traditional lands, and it was thought the boycott would probably find support among the world museum community than the sports people who could be expected to have less interest in Native issues. The Lubicon claimed that sponsorship by Shell and the federal government was an attempt to make the sponsors appear supportive of Native peoples, whereas they were actually destroying Native existence with their drilling activities or their hard-line stance on the Lubicon land claim negotiations.

The boycott effort began with a massive letter-writing campaign by Lubicon supporters and staff. It was financed by funds given to the Lubicon band by the federal government to prepare their case for land claims negotiations. Organizations such as the World Council of Churches, the European Parliament, some national and regional Native political bodies, and some segments of the academic community and general public added their support.

In July 1986 when other members of Glenbow staff, the Lubicon representatives, and I met, the Lubicon registered no objection to the content of the exhibition but only to its sponsorship and association with the Calgary Olympics, which they were boycotting. It was agreed at that time that both the Lubicon and Glenbow would continue in their respective directions.

In the end twelve institutions out of the 110 approached by Glenbow supported the boycott and did not, therefore, lend to *The Spirit Sings*. The Lubicon band and Glenbow disagreed concerning the number of institutions who actually supported the boycott. The confusion was due to two main factors: the official reasons for denying a loan as communicated to Glenbow were often different from those given to the Lubicon, and the Lubicon gained support from several museums from which the Glenbow did not request material.

In organizing *The Spirit Sings*, Glenbow attempted to restrict its actions to the political realm in the broadest sense (this follows on the assumption that every action is political) rather than to advocate for one specific cause. By doing this the museum intended to promote better and wider understanding of Canada's Native peoples rather than one solution to their struggles. Lubicon supporters claimed that Glenbow had taken a definite political stand because it had accepted money from an oil company which had drilled on land they claimed.

Several Native leaders from across the country gathered in Calgary at the time of the opening of *The Spirit Sings* to show their support for the Lubicon Indians. A group of Mohawk chiefs who came to Calgary succeeded in obtaining a two-week court injunction to have a False Face mask lent by the Royal Ontario Museum in Toronto removed from the exhibition. They also submitted a statement of claim to the museum requesting the return to the Mohawk of eight other objects in the exhibition. The items in question were claimed by the Mohawk Nation as they asserted "the exclusive right, title, and interest in and to all artifacts produced by or in any originating from Mohawks."[6]

The claim concerning the mask was that it should not have been on view to the public since it was only to be seen by members of the respective medicine societies of the Six Nations Iroquois Confederacy. The court ruled that the mask has been both on view and reproduced in numerous publications since 1922, and that its exhibition at this time would cause no one irreparable harm.[7] In the end the mask was removed from the exhibition only for the two-week period of the injunction.

The curatorial decision to include the mask in the exhibition in the first place was made "after examining past agreements between the Royal Ontario Museum and Iroquois False Face Society Faith Keepers which indicated that no offense would be caused by exhibiting the mask."[8] But things change in a political crisis. The action by the Mohawk chiefs was imbued with a genuine concern for the sacred nature of some false face masks, but it also succeeded in garnering more publicity for the Lubicon, their land claim and their attacks on *The Spirit Sings*. (The mask was removed from the Ottawa showing of *The Spirit Sings* after Glenbow received a letter from the appropriate leaders of the reserve from which the mask had originated.[9] These leaders were not involved in the Mohawk court injunction.)

Conditioned by a professional need to "see for innocence," the Glenbow museum like other similar institutions in Canada failed to see these issues early in the development of the project. Possession of collections was assumed to give museums the power to present and interpret them. But the very themes the museum chose provoked a challenge to that "innocence" when they were placed in the context of the late 1980s, the Olympics, and the political and cultural climate in Canada during that time, particularly in reference to the Native Canadian community.

The political and cultural climate surrounding *The Spirit Sings* raised many scholarly, practical, and ethical issues. What is the value of history to the contemporary world? Who has the right to interpret history? How does one define the appropriate representatives of a people? What is sacred? Which generation defines the term? What are the ethics of corporate sponsorship? Can one "own" another's heritage? What are the ethics of a boycott strategy? The organizers of *The Spirit Sings*, the lending institutions, and the audiences who viewed the exhibition were forced to respond to these issues in some way.

THE RESPONSES TO *THE SPIRIT SINGS* AND THE BOYCOTT

The Museum Community

In the spring of 1986, requests for loans to *The Spirit Sings* were sent out to 100 European, American, Australian, and Canadian institutions and individuals. The rather arduous negotiations extended over the next eighteen months. Several loans were refused for purely museological reasons (the items were too fragile to travel, were committed to other exhibitions, were on permanent exhibition and could not be removed, or the museum that owned them simply did not lend their collection). The decision to lend or to boycott became embroiled in a moral and ethical debate among the staffs of some museums. Should they lend to an exhibition which did not have the support of Canadian Native organizations and specific bands? As with any controversy which involves a large and diverse constituency, many Native people had no direct vehicle to voice their support or objection to the boycott. However, it was generally assumed by all those involved on both sides of this issue that even if some Native peoples did not support the boycott strategy, they would unquestionably support the issues for which it stood.

Despite the volume of information disseminated by the Lubicon supporters and the campaigns of the various Native support groups in Europe, there was confusion over the issues. Some museum people thought that the Olympics were being held on Lubicon lands, some that the exhibition was about the Lubicon, others that Native people were not involved in any aspect of either the exhibition or the Olympics.[10]

A few museums refused to lend to *The Spirit Sings* because of a resolution passed at the October 1987 triennial meeting of the International Council of Museums (ICOM) in Buenos Aires. This resolution stated, "Museums, which are engaged in activities relating to living ethnic groups, should whenever possible, consult with the appropriate members of those groups, and such ... museums should avoid using ethnic materials in any way which might be detrimental to the group that produced them." Both the Secretary General of ICOM and the president of the International Committee for Museums of Ethnography (ICME), which brought forward the motion, denied that the resolution was intended to refer to *The Spirit Sings*.[11] Several institutions and a number of Lubicon supporters nevertheless cited the resolution as a reason not to lend to Glenbow.

The general atmosphere of tension that developed around the exhibition fuelled concern for the safety of many of these objects and thus prompted replies such as that from the National Museum of Denmark: "The tense political situation which has arisen as a result of the call made by a number of indigenous organizations for a boycott of the arrangements, has caused that we do not find it safe to lend our museum artefacts for the purpose of the exhibition."[12]

Some museums expressed concern that although this was a historical exhibition, the climate that had grown up around it necessitated that Glenbow recognize in some way the contemporary dimensions and struggles of Native life. The Glenbow agreed to put a panel in the exhibition with the following statement:

The importance and the reality of continuity in the cultures of Canada's Native Peoples is integral to the exhibition, *The Spirit Sings*. Consistent with that principle, the participants in the exhibition, listed below, express their hope for an expeditious and just resolution of all Canadian Native land claims, and the related issues of compensation, self-determination, and self-government.

Each lending institution was then approached about listing its name. A total of thirty-five lenders appeared on the panel; some felt the statement was too political.

What was the feeling in the Canadian museum community about the whole affair? All the Canadian institutions which were approached to lend did so. Many discussed at length the implications of lending and felt that the direct mix of culture and politics inherent in refusing the loan would put museums in a very vulnerable position and sacrifice a significant degree of their autonomy to control their collections and activities. (The response to this stand was that all actions are political; lending was as political an action as not; Trigger 1988:71–9.)

The annual conferences of professional associations provide a certain weather vane for assessing the feeling and mood of the membership. The Canadian Museums Association conference in June 1988 reflected an atmosphere of confusion over the issues and a desire to learn as much about the Glenbow response as possible. In general the membership expressed a degree of nervousness over the whole issue. No Canadian museum exhibition had ever been the focus of a boycott before nor had an exhibition ever received as much publicity as *The Spirit Sings*. Such a predicament was a mixed blessing. What could the community learn from the experience? How could they avoid a recurrence?

Exhibitions are a large part of museum work. The presentation of information and ideas through objects is what makes museums a unique educational experience. The museum community would in principle, it is assumed, resist any effort to suppress an exhibition, but many Canadian museum staff were ethically torn over the issue of what to do when a segment of the people who are the subject of an exhibition attempt to stop it.

A key issue in the debate over *The Spirit Sings* was Shell's sponsorship. In this time of dwindling funding from governments and the subsequent need for cultural institutions to turn to the private sector, museums and universities can find themselves in a hopeless search for "clean" money. Cultural institutions have to be aware of all the sensitive areas and weigh each potential sponsor and project accordingly. In the end this exercise is a very healthy one, for it clarifies with stark reality the merits of any project and ensures that the reasons for doing a project are clearly understood by everyone involved. It also behooves the institution to understand the objectives of the sponsor and ensure that it can work within them.[13] The decision by a corporate sponsor to support the arts is usually done if it is deemed to be beneficial to a company's image. Such an improved image is assumed to ultimately increase profits.

Glenbow's perseverance with *The Spirit Sings* was seen as an important precedent for the profession to ensure that museums retain control over what they do. But this control must be administered within the context of frank dialogue and discussion which stems from an understanding of the needs of those whose culture is being exhibited on the one hand, and the roles of a museum on the other. Several lengthy discussions at all levels of Glenbow management considered the feasibility of continuing with *The Spirit Sings* during the height of the boycott fervour. But the merits of doing the exhibition continued to be seen as more positive than what would be gained by cancellation. As Glenbow's staff recognized, refusal to cancel the exhibition provided a focus for the Lubicon attack which ensured ongoing press coverage throughout the two years preceding the opening. (The irony of this is that the decision to continue with the exhibition inadvertently helped the Lubicon at least as far as making their plight and presence known to the general public. Such cognizance put pressure on the federal and provincial governments to give priority to the negotiations concerning the Lubicon land claim.)

A museum must work closely with the subject groups of an exhibition to determine what messages to transmit. Once having determined these messages, the museum must balance them in the context of its wider audience. While it may be legitimate to mount political action around any activity of a public institution, it would destroy the credibility of those institutions if they were forced to espouse the political causes of one pressure group after another. Museums specify that the institutions should remain as nonpartisan as possible.

Such legalities have ensured that museums remain conservative and have defined a moral authority for them to do what they have always done. This framework, however, hides their "seeing for innocence" – their use of history and the cultures of "others" to demonstrate their usefulness and importance as institutions. Actions such as the Lubicon boycott attempt to elucidate such thinking.

Glenbow faced (and others will face) a sheerly practical predicament in the planning of *The Spirit Sings*, a predicament exacerbated by their own "seeing for innocence." To whom should the museum have turned in the Native community who could speak with a national representative voice? Is it fair to expect the Native community to have a national representative voice? If not, how best can the museum community address this issue? Why do not all museums who hold even the smallest collection of Native materials have some form of localized advisory board from which to seek advice on such matters? Who should be hired to a job if qualified people do not exist within the Native community? (When the project began there were no Native curators with the broad knowledge of regional collections who also knew European collections and who were available for the time that the project entailed.) What is the role of the non-Native specialist? Closer relations with the Native and the academic community are the only way to find answers to these questions.

The Public

Nearly 230,000 people saw *The Spirit Sings*.[14] Monitoring the response of museum visitors is difficult, but both in Calgary and Ottawa visitors were invited to fill out "comment cards" which were then displayed at the exit of the show. In addition to this, Glenbow and the CMC received many letters and phone calls from people who had visited the exhibition, and letters to the editors of local papers were also common.[15]

Reactions were varied but rarely ambivalent. Visitors wrote:

- A great exhibition from anthropological point of view, it shows how advanced and sophisticated native people's culture and philosophy is – but the exhibition fails to show how they became Canada's poor and alienated in their own land.
- Is this show not the containment and pinning of a culture's spirit?
- How can the spirit sing under plexiglass?
- I feel that the spirit does indeed sing, but in the living artifacts of our time.
- You can imagine the lives of these first Canadians; you leave a little wiser.
- I find it difficult to understand why some Indians do not want to share with us their history.
- What a disservice the Lubicons have done to native people.
- This whole experience has led to much greater understanding of what native groups are so justifiably trying to preserve.
- Perhaps one day people will learn to respect [Native] political and economic rights.
- Extremely beautiful, intellectually and artistically stimulating, and very sad.

- This exhibit may do more for the indian [sic] as a nation among nations than anything to date.
- The Sun does shine and the winds to [sic] blow but the Spirit lives on forever!
- Tragic most of it belongs to others.
- Enriched my understanding of aboriginal peoples.
- This is real Canadian history not just the white settlers that we are taught in school.
- I would hope that Shell and Glenbow will now put as much effort in preserving and fostering the talent that exists in native people today.
- I believe Indian peoples (future curators) must have a part (large) in these presentations.
- I would also have liked to have seen something about Indian life today ... that's something I know about.
- I would have liked to have seen Indian guides.
- There are ghosts here.
- Let's elect an Indian chief Prime Minister.
- How do we give this strength and beauty back to the people who created it? We must find a way!
- Let's use some of the power in this exhibit to point the way to a just settlement of the Lubicon land claim.
- Elated, sad, overwhelmed, ashamed, awed, impressed, respectful, thankful, warned, hopeful, thrilled, spirited.
- I hope the feeling of this day long remains.
- The most I gained was a sense of the importance of trying to see a people and each person from their eyes – to get a sense of the world as they see it – to reveal our uniqueness as well as the common spirit within us all.[16]

A variety of officials spoke at the opening in Calgary, and the tone of the speeches reflected a recognition of the issues that the exhibit and the Lubicon boycott had raised.

We all have much to learn and if this program has served the public interest in drawing attention to contemporary native issues – then, it is all to the good. For such awareness of native culture is what the exhibition hopes to achieve.[17]

We also welcome this exhibition for a more contemporary and important reason ... The correct interpretation of the function and meaning of native artworks depends upon an understanding and appreciation of the ways of life, the values, and the principles of the peoples themselves.[18]

These comments set the tone for the response to the exhibition. They predicted comments made many months later by Tom Hill, an Iroquois, from the Six Nations reserve in southern Ontario: "There is no break between our past and our present. The past is part of the present."[19]

Many visitors in some way absorbed the message. Such a response to *The Spirit Sings* made people think about Canada's Native peoples. As one visitor put it: "I [found] myself lost in thought at the original owners, artist creators, of the objects displayed ... [*The Spirit Sings* has fundamentally] affected my own perception of [Canada's] native peoples."[20]

The Academic Community

Glenbow came under heavy criticism from the Canadian academic anthropological community;[21] criticism largely channelled through the Canadian Ethnology Society (CESCE), a professional association with about 300 members drawn almost entirely from the academic community. The most vocal members of the society wanted Glenbow to take some kind of affirmative action which would bring attention (and it is assumed, support) for the plight of the Lubicon. To show support for the Lubicon, CESCE executive in November of 1987 passed a motion which read:

Whereas the Executive of the CANADIAN ETHNOLOGY SOCIETY/LA SOCIETE CANADIENNE D'ETHNOLOGIE (CESCE) supports the resolution of the General Assembly of the International Congress of Museums (ICOM) that "museums which are engaged in activities relating to living ethnic groups should, whenever possible, consult with appropriate members of those groups, and such museums should avoid using ethnic materials in any way which might be detrimental and/or offensive to such groups," we, the Executive of the CESCE, support the Lubicon Lake Cree people and other Native peoples in Canada in their opposition to the Olympic exhibition, "The Spirit Sings."

Subsequent discussions between the CESCE executive and me as Glenbow's curator of ethnology raised several points concerning the motion. Executive members assured me that it was not directed at Glenbow, the work of museums in general, or me personally. It was an attempt to take a stand in support of the Lubicon and against the sponsorship of the project by Shell, which was trying to portray itself as a corporation interested in the cultures of Native people while at the same time actively drilling on the traditional lands the band claimed. But the official circular had included none of these points.

The Spirit Sings was also criticized because it dealt only with the past; it was said to ignore the contemporary situation of Canada's Native peoples. No exhibition can deal with every issue, and this was not an exhibition about land claims. Glenbow offered to host a public forum on contemporary issues, but the Native Liaison Committee, wishing to keep politics out of the museum, advised against it.[22]

When asked why the executive had not contacted me at Glenbow (I was an active member of the society) to discuss their concerns and actions under consideration, there was some recognition that this was an oversight on their part. No effort was made at any time by the CESCE executive to inquire about the "professional culture" (i.e., that of museums) within which museum curators work, and, therefore, how the actions of the museum made sense in that context. As co-ordinating curator, I had personally addressed the ethical and practical issues of the project, and had concluded that there were valid and correct reasons to continue. Museums are important reference points in Canadian history and culture, and while these institutions need to rethink the limits of their mandate, they do serve to affirm the very nature of this country. My personal goal was to ensure that the exhibition was done in the most respectful way possible as I hoped that this would be the pervasive message absorbed by the visitors who came to see it – Canada's Native cultures demand respect and thus to be treated justly and fairly within this nation. Furthermore, the executive offered no clear reason as to why the society had not passed a motion to boycott Shell rather than the museum if their main concern was with the ethics of the oil company's actions.

Two prominent members of Canada's anthropological community took up the debate of the Lubicon boycott of *The Spirit Sings*. Michael Ames and Bruce Trigger initially debated the issue on a national radio program aired the day the exhibition opened in Calgary. The debate became embellished, eventually being written up in at least three journals. It is interesting to note that editors of national journals of anthropology, contemporary art, and museology all felt the issue to be of significance to their readers. The Lubicon boycott was not something to be ignored (see Ames 1988a, 1988b; Hill 1988; Trigger 1988).

Trigger argued for greater Native involvement in anthropology. In museums, Natives must be employed as curators to ensure that the exhibitions are mounted, collections collected, and documentation amassed with the sanction and support of the Native community. He further suggested that Canadian anthropology in general needed to have more Native anthropologists. Ames supported this, and the museum of which he is director, the Museum of Anthropology at the University of British Columbia, has set many precedents in this regard.

Trigger failed to address the issue of whether many Native people are interested in anthropology and/or museums. Ames's experience (and that of other Canadian museums) is that often no matter how wide the doors are opened, large museums as places to work (or even visit) are not generally part of Native thinking. This may change in time but the impetus for that change must come from within the Native community. Much more can be done to encourage Native people to come, but they cannot be forced to do so.

The main point of disagreement between Trigger and Ames was the correctness of any attempt to suppress an exhibition intended to support the position of Native people, which was also the result of extended scholarly research and study. Trigger felt that the exhibition should have been shut down because of the support for the boycott among the Native community; Ames felt that this support was not necessarily based on any real understanding of the objectives of the exhibition, and was an overt politicization of a body of work. Furthermore, he believed that the advocacy of the suppression of any information for political purposes was the worst form of censorship in which a group could engage. The last group to support this kind of action should be academics who value freedom of expression as a basic right of their profession.

Trigger presented his point of view, much elaborated from the original radio interview, during the Harry Hawthorne lecture at the annual conference of the CESCE in May 1988 where the Lubicon situation, the boycott, and *The Spirit Sings* were popular and impassioned topics. It is difficult to generalize about the mood of the conference concerning the issue. Some academics just wanted to "lay low" until the whole controversy blew over; others lauded the efforts of several key members of the society who had taken a very active role in the boycott; some considered the actions of the CESCE executive to be a strong statement against museums;[23] others supported the work of the museum and felt that the stance of many of the anthropologists against the actions of Glenbow were unrealistic and naïve; and still others considered my continued participation in the exhibition was ethically questionable.

If any generalization can be made, it would be that the Lubicon boycott of *The Spirit Sings* raised many issues for CESCE members. The leading role taken by the executive in passing their motion set the tone of the meeting in support of the Lubicon and against the Glenbow exhibition. Glenbow staff in general supported a swift and just settlement of the Lubicon land claim, but were powerless to do anything which would move along the negotiations between the Lubicon and the government. Contrary to the thinking of the Lubicon supporters, museum staff have little influence on those who hold power in Canada. Also, the Glenbow board of governors would have been in a breach of contract with sponsors had they pulled out of *The Spirit Sings* at any time. Furthermore, the staff of the museum fundamentally believed both that the messages in the exhibition were socially relevant and that its production was a responsible action. The museum was (and is) committed to the idea that museums must remain independent of external political pressures so that they can determine their own political stand, which in this case was to promote a wider understanding of the continuing relevance of Native heritage.

Most people would support the plight of the Lubicon. But was a boycott the best route to go?[24] Why was there no independent or neutral investigation of the circumstances surrounding *The Spirit Sings* and the boycott? Passion, idealism, emotional fervour, and frustration are also all elements of the process presented above. Independence from the issues or neutrality of position were not assumedly seen to be possible or even desirable on the part of anyone who would be qualified to have done such an investigation. Also, time was critical: there was not time for such a neutral investigation. Such are some of the processes of "seeing for innocence." The "essential goodness" of such actions by the academic community confirmed their authority to promote their actions in support of the boycott.

The Native Population

When Bernard Ominayak, Chief of the Lubicon Cree, was asked whether there was any value in "putting ... artifacts ... in a museum" he admitted that he hadn't "really thought about it" (Elton 1987:31).

His comments were published in the magazine *Last Issue* in the fall of 1987, although the interview had been conducted several months earlier. In contrast, a year later, at the conclusion of *The Spirit Sings* in Ottawa, Georges Erasmus, president of the Assembly of First Nations (AFN), the national political body representing status Indians in Canada, stated that "the AFN was going to have to decide how long it was going to stay in the museum business."[25] The Assembly of First Nations in conjunction with Indigenous Survival International had worked with the Museum of Mankind in London to produce an exhibition entitled *The Living Arctic*, which presented contemporary life of Native trappers in northern Canada in an effort to counter-balance the anti-fur lobby in Europe. The AFN also organized, with the Canadian Museums Association, the Preserving Our Heritage Conference, in November 1988 to address many of the issues raised by *The Spirit Sings*. While individual Native people were not thinking about museums, a major Native political body had obviously become very involved with them. Ominayak's response was typical of many Natives in Canada prior to the exhibit. Why should they think about museums, particularly those institutions located in large cities, many miles from their homes? This was part of the problem Glenbow faced in getting fair representation on the Liaison Committee. There was a great void between the cultural reality of a remote Native community and an urban museum controlled and staffed by members of the white population. In addition, the announcement of the Lubicon boycott strategy early in the planning stages of *The Spirit Sings* created a difficult situation for those Native people who may have wanted to participate but also wanted to support the Lubicon.

But how then did the AFN, a political lobby organization upon whose agenda museum issues were always near the bottom (if they appear at all), become involved in the "museum business?" They came to know the business because *The Spirit Sings* became a political tool in their hands. (The sanctioning of the boycott by AFN gave the whole campaign much more clout in museums around the world.) But in the end AFN also came to see some of the value of the work museums do, and could do, and the important dimension of Native heritage in museum collections. The organization also began to seriously ponder the question of who had the right to hold this heritage. In the end the political bodies representing the Native populations in Canada came to see museums as potential allies in their struggles to gain recognition.[26] This recognition may entail regaining control over portions of Native heritage which are housed in museums; this can best be achieved by working with, rather than against, museums.

Comments by Native people who visited *The Spirit Sings* included:

- IT MAKES ME PROUD TO BE AN INDIAN.
- Now I can understand my Cree ancestry.
- Maybe someday through efforts such as these our people will unite again and all shall know how to feel their own spirit.
- In spite of all the turmoil this has caused I feel some good must come out of it.

- We're still around!
- This art exhibit has stirred my own Indian spirit within me.[27]

There were unquestionably many Native people who could have come, but chose not to either in support of the Lubicon or because they could see no personal relevance in the exhibit. (The same applies, of course, to segments of the white population.) A few arranged to see the show in Ottawa when the boycott strategy had been essentially abandoned for a much more positive strategy. At the press conference to announce that *The Spirit Sings* was going to Ottawa, the AFN requested a conference with the Canadian museum community to discuss the issues that had arisen with the exhibit. As mentioned earlier, such a conference was held in Ottawa in November 1988. At a planning meeting in the early fall of the same year, it was decided that the conference should be jointly organized by the AFN and the Canadian Museum Association (CMA). Apart from many Native individuals who attended the conference, representatives of the Assembly of First Nations, Dene Cultural Institute, Inuit Cultural Centre, Inuit Tapirisat of Canada, Metis National Council, National Association of Friendship Centres, Native Council of Canada, Native Indian and Inuit Photography Association, Native Women's Association of Canada, Prairie Treaty Nations Alliance, and Society of Canadian Artists of Native Ancestry were also there. (Some of these groups only attended one of either the conference or the planning meeting.) Throughout the planning and the actual conference there was discussion of who should represent the Native community. There was some disagreement as to whether representatives of Native cultural centres were appropriate as, according to one delegate, "cultural centres were not involved with traditional culture."[28] Erasmus suggested, however, that it might be appropriate for the National Organization of Cultural Centres to take over from AFN's role in order to "get AFN out of the museum business."[29]

Agenda items included repatriation of artifacts, strategies for working together (with examples of museum exhibitions both in Canada and abroad where there was close co-operation), the role of elders, the access of Native peoples to collections, the role and place for contemporary Native art, and sponsorship and funding. A visit to *The Spirit Sings* for conference delegates was also arranged at the request of AFN. This allowed many people to see the exhibition in a context of understanding and open-mindedness rather than antagonism and tension. In all stages of the conference planning, as well as during the actual conference sessions, representatives of both the

Native community and the museum community took very nervous steps toward a better understanding of each others' perspectives. Members of the Native community articulated the extent of the cultural and political void that exists between the two groups, a void not only fuelled by the reality of the two solitudes in which the communities exist, but also by the fact that the behaviour of museum professionals has not historically always been of the highest order. Native peoples described their definitions of what a museum could or would be in their own communities.

The Native community learned of the new and changing climate within the museum community. The co-operative projects that have occurred between many museums and local Native communities are not usually known on a national scale and thus it is assumed that they have not happened. Several publications such as a special issue of MUSE (the journal of the CMA) entitled "Museums and First Nations," an issue of the *Native Studies Review* devoted to the same topic, and other articles document some of these projects and the changing attitudes in museums (see Ames 1986a, 1986b; *MUSE* 1988; *Native Studies Review* 1987). Through very frank dialogue major steps were taken towards shifting the Native perception of museums as "the enemy" to one of them as potential allies. There was unanimous agreement at the conference that the AFN and the CMA appoint a task force to ensure continued co-operation. All of this was a fitting conclusion to *The Spirit Sings*. As one Native person said upon the conclusion of the conference, "Many circles have been completed."

THE FUTURE

The open dialogue at the conference organized by the AFN and CMA contributed greatly to the breaking of the "seeing for innocence" in which both the Native and museum communities have historically indulged. It lessened the intent to "use [the] other as a means to [their] own goodness and superiority." At the conference tentative steps were taken toward answering some of the questions raised throughout this paper, questions which were admittedly not at the forefront of museum thinking at the beginning of *The Spirit Sings*. The general public and the academic community have asked for greater dialogue between museums and Native peoples. This dialogue is happening, and significant strides had been taken even before *The Spirit Sings* opened. An increasing number of Native people now use museum collections and expertise as part of their cultural development programs. As time passes Natives are increasingly aware of the relevance to them of these collections. Native internship and training programs offered in museums are very concrete steps toward increasing the exchange between these communities.

What of the Native community and the academic community? Can they come closer together? Have there been any meetings of these two groups on a national scale to seek ways to improve the university teaching? Is there ongoing dialogue on this subject? Museum anthropologists are potentially on the forefront here as they are taking steps toward actively involving Native people in their work. On local levels there is probably more dialogue between academics and Native peoples than the Native community, funding agencies, or the general public perceive. Much could be done to improve the public image of anthropology and its relation to its subjects if such dialogue were made known through popular lectures, media coverage, general interest writings, and direct involvement of "the subjects" of anthropological study from initial research to final writings. Anthropologists must fully address their responsibility to society. There is a role for academic and museum anthropologists to speak to the non-Native community of the need for respect of other cultures, specifically the Native peoples of Canada. Native people themselves can then readily confirm that they are not just something to be seen in museums, that they are not works of art. It is they who can best relate this message, not academics or non-Native museum staff. Museum anthropologists need to take a more active role in the world of academic anthropology; they must see themselves as anthropologists with obligations to the professional community as a whole; they need to see developments in the thinking of Canadian anthropology as relevant to their own professional activities; they must work to become more accessible to the academic community and to promote their collections as viable sources of data. To this end the work done by museum anthropologists will be better understood and assumedly judged more fairly. Academic and museum anthropologists should begin to recognize the parallel nature of the data they collect – one in the form of recorded information; the other in the form of objects. Academic anthropologists should recognize the significant recent changes in museum ethnology. Museums are not the dusty, musty places that they were once characterized to be. Ethnology departments are not only interested in the past; many have active campaigns to acquire a broad range of expressions of contemporary culture.

The academic and museum anthropological communities must both stop assuming that they see the issues more clearly and know the "correct" route to go; they need to begin to work together. It is tragic that two segments of the same community seem to have the greatest reluctance to really recognize each other's value and worth. Between these two groups there are yet "many circles to be completed." *The Spirit Sings* and all that developed around it ushered in a new era for museums, museum policy, and political issues. Never again could museums assume distance from the latter, particularly in relationship to Canada's Native populations. On one level the controversy initiated the development of policies within museums as they drafted more formal stands on repatriation, community involvement in programming, the nature of programming in general, and museums' responsibilities to their various publics. Such actions formalized things that in some cases had been happening informally for years; in other cases they defined totally new relationships. This thinking took museums into new dimensions about the right to do what they do and challenged the very nature of the power of these institutions. The debate prompted by *The Spirit Sings*, which turned to dialogue between museums, Native peoples, and the academic community, predicts a challenging and productive future for these three groups, as each now has an entrée to begin to question the assumptions which drive its relationships with the others. The policies and programs being developed by museums are only the first step in this process.

POSTSCRIPT (JUNE 1992)

Since the time this article was first drafted in the fall of 1989, much has happened in Canada concerning the nation's awareness of its Native populations. All the events described above happened well before the fall of Meech Lake, the events of Oka, and recent constitutional discussions. The political and real power of Native peoples is now more fully recognized. During these last turbulent years, the task force discussed at the 1988 conference has been steadily working to define the nature of a new relationship between Canada's Native peoples and museums. Its report should lead to further developments in museum policy and cognizance of political issues and power. Museums, working as partners with Native peoples in this highly charged time, have much to contribute.

NOTES AND UNPUBLISHED REFERENCES

1 Rita Joe is a Micmac poet. She wrote this poem after receiving her copy of *The Spirit Sings* book in which some of her poems were quoted.

2 This paper is based on one originally presented at the CESCE annual meetings in Saskatoon, Saskatchewan, 1988.

3 The curatorial committee included Ted Brasser, formerly of the Canadian Museum of Civilization; Bernadette Driscoll, Johns Hopkins University; Ruth Phillips, Carleton University; Martine Reid, Independent Scholar; Judy Thompson, Canadian Museum of Civilization; Ruth Whitehead, Nova Scotia Museum; and Bill Reid, Haida Artist, who attended some meetings.

4 A similar, smaller program was also organized in Ottawa.

5 The latter's contribution was entirely in staff hours and services with no direct funds coming from Glenbow's operating budget.

6 Affidavit between The Mohawk Bands of Kahnawake, Akwesasne, and Kanesatake and Grand Chief Joe Norton, Grand Chief Mike Mitchell, Grand Chief Alex Montour, and the Glenbow-Alberta Institute. 14 January 1988, 2–3. *The Spirit Sings*, Administration files, Glenbow Museum.

7 "Controversial Iroquois mask returns to Glenbow." Glenbow Press Release. 29 January 1988. *The Spirit Sings*, Administration files, Glenbow Museum.

8 Letter to George MacDonald from Ruth Phillips. 11 April 1988. *The Spirit Sings*, Administration files, Glenbow Museum.

9 Letter to Duncan Cameron from Thomas Longboat, Jr. 9 May 1988. *The Spirit Sings*, Administration files, Glenbow Museum.

10 Native people were involved in several dimensions of the Olympics. There were also close to 150 Native people involved in *The Spirit Sings*.

11 Personal communication with H. Gansylmayr, president, International Committee of Museum Ethnology. Letter from G. Lewis to H. Ganslmayr. 26 August, 1987. ICOM, Ethnology Department files, Glenbow Museum.

12 Letter to D. Cameron from T. Lundbaek. 28 November 1986, ref. 3364. National Museum of Denmark, *The Spirit Sings*, Ethnology Department files, Glenbow Museum.

13 Shell took the position that they played no role in land claims as they were something to be settled between the government and the band. Once the land claim was settled Shell would simply deal with the new landlord; until such time the company would continue to negotiate their oil leases with the government.

14 In Calgary 127,506 people saw the exhibition; 101,040 people saw it in Ottawa.

15 Due to the Olympic connection of *The Spirit Sings* and the furore of the Lubicon boycott, the exhibition prompted much greater tangible public response in Calgary than in Ottawa.

16 These comments are taken from anonymous comment cards from Calgary and Ottawa.

17 J.E. Czaja, vice president, Shell Canada Limited. Opening Ceremonies, *The Spirit Sings*, Ethnology Department files, Glenbow Museum.

18 Ralph Klein, Mayor of Calgary. Opening Ceremonies, *The Spirit Sings*, Ethnology Department files, Glenbow Museum.

19 Comments made in discussion during the planning meeting held 9 and 10 September 1988 for the conference Preserving Our Heritage. Canadian Museums Association, Ethnology Department files, Glenbow Museum.

20 Letter to Julia Harrison from Robert Doyle, Costume Studies, Dalhousie University, Halifax. 19 August 1988. Comment Gallery, *The Spirit Sings*, Ethnology Department files, Glenbow Museum.

21 For further discussion of the academic support for the boycott see Julia D. Harrison and Michael M. Ames. "Why Did Anthropologists Boycott an Anthropology Exhibit? The case of *The Spirit Sings*." Paper presented at the 87th Annual Meeting of the American Anthropological Association. Phoenix, November 1988.

22 Minutes of 12 September 1986 meeting of Native Liaison Committee, *The Spirit Sings*, Ethnology Department files, Glenbow Museum.

23 Letter to Carmen Lambert from Julia Harrison. 18 May 1988. Canadian Ethnology Society, Ethnology Department files, Glenbow Museum.

24 Glenbow was indirectly asked by a Lubicon supporter to include a section in the exhibition on the Lubicon. Glenbow declined as *The Spirit Sings* was not an exhibition about land claims. Glenbow's subsequent offer of a public forum on contemporary issues as part of the Celebration of Native Cultures was rejected by the Native Liaison Committee. In spite of this offer and the relevance of history to the contemporary situation, working with Glenbow to promote *The Spirit Sings*, as a positive statement about Native cultures seems to have been given little consideration by Lubicon supporters.

25 G. Erasmus, closing remarks, Preserving Our Heritage Conference. Ottawa, 5 November 1988. Author's notes.

26 In his opening remarks to the "Preserving Our Heritage" conference Georges Erasmus stated that museums a.id Native people were "two possible strong allies." Canadian Museums Association, 1988, Ethnology Department files, Glenbow Museum.

27 These comments are taken from anonymous comment cards.

28 Comments made by Nicholas DeLeary, Native studies professor, Laurentian University, 10 September 1988 during the planning meetings for a Preserving Our Heritage Conference, Canadian Museums Association, 1988, Ethnology Department files, Glenbow Museum.

29 G. Erasmus, closing remarks Preserving Our Heritage Conference. Ottawa, 5 November 1988. Author's notes.

REFERENCES

Ames, M. 1986a. *Museums, the Public and Anthropology: A Study in the Anthropology of Anthropology*. Vancouver: University of British Columbia Press.
- 1986b. "Report from the Field: The Democratization of Anthropology and Museums." *Culture* 6(1):61–4.
-, and B. Trigger. 1988a. "Share the Blame." *Vanguard* 17(2):15–19.
- 1988b. "The Liberation of Anthropology: A Rejoinder to Professor Trigger's A Present of Their Past." *Culture* 8(1):79–88.
Elton, Heather, L. Doolittle, et al. 1987. "Appropriation: A Case in Point." *Last Issue*. Autumn: 20–31.
Harrison, Julia. 1987. "Introduction." *The Spirit Sings: Artistic Tradition's of Canada's First Peoples. A Catalogue of the Exhibition*, 7–8. Toronto: McClelland & Stewart; Calgary: Glenbow-Alberta Institute.
Hill, Tom, ed. 1988. "Museums and First Nations." Special Issue *MUSE* 6(3). *Native Studies Review*. 1987. 3(2).
Steele, Shelby. 1988. "I'm Black, You're White, Who's Innocent?" *Harper's* 276(1657):45–53.
Whitehead, R., R. Phillips, et al. 1987. *The Spirit Sings: Artistic Traditions of Canada's First Peoples*. Toronto: McClelland & Stewart; Calgary: Glenbow-Alberta Institute.
Trigger, Bruce. 1988. "A Present of Their Past? Anthropologists, Native People, and Their Heritage." *Culture* 8(1):71–9.

Contributors

PEGGY MARTIN BRIZINSKI received her Ph.D. from McMaster University in 1989. She has taught in the Native Studies Department at the University of Saskatchewan, and is currently a special advisor to the Treaty Commissioner in Saskatchewan; she does research and practice in the areas of land entitlement and the treaty right to education.

JULIE CRUIKSHANK worked for several years at the Yukon Native Language Centre. Her books, written in collaboration with Yukon elders, include *Life Lived Like a Story* and *Reading Voices: Dan Dha Ts'edenintth'e*. She is currently associate professor of anthropology at the University of British Columbia where she also works at the Museum of Anthropology.

NOEL DYCK is an associate professor of anthropology at Simon Fraser University, the editor of *Indigenous Peoples and the Nation-State: Fourth World Politics in Canada, Australia and Norway* (Institute of Social and Economic Research, 1985), and the author of *What Is the Indian "Problem": Tutelage and Resistance in Canadian Indian Administration* (Institute of Social and Economic Research, 1991).

PETER DOUGLAS ELIAS earned a B.A. at the University of Manitoba and a Ph.D. in anthropology at the University of Toronto. In 1989 he joined the Faculty of Management at the University of Lethbridge as Assistant Professor teaching in the BESS Program, a specialist course of studies for Indians, Inuit and Metis who work in an environment of aboriginal people's issues. In 1991, as associate professor, he was appointed co-ordinator of the BESS Program. Publications include *The Dakota of the Canadian Northwest* (University of Manitoba Press), *Development of Aboriginal Peoples Communities* (Captus Press), and several pieces in scholarly journals.

JULIA D. HARRISON is a D.Phil. student in anthropology at Oxford University. Her research is in institutional change in museums. From 1979 to 1989 she was curator of ethnology at the Glenbow Museum.

RON IGNACE has a master's degree in sociology from the University of British Columbia and is the chief of the Skeetchestn Band in British Columbia. He is also a member of the Shuswap Tribal Council and president of the SECWEPEMC Cultural Education Society.

JOSEPH M. KAUFERT is a professor in the Department of Community Health Sciences at the University of Manitoba. He is a medical anthropologist who has published widely, most recently in *Sociology of Health and Illness* and *Social Science and Medicine*. He is currently engaged in ethnomedical research on medical interpreting and renal disease among Native Canadians and sociological research on aging with a disability and impact of life support technology.

PATRICIA LEYLAND KAUFERT is associate professor in the Department of Community Health Sciences, University of Manitoba. She has published numerous articles about women's health issues, most recently *Social Science and Medicine, Maturitas* and *Culture, Medicine and Psychiatry*. She is currently investigating childbirth and mid-life among Inuit women.

WILLIAM W. KOOLAGE, Ph.D. is an associate professor in the Department of Anthropology at the University of Manitoba. His research has focused on the role of intermediaries in health services for Native people. He is currently working on the index for the *Arctic Blue Books*.

JOHN D. O'NEIL, Ph.D., is an associate professor of medical anthropology in the departments of Community Health Sciences and Anthropology at the University of Manitoba. Current research interests include a collaborative suicide prevention project with Pauktutit

(Inuit Women's Association), an investigation into the cultural construction of environmental health risks in aboriginal communities, and international comparative work on community-controlled health services in indigenous communities.

JOE SAWCHUK is assistant professor, Department of Native Studies, Brandon University. His research focuses on the internal operations of Metis and non-status Indian organizations in Canada and the effects of government funding and policies on these organizations. Publications include *Métis Land Rights in Alberta* (co-authored with Patricia Sawchuk and Theresa Ferguson) and *The Métis of Manitoba: Reformulation of an Ethnic Identity*. He is currently editing a volume of readings on the effects of state structures and policies on aboriginal identity.

COLIN H. SCOTT (B.A. University of Saskatchewan, M.A. and Ph.D. McGill University) is an assistant professor in the Department of Anthropology at McGill University. He has served as a consultant to the Grand Council of the Crees of Quebec, and to other aboriginal, and provincial and federal government offices.

DEREK G. SMITH studied at the University of British Columbia, and holds an A.M. and a Ph.D. from Harvard University. He is associate professor of sociology and anthropology and co-ordinator of the graduate program in anthropology at Carleton University in Ottawa, where he has taught since 1971. His current research concerns state and state-linked practices of domination in the Canadian North.

GEORGE SPECK has a B.A. in anthropology and has conducted graduate research in the discipline. He has been a fisherman and is a member of the Nimpkish Band Council administration and a hereditary chief.

RENEE TAYLOR is a Vancouver lawyer and a member of the Nimpkish Band, Alert Bay, British Columbia. In the past she has assisted anthropologists conducting research in her home community.

PETER D. USHER is a geographer (Ph.D., University of British Columbia) who has been involved in social impact assessment in the North for over twenty years. He co-ordinated the socio-economic component of the Committee for Original Peoples' Entitlement's intervention at the Berger Inquiry from 1974 to 1976. Since then he has been involved in impact assessments of mercury pollution in north-western Ontario, hydro-electric development in northern Manitoba, Ontario, and Quebec, oil and gas development in the Beaufort Sea, and oil pollution in Alaska. He maintains an independent consultancy in Ottawa, which provides research and advice on impact assessment, resource management, and Native claims, and is also research director at Inuit Tapirisat of Canada.

JAMES B. WALDRAM (B.A. Waterloo 1978, M.A. Manitoba 1980, Ph.D. Connecticut 1983) is a medical and applied anthropologist and professor of Native Studies at the University of Saskatchewan, Saskatoon, Saskatchewan.

SALLY M. WEAVER, Ph.D., is a political anthropologist and professor in the Department of Anthropology, University of Waterloo. Her research interest is in the processes by which governments develop policies with and for indigenous peoples in western democracies such as Canada, Australia, and Norway.